MW00629759

Maria Soldat
83 Liberty St
Bloomfield, NJ 07003

Buying into Change

BUYING INTO CHANGE

Mass Consumption, Dictatorship, and Democratization in Franco's Spain, 1939–1982

ALEJANDRO J. GÓMEZ DEL MORAL

UNIVERSITY OF NEBRASKA PRESS | Lincoln

Portions of this manuscript originally appeared as "Refashioning Spain: Fashion, Consumer Culture, Gender, and International Integration under the Late Franco Dictatorship," in *The Global 1960s: Convention, Contest, and Counterculture*, edited by Tamara Chaplin and Jadwiga E. Pieper Mooney, 159–175 (New York: Routledge, 2017); and "Buying into Change: Consumer Culture and the Department Store in the Transformation(s) of Spain, 1939–1982," *Enterprise and Society: The International Journal of Business History* 16, no. 4 (December 2015): 792–810.

Library of Congress Cataloging-in-Publication Data
Names: Gómez del Moral, Alejandro J., author.
Title: Buying into change: mass consumption, dictatorship, and democratization in Franco's Spain, 1939–1982 / Alejandro J. Gómez del Moral.
Description: Lincoln: University of Nebraska Press, [2021] | Includes bibliographical references and index.
Identifiers: LCCN 2020037081
ISBN 9781496205063 (hardback)
ISBN 9781496226303 (epub)
ISBN 9781496226310 (mobi)
ISBN 9781496226327 (pdf)
Subjects: LCSH: Consumption (Economics)—Social aspects—Spain—History—20th Century. | Consumers—Spain—History—20th century. | Democratization—Spain—History—20th century. | Spain—Politics and government—1939–1975. | Spain—Politics and government—1975–1982.
Classification: LCC HC390.C6 G66 2021 |
DDC 330.946/082—dc23
LC record available at https://lccn.loc.gov/2020037081

Set in Garamond Premier Pro by Mikala R. Kolander.
Designed by L. Auten.

For Kat, Cesc, and Joan

CONTENTS

ILLUSTRATIONS

Table

ACKNOWLEDGMENTS

I once wrote that completing my PhD was a long, daunting, and difficult process that would have been impossible without the advice and support of a number of individuals. This is still truer of a scholarly monograph, especially a first book. I would like to start by again thanking Temma Kaplan, my PhD adviser, for the guidance she provided over the course of my doctoral studies as well as the subsequent process of turning my dissertation into this book. I'd also like to thank the other two internal members of my dissertation committee, Seth Koven and Jochen Hellbeck, for their contributions to the dissertation out of which this book has developed. And I would like to offer a special word of thanks to my enormously helpful and intellectually generous external reader as well as personal friend, Aurora Morcillo, whose untimely loss surely remains tragic and shocking to all of us who were fortunate enough to know her.

The list of other colleagues and collaborators who have made this book possible is quite possibly too long to list here, but I will try. I would like to thank Phyllis Mack for guiding the research that was the germ of this book's source dissertation. I would similarly like to thank a number of colleagues and institutions based in Spain, without whom this research would not have been possible. Colleagues include Javier Muñoz Soro, Stephen Jacobson, and Pilar Toboso Sánchez. Individuals at institutions include Igor Cacho Ugalde at the Archivo General de la Universidad de Navarra; Javier Tébar at the Fundació Cipriano García–Arxiu Històric de cc.oo. de Catalunya; Antonio Mingo at the Fundación 10 de Mayo–Archivo de Historia del Trabajo; and the archivists and librarians at the Archivo Regional de la Comunidad de Madrid, the Archivo General de la Administración, and the National Libraries of Catalonia and Spain. I must similarly thank quite a few colleagues in the United States for their help and support, including Montserrat Miller, Jessica Davidson, Samuel Pierce, Nick Saenz, Clint Young, Antonio Cazorla, Karl Trybus, Andrea Davis, Pamela Radcliff, Andrew Lee, Scott Eastman, Julia Hudson-Richards, Allison Salazar, Louie-Dean Valencia-García, Sasha Pack, and the rest of the very special scholarly family that is the Association for Spanish and Portuguese Historical Studies (ASPHS). I would like to thank Westley Follett, Douglas Bristol, Deanne Nuwer, and my other former colleagues at the University of Southern Mississippi (USM) for their collegiality and advice during my first years as a junior faculty member. I also thank the staff at the Rockefeller Family Archives for their help during my dissertation research. Moving back to Europe, I thank my colleagues in the Economic and Social as well as Political History Departments here at the University of Helsinki, both for taking a chance on a twice-foreign scholar (Spanish and American, but certainly not Finnish) as well as for the generous support, encouragement, advice, and friendship they have shown me and my family since our move to Finland. They too are many in number, but they include Hanna Kuusi, Sakari Saaritsa, Antti Häkkinen, Jari Eloranta, Laura Ekholm, Matleena Frisk, Aappo Kähönen, Henrik Forsberg, Riikka Taavetti, Heikki Haara, Sophy Bergenheim, Juri Mykkänen, and Hannu Nieminen. Kiitos paljon kaikesta avustanne. And I would like to thank my editor, Matt Bokovoy, as well as the rest of the staff at the University of Nebraska Press (UNP) for their help and the regard they have shown for this manuscript; my warmest thanks too to Alisa Plant of Louisiana State University Press, who believed in this book when it was not even a completed dissertation and brought it to UNP during her tenure there as editor in chief.

The research for this book would have similarly been impossible without support from several generous funding organizations. These include the Program for Cultural Cooperation between the Spanish Ministry of Culture and United States Universities, the Mellon Foundation, the Rutgers University Graduate School-New Brunswick, the

Rutgers Department of History, and both USM and the University of Helsinki, all of which at various points subsidized the research that forms the core of this book.

Most of all, I thank my family and friends, whose support has been invaluable. I thank my colleagues, Arnout van der Meer, Steve Allen, Adam Zalma, Annie Kinkel, Elizabeth Churchich, and Patrick Zimmerman, for their moral and professional support. Arnout, Adam, Steve—without those Hungarian Pastry Shop sessions, neither my dissertation nor the book that has grown out of it would have happened. I thank my friends Joke van Oers and Peter Bulmer for their solidarity over the years. I cannot thank my parents, Al Ritchie and Maria de Lourdes Guerra, nor my in-laws, Jack and Colleen Mahaney, enough for their love and support over the many years it took to reach this point. I thank the whole Guerra clan for bearing with my work-induced silences, and offer a sincere *gracias* and *gràcies* to my family in Spain and Catalonia, including my grandmother María Luisa Peire, my uncles Carles and Luis Gómez del Moral, and my aunts and cousins for their unflagging support along this journey. I offer a special thanks to the Gómez del Moral-Buisán family for providing me a copy of my great-uncle Alfonso Buisán Pérez's memoirs, which proved a key source when drafting chapter 5.

Finally, and most of all, I would like to thank my wife, Dr. Kathryn (Kat) Mahaney, for her immense love, support, forbearance, and valiant (if mostly unsuccessful) attempts to keep me sane during this process, as well as the many revisions and advice she has provided me over the years as a respected colleague. There are no words to encompass how much you have done for me. This book is dedicated to you and to our two extraordinary and occasionally perplexing little monsters, Cesc and Joan.

Buying into Change

Introduction

On the morning of 4 October 1934, readers of the leading Madrid newspaper *A.B.C.* unwittingly bore witness to a turning point in Spain's history. What they encountered as they paged through the paper surely seemed unremarkable: an interview with an obscure businessman named José Fernández Rodríguez—"Pepín" to his friends, "Don José" to employees—who publicized the recent opening of his new Sederías Carretas department store just steps away from Madrid's central Puerta del Sol plaza. Yet this was only the first of several pieces on Pepín's store that ran in *A.B.C.* that month, and in them the entrepreneur made claims that were anything but ordinary. He predicted that Sederías would soon revolutionize Spanish retailing, making it into something nobler than simple business—a "service to the public." This, he promised, was the store that Madrid "had been waiting for," featuring the latest American commercial methods imported from Havana's prestigious El Encanto department store, where he himself had learned his trade. Curious crowds had flocked to the store's grand opening on 2 October; perhaps emboldened by this early success, a boastful Pepín declared the launch nothing short of "transcendent" in significance.[1]

In fact, over the next half-century Sederías and other retailers like it transcended not only Pepín Fernández's expectations for his store, but the confines of the commercial sphere in which they operated, broadly impacting Spanish society, culture, and politics into the 1980s. Spain's mid-twentieth century was politically turbulent. Mere hours after Pepín's first interview ran in *A.B.C.*, a violent miner's strike in the industrialized northern province of Asturias set in motion a series of political clashes that ultimately sparked the Spanish Civil War (1936–1939), which Generalissimo Francisco Franco's Nationalist forces won.[2] Sederías grew into Galerías Preciados, Spain's premier retailing chain, under Franco's subsequent four-decade dictatorship (1939–1975). And the store fell into bankruptcy as the nation transitioned from dictatorship to its present democracy during the late 1970s and early 1980s. Socially and culturally, the changes were equally severe. The 1940s were years of famine, international ostracism, and peak repression in Spain, during which Franco's new regime executed thousands, banned virtually all political life, and, alongside the Spanish Catholic Church, imposed deeply conservative social and moral strictures. In the 1950s and 1960s, Spanish diplomatic and economic fortunes rebounded, epitomized by a dramatic boom (1959–1973) during which Spain possessed the world's second-fastest-growing economy and began to receive a flood of foreign investment and tourists as well as the social and cultural alternatives to Francoist orthodoxy they brought with them.[3] By the time of Franco's death in 1975, Spanish society had transformed. Migrations and the boom had swelled Spain's cities and once-miniscule middle class; women's legal status was improving; exposure to social movements abroad had emboldened Spanish dissidents; and, most of all, as historian Sasha Pack has noted, contact with European tourists, media, and products encouraged Spaniards to similarly identify with Europe— its democratic traditions included.[4]

This book examines how Spanish department stores like Sederías Carretas and its principal competitor, El Corte Inglés—now one of Spain's most powerful companies—contributed to these changes alongside other actors such as consumer magazines, the Spanish advertising industry, and foreign-influenced supermarkets that came to Spain in the late 1950s and 1960s. It is one of just a handful of studies on mid-century Spain's department stores and supermarkets, and is similarly one of the only accounts of how such enterprises, often working in tandem with the Franco regime, contributed to the development of a Spanish mass consumer society and to Spain's insertion into a larger European and American consumer sphere.[5]

Initially apolitical, or otherwise aligned with the regime, Spanish retailers, journalists, and admen drove the formation of this mass consumer society from the 1940s onward by pursuing the very goal that Pepín Fernández had espoused in 1934: namely, the modernization of Spanish commerce through the adoption of new, foreign ways of buying and selling. In so doing, I argue, they (sometimes unwittingly) became politically subversive, contributing to a popular adoption of American and Western European consumer ways and sociocultural notions—an Americanization and Europeanization of Spanish lifestyles—that undermined the Franco regime's social project.[6] For Francoism consisted of not just political and moral coercion, but a dense ideology that included a patriarchal system of gender relations as well as a semi-mystical, exceptionalist conception of Spain as a nation apart with a special destiny, and it is these concepts that Spain's foreign-influenced mass consumption most subverted.[7] This process was hardly one-sided. As in much of postwar Europe, Americanization advanced in Spain less by wholesale cultural imposition than through myriad local acts of selective appropriation and adaptation of American culture, and Spanish responses to Northern European cultural imports were often similarly discriminating.[8] Thus, Francoist officials and allies could often politically co-opt Spain's nascent consumerism, despite the liberal foreign cultures that influenced it, as when the Ministry of Commerce publicized boom-era improvements in the Spanish standard of living to improve the regime's image abroad.[9] In the end, though, the merchants and media-makers who championed this new consumption drove forward social changes that prepared the way for Spain's remarkably rapid transition to democracy.

The speed and apparent ease of this transition quickly became and remains a subject of ongoing debate in the study of contemporary Spain. This debate has ranged from early, largely political narratives, to later sociocultural analyses rooted in sociologist Victor Pérez Díaz's argument that a resurgence of Spanish civic life in the 1960s produced the liberal political culture that fueled Spain's transition, to recent multi-causal accounts that combine the political, social, and cultural.[10] However, scholars have paid far less attention to the role that mass consumption played in the liberalization of Franco-era Spanish society, or how it could conversely serve—and after the regime's end, preserve—Francoist policies and mores.[11]

It is such an analysis, one that takes consumption seriously as an agent of sociopolitical change, that this book contributes to both the current multicausal transitional model and to a much-needed recent upsurge in scholarship on the socially and culturally turbulent late Franco era (1959–1975).[12] This merits a pause: by "consumption," I mean not just the purchase of items, but, following Jean Baudrillard, a "systematic manipulation of signs"—that is, the transfer of qualities such as "middle-class," "modern," or "European" from products to their consumers. And by a mass consumer society, I mean a society organized around mass access to, and participation in, such consumption.[13] Inclusion of mass consumption as a driving force in the transition matters because of its ubiquity—what Baudrillard and Guy Debord have described as consumption's pervasion of every aspect of modern life and consequent "totalitarian" inescapability.[14] And indeed, once rising prosperity and greater access to credit made consumer products widely accessible, they pervaded Spanish daily life.[15] Shopping at Spain's new self-service grocery stores, for instance, was an everyday occurrence for housewives in small-town Yecla (Murcia) as well as in metropolitan Barcelona, and so were shoppers' encounters there with foreign products and efficiency-oriented sales methods that disseminated notions of a European rather than provincial Spain. These were the same kinds of cultural encounters that Spanish tourism facilitated—indeed, the tourist industry and mass retailing often functioned in dialogue, each fueling the other—but shopping took place with greater frequency.

These encounters furthermore offer intriguing opportunities for comparison with other cases of consumption-driven sociopolitical change, both in Southern Europe's other dictatorships—Portugal and

Greece—and also, less obviously, in the 1960s Soviet bloc and post-Maoist China, which experienced a dramatic but uneven consumerist turn in the 1980s.[16] Much as McDonald's restaurants in China served as international spaces in which patrons could behave like affluent Western consumers, briefly escaping local socioeconomic constraints, *Buying into Change* shows how foreign product exhibitions turned 1960s Spanish department stores into sites of cosmopolitan consumer fantasy in which Francoist notions of national particularism were temporarily suspended.[17] Alongside recent work on Soviet consumption, this book also counters established notions of 1960s-era social transformations as a priori countercultural, showing how such shifts could develop within politically conformist technocratic networks whose activities had unintended counterhegemonic consequences. Where communist authorities who adopted Western design and urban planning methods inadvertently reproduced the same social inequalities they deplored in the capitalist world, the foreign consumer culture that mid-century Spanish officials and retailing professionals embraced likewise helped to sharpen socioeconomic disparities and undermine Francoist hegemony in Spain.[18] Indeed, by the 1970s, both Soviet and Francoist authorities had begun to abandon earlier efforts to articulate hybrid modes of consumption that reconciled their sociopolitical doctrines with a foreign capitalist consumerism, motivated by a need to keep pace with Western European and American consumer modernity that increasingly trumped their desire to preserve systemic purity amid this modernization.[19]

At the same time, such comparisons can also highlight the limits of mass consumption's democratizing effects on both sides of the Iron Curtain. In China, even though diners could eat in McDonald's, their choices were still highly subject to state control, and early 1990s anonymous advice hotlines that ostensibly allowed for freer discourse often addressed female callers in ways that instead reproduced traditional gender norms.[20] In the Soviet bloc, state-driven consumer initiatives were often intended to extend socialist hegemony, as when communist planners promoted a kind of tourism abroad that was designed to reinforce travelers' socialist loyalties, or flooded the East German market with state-produced plastic consumer goods that subtly disseminated an official socialist view of plastic, not as cheap and disposable, but prized and futuristic.[21] Meanwhile, in the West, early 1960s Spanish supermarkets that were ostensibly privatized bastions of foreign modernity in fact remained heavily regulated by an interventionist Franco regime that, as in its fascist early days, continued to view food distribution in nationalistic terms as a vehicle for international economic clout and as a means to cultivate "biopower." By this last term, I mean political power over a population secured intentionally through measures that, in explicit terms, seek to control the physical body and its biological processes, for example, through nutrition.[22]

Even the cornerstone of this global consumerist turn—the U.S. Cold War pursuit of soft power through export of its consumer culture—faced similar limits. For instance, the introduction of the supermarket to late 1950s communist Yugoslavia, which, as in Spain, was initiated by a regime seeking to modernize the nation's food distribution, failed due to logistical difficulties that persisted, despite receiving extensive support from a U.S.-government-backed "Supermarkets U.S.A." traveling exhibit that visited Spain two years later.[23] Of course, in Spain the supermarket did succeed, and U.S. "consumer diplomacy" certainly did play a significant role in transforming late Franco-era Spanish society and commerce.[24] Yet, as recent scholarship has noted, this policy never fully achieved its larger aim of securing public support for the United States, whose pursuit of good relations with Franco ultimately left many in Spain disillusioned. And, moreover, this book adds, Spain's mass consumer society resembled others in postwar Europe inasmuch as it was shaped significantly by internal European commercial and social exchanges, not just transatlantic American influences.[25]

These exchanges began to take place considerably before the Spanish economic boom as well, revising our understanding of when mass consumption developed in Spain. Before the late 1960s, scholars long argued, Spaniards simply lacked the buying power to consume *en masse*.[26] And indeed, poverty remained sufficiently widespread into the 1970s that in 1973 half of Spain's households earned less than 10,000 pesetas per annum (about half of what the average income had been ten years before) and in 1970 Spaniards still consumed three hundred calories fewer per day per capita than other Western Europeans.[27] However, I propose that, despite these hardships, a socially transformative *imagined* mass consumer society formed in Spanish discourse as early as the 1940s. In the late 1940s and early 1950s, an American hunger for Cold War allies, coupled with Franco's anti-communist reputation, fueled his regime's diplomatic rehabilitation. This culminated in a 1953 treaty with the United States that brought Spain respectability abroad, over $62 million in exchange for allowing American military bases on Spanish soil, and an influx of American soldiers and tourists as well as the customs they brought with them.[28] Pro-American sentiment meanwhile grew in the treaty's wake, such that when Francoist attorney Gregorio Marañón Moya co-founded a Spanish Association of Friends of the United States later that year, he received a flood of supportive correspondence from across Spain.[29] As the economy improved, department stores like Galerías Preciados spread across Spain, consumer magazines proliferated, and both stoked interest in foreign (especially American) products and lifestyles, including Parisian fashions and American-style home appliances that arrived laden with promises of convenience and modernity.[30] Meanwhile, these enterprises courted not just the few who could afford to buy such goods but also the many who aspired to do so, through content aimed at working-class as well as bourgeois readers, new store credit systems that made these products more affordable, and spectacles like escalators, then still a novelty.

Thereby, these retailers and journalists sold consumption to the masses as an activity to which they could legitimately aspire and through which they could shape their identities—core traits of a mass (as opposed to a typically nineteenth-century, bourgeois, and class-constrained) consumer regime.[31] Put differently, they represented Spanish society to itself as already engaged in mass consumption. Spaniards responded by internalizing and acting upon this vision: in 1957, for instance, they overwhelmed national automaker SEAT with orders for the new 600 model despite the car's expensive price, which was more than triple the average Spanish annual income.[32] The result was Spain's first, albeit largely imagined mass consumer society, which nevertheless produced the commercial structures that later under-pinned the full realization of mass consumption in Spain during the 1960s, when rising incomes at last made material rather than strictly aspirational consumption of products available to the masses.

This book furthermore reveals that store managers, journalists, and regime officials all explicitly politicized this new consumption, and so qualifies arguments that have declared it apolitical or depoliticizing in nature—a spectacle of unfettered consumerism behind which the Franco regime hid its brutality, or a safety valve for Spanish liberaliz-ing aspirations.[33] Rather, Spain's department stores, consumer media, and, eventually, its supermarkets, all occasionally aided the regime in its aims. Indeed, it was a government agency, the Comisaría General de Abastecimientos y Transportes (Commissary-General for Supply and Transport, henceforth, CAT) that imported the *autoservicio*, or "self-service" grocery store—the supermarket—in 1957–1958 as part of a larger state-led push to project a more modern image of Franco's Spain abroad.[34] Pepín Fernández, meanwhile, was a longtime Franco supporter,[35] and his store's paternalistic employee code of conduct extended early Francoist attempts at a totalizing control of Spaniards' private morality by claiming managerial authority over nearly every aspect of employees' lives. Notably, inasmuch as the regime pursued such social control through proxies like Galerías or, more famously, the Spanish Catholic Church, this qualifies sociologist Juan Linz's thesis that Francoism was authoritarian and not totalitarian for lack of such forms of social coercion.[36]

And then came the economic boom of the 1960s, and with it a sharp rise in both material consumption of goods among Spain's masses and foreign influence on their lifestyles. Victoria de Grazia has argued that the export of American consumerism to twentieth-century Europe resulted from a sometimes-unwitting collaboration between the American government and private business interests, who initially pursued their frequently conflicting agendas separately, but by mid-century acted complementarily, motivated by a shared Cold War "national interest."[37] Similarly, Spanish government officials and commercial professionals in the 1940s, 1950s, and especially the 1960s, embraced a foreign brand of mass consumption out of a common desire to raise Spain to a perceived European and American standard of modernity and prosperity—what Sasha Pack has termed a "myth" of modernization.[38] Thus early 1960s technocrats like Minister of Commerce Alberto Ullastres and Minister of Information and Tourism Manuel Fraga courted foreign investment and tourism, seeking to improve Spain's economic fortunes and international prestige by modernizing its industry and commerce to match achievements abroad.[39] Rising incomes meanwhile swelled the ranks of the middle class, who, alongside the growing flood of tourists, flocked to shop at the nation's department stores.[40]

These retailers responded by expanding more aggressively than ever before. They built new branches in cities like Barcelona, and, reflecting the growing Spanish focus abroad as well as the myth of modernization that underpinned it, laid claim to modern cosmopolitan identities by representing themselves as world-class establishments both internally and to the public. They also staked these claims indirectly through initiatives like foreign employee exchanges and by adopting the sleek concrete storefronts and shopping centers pioneered in the United States and Northern Europe, which led Spain's urban landscapes to increasingly resemble cities abroad.

In near unison, Spain's consumer press, grocers, and advertising industry joined in this turn abroad. They celebrated Spanish participation in foreign trade shows and conferences. They affiliated with multinationals like the Dutch self-service grocery chain SPAR, or international bodies like the International Public Relations Association (IPRA), which Spanish Public Relations pioneer Joaquín Maestre Morata joined in 1964.[41] And they acted as part of a larger effort to professionalize their trades, again along foreign lines, which the Franco regime supported. Thereby, these stores, advertising agencies, and magazines further exposed Spanish consumers to foreign products and mores. The 1964 arrival of the quintessentially American department store chain Sears, Roebuck and Co. epitomized this influx. Sears offered products so alien that local manufacturers thought them impossible to sell, and cultivated an international workplace by shuttling company veterans between its branches in the Americas and the new Sears, Roebuck of Spain, meanwhile stressing that its employees all belonged to a single, integrated, global organization that transcended social, cultural, and even political borders.

The sociopolitical implications of Spain's commercial growth and newfound cosmopolitanism were broad, with dire consequences for the Franco dictatorship. Regime officials continued to encourage mass commerce and consumption, now hoping to shore up public support as the Spanish standard of living rose, or at least defang the regime's increasingly restive opponents—efforts that met with some success.[42] Yet the foreign orientation that this new commerce displayed placed Spanish merchants and shoppers ever more into contact with their European and American counterparts. And via these points of cultural exchange, foreign ideas that subverted Francoist orthodoxy began to arrive alongside the products that Spanish consumers coveted and the commercial innovations used to sell them.

Specifically, the countercultural, independent-minded youth culture of the 1960s, and the gender-bending unisex fashions of London's Carnaby Street, arrived in magazines like the men's journal *Don* (founded 1962) and at new "youth" store departments introduced by Galerías Preciados, El Corte Inglés, and Sears during the late 1960s and early 1970s. Among adult Spaniards, tradition, age, and life experience had long been part of the dominant masculine ideal. As the 1960s advanced, however, the values of youthful inquisitiveness (*inquietud*), innovation, and "*ye-yeismo*"—the open-minded youth culture associated with the British Invasion[43]—soon became fashionable. Alongside, a strain of the same rebellion against conservative paternal authority then unfolding in late-1960s Europe and the United States began to gain popularity in Spain, where it could also involve a rejection of Francoist political repression.[44]

The consequences for National-Catholic gender relations were similarly marked, particularly for Francoist constructions of masculinity, which have only recently begun to receive scholarly scrutiny.[45] This study reveals that Spain's mid-century influx of foreign consumption drove shifts in Spanish discourses of masculinity that subverted Francoist gender orthodoxy as a whole. Spanish department stores' new unisex-oriented youth sections allowed teenagers to mingle freely with members of the opposite sex while shopping for garments whose lack of strong gendering deemphasized the gender differences and patriarchy central to Francoism's social order. In particular, such contact undercut a misogynistic, conquest-based masculinity that had long enjoyed wide currency alongside the official, chaste Catholic masculine ideal, as well as Francoist society's contrasting, Manichaean division of women into respectable ladies and sexually impure "fallen" women who failed to meet this standard.[46] As Spanish magazines meanwhile embraced the experimental fashions of the 1960s, this stripped away a key Franco-era sartorial marker of male sobriety and thus superiority.[47] A few also tested their ability to print risqué, avant-garde content without provoking censors from the regime's Ministry of Information and Tourism (MIT), anticipating later expansions of sexual expression in the late 1970s, such as a craze for cinematic nudity known as the Destape, or "removal of tops."[48]

With that said, mass consumption in the late Franco era remained sociopolitically contested terrain. On the one hand, officials like

Alberto Ullastres certainly tried to use the spectacle of Spanish economic modernization and rising living standards to whitewash the Franco regime's repressive reputation at home and abroad. Also, while measures like the supermarket's introduction significantly transformed Spanish society, this impact nevertheless had limits. Spain's homemakers gained new social prestige because they could use supermarkets to maximize family budgets and improve nutritional levels nationwide, but their traditional caregiving roles otherwise changed little.[49] And if American consumer culture gained currency in Spain during the late Franco years, so did anti-American sentiment that was fueled by a growing fear—then common in Europe—of American cultural and economic domination.[50]

Ultimately, though, the development of a Spanish mass consumer society had significant consequences that the Franco regime was unable to truly limit or control. Most especially, as they exposed consumers to imported goods and lifestyles, joined international professional communities, and branded themselves publicly as cosmopolitan, Spain's new, foreign-influenced retailers and consumer media drove a shift in popular discourse on Spanish national identity. Spaniards on both sides of the shop counter began not only to buy and sell like Western Europeans, but to think of themselves as such. In the process, they abandoned the remains of early Francoism's foundational discourse of Spanish national difference, and instead embraced the idea that Spain's future lay as part of a prosperous, capitalist, and democratic Europe, establishing a foundation of popular support for the Spanish transition to democracy.

The Spanish Department Store's Long Pedigree

While Spain's socially transformative mass consumer revolution unfolded most dramatically between the late 1950s and the early 1970s, it built upon a Spanish interest in foreign consumer ways, particularly an embrace of department stores, that was far older and dated to these stores' origins in mid-nineteenth-century Europe and the United States. For while historian Pilar Toboso has argued that the modern department store only came to Spain in the 1940s at the hands of Pepín Fernández and his archrival (and cousin), El Corte Inglés founder Ramón Areces, who were indeed both instrumental in modernizing Spanish retailing, other Spanish department stores had begun to adopt foreign methods decades before either businessman arrived in Madrid.

Aristide Boucicaut's Bon Marché, which opened in Paris in 1852, is generally regarded to be the first department store and was in 1883 still so synonymous with that commercial genre that it served as the inspiration for Émile Zola's novel *The Ladies' Paradise*, a portrait of the fin-de-siècle Parisian department store.[51] Boucicaut's innovation quickly spread across Europe and the Atlantic: by the early twentieth century, well-known retailers like Galeries Lafayette, Harrods, Selfridges & Co., R. H. Macy's, and Marshall Field & Company had all opened, as had Havana's landmark El Encanto department store (1888), as well as Harrods' sole branch store, Harrods of Buenos Aires (1914).[52] In these cathedrals of bourgeois consumption, the department store developed its characteristic traits, including fixed low prices, high sales volume, widely varied inventory sold in specialized sections spread out across vast square-footage and multiple floors, as well as spectacles like fashion shows and eye-catching window displays. Zola himself stressed the power of these stores' visually lush displays, describing how maverick window-dresser Octave Mouret seduced and "transfixed" Parisian shoppers with "dazzling combinations [of cloth] . . . avalanches . . . blazing with the most flamboyant colours . . . [such] that the customers should have sore eyes by the time they left the shop."[53]

Spain's first department stores opened contemporaneously, led by Barcelona's Almacenes El Siglo (1881). Despite Spain's absence from scholarship on the nineteenth-century department store, El Siglo was just such an establishment: it sold a wide range of products across nineteen departments and two stories (later twenty-nine sections on five floors); featured spectacles typical of this commercial genre, including an elegant central staircase, cutting-edge gas lighting, and elevators; and even published a customer newspaper. Other department stores soon followed, including Madrid's Almacenes Madrid-Paris; Almacenes Siro Gay of Salamanca; Oviedo's Almacenes Botas Roldán; and, in Barcelona, Almacenes Jorba, whose palatial five-story structure became a city icon by the 1950s.[54] Less-heralded but hardly latecomers, these stores opened alongside their famous European counterparts, and were moreover part of a network of intellectual exchange that led the Bon Marché to inspire innovations at Marshall Field's, and El Encanto's Bernardo Solis and Aquilino Entrialgo to seek out the latest American and Parisian methods and products.[55] El Siglo owners Eduardo Conde and Pablo del Puerto, for instance, adopted American retailing methods they had learned while working in nineteenth-century Cuba, and in the 1920s, Jorba's advertising department studied ads that Harrods of Buenos Aires ran in the Argentine newspaper *La Nación*.[56]

It was into this environment of transnational professional exchange that Pepín Fernández and Ramón Areces respectively arrived in 1908 and 1920, when each left Asturias for Cuba, following an established Asturian tradition of emigrating to the Americas with the dream of amassing a fortune. Both boys—neither was older than sixteen—soon joined El Encanto as general-purpose errand runners, partly thanks to the intervention of top store executive Cesar Rodríguez, who was Pepín's cousin and Areces's uncle. During their combined thirty-six years working at El Encanto (1910–1931 and 1920–1934, respectively), the pair internalized its often foreign-influenced methods and attention to professional developments abroad, which later marked their own stores' principles. These included a paternalistic company ethos that asked employees to completely identify with and sacrifice for the store; a stress on customer service and its use in marketing; the employee rank of *interesado*, a kind of profit-sharing partnership in the company; and cutting-edge American window-dressing techniques acquired from a Gimbel Brothers department store window dresser who El Encanto hired in 1922.[57] Pepín in particular embraced these methods, which later informed moves like his aggressive use of the press to publicize Sederías Carretas' launch.[58] Finally, both men absorbed American commercial expertise directly during business trips to the United States, including a four-year stint (1924–1928) that Areces spent at El Encanto's New York buyer's office. So equipped, they each returned to Spain in the early 1930s and launched their stores in 1934 and 1935, on the eve of the Spanish Civil War.[59]

The Franco Regime: An Overview

The society that emerged from this conflict—or more to the point, the sociopolitical context in which Spain's mass consumer society took shape—warrants a brief review before proceeding. As noted previously, postwar Spain was a diplomatically isolated nation in economic tatters, and remained so for much of the 1940s, a period known in Spain as the "Years of Hunger."[60] Food shortages and rampant black marketeering that flouted government efforts to ration the nation's limited food supply left thousands sick and starving. Agrarian wages plunged below subsistence levels, where they stayed into the 1950s. And Franco's embrace of autarky—a policy of economic self-reliance based on industrialization and import substitution—only compounded these problems.[61] So did the defeat of his main allies, Nazi Germany and Fascist Italy, in 1945, which left Spain ostracized as a fascist relic and excluded from initiatives like the United Nations (founded in 1945) and the U.S. European Recovery Program (1947), better known as the Marshall Plan.[62]

These were also the peak years of Francoist social and political repression. Authorities persecuted former Republican civil servants, political militants, and military veterans, all judged guilty of having served a morally decadent, Judeo-Masonic, and communist "anti-Spain" responsible for the loss of Spain's former global empire. By December 1939, Spanish jails housed 270,719 political prisoners, thousands had been executed, many more faced civil penalties up to and including exile, and a climate of fear reigned.[63]

In place of this anti-Spain, the Franco regime and Spanish Catholic Church imposed a new, deeply conservative social order. The regime banned all political parties save for the official Movimiento Nacional (National Movement), which grew out of and was largely synonymous with the fascist Falange Española Tradicionalista y de las J.O.N.S. (henceforth, Falange).[64] Spain became a confessional state, with "National-Catholicism," a new and nationalistic brand of Catholicism, the sole permitted creed.[65] Franco and his ecclesiastical allies imposed a patriarchal system of gender relations that strictly policed gender roles and sexual morality, and demanded unquestioning obedience to male authority.[66] Finally, women lost the right to vote, to divorce, and, once married, to freely pursue extradomestic work; those who retained career ambitions or lacked interest in marriage risked the social stigma of being deemed bound for spinsterhood.[67]

By contrast, the Francoist ideal of "True Catholic Womanhood," as Aurora Morcillo has termed it, which drew heavily on early modern Catholic sources like the sixteenth-century women's manual *La Perfecta Casada* (The perfect married lady, 1583), stressed patriotism, self-sacrifice, and chastity. New pronatalist policies only underscored this domestic ideal, as did its principal champion, the Sección Femenina (Women's Section) of the Falange.[68] Founded in 1934 by Pilar Primo de Rivera, sister to Falange founder José Antonio, the Sección Femenina enshrined Francoist femininity, particularly its emphasis on obedience, in its eighteen-point creed. After 1939, this group also took on the task of instructing women in the docile domesticity now expected of them through didactic publications as well as programs like the compulsory Social Service (a female counterpart to men's military service requirement), which trained them in household management.[69]

Meanwhile, their privileged status notwithstanding, men had to similarly conform to a strict conservative model of masculinity. Certainly, they controlled female access to the public sphere, as married women needed spousal permission to secure work or open a bank account, but this privilege came with obligations as well. National-Catholic authorities and the prevailing social norms of the era held men responsible for ensuring the stability of Spanish society by policing female relatives' moral conduct and for disciplining their own sexual urges—though prostitution, seen as a necessary release for male sexual voracity, remained widely tolerated into the mid-1950s.[70] The Falangist view of masculinity led to an expectation that men be "man-warriors," displaying a virile, competitive desire to succeed socially and professionally.[71]

The Francoist State devoted considerable resources to publicly enforce these moral demands. National-Catholic authorities like Archbishop Pedro Segura, who had numbered among the secularizing Republic's chief ecclesiastical foes, as well as Bishop Enrique Plá y Deniel of Salamanca, one of the foremost defenders of Franco's rebellion as a just "crusade," imposed a heavy moral stigma on myriad supposedly immoral practices that were often also subject to new legal penalties.[72] They deemed prolonged interaction between the sexes an invitation to sin; consequently, the state banned coeducation after the age of six, and police as well as society at large monitored adults carefully, particularly on Spanish beaches, where police patrols detained immodestly dressed bathers.[73] Press censorship underpinned this coercive system: under the restrictive Press Law of 1938, official censors enjoyed near-total control over the press, subjecting every published word that circulated in Spain to prior scrutiny, and vigorously prosecuting all who offended "public morality."[74]

The early 1950s and Spain's rapprochement with the United States brought an initial wave of economic growth, but resulted in only limited social and political reforms, which were made largely to placate the nation's new foreign allies. In 1951, Franco reshuffled his cabinet to present a more palatably liberal image abroad. Subsequent economic reforms and heavy investment by his new ministers of

Commerce and of Industry, as well as the newly minted Ministry of Information and Tourism, doubled both tourist visits and industrial production figures by the late 1950s, boosted foreign investment, and lifted average incomes to pre-Civil War levels in 1955.[75] Otherwise, however, the regime conceded little beyond marginalizing the fascist Falange in future cabinets and a 1958 revision of the Spanish Civil Code that sought to reconcile Francoism's womanly ideal with new, more liberal notions of femininity arriving from abroad by cautiously bettering women's legal status while reiterating their subordination. Housewives still needed permission to work, censorship remained in force, and even autarky lingered, producing economic dysfunctions that halted Spain's tenuous growth in 1956 and drove inflation—at a postwar nadir—skyward.[76]

And yet, Franco's response to this crisis, which was to reshuffle his cabinet anew in 1957, helped sparked Spain's economic boom by placing a new crop of technocrats—the boom's architects—in key ministries. More reforms followed from the appointments of Minister of Commerce Alberto Ullastres, Laureano López Rodó (Office of the Presidency), and others, culminating in 1959 with the rollout of a groundbreaking Stabilization Plan that ended autarky and opened the economy fully to foreign money, bringing Spain in line with a European push for economic integration that meanwhile produced the European Economic Community (EEC, or Common Market) in 1958.[77] A growing Spanish population; tourism figures that continued to rise, fueled by a larger European economic upswing; and three national development plans spearheaded by López Rodó during the 1960s only magnified the impact of these reforms.

The resulting economic, social, and political changes, sometimes termed the "Spanish Miracle," were dramatic.[78] Between 1961 and 1964, Spain's gross national product grew by an unprecedented 8.7 percent per annum; tourism revenues soared from $71 million in 1958 to $3 billion in 1973; and, by 1975, Spain was the world's eleventh-largest industrial producer.[79] Spanish foreign relations similarly improved.

In 1959, Dwight Eisenhower became the first U.S. president to visit Franco's Spain. In 1964, newly appointed Minister of Information and Tourism Manuel Fraga Iribarne debuted a new "25 Years of Peace" ad campaign and revived an existing tourist slogan that declared "Spain Is Different," which together rebranded Spain as an exotic tourist destination and also a modern European state. So too, though his repeated attempts to join the EEC after 1962 were all rebuffed, did Franco secure a preferential trade agreement with the organization in 1970.[80] Finally, ordinary Spanish lifestyles transformed. Declining religious piety and rising sexual freedom along the tourist-heavy coast alarmed National-Catholic authorities.[81] Consumption of new, modern conveniences by the growing urban middle class shot upward—just 4 percent of households owned refrigerators in 1960, but 87 percent did in 1975—as the "Model Mrs. Consumer" feminine archetype, a consumer-homemaker of American creation that Victoria de Grazia has shown was spreading elsewhere in Europe, reached Spain.[82] And, as the standard of living rose and this foreign-tinged consumerism spread, anti-American sentiment continued to plummet through the mid-1960s.[83]

Yet serious social problems had also begun to fester. Censorship remained heavy, despite the passing of an ostensibly more liberal press code in 1966, because while publishers could now print what they wished, the new code harshly penalized politically or morally offensive content, leading the press to police itself.[84] Incomes rose mainly in Spain's largest cities, resulting in mass migration to these urban centers, housing crises, and swollen outlying neighborhoods like Orcasitas (in Madrid) that struggled with poverty well into the 1970s.[85] For those whose lot improved but still could not achieve their media-fueled consumer aspirations, the results were raised benchmarks for the so-called good life and consequent frustration.[86] Wanting wages that would let them to reap the benefits of the consumer society their work fueled, as well as the right to strike, factory workers formed the first chapters of Comisiones Obreras (CC.OO., workers commissions), the period's most powerful clandestine labor syndicates.[87] Illegal stoppages multiplied, often fueled by political grievances like the 1970 trial of six Basque terrorists, which was itself a symptom of growing tensions between the regime and Spain's long-persecuted minority regional cultures.[88] Meanwhile, the once dependably loyal clergy began to criticize the regime's sociopolitical immobilism, particularly after the liberalizing Second Vatican Council concluded in 1965.[89]

These tensions continued to mount through the mid-1970s, hastening the regime's collapse after Franco's death in late 1975. Fraga was an early casualty, swept out in 1969 following a major financial scandal. Franco's prime minister and trusted lieutenant, Admiral Luis Carrero Blanco, became another when a Basque terrorist attack took his life in 1973, mere months before the Spanish boom met its own end during the global oil crisis of 1973–1974, which sank Spain into a nearly decade-long recession.[90] The ailing Franco had charged Carrero Blanco with ensuring that his successor, Prince Juan Carlos of Spain, remained faithful to Francoism; by contrast, the admiral's replacement, Carlos Arias Navarro, proved unequal to this task as well as the challenges posed by a stalling economy, continuing labor strikes and terrorism, as well as growing pressure for reform emerging from Spanish civil groups, universities, and intelligentsia.[91] Arias Navarro tried to quell this unrest by means of police batons, which seriously harmed the regime's reputation abroad, and, in July 1976, the newly crowned King Juan Carlos duly replaced him with National Movement Secretary-General Adolfo Suárez, a supporter of reform despite his Francoist political pedigree.[92] Amid a crescendo of strikes, months of negotiations followed, with both the illegal leftist opposition and increasingly nervous Francoist diehards in government, ending in an unprecedented Law of Political Reform that outlined the framework for a new democratic government and called for elections. On 15 June 1977, after more negotiations and the controversial legalization of the Spanish Communist Party (PCE), those elections took place, with Adolfo Suárez emerging as the winner and the Spanish Socialist Party

(PSOE) heading the opposition. The struggle to redefine Spanish society and political culture after Franco would continue—and still does—but with this new democratic process in place, Franco's political system was essentially defunct, a transition to democratic governance that became formal with the drafting and ratification by referendum of a new Spanish constitution between July and December of 1978.[93]

This book explores the role that consumption played in these upheavals over the course of five chapters. Chapter 1 examines the genesis of a mass consumer society in Franco-era Spain by considering how its department stores, a telltale feature of mass consumption, took form and spread during the early dictatorship.[94] Starting with the years surrounding Franco's consolidation of power in 1939, this chapter reveals that as these stores grew, they shaped the venues in which the mass consumption of the 1960s would take place, as well as patriarchal and paternalistic institutional cultures that at Galerías Preciados and El Corte Inglés could verge on totalitarian. It argues that this process was profoundly political, most especially insofar as these retailers' totalizing workplace cultures extended regime efforts to impose and enforce a National-Catholic moral and gendered order. At the same time, it concludes, Spanish commercial modernization had already begun to display a marked international orientation that would soon pose an even stronger sociopolitical challenge to the regime.

Chapter 2 considers this process from the other side of the shop counter, through the lens of the Spanish press, which it shows drove the discursive construction of mid-century Spain's first, imagined mass consumer society. During the 1940s and 1950s, the number of Spanish consumer magazines rose sharply; this chapter argues that as they multiplied, these periodicals encouraged readers to consume and perform middle-class identities through products like American home appliances, and to imagine themselves as part of a mass consumer society in which all could aspire to this. As at Spain's department stores, the products and lifestyles that these magazines promoted were often foreign and especially American in origin, the result of a foreign focus that marked these magazines, and Spain's burgeoning mass consumption, from their inception. Finally, this chapter emphasizes this foreign turn's extensive sociopolitical consequences. While at first magazines like the women's journal *Mujer* actively promoted National-Catholicism's conservative feminine model, the arrival of American consumerism challenged this domestic and self-abnegating feminine ideal. Some Spanish magazines began to encourage housewives to consume for their own pleasure and pursue careers, while others fought a rearguard effort against these changes, stressing women's traditional duty to home and family. Most of all, though, the embrace by the Spanish consumer press of foreign consumer culture, in tandem with Spanish department stores' own outreach, advanced Spain's integration into an international network of American and European retailers, fashion professionals, consumers, and, more broadly, of nations—the last of these soon to be given a measure of formal political reality in the EEC.

Chapters 3 and 4 explore the culmination of these processes during the years of the Spanish economic boom, Franco's death, and the subsequent transition to democracy, or roughly from 1956 through 1980. Chapter 3 focuses on the arrival of the supermarket in Spain in the late 1950s and early 1960s, while chapter 4 examines the contemporaneous professionalization of the Spanish advertising industry and expansion of Spain's consumer press, in both instances using these developments as case studies for how Spain's consumption-mediated international integration accelerated during its economic boom. Between 1956, when the Spanish Ministry of Commerce first contacted its U.S. counterpart for information about supermarkets, and the 1966 annual meeting of IPRA, hosted in Barcelona by Spanish public relations pioneer Joaquín Maestre Morata, both the food distribution and advertising industries expanded at a breakneck pace. They did so, these chapters argue, for the same reason that drove Spanish department stores' foreign outreach: concern over the economic challenge that the EEC posed, and a consequent fixation on modernizing their industries, as well as spurring a broader, national rise to modernity, through professionalization.

Both chapters also reveal that food retailers and admen alike undertook this concentrated expansion in close dialogue with the Franco regime, which wielded an often heavily regulatory hand and in particular sought to harness the supermarket's spread to its goal of promoting Spanish national prosperity and international prestige. Meanwhile, Spain's consumer journalists and fashion professionals likewise turned their focus increasingly abroad as the consumer press continued to expand. As they did so, shifts in gender norms and women's access to the public sphere, as well as the newly arrived youth culture of the 1960s, played out in Spain's consumer press, especially men's magazines, which ultimately reinforced the same fixation with foreign lifestyles and international affiliation sweeping through the food distribution and advertising industries. In all cases, the result was a new and especially strong penetration of foreign products and lifestyles into rural as well as urban consumers' lives, and a growing perception among these consumers as well as Spanish food retailers, admen, journalists, and fashion industry professionals, that their nation's future best lay in a further economic, social, and, if necessary, political convergence with their Western Europe neighbors.

Chapter 5, finally, returns to the nation's department stores, examining how the social upheavals of the dictatorship's last fifteen years (1960–1975) unfolded in these venues, focusing especially on shifting gender roles and conceptions of Spanish national identity. Over a longer span of time than at SPAR's supermarkets or Joaquín Maestre's public relations agency, and in dialogue with the shifts taking place in Spain's consumer press as detailed in chapter 4, Spain's department stores helped develop its mass consumer society and hastened its insertion into a larger international community. This chapter examines Galerías Preciados' and its competitors' spread during the economic boom years, as well as their efforts to gain world-class, cosmopolitan reputations, but also the challenges that the changing times posed to their carefully constructed institutional cultures. It then follows these trends as they culminated during the 1970s and the end of the dictatorship in the halls of not just a foreign-influenced store but a truly hybrid Spanish-American enterprise: Sears, Roebuck of Spain. Aided by its parent company's multinational structure, this store thrust its employees and customers into the most extensive international commercial network they had yet experienced, a remarkably fluid transnational flow of people and ideas that, as one contemporary put it, caused borders—and increasingly, one might add, notions of Spanish social and political difference—to cease to exist.[95]

CHAPTER 1

World-Class Stores and (Inter)national Ambassadors

The Department Store and the Formation
of a Spanish Mass Consumer Society under
the Early Dictatorship, 1939–1957

On 15 November 1941, Francisco Casares, secretary of the Spanish National Federation of Press Associations and an official within the newly established Franco regime, crossed central Madrid to deliver a speech at Sederías Carretas, by then an up-and-coming retailer in the capital. Standing before the store's assembled staff, Casares emphasized that, true to founder Pepín Fernández's well-known maxim that "commerce is a social function," stores like Sederías were important for providing people "what they need to live, to reward their senses, or to lead more elegant lives." Commerce, Casares added, "is as useful and noble [a task] as that of the public official, the human instrument of the State."[1]

Inasmuch as they perceived that retail commerce in early Franco-era Spain was a site of social and political power, Casares and Pepín were fundamentally correct. The period from 1939 to 1957—the era of Spain's postwar isolation as well as its initial diplomatic and economic recovery—saw the genesis of a mass consumer society in which ordinary Spaniards lived lives steeped in advertising charged with various hidden meanings, most especially promises of achieving social respectability through consumption.[2] As noted previously, scholars to date have largely argued that, though the economic recovery of the 1950s laid the foundations for the boom of the 1960s—when enough of the populace at last gained the buying power to support mass consumption—the initial effects were limited.[3] Yet, in fact, during the eighteen years between the end of the Spanish Civil War in 1939 and Franco's politically transformative cabinet change in 1957, department stores like Sederías Carretas/Galerías Preciados, Ramón Areces's El Corte Inglés, and Almacenes Siro Gay expanded into a host of Spanish cities. They likewise reached rural areas through new mail-order services. And, by so doing, they achieved unprecedented success and influence over the nation's commerce and consumer life.

As they grew, these stores played a key role in the development of mass consumption in Spain. They provided new, modern, purposely built venues for this mass-oriented commerce. They helped professionalize the nation's retail commerce through training programs, trade journals, and internal bulletins that rendered their workforces more technically proficient, held together their flourishing networks of store branches, and meanwhile produced workplace cultures that were the backdrop against which shoppers and store clerks later experienced the socioculturally turbulent 1960s. And, as Spain's diplomatic fortunes improved from the late 1940s on, these retailers increasingly embraced imported commercial methods, nurtured ties to foreign retailers like Havana's El Encanto, and pursued affiliation with international retailing organizations like the International Group of Department Stores (IGDS), all of which reinforced and extended Spain's existing commercial ties abroad.

This had political consequences, and indeed, early Franco-era Spain's embryonic mass commerce was often politicized, particularly by the Franco regime and its supporters within the retail sector. On the one hand, after 1939 stores like Galerías Preciados professed loyalty to the new regime and began imposing Francoist values—especially gender norms—on their staff through new official employee codes of conduct and other similar policies. So armed, managers aggressively regulated workers' private moral conduct and even their choices as consumers. These efforts in turn extended Francoist moral authorities' ability to control Spaniards' private lives and so contributed to the early regime's efforts to attain an extensive and invasive degree of control over Spanish social mores and public morality. At the same time, the emergence of modern department stores in early Francoist Spain laid the foundations not only for the nation's subsequent consumer boom but, concomitantly, for an undermining of Francoist social hegemony. Inasmuch as they drew on imported methods and sought ties abroad, these retailers' new management policies and efforts to expand physically helped build pathways through which other foreign products, consumer ways, and, eventually, subversive sociopolitical notions would enter Spain during the tumultuous 1960s. This chapter examines the roots of those relationships, and shows how, by advancing Spain's integration into the socioeconomic fabric of Western Europe—and importantly, popular awareness thereof—this foreign outreach also set in motion an erosion of Francoist notions of national difference.

The Spanish Department Store Begins to Spread

The modern department stores of the Franco era began to develop almost immediately after the dictatorship established itself. Yet, at first, the economic disarray of the Spanish postwar period and the absence of any appreciable middle class, even in Madrid, made this far from easy. Revenue was so low that Sederías Carretas had to cut back on advertising, one of the cornerstones of the store's message-oriented commercial philosophy.[4] In addition, such retailers found virtually every aspect of their daily operations beset with obstacles. During 1941 and 1942, the years of greatest shortage in Spain, scarcity translated into an ongoing struggle to even fill shelves. In 1941, for example, Sederías's merchandise buyer's office in Barcelona found itself unable to procure stockings, a popular product, as well as semi-luxurious fabrics like Scottish wool—difficulties that disruptions caused by World War II, which engulfed Europe through 1945, surely exacerbated.[5] Government rationing of textiles, meanwhile, proved yet another hurdle, as their sale required a special license that even Pepín Fernández, who was otherwise politically well connected, was still struggling to secure in 1948.[6]

The economically hard times also circumscribed these stores' clienteles. Per-capita incomes in Spain dropped sharply during the 1940s, and the majority of Spaniards barely earned enough to subsist—much less shop for pleasure—in part because the Franco regime kept worker wages artificially depressed.[7] A pair of factors mitigated the effects of this lack of buying power. First, stores like Sederías Carretas initially traded mainly in textiles; particularly the lengths of unfinished cloth needed by Spanish housewives who sewed or had a seamstress sew their families' clothes rather than buying off the rack.[8] Second, these stores operated in Spain's principal and wealthiest cities. Here they could sell to postwar Spain's small upper class and the nouveau riche who were making fortunes in the black market, as well as to working-class city dwellers who, as Civil War chronicler Gerald Brenan observed on a return visit to Madrid in 1949, faced pressure to dress well in order to remain employable, despite having to live on one meal a day.[9] Despite the hard times, such efforts provided a starting point for the subsequent development of an imagined consumer society in Spain, as the nation's department stores advertised to a public that for the most part could only aspire to consume.

Indeed, Sederías Carretas, along with fellow Madrid newcomer El Corte Inglés (founded in 1935) and older stores like Almacenes Siro Gay, soon began to expand across the country. They enlarged existing stores and built branches in new cities, hired more staff, and introduced foreign technical innovations like Spain's first escalators and professionally designed window displays. In so doing, they provided Spain's cities with spaces in which a new mass commerce could take place and introduced the chains, entrepreneurs, and legions of ordinary sales clerks who would ply that trade. And, as these department stores turned their attention to foreign commercial methods, they exposed Spaniards to these new ways of buying and selling and began to integrate the nation into international European and American retailing circles.

These changes unfolded most dramatically at Sederías Carretas and the retailing chain it spawned, Galerías Preciados. In 1943, the retailer debuted this new commercial identity with the opening of a flagship store bearing the name in Madrid's city center, on a stretch of street—Calle Preciados, the rechristened chain's namesake—between the commercially important Puerta del Sol and Callao plazas (henceforth, Galerías-Callao).[10] In 1943–1944, Galerías created a mail-order department that enabled it to reach customers nationwide.[11] Either in 1941 or 1947—sources disagree on the date—the chain opened its first satellite location in the Moroccan city of Tangier, which was under Spanish military occupation between 1940 and 1945, with the aim of breaking into a market with few Spanish competitors and known to be friendly to shopping via catalog thanks to the longstanding presence of outposts run by many major Parisian retailers.[12] Then, expansion accelerated: between 1947 and 1956, Galerías Preciados built six branches, expanded its flagship store, and opened a textile factory in Madrid, Talleres Coppelia, to cope with the shortages of the 1940s (see table 1).[13] In 1953, Galerías also moved its Tangier location to a larger space on the Boulevard Pasteur, a commercial thoroughfare that anchored the city's new international district, where an eclectic mix of Spaniards, Britons, and Frenchmen drank in cafés, browsed the bookstore run by French publisher Gallimard, and took nightly strolls along the avenue.[14]

Yet, the case of Galerías Preciados was not unique. In 1940, El Corte Inglés opened its flagship store in Madrid on Puerta del Sol, where it remains today. The branch expanded in 1946; over the course of the next eight years, El Corte Inglés went on to found its own Tangier branch as well as a manufacturing division, Industrias y Confecciones (INDUYCO), incorporated, and expanded its flagship a second time.[15] It was to El Corte Inglés as well as Galerías Preciados that the 1956/1957 Annual Guide to Industry and Commerce in Madrid likely

TABLE I. Expansion of Galerías Preciados, 1939–1956

YEAR	NEW BRANCHES	OTHER EXPANSIONS
1934	Sederías Carretas-Madrid	—
1941/1947	Tangier (Morocco)	—
1943	Galerías Preciados Flagship Branch (Galerías-Callao)	"Postal Department" Catalog Service—Madrid (1943/1944)
1947	Badajoz	Talleres Coppelia Manufacturing Wing—Madrid
1948	Galerías Preciados Annex-Madrid; Tetouan (Spanish Morocco)	—
1949	Melilla; Don Benito (Extremadura)	—
1950	Santa Cruz de Tenerife (Canary Is.)	—
1953–1954	—	Expansion of Sederías Carretas, Expansion of flagship to Plaza de Callao, Relocation of Galerías-Tangier to Boulevard Pasteur
1956	Córdoba	—

Source: Author's compilation from Toboso, *Pepín Fernández*, 159, 177–178, 230; Zafra Aragón, *Méritos, errores, ilusiones y personajes de Galerías Preciados*, 38–46; and, Jiménez Artigas, Pineiro Alonso, and Ranedo Fernández, *Galerías: Ayer, Hoy y Mañana*, 2:42.

referred when it noted that "some . . . department stores manage sales of over one million pesetas daily."[16] This sum was equivalent to more than 2,200 satin-lined men's wool overcoats, then selling at Galerías for 450 pesetas (ptas); more than 500 portable children's swimming pools, which El Corte Inglés priced at 1,950 ptas; and roughly 6,250 times the average daily wage of a well-paid store manager.[17]

Beyond the capital, Almacenes Siro Gay of Salamanca expanded even more quickly than Galerías, adding a new branch every two years between 1942 and 1952. And in Oviedo, capital of Pepín's native Asturias, Almacenes Botas underwent a series of relocations and expansions that won it a national reputation for visual splendor by 1945. That year, a column in Madrid's *A.B.C.* heaped praise on one of the store's "cheerful, luminous, and alluring" entrances and deemed it "forceful and attractive enough" to single-handedly guarantee Oviedo's status as a great city—acclaim that echoed Botas's own marketing slogans that declared it "Spain's best commercial establishment" and its wares likewise "always the best."[18] Finally, a constellation of smaller, local department stores flourished, including Barcelona's Almacenes Jorba, Madrid's Almacenes Simeón, and a host of bargain-priced retailers that flooded Barcelona's newspapers with ads promising deep savings during the hardscrabble 1940s. These establishments did so well in Madrid that they helped more than triple total yearly sales in the capital between 1940 and 1954.[19]

This expansion fueled a similarly rapid increase in hiring, which notably included a number of foreign-trained specialists who, by applying their imported expertise, began to integrate Spain's commercial sector into the larger international retailing community. Almacenes Botas, for instance, took on not just a steady flow of locals like Rafael Álvarez Fernández, a native of neighboring Limanes parish who rose from novice textiles department clerk in 1940 to head of Menswear in 1955, but also American-trained Luis Botas Rezola, son of the store's founder, who joined in 1944 and over the next two decades spearheaded a variety of modernizing professional-development initiatives.[20] At Galerías Preciados, payroll grew from 12 employees in 1934 to 830 in 1948, 1,000 in 1951, and triple that figure in 1957.[21] Among these new hires were Paris-based merchandise buyer José Corominas, formerly of El Encanto, who brought his foreign contacts with him to Galerías in 1941; Pepín's eldest son, José Manuel, hired in 1948 after stints at several American stores, who patterned the store's new employee bulletin on another circulating at Macy's; and Head of Accounting Ramón Granda Lanzarot (hired in 1956), who standardized the store's accounting practices and oversaw the creation of a teletype network that connected Galerías's branches.[22]

Expansion drove these stores to import other technical advancements, too, which exposed Spanish consumers to new foreign commercial experiences. During the early and mid-1940s, modern foreign store window-dressing techniques—a staple of commercial advertising during Spain's 1960s mass consumer boom—came to Spain. Early in the 1940s, Spanish department stores began to abandon their traditionally cluttered and amateur window displays in favor of the larger, well-lit, professionally designed ones that stores like Macy's had pioneered several decades before. In 1940, for example, El Corte Inglés featured a display that, in lieu of merchandise, simply offered a series of placards listing the store's many services and long hours. In 1943, the newly opened Galerías Preciados similarly marked the line between old and new when it commissioned foreign-trained window dressers Aycuens and Domenech to produce a pair of attention-grabbing displays for perfumes and woolen goods that, store ads later boasted, were an "artistic" departure from the tradition of "purely commercial" window designs.[23] And in April 1945, Spanish window dressers got their first dedicated trade journal, *Escaparate*.[24] As the spread of such journals had done in late nineteenth-century Britain and the United States, *Escaparate* shaped the window draper's profession in Spain, spreading principles of good (often foreign) design, and arguing for the trade's legitimacy by identifying successful Spanish members.[25] In an early article from 1945, for example, the magazine wove a legitimating narrative of past success for the profession both by referencing a prize that Aycuens (now Galerías Preciados's artistic director) had won in 1939, and by quoting him, stating that store displays in Spain's major cities had much improved in the years since his award, as now, in 1945, these were far more carefully designed.[26]

Other foreign innovations followed. Physically, Galerías Preciados, Almacenes Jorba, and other stores continued to evolve. The escalator, an early twentieth-century American invention designed to maximize customer flow in department stores, had been exhibited in Spain in 1929, and was first installed for regular use at a retailer, the bargain-price outlet SEPU (Spanish Fixed-Price Company) in 1935. By the late 1950s, the invention had become synonymous with modernity and national progress in Spain, and both Galerías-Callao and Jorba had linked most (in the former case, all ten) of their shop floors with escalators. Tellingly, Pepín Fernández justified the exorbitantly expensive project by calling it necessary if Galerías was to be world class. This symbolic importance is only underscored by the reactions that followed Siro Gay's installation of an escalator in its new Valencia branch in 1961. Among the local public, the device drew what the store deemed "considerable attention," while the store's own bulletin as well as local Valencian newspaper *Las Províncias* saw in it a "symbol" of "Man's ingenuity and desire to excel," or, more pointedly, of the store's preeminence in Valencian commercial life and extensive clientele.[27]

Finally, Almacenes Jorba introduced two other notable innovations during the mid-1950s, new and at the time rare customer services that both cultivated public goodwill and boosted sales. First, in 1953 the store launched *Revista Jorba*, a fashion and women's magazine that served as a platform for ads, publicized store events, and, more generally, let Jorba insinuate itself further into customers' lives. It was different from other store periodicals: more so than earlier store magazines aimed at customers, Jorba's new journal featured attractive images and graphic ads, a color-illustrated cover, and fashion and child-rearing columns as well as short stories, all targeted at a similarly new mass audience. And, at first, it had no direct competitor: at the time, its sole contemporary was Galerías Preciados's bulletin, a professional journal.[28]

Beyond the sheer fact of its novelty—and its popularity, for the magazine enjoyed a sizeable circulation of 25,000–30,000 copies per issue, with readers across Spain and abroad—*Revista Jorba*'s appearance represented a milestone in the trajectory of Spanish consumer culture. It actively participated in the various liberalizing and conservative currents in motion within domestic consumer discourse throughout the 1950s. In several of its recurring columns, perhaps most notably the journal's *consultorios femeninos*, or "women's advice" columns, the magazine offered content that reinforced traditional notions of proper femininity against the challenge that new, more liberal models of feminine behavior posed, a struggle that historian María del Carmen Muñoz Ruiz has shown later pervaded such columns in the 1960s.[29] For instance, in early 1955 Jorba advice columnist Macrina counseled a young career woman named Paulina to be careful of her new boyfriend, because the places to which he took her—unchaperoned— were "not very appropriate for a young woman," imperiling her virtue and good name. Several months later Macrina likewise scolded another reader, "R.N.," for having indulged in "that modern practice, like something out of a novel, of women declaring their intentions toward men, which fortunately tends to end badly in Spain."[30]

Revista Jorba also served as an early example of a phenomenon that would eventually become commonplace in other sectors of Spanish commerce: the store-published consumer magazine. In 1959, Galerías Preciados experimented with such a periodical, a short-lived women's magazine titled *Galerías*. At least one supermarket chain, once supermarkets arrived in Spain in the late 1950s, published a magazine meant for the housewives who shopped there, one that was separate from its internal company bulletin. And much later, in the late 1980s, Galerías would again experiment with the genre, publishing a glossy full-color fashion magazine titled *Galerías Marcando Estilo* (Galerías setting fashion).[31] But such customer-oriented magazines remained rare in the 1950s. Department stores more commonly incorporated elements from traditional consumer periodicals, such as fashion columns and serialized stories, into their employee bulletins—Galerías, El Corte Inglés, Almacenes Botas, Siro Gay, and, once it arrived in the late 1960s, Sears, Roebuck, would all do so to varying degrees. *Revista Jorba* was the first modern example of a store magazine published specifically for customers, and may have even inspired the short-lived *Galerías*.

Jorba's second innovation, which debuted in 1955, was a consumer credit system of payment by installments, which the store publicized especially to housewives.[32] The significance of this measure should not be underestimated. First, as Aurora Morcillo has noted, availability of consumer credit was a key factor in the initial emergence of a mid-century Spanish consumer sector. While the comparatively prosperous residents of Madrid's and Barcelona's city centers shopped at stores like Jorba, most Spaniards—including many in these cities' peripheries—lacked for food and basic services like running water. In between these two extremes lay urban populations whose incomes rose somewhat amid Spain's initial mid-1950s economic upturn, and who wished to consume but could not quite afford to do so. For them, credit made shopping possible and added a dose of material reality to fantasies of consumption in which ordinary Spaniards had begun to imagine themselves engaging.[33]

In adding this service, Jorba also preceded its larger Madrid counterparts, Galerías and El Corte Inglés, by over a decade. Pepín Fernández and Ramón Areces remained suspicious of and reticent to adopt installment payment services as late as 1964, when, by their own admission, establishing a credit service had become unavoidable.[34] The Catalan retailer may in turn have been following the example of foreign department stores like Macy's and El Encanto, which introduced this innovation decades earlier still. This seems especially likely given Jorba's history of monitoring such stores' methods as well as credit's well-established impact abroad: when Jorba introduced its installment program in 1955, U.S. consumers' credit use was already so extensive that it sparked public anxiety over the influence this kind of spending was having on private debt, then steeply on the rise.[35]

By the mid-1950s, then, Spanish department stores had developed the nation's first commercial infrastructure devised to serve a mass market. Twenty years earlier, Madrid, Barcelona, and a handful of other Spanish cities had hosted a variety of bargain stores, outlets of purely local appeal and of unremarkable quality, as well as a few establishments of a bourgeois, nineteenth-century character, such as Barcelona's El Siglo and Jorba. In the period roughly spanning 1940–1956, by contrast, stores like Galerías Preciados founded branches in an impressive list of Spanish cities, including eleven provincial capitals. They dramatically expanded their ranks—in Galerías's case, growing from forty-three workers in 1939 to three thousand in 1957—introducing some of the key names in 1960s Spanish retail in the process. And they incorporated foreign technical and technological innovations laden with notions of modernity.[36] Yet this was only half of the sea change taking place in the culture of Spanish retail commerce—alongside this physical, infrastructural, "external" expansion, there took place another, and perhaps still more transformative, management-oriented, "internal" one.

Internal Expansion and International Influences at Spain's Developing Department Stores

During these same years (1939–1956), El Corte Inglés, Almacenes Botas, and especially Galerías Preciados also implemented a series of internal personnel policies and programs, including employee codes of conduct, store bulletins, and professional-education departments. Such measures, again often of foreign origin, profoundly shaped these stores' evolving policies and organizational structures. More generally, they also influenced the workplace cultures through which store staff experienced and contributed to the birth of a Spanish mass consumer society during the 1950s, and later experienced the economic growth and social turmoil of the 1960s. In particular, this professionalization of Spanish department store retailing functioned as a site for the politicization of the nation's emergent mass commerce, often in the form of alignment with rather than against Francoism's sociopolitical project. At the same time, such imports also established a precedent for a further importation of foreign commercial methods, products, and consumer ways in the boom years of the 1960s, all of which arrived accompanied by associated (and to Francoist eyes, subversive) notions that would in time have significant sociocultural consequences for Francoist society and the Franco regime itself.[37]

The first and most fundamental of these policies was having a store code of conduct, known as the *Normas* at Galerías Preciados and Botas, and which existed under other names at El Corte Inglés. Galerías again led the way: its *Normas* already existed in some form by the time of Francisco Casares's 1941 speech, which mentioned the code, and it began to circulate as a handbook penned by Pepín himself shortly after the first Galerías Preciados opened in 1943. Almost immediately, the book became standard issue to all new hires and a cornerstone of the store's culture—an employee bible that entered a second, expanded edition in 1951. El Corte Inglés also introduced a handbook in 1943, an adapted American sales manual titled *El Arte de Vender* (The art of selling) that was the first of several such handbooks that the store published from the 1940s on, including several editions of a code similar to the *Normas*. And Almacenes Botas's own *Normas de Botas*, a near-verbatim copy of Galerías's code, appeared soon after at the hands of Luis Botas Rezola, son of the store's founder, who joined Botas in 1944.[38]

Over the course of the 1940s and early 1950s, Botas, Galerías, and El Corte Inglés also began to adopt measures that pushed their staff to pursue constant personal and professional self-improvement, something that was already fast becoming a core institutional value at all three establishments. By the end of the 1940s, Galerías and Botas had both launched professional-education programs. These were initially modest—in 1950, future menswear department head Jesús Méndez González went through Botas's program seated on a merchandise counter rather than in a classroom—but they soon expanded. As of 1960, Galerías was running a broad range of courses at its smaller provincial stores as well as its core branches, including an economics colloquium series at its then new Bilbao location and a special course for saleswomen at the likewise new (and small) Murcia branch. This programming also coincided with a new wave of hires that included many budding young university-trained technocrats, popularly termed *los universitarios* (the university students). These were men like José Luis Botas Rodríguez, Galerías Preciados's director of technical services from 1963 through 1975, who arrived armed with extensive professional knowledge and familiarity with the latest methods being pioneered abroad. Botas Rodríguez, for instance, introduced the first computers at Galerías in the early 1960s.[39]

Yet this growing stress on professional development was perhaps most evident in the employee bulletin that the recently returned José Manuel Fernández launched at Galerías in 1948, the *Boletín de Galerías Preciados*. This new monthly periodical quickly became management's main means of communicating with staff company-wide, often to didactic ends. It was the first and, until the late 1950s, the only such publication in Spain, as *Revista Jorba* catered to customers rather than staff. Along with the *Normas*, it was arguably also one of the store's most notable early foreign imports: Pepín had based his handbook on another he had penned in 1926 for El Encanto, itself patterned off still earlier ones used at U.S. department stores Lord & Taylor and Wanamaker's; likewise, an employee bulletin at Macy's inspired José Manuel to create the *Boletín*.[40]

Throughout its print run, which lasted through the end of the dictatorship in 1975, the *Boletín* regularly ran columns that called on readers to pursue greater technical mastery in retailing, as dedication to their trade and to its underlying service ideal demanded—that is, to engage in what scholars term "professionalization."[41] A series of articles submitted by employees to the bulletin for a 1953 contest, for instance, declared that "to be a good salesperson one needs preparation [professional education], art, and hard work," and that "there is nothing further from the true salesperson than the anachronistic clerk lacking adequate training and knowledge about his customers and products." Other columns described professionalization as a safeguard against the store's moral and commercial degeneration and as a way to shore up both the store's and employees' own personal fortunes, and saw a lack of interest in retailing's technical aspects as a sure sign of a bad salesperson.[42] Meanwhile, the employee handbooks introduced at Galerías Preciados, Botas, and El Corte Inglés sought to similarly spur employees to better themselves. Indeed, in 1957, the *Boletín* pointed proudly to the *Normas'* insistence on professionalization as proof that Galerías "[had been] the standard bearer of progress ... [in] the transformation of commercial methods in the Spanish capital."[43]

For their efforts, these stores paid their workers well—especially Galerías Preciados—which only reinforced the carefully cultivated aura of prestige that these establishments enjoyed in the public eye. This was the point. Tellingly, Sederías Carretas's *Reglamento de Régimen Interior*, the charter that legally regulated the store's internal workings, not only set many workers' base salaries as high as double what well-compensated trades like cabinetmaking and tailoring paid, but stipulated an additional and permanent 15 percent pay bonus for all staff in order to reflect the store's "first-class" and "special" status.[44]

Finally, starting in the early 1950s, Galerías founded a system of company social clubs, the Club de Galerías Preciados, through which it provided cultural and social activities for off-duty employees. Some chapters also had physical spaces: Madrid's Club, which lay just minutes from the Callao flagship store, offered board games, live music, and an inexpensive bar that, to underscore the club's central place within the Galerías organization, was first tended by future Cafeteria Department head Rafael Molina Santander.[45]

These measures all displayed a didactic impulse akin to the disciplinary, training, and social programs, sometimes termed "welfare work," by which turn-of-the-century American department stores had sought to raise employee morale and professionalism, and so yield better customer service. Employee handbooks—forebears of the *Normas*—had become common at those stores by the late 1920s.[46] Their latter-day Spanish counterparts and other such measures likewise sought to preserve customer service quality, which (especially at Galerías) managers feared would decline as untested novices flooded stores' growing ranks, and Spain's continued economic woes hindered these often undereducated and poorly dressed hires' efforts to meet employers' exacting professional standards.[47] Meanwhile, amid this climate of economic uncertainty, the prospect of earning a steady and, in some cases, unusually high salary made working at these stores worth enduring their supervisors' pedagogical zeal and close oversight.[48]

For indeed, these initiatives responded to managers' concerns with a heavy-handed brand of paternalism that sought to regulate every aspect of the workplace. Store handbooks such as the *Normas* and El Corte Inglés's code were comprehensive and naked in their pursuit of maximum control over worker conduct, for much the same reasons as their American predecessors. For instance, they sought to ensure that saleswomen were neither snobbishly overdressed nor carelessly underdressed in stained and wrinkled uniforms, both of which could put customers off and hurt sales.[49] The *Normas de Galerías Preciados* in particular included rules governing employees' behavior in virtually every workplace situation, including how they ate lunch in the company café (alone, to avoid time-wasting conversation), how often they bathed and changed underclothes, and how they greeted clients. Thus, in response to the poor state of oral hygiene in Spain, to which the era's material hardships only contributed, the *Normas* painstakingly ruled:

The mouth requires . . . very special attention. There are people who . . . cannot stand to be near someone who has bad breath. We must, then, care for our oral hygiene with maximum rigor. We must clean our mouths meticulously and patiently for a few minutes' time at least twice a day, when getting up and going to bed. When a toothbrush has softened, it must be replaced. One must brush both inside and out, leaving not one tooth untouched. Cavities appear frequently. . . . It is therefore essential to visit the dentist at least once a year, even if free of symptoms. Cavities caught in time are easily treated, while those that are ignored become more serious later on and can infect other, healthy teeth. Such small details . . . have many times decided one's fate in life.[50]

Employee training programs similarly aimed to build on employees' often sparse formal schooling, making them more capable workers and especially better able to serve foreign customers.[51] Meanwhile, the club echoed American welfare work initiatives in providing employees (whose private moral conduct was of acute concern to Pepín Fernández) with store-sanctioned, wholesome, and often educational leisure activities that also reinforced their loyalty to the store.[52] Making this debt all but explicit, Pepín would in 1971 cite El Encanto—an avid student of American store methods in its day—as the inspiration for founding the club.[53]

These measures also had the vital purpose of preventing the chain's atomization into a collection of disjointed, far-flung branches—another peril of an expansion that, by the late 1950s, left Galerías with outposts as distant as Tenerife. Beginning in the mid-1950s, a handful of columns in each *Boletín* issue offered news from the store's branches; coverage of recent births, nuptials, and deaths within its ranks; and profiles of departing well-known employees, all to preserve a sense that, distances notwithstanding, every branch and employee belonged to a single Galerías family. Thus, in a 1953 article on the store's Tangier branch, *Boletín* regular Agustín Olivera wrote of branch head Luís García, "As all or nearly all of us know, he is in charge of our branch [there]. He does not, I assure you, wear a turban nor does a snake dance about his feet. Despite his years [in Morocco] García seems as if he never left Madrid. He has neither a camel, nor a blonde with the look of a spy and the gaze of a Marilyn Monroe."

Lying just underneath the levity was Olivera's more pressing point: that García and his distant branch were still recognizably part of Galerías, a point that García himself underlined in the subsequent interview. In it, he noted that the Tangier branch's clientele was mostly Spanish, described their policies and methods as "a little piece of Galerías, brought over to Morocco . . . [such that one] enters and thinks oneself in Madrid," and requested that the *Boletín* report on them, "so that [in Madrid] they'll remember us and know we exist."[54]

Yet the ambitions underlying these initiatives ran still deeper. Both Ramón Areces and Pepín Fernández, and, later, other retailers like Luis Botas Roldán, saw their stores as more than just a place to work or buy goods. This perception was rooted in Areces's and Fernández's own experiences at El Encanto in early twentieth-century Havana, where the store's errand boys had slept overnight on the counters they worked during the day, received an allowance and board in lieu of pay, and had little time off—perhaps a single afternoon per week. The Cuban store had demanded that employees devote their lives almost completely to the store. As Areces and Fernández crafted their own stores' internal politics and oversaw the stores' physical expansions, both men sought not only to manage the growing number of staff this expansion generated but to similarly absorb their growing ranks further and further into the company, centering workers' lives around the store.[55]

To that end, measures like the *Normas* sought to control aspects of employees' lives that were only loosely related to the store. As an attempt to colonize workers' leisure time, the Club de Galerías Preciados represented one such effort, though its aim was specific (and thus limited) and participation remained voluntary. Not so for the *Normas*. Galerías's, Botas's, and El Corte Inglés's handbooks all warned readers that their conduct always reflected back on their employers' reputations, whether they were in or out of uniform, and so they were expected to adhere to these stores' high standard of conduct in their private as well as work lives and internalize their cultures of self-discipline. El Corte Inglés's code claimed exclusive rights to employees' work lives, forbidding any outside work, even self-employed labor.[56] Pepín's manual (and Botas's close copy) meanwhile sought to police both what workers read as well as with whom they spent their free time, calling on them especially to avoid morally corrosive friendships and pastimes and instead "care for their spiritual lives." Ominously, the *Normas* followed these moralistic commands with a thinly veiled threat for those who would disregard them: "How many youths, having given in to such stimulations, have *lost their jobs* [emphasis mine] and have been unable to put their lives back together!"[57]

Most ambitious was the store's injunction against what Pepín termed *Traición a la Casa*, or "treason against the store," which was one of the worst sins a Galerías employee could commit. The act itself was a seemingly commonplace one, nothing more than purchasing something that Galerías Preciados sold from a competitor instead. Yet the *Normas* considered such "treason" deeply serious. The handbook described it as a betrayal of trust, "sabotage of [the store's] name," and dereliction of the fundamental duty to never actively harm the store's interests—in short, a moral transgression, not just a breach of store policy. Its severity was visually underscored by the black border that surrounded the bylaw's text in the *Normas*, a distinction reserved for the store's most important, absolute principles (see fig. 1).[58]

Given the comprehensiveness of Galerías's inventory, which ranged from textiles to religious paraphernalia to automobiles, the store's policy effectively claimed control over staff members' lives and choices as consumers, just as Galerías's, Botas's, and El Corte Inglés's codes otherwise laid claim to workers' private morality and, in the last

TRAICION A LA CASA

El personal de GALERIAS PRECIADOS no puede, sin daño material y moral para nuestra Casa, comprar en otras lo mismo que nosotros tenemos. Comprar en establecimientos competidores nuestros sería una acción desleal, un acto de traición, un verdadero sabotaje contra nuestro nombre y contra el prestigio y los intereses de nuestro negocio. No se trata simplemente de la materialidad de la compra. Eso no significa nada. Se trata de lo que ello representaría en un orden más elevado y más importante. ¿Qué pensaría de nosotros, en cualquier sentido, la casa donde comprara alguien de nuestro personal los mismos artículos que nosotros vendemos? ¿Cuál sería el efecto causado en el público? Una hipotética diferencia en el precio no puede ser explicación o justificación en ningún caso. Si tal diferencia existiera, real o aparente, infórmele al Jefe de sección, a fin de que haga la comprobación debida. Pero en todo caso tenga en cuenta esto tan sencillo y elemental en una conciencia justa, honrada y lógica: Usted trabaja aquí; aquí gana su vida; de la vida del negocio depende la suya; si el negocio va bien, tiene usted asegurado en él su presente y su porvenir; si va mal, los pierde. *Vea, pues, cómo ambas vidas—la del negocio y la de usted—están tan fundidas y enlazadas, que vienen a ser una sola.* Una misma vida, física y espiritual. Siendo esto así, constituyendo una profunda realidad humana, ¿no es para todos nosotros un deber natural, fundamental, hacer cuanto de nosotros dependa en beneficio del negocio y no hacer absolutamente nada que pueda perjudicarlo material o moralmente?

FIG. 1. "Treason against the Store." Galerías Preciados Collection, ARCM, File 124661/8.

GALERÍAS PRECIADOS staff cannot buy elsewhere anything that we sell without morally and materially harming our store. Buying from our competitors would be a disloyal act, an act of treason, veritable sabotage of our name and our enterprise's prestige and interests. It is not about the material purchase itself. That is nothing. It concerns what this represents on a higher and more important level. What would a store think of us, if our employees bought things there that we sell? What would be the public impact be? A possible price difference is never a valid reason. If faced with such a real or apparent difference, inform your section head, who can look into it. But in any case, consider what is to the just, honorable, and logical mind a simple and basic fact: you work here; here is where you earn your living; your life depends on the store's; if business is good, your welfare is assured; if business is bad, you lose it. *See, then, how both lives—the store's and yours—are so fused and intertwined that they become one.* [Emphasis mine.] One life, physical and spiritual. This being the case, being a fundamental human reality, is it not for us all a natural, fundamental duty to do all in our power to benefit the business and do absolutely nothing that could harm it materially or morally?

case, to their professional lives as well. There was little a Galerías employee might want that they could not buy from their employer, so there were few purchases they could make that were not subject to this policy and to the store's control. This was especially so because these policies, including Galerías's rule on professional "treason," had real teeth. Managers at Galerías Preciados were manifestly willing to carry out the consequences threatened in the handbook, firing one female employee, for example, for immoral behavior in March 1958. Ramon Areces shared this reputation for strictness, even if he was more forgiving toward minor offenders.[59] Meanwhile, if the disciplinary regime at Almacenes Botas is less well known, the *Normas de Botas* (once again, a nigh-verbatim copy of Galerías's handbook) included a commercial treason clause that differed only cosmetically from Pepín Fernández's original handiwork, and in particular preserved its black border, suggesting a similar view on employee discipline.[60] Indeed, to the degree that its own inventory spanned a broad range of goods, Botas had in its treason policy a similar means by which to colonize its staff's private consumption.

Such severity followed naturally from what these stores and their employee codes deemed to be fundamentally at stake—their public reputations—concern for which bordered on the obsessive among the managerial ranks at all of these retailers. At Galerías, it conditioned the store's relationship with the public from its very founding: Pepín's comments to the press following Sederías Carretas's 1934 launch had stressed the size of the attending crowd as well as the store's novel methods in order to quickly establish its public prestige. This concern is likewise evident in the *Boletín*'s penchant for printing letters from visitors that praised the store's customer service. In 1955, for example, the journal used a letter by a visitor from Pakistan, which thanked the store's staff for the warm reception the writer had received as proof of the "great prestige that Galerías enjoys not just within but beyond our borders"—that could nonetheless easily be lost if staff became complacent, as another customer's letter warned.[61] The *Boletín de*

Botas similarly preached the need to protect the store's image. In 1963 it reprinted an *Escaparate* column in which Samuel Venero, a veteran of Galerías and El Corte Inglés, warned Botas that its sterling national reputation would last only as long as staff kept taking personal responsibility for their work. Tellingly, the recurring column that featured Venero's comments was titled, "What Others Think of Us."[62] Most of all, this concern over public perceptions introduced a degree of invasive unpredictability to Galerías's and El Corte Inglés's draconian disciplinary regimes: thus, though the *Normas* did not explicitly ban smoking, a new Sederías hire once nearly lost a raise because the manager who found him doing so on the street after work considered it an ugly habit.[63] And, attracting such unwelcome attention, particularly from the founders themselves, was a real danger, as both men regularly inspected their stores—Pepín did so daily—visits that inspired respect and even fear among workers.[64]

Indeed, as the point where retailers' carefully curated marketing met the public's real shopping experiences, sales personnel occupied so fraught a role at Galerías and Botas that, in seeking to limit employees' ability to tarnish the stores' reputations, their policies on commercial treason abandoned the American commercial and management philosophies the retailers otherwise so emulated. As it developed in the early twentieth-century United States, mass consumption quickly took on significant political meaning, inasmuch as American citizen-consumers' freedom of choice, like the freely exercised franchise, became a cornerstone of what it meant to live in a democratic and capitalist society.[65] In these terms, Galerías's policy by contrast disenfranchised a whole category of consumers—the store's employees. This was striking both because it came not long after America's own enshrinement of consumer choice, of which the Havana-trained Pepín had to be aware, and because Galerías meanwhile took pains to remind these same clerks that poorly treated customers had and could exercise this very right, voting with their feet and pocketbooks by shopping elsewhere. Another of the *Normas*'s black-rimmed tenets, for instance, warned that customers did the store a favor by shopping there, and that wasting their time with inexact information would "cause them to leave . . . resolved never to return."[66]

Yet, again, there was a logic to this, one that was also shaped by the Francoist sociopolitical context in which Spain's mass-oriented department stores developed. Galerías's treason clause was symptomatic of how the store envisioned its employees not as consumer-citizens of a Spanish polity but rather as akin to military servicepersons: like soldiers or priests (both highly regarded roles under Francoism), the store's clerks surrendered certain basic freedoms—namely, consumer freedom of choice—in the line of duty. They similarly served a cause greater than themselves, which was both the greater good of the store, and, following Pepín Fernández's oft-repeated maxim that "commerce is a social function," the whole of Spanish society. Indeed, another *Normas* tenet fascistically called on employees to sacrifice their own desires for the store's benefit, which it likened to the nation's highest interests. And the store's treason policy similarly blurred the line between store and self, describing these as "so fused and intertwined that they become . . . one life, physical and spiritual," such that workers' efforts (and the store's treason policy) benefited them as much as their employer.[67] The *Boletín de Galerías Preciados* only reinforced this metaphor through columns that fetishized military service. Some directly celebrated colleagues who left the store to serve in the Spanish military (see fig. 2) or, in one case from 1956, who had joined the French Foreign Legion.[68] Another pair of articles from 1960 used military terms to describe workers' efforts to ready the launch of Galerías's first Bilbao branch—one praised the branch's "shock troops" for "taking Bilbao without a single casualty." Notably, this language reportedly originated not in the bulletin, but among the store's ranks, among whom such discourse was seemingly already well established.[69]

Perhaps unsurprisingly, this militarized discourse and the controlling policies that underpinned it were likewise in line with the Franco regime's illiberal politics, and reveal the extent to which these

4 RECLUTAS, 4, SE DESPIDEN

Ante la imposibilidad de estrechar, una a una, las manos de dos mil ochocientos compañeros, Luis Larumbe, José Bayo, Antonio López y Santiago Piqueras, los cuatro del Departamento Postal, dedican, a través del BOLETIN, un saludo a la afición horas antes de incorporarse a la vida militar. Cuando usted, amigo lector, vea publicada esta foto, ellos ya habrán cambiado sus elegantes trajecitos grises por sendos uniformes de color caqui, y sus cabecitas se tocarán con el clásico gorrito de borla roja. ¡Animo, muchachos! A estos colegas, así como a cuantos dejan de estar con nosotros una temporadita por las mismas causas, les deseamos mucha suerte y les recomendamos un comportamiento tan digno como el que han tenido en «Galerías Preciados».—A. E.

FIG. 2. "Four Recruits, Four [Store] Resignations." *Boletín de Galerías Preciados*, no. 61, Year VII (April 1956), 6. Galerías Preciados Collection, ARCM, File 88011/1.

stores were shaped by the authoritarian context in which they developed. If in the United States consumer choice was linked to democratic values, the Franco regime vilified these values in its first decades, later enacted cynical and at best superficially liberalizing reforms, and meanwhile sought to politically demobilize its populace throughout its tenure. Put differently, if American consumer choice derived value from its metaphorical link to a culturally sacred democratic franchise, in Franco's Spain the vote was neither valued nor even existed. To the contrary, the regime idealized self-sacrificing service to the nation, particularly military service, which the *Boletín de Galerías Preciados* and *Normas* echoed.

Indeed, during the Franco dictatorship's most fascistic early years, handbooks like the *Normas* could themselves be directly political. The demands that these codes made on workers represented a colonization of their lives by the stores that issued them. This rendered the resulting work cultures at Galerías Preciados and El Corte Inglés, for which the stores' *Normas* functioned as foundational texts, in a sense totalizing—that is, systems characterized by the desire to construct model employee-citizens wholly defined by, and committed to, their service to the store. El Corte Inglés termed such individuals *personas Cortty*, or "Cortty people."[70]

These aspirations to total citizenship fit directly within the Franco dictatorship's larger sociopolitical project. In the late 1930s and early 1940s, myriad voices around the new regime declared it totalitarian, in line with the Falangist tenet that the Spanish state ought to be "a totalitarian instrument in the service of the integrity of the Patria [Fatherland]." Sociologist Juan Linz and others later argued convincingly that the dictatorship abandoned these totalitarian pretensions after 1945 and instead evolved into a "stabilized authoritarian regime" that lacked both a clear ideology and extensive political mobilization, and exercised power by ill-defined yet predictable means.[71] Yet an important continuity remained: the Franco regime had in fact never sought to wield total authority alone, even initially. Rather, its aim was always to centralize political power in order to better compel public support for its project of national renewal, and not, for example, to take over the Spanish Catholic Church, or expand the state's authority for its own sake. Rather than assume direct control over every aspect of life, Franco's "subjective[ly] totalitarian" Spanish state, as Jesuit theorist of Spanish corporatism Joaquín Azpiazu termed it in 1937, assumed a "directive" role, aiding rather than absorbing the Spanish Catholic Church and its mission of saving souls, and working together to disseminate the politicized brand of Catholicism they termed National-Catholicism.[72] In other words, they worked toward a kind of delegated and at least partial totalitarianism.

In their will to control, El Corte Inglés and Galerías Preciados—especially the latter—existed in a relationship to the early Franco regime analogous to that of the Church. In her study of the Coros y Danzas, a folkloric dance troupe run by the Falange's Sección Femenina, historian Pilar Amador Carretero has noted that states transmit ideology both through official mechanisms and also "accidental ... agents ... with their own distinct aims but which ultimately

also serve as [ideological] transmitters."[73] Galerías Preciados functioned as just such a private, separate, yet allied and at times explicit
agent of Francoist "subjective totalitarianism," and at times the regime
intentionally used the store thusly. Only in this case, rather than disseminate National-Catholicism (though the store was public in its
official Catholic fervor), it worked alongside the regime to advance
the latter's vision of a unified, corporatist reorganization of Spanish
society and, most especially, of labor and commerce at the service of
Spanish national greatness.[74]

It was in these terms that, in his 1941 speech at Sederías Carretas,
Secretary Francisco Casares described the role he believed Pepín's
store and its *Normas* played as paragons and champions of the new
Francoist Spain's fundamental ideology. The store's code, Casares
declared in Falangist and National-Catholic terms, had established a
model for how organizations could develop a fraternal, collaborative
workplace ethos that cut across internal hierarchies and rooted itself
in the shared experience of daily labor toward a common goal. This
"honest, Christian worldview" embraced early Francoism's notion of
work as the morally imbued key to the regime's pursuit of national
greatness, which could only be achieved when "those working in
the same place fus[ed] their wills, intelligence, and physical efforts
together toward one shared end." This was the same spiritual com-
munion that Pepín Fernández sought to build when he called in the
Normas for total dedication to the store's cause and warned that "a
firm like Sederías Carretas . . . which requires the collaboration of
many spirits, cannot reach a high grade of efficiency if everyone is
not governed by the same obligations. [These are] duties from which
no-one can be exempted. The well-being of the company and the
prestige of our name demand it."[75]

The shared end to which Galerías's workers so dedicated
themselves—commerce—could itself also take on a political charge.
In his speech, Casares ranked it with the Church and the Spanish military as a central pillar of Francoist Spain's new society. Two decades

before Galerías-Bilbao's "shock troops," and echoing the Falange's bellicose "man-warrior" masculine ideal, he argued that Galerías's clerks bore just as much a duty to the nation as did Spain's soldiers and likened the store's commercial-cum-social philosophy with Falange founder José Antonio Primo de Rivera's own thinking. He further-more naturalized the handbook's totalizing expectation that workers identify completely with the store by comparing this dedication to soldiers' and priests' devotion to their calling. Casares even went so far as to say of the *Normas*:

> One could call [it] your breviary, or in more mystical, but to my mind not exaggerated terms, your book of hours. . . . For this store's staff, it is more a reminder of conduct than a new, never-before-seen law. We who are [Catholic] believers pray the same prayers every day, not to learn of some moral obligation of which we were previously ignorant, but rather to practice the discipline of restating [moral] purpose and renewing devotion every day. There is, then, a renewal . . . of your own conduct in these norms that you have been given. . . . There is a spiritual commerce, which is that of treating others well, that is far greater interest to your managers than that other one that consists of the simple mechanism of selling, counting, weighing, and measuring.[76]

Comparing observance of the code's precepts to the Catholic self-discipline of daily prayer, Casares effectively sacralized its contents much as the store's own discourse did, particularly in the *Boletín de Galerías Preciados*, which fetishized the handbook.[77] Indeed, he closed by counseling that obedience to managers and the *Normas* was "the truest way to feel oneself to be Spanish."[78] In sum, Galerías and its code could readily serve as an example in microcosm of the corporatism that the early Franco regime sought to implement and, in cases such as the introduction of the supermarket in the late 1950s, would continue to advance years later.

Moreover, though Casares's own right-wing and Francoist allegiances were well established, dating back to the Second Republic, he was not in this instance imposing a purely fabricated political reading on the store's institutional culture.[79] He had been invited to speak by the famously controlling Pepín Fernández himself, and the views Casares offered not only anticipated the store's later militaristic discourse but also fit Pepín's own Francoist leanings. By then, the latter had already joined Foreign Minister Ramón Serrano Súñer's effort to cultivate Spanish-Latin American diplomatic ties by creating a new Consejo de la Hispanidad (Hispanic Cultural Council), to which Pepín recruited several former Havana colleagues. He had also begun to build ties to the regime through personal friendships with top figures like Serrano Súñer and the Spanish First Lady, Carmen Polo.[80] In sum, Casares's speech manifestly reflected the store's own political alignment at the time, which was eagerly at the regime's service.

It is by no means certain that such a politicization of work achieved currency at other retailers. El Corte Inglés was comparatively apolitical. Botas's nearly identical employee code included the same intrusive policies present in the *Normas*, but, as at El Corte Inglés, it does not perforce follow that this paternalism was ideologically Francoist. The *Boletín de Botas*'s references to that store's handbook, while reverential and at times heavy-handedly didactic, likewise tended to simply enjoin clerks to "always be ready to serve" rather than indulge in the kind of military and religious metaphors favored at Galerías. And the closest another store came to Galerías's ties to the dictatorship was Almacenes Siro Gay, whose founder won the regime's Silver Medal for Merit in Work in 1960, an award that Pepín won twice, in 1962 and 1974.[81]

Yet it is suggestive that by the end of the 1950s Galerías's example was otherwise widely emulated by Spanish department stores. Botas in particular frequently voiced its admiration for Galerías's methods and its founder, celebrating Pepín's Asturian background on numerous occasions. Indeed, not only did the store's *Normas* mimic its model almost exactly, but Botas's official discourse also paid its employee code the same kind of reverence expressed at Galerías, for instance, citing the handbook as the basis for the store's success.[82] After the 1958 launch of its version of the Club de Galerías Preciados, the Club de Botas, the Oviedo retailer could likewise aspire to colonize its employees' leisure time as Galerías Preciados did.[83]

Discipline and Daily Life

These cultures of control fundamentally shaped store workers' daily experiences, particularly (but certainly not exclusively) at Galerías Preciados and El Corte Inglés. As these disciplinary cultures developed, they drove the formation of distinctive workplace rhythms of life and practices whose tone as well as specific policies were largely conservative and reflective of the early regime's own social values.

Rigid discipline and an emphasis on hierarchy reigned within the workplace cultures at both Galerías Preciados and El Corte Inglés, following naturally from El Encanto's formative example. At Galerías, potential hires faced a scrupulous and systematic evaluation process involving presentation of an employment application, an entrance exam, a fifteen-day trial under close observation, and a barrage of psychological evaluations, any of which could doom a candidacy.[84] Once hired and situated within these stores' extensive and rigid hierarchies, new employees faced long work hours as well as frequent calls from superiors to work well beyond their allotted shifts. And, as noted above, employees were all the while subject to exacting standards of conduct, with even the lightest infractions punishable by stiff penalties. These demands were rooted in the *Normas*'s expectations of *entrega total* (complete employee identification and self-sacrifice), which the *Boletín de Galerías Preciados* romanticized in columns such as José Javier Aleixandre's tribute to the overtime work done by Galerías-Bilbao's "shock troops."[85]

Managerial authority was autocratic, obedience total, and the penalties for disobedience were severe. In the mid-1950s, for instance, manager Valeriano Rojo forced store accountant Manuel Zafra to undo a reform he had been authorized to make to the store's bookkeeping practices purely because Rojo himself had not personally approved it.[86] Zafra dared not complain, for insubordination could get one suspended or fired, as could the seemingly harmless act of accepting a tip from a customer, which Galerías Preciados and El Corte Inglés both expressly forbade.[87] Nor were all such infractions obvious or even codified, as in the case of the Galerías clerk who nearly lost his raise for smoking after hours. And attracting such unwanted attention from not just any ordinary manager, but the store founder himself, was a daily possibility. Both Pepín Fernández and Ramón Areces made a habit of regularly inspecting their stores—visits that inspired considerable fear.[88]

Humor columns in Galerías's bulletin that gently poked fun at certain managers' idiosyncrasies only reinforced this control by serving as a store-sanctioned safety valve for the tensions such an autocratic management style could engender. The *Boletín de Galerías Preciados*'s humor pages—tellingly titled "Humor and a Bit of Controversy"—also served as a means of airing problems generally akin to, though usually less serious than, Manuel Zafra's frustrations with Valeriano Rojo. Several columns to this effect appeared in each issue. Using the pseudonyms "Boliche" and "Dorotea," which were the names of the Interior Design Studio's cats, Advertising Department artist Agustín Mencía Sanz penned at least two such columns. One was a recurring comic strip that gently mocked salespersons' bad habits (see fig. 3).[89] The other, "¡¡Veinte al Bote!!" (roughly translated as "Twenty in the Tip Jar!"), which debuted circa 1953, often worked in reverse, offering a list of twenty observations, suggestions, or even complaints about store policies and the foibles of Galerías managers like Rojo, whose authority otherwise protected them from criticism from below.[90] Thus, for instance, the column's first entry took a Stationery Department manager to task for denying the Catalog Division permission to use one of his saleswomen as a model. It criticized the Annex's management for placing a store bar where employees smoked next to the Mail Order Department's baskets full of outgoing merchandise,

FIG. 3. Comic Strip, "Boliche, El Gato del Estudio" [Boliche, the Studio's Cat], *Boletín de Galerías Preciados*, no. 50, Year VI (Undated, ca. 1954), 2. Galerías Preciados Collection, ARCM, File 88011/1.

which Mencía deemed a fire hazard. And, as it would happen, the article teased Valeriano Rojo for ambushing put-upon salespersons with accounting minutiae. Another edition criticized management for so restricting employees' movements that they did not know where departments on other floors were located, even after internal memos circulated with precisely that information.[91]

Boliche's pointed cattiness was ultimately meant to be prophylactic, stabilizing, even functioning as a vehicle for reasserting aspects of the store's institutional culture. Mencía's comic strip obliquely underlined a tenet from the *Normas*: that every customer's business was important, no matter how small. And the inaugural "¡¡Veinte al Bote!!" meanwhile scolded "whoever it was who spread the false rumor that employees were being tape-recorded during their annual performance reviews," both because it was false, and also, presumably, because such behavior, which threatened store discipline, violated Galerías's core values of devotion and obedience. Mencía's own loyalist critique, by contrast, was more measured.[92]

Boletín de Galerías Preciados contributors also used humor to continue the bulletin's and the club's work of cultivating the notion among readers that a warm, intimate camaraderie still tied the store's increasingly far-flung members together into a single "great family."[93] Authors sought to conjure this feeling by using descriptors like *entrañable* (situationally translating as "dear," "fond," or "close"), and *íntimo* (intimate).[94] Agustín Olivera's initial, joking tone in his 1953 report on Galerías's Tangier branch represented one such deployment of humor.[95] An especially rich instance was "La Mampara de Jacometrezo," a long, comically exaggerated account of the decision-making process to install a room partition at the store's Calle de Jacometrezo office in late 1959. The pseudonymous author, "Don Nuño," described the discussion as "a dialectical bombardment that dwarfed what neutrons and protons undergo [in a nuclear explosion]," and caricatured a succession of Galerías notables, including Ramón Granda and store co-founder Adolfo Pérez Piqueras, who was a veteran of the chain's expansion projects. Of Piqueras, the author wrote,

On hearing the words "division" and "partition" he did not let us finish. He picked up the phone and called Mr. Sabio to tell him to prepare fifteen squads of construction workers, three bulldozers, twelve garbage trucks and an explosives team in case some load-bearing wall should offer unexpected resistance. When he finished ... and we continued explaining the project, he gave us a look of such hypnotic force that we ran out of his office. It was then that we realized our mistake in going to Mr. Piqueras, who had spent almost thirty years [living and] breathing lime, plaster, cement, and iron, [to ask] about a humble wooden screen.[96]

Good-natured rather than malicious, the net effect of the caricatures was endearing and bred a sense of familiarity with their subjects. This was especially important for employees in far-off Tenerife and Tangier, who had quite possibly never met these company notables.[97]

Finally, many of the comic strips and humor columns published in the *Boletín de Galerías Preciados*, as well as the entire humor page in "*Gay*," an employee bulletin that Almacenes Siro Gay launched in 1958, aimed not to engage in internal critique or proselytism, but simply to amuse.[98] Yet even such comparatively unpolemical content also reflected and reaffirmed the regime's social discourse. And it reveals how these stores' organizational and disciplinary infrastructures shaped their workplace cultures, particularly as regarded notions of gender and the gendering of social roles in Franco-era Spanish society, which was a subject on which much of this frequently patriarchal and misogynistic humor hinged.

For, just as Franco-era social orthodoxy displayed an acute concern over gendered domesticity, management of the household, and obedience to husbandly authority as women's rightful destiny, several of Spain's premier department stores placed a similar importance on gender difference. These retailers produced and circulated a canon of notions concerning women in their roles as shoppers and, within the stores' own ranks, as fellow retail workers. In myriad articles, interviews, and, most especially, humor pages, both *"Gay"* and the consumer-oriented *Revista Jorba* painted a picture of women as at once painstaking shoppers and profligate spenders.[99] Cartoons published in early issues of *"Gay"* dealt in well-worn stereotypes of women as henpecking viragos and spendthrifts: one, for instance, shows two lines in a bank—one male, one female—the male line stretching from the deposit window, and the female from the withdrawal, juxtaposing women's supposed financial profligacy with the bourgeois sobriety of their harried husbands, one of whom in fact regards the women nervously.[100] Another depicts a sister and brother playing a game of pretending to be "mommy and daddy," the former waiting, rolling pin poised to strike, for the latter's late (and perhaps drunken) arrival home (see fig. 4). Several years earlier, a similarly acute concern over gender difference permeated these stores' policies concerning their saleswomen, reproducing the deep gendered divisions that existed in Franco-era Spanish society as a whole. At Galerías, even though women made up nearly 70 percent of the store's workforce as the 1950s ended, the perception reigned, even reaching as high as the founder himself, that women's work was second-rate. In a 1960 interview printed in *"Gay,"* Pepín explained:

> With women there is a strange phenomenon. All of them, up to a certain age, are enchanted with ... marrying, and this keeps them somewhat aloof toward the firm; it is as if they do not entirely identify with it, because, "since they're going to get married. . . ." But then, when they turn 27, for example, it isn't that they lose the desire to marry, but they tend to think more of the store as a career, and this makes them feel more responsible, they take greater interest. I could tell you of many who now occupy positions of responsibility.[101]

Yet, as Pilar Toboso has shown, the number of female managers was low throughout this period, particularly at the highest levels of management. During the late 1940s, Sederías Carretas's three depart-

LA MEJOR PRENSA

La revista inglesa «The Reporter» cuenta la siguiente anédota que revela la actitud del soldado ruso hacia la prensa.

— ¿Qué diario prefieres? — preguntan a un sargento del ejército rojo.

—Creo que el mejor es «Pravda», seguido de «Izvestia» y «Estrella Roja». Los demás se hallan casi igualados. En cuanto a los periódicos alemanes, son muy malos y no se pueden comparar en modo alguno con los nuestros.

— ¡Ah! — responde el informador—, ¿Entonces lee usted el alemán?

— ¿Quién habla de lectura? Los fumamos. El papel nos sirve para liar nuestros cigarrillos y el de «Pravda» es el mejor. Los alemanes irritan la garganta.

—No, mamá, no viene nadie; es que Pepita y yo estamos jugando a papá y mamá.

41

FIG. 4. "No, Mama, nobody's here; Pepito and I are playing house." *"Gay,"* no. 9, Year II (August–September 1958), 41.

ment heads were all male, as were six of the store's seven most senior salespersons, while over a decade later, in 1962, no women figured among the chain's 104 top officers. Instead, women abounded among the rank and file. Indeed, before launching his flagship store in 1943, Pepín had gone so far as to personally recruit the daughters of well-respected local families, swaying their parents with the promise of the strict moral oversight enshrined in his *Normas*.[102]

And, just so, the perception—indeed, the expectation—similarly persisted at both Galerías Preciados and Siro Gay that "shop girls" were destined for marriage rather than management and could mainly be counted on to leave the store in short order. Official store policy at Pepín's store codified this expectation in an echo of extant legal restrictions on women's right to work. Both Sederías Carretas's 1948 internal regulatory code and a second company-wide code enacted in 1959 mandated the automatic dismissal of female employees who married, with exemptions allowed only for women who were heads of households. The former code—but notably, not the latter, which specified equal pay for equal work—also expressed this wariness toward women's work in explicit, financial terms, paying female employees only 80 percent of what their male colleagues earned.[103] *"Gay"*'s editors, meanwhile, revealed similar preconceived notions regarding women's work in a March 1962 editorial reacting to the recently passed Women's Political, Professional, and Labor Rights Law of 1961, which mandated greater pay parity between men and women. Equal pay was fine, the editorial grudgingly warned Siro Gay's saleswomen, but henceforth they would also have to work equally as hard as their male colleagues—the implication being that this had not previously been the case.[104]

The notion that employment at a department store was something Spanish women only did until they could find a husband even penetrated the public consciousness, as evidenced by the feature film *Las Muchachas de Azul* (The girls in blue, 1957). The movie, which starred three of the nation's leading stars, Analía Gadé, Tony Leblanc, and film legend Fernando Fernán Gómez, launched an entire genre of lighthearted Spanish comedies. It followed a trio of blue-uniformed Galerías Preciados shopgirls as they worked to offer excellent service and, more importantly, to land a husband, most especially the film's male lead, sales clerk Juan Ferrándis. Leaving no question as to the film's base assumption that a woman's ultimate aim was always marriage, a common belief in Spain at the time, screenwriters Noël Clarasó and Juan Dibildos opened the film with a voice-over sequence featuring images of an idyllic urban Madrid of cafés, bustling pedestrians, stylish automobiles, and, finally, a groom waiting nervously in front of a church. The male narrator declared: "With regard to the admiration [that women have] for men, we need not say anything ... it is infinite.

They admire him so much that one look will not do—they want to admire him comfortably, for a lifetime. And to better show him their admiration, they dress him in the husband's uniform, the glorious and heroic morning coat."[105] Still, the narrator continued, "it is not so easy to get a man to put on this coat," and as the misadventure-filled film concluded, he stressed, "all of this [the film's events] had to take place so that [the saleswomen's new husbands] might wear the marvelous morning coat."[106] Even the movie's poster pushed this message, showing an alarmed Ferrándis fleeing from three shopgirls, each wielding a net with which to catch him in marriage.[107]

Such assertions and deployments of gender difference likewise abounded at other stores and on other questions. "Gay"'s August 1961 issue, for instance, included a farewell letter from well-known Siro Gay manager María Begoña in which she announced her coming marriage and departure, wishing her female coworkers luck, happiness, and the chance to similarly marry their beloveds soon.[108] Other columns in the Boletín de Galerías Preciados, Botas's bulletin, and "Gay" contained feminine-gendered content that reproduced stereotypes of feminine flightiness, workplace moodiness resulting from private, often romantic troubles, and even a tendency toward immorality. Thus, one July 1960 "Gay" article offered readers the cautionary (albeit fictional) tale of a saleswoman who was irritable due to problems with her boyfriend, brushed off a customer looking to exchange a pair of stockings, and so nearly lost the store a customer before a more sensible female colleague intervened and, subsequently, lectured her about leaving personal issues at home.[109]

Official store policies could likewise reflect such notions of feminine instability, just as they did assumptions concerning saleswomen's marital ambitions. Galerías's and El Corte Inglés's employee rulebooks required female employees to wear uniforms—the blue dresses that gave Las Muchachas de Azul its title—but did not require the same of their male colleagues. Following arguments such as Jennifer Paff Ogle and Mary Lynn Damhorst's contention that men's business suits reproduce the hegemony of white male businessmen, one can read this policy as more than a simple visual representation of gender difference. Rather, it was also underpinned by a perceived need to impose discipline on saleswomen's bodies, something that menswear's staunch conservatism had already ensured in the case of their male colleagues.[110] Donning a uniform, in other words, was an act that made these women stable and reliable enough to represent the company on the shop floor.[111] Even so, as the 1950s closed, managers at Galerías remained concerned about maintaining uniformity in saleswomen's attire, and most especially about the sexual danger posed by insufficiently high uniform necklines and slips peeking out from under skirt hems. The latter fear, which the *Normas* expressly voiced, was such that in 1960, Agustín Mencía Sanz, as "Boliche" in "¡¡Veinte al Bote!!," called for that winter's seasonal uniforms to button up to the neck, or alternatively to include a uniform sweater.[112] These efforts, moreover, faced little resistance on principle from Galerías Preciados's and El Corte Inglés's saleswomen, who had internalized their employers' rivalry and cultures of store pride, and for whom these uniforms represented not an imposition, but a status symbol. In Madrid these saleswomen often remained in uniform when they left for lunch, reveling in the public display of their ties to the capital's leading retailers and in the rivalry they felt when they encountered the competition.[113] Quite possibly because these women chose to wear their uniforms in this way outside the workplace, when Galerías saleswomen complained about them—and by the early 1960s, such complaints had become common—it was a particular seasonal uniform's colors and style, and not the fact of a uniform, with which they took issue.[114]

Indeed, for both the men and women who worked at stores like Galerías, Botas, or El Corte Inglés during the 1940s and 1950s, the clothes they wore to work could represent a considerable perk of the job. As noted previously, British author Gerald Brenan observed in 1949 that urban Spaniards, particularly middle-class Madrid residents, faced rising pressure from employers and society as a whole to dress elegantly, even though severe poverty and persistent goods shortages remained daily realities for many of these city dwellers. Under these circumstances, a 15 percent discount on tailored menswear that Sederías Carretas's *Reglamento* afforded its male employees—a provision meant to help them procure suitable work attire—offered an added benefit: it helped these clerks meet society's sartorial dictates by reducing the out-of-pocket cost of building up wardrobes they could just as readily wear to a dinner as onto the shop floor.[115] Though not as versatile, the uniform dresses issued to women workers were likewise useful, inasmuch as they not only constituted comparatively inexpensive workwear, but, as illustrated by some saleswomen's practice of keeping their uniforms on while out on a break—again, against company policy—these were garments that wearers could reasonably expect would not harm, and might even enhance, their personal public image.[116]

Intern(ation)al Expansion

Finally, this growing internal organization at Spain's premier department stores increasingly exposed those stores to foreign commercial practices, and with them the notion that Spain was and should aspire to be part of a larger international commercial community. It was, in other words, the beginnings of the internationalization of Spanish mass retail commerce in the Franco era. The innovations that these retailers introduced during the 1940s and 1950s were overwhelmingly foreign in origin. More specifically, they often arrived having followed a roughly triangular path that led from the United States through Latin America (especially Havana) to Spain, as in the case of Galerías Preciados's *Normas* and club, both developed from Cuban models that were in turn based on North American predecessors, and which later inspired counterparts at Botas.[117] Such measures also included El Corte Inglés's adapted American sales manuals; the *Boletín de Galerías Preciados*, which José Manuel Fernández modeled after a newsletter circulating at Macy's; and one of the foundational features of both Madrid retail giants' internal hierarchies, the rank of *interesado*, original to El Encanto. Epitomizing this early linkage process, in 1951 Galerías Preciados joined the Intercontinental Group of Department Stores (IGDS), a group of mostly Western European department stores that pooled their expertise and ordered inventory collectively in order to bolster their international competitiveness.[118] Meanwhile, the *Boletín* and, after 1958, *"Gay,"* printed a steady and insistent stream of articles that praised the experience of shopping in Europe's great capitals and called for further foreign-inspired advances in areas such as advertising. For instance, in 1956, *Boletín* editor Alfredo Marquerie called for Galerías to modernize its marketing practices following the example of Italy's La Rinascente department store.[119]

For those who opined on this issue, what was at stake was nothing less than achieving a foreign modernity that held the key to a prosperous future for Spain. In 1934, this ambition had underpinned Pepín's 1934 declaration that Sederías Carretas was the store that Madrid, *as a world-class commercial city*, had been waiting for; in the 1950s, it drove Spanish retailers' adoption of the escalator, and the Spanish public's enthusiastic reception thereof, an enthusiasm that in 1960 led working-class Almerian E. Chacón to include a stop at the flagship Galerías Preciados branch during a family trip to the capital.[120] And thus Alfredo Marquerie's insistence in 1956 on the need for Galerías to bring its advertising up to a foreign standard, warning that, "in Spain, where we look too often inward, modern [commercial] art cannot seem to lay down strong roots, because our gaze never roams far enough."[121]

Like the Franco regime itself, department store commerce in Spain at the close of the 1950s looked radically different from two decades earlier. Between 1939 and 1957, the regime had moved from the openly fascist posturings and autarkic policies of its first years toward an increasingly internationally integrated market economy and an equally open, if also disingenuous, avowal of the regime's democratic nature. The transformation at Spain's department stores was similarly radical: from a single neighborhood store, Sederías Carretas had grown into a national chain with locations even in Spanish Morocco (meanwhile adopting a new commercial moniker), and underwent an internal complexification to match. The chain developed an employee club structure, professional-development programs, an internal bulletin, and a set of rigid principles, its *Normas*, which would, after their introduction in the early 1940s, serve as the store's bible—all measures that the rechristened Galerías Preciados's competitors also undertook to varying degrees.

One consequence of this expansion was that, as these stores opened branches in Spanish provincial capitals as well as towns such as Eibar and Don Benito, they provided these places with modern department stores in which the consumer revolution of the 1950s and 1960s could unfold. Crowds in Valencia could now marvel at Siro Gay's escalator or take advantage of Jorba's new sale by credit system in Barcelona. Meanwhile, Galerías Preciados and El Corte Inglés developed internal policies that increasingly sought to bring employees' lives completely under their purview, echoing the early Franco regime's own totalizing impulses. As they did so, these stores shaped the workplace cultures through which their salespersons would experience the mass consumer revolution and social upheavals of Spain's tumultuous 1960s.

And in this same vein, these measures had a profound impact on current and future politics of national identity in Spain, at times in keeping with the regime's agenda, but also, crucially and increasingly, in ways that undermined Francoist orthodoxy on this question. As foreign innovations like cutting-edge window-dressing methods arrived in Spain, and Galerías Preciados joined the IGDS, these measures rendered Spain commercially more like other nations and fostered a sense of connection between Spanish retailing and its American as well as Western European counterparts that would only continue to grow from the 1960s onward. During the 1940s, 1950s and into 1960s, the Franco regime could still insist on Spain's national social and cultural as well as political difference, but, from a commercial perspective, Spain was beginning to seem less and less different from its Western democratic trading partners.

CHAPTER 2

Imagining a New Señora Consumer

Emerging Mass Consumption, Gendered
Consumer Magazines, and the First Rumblings
of Boom-Era Cosmopolitanism, 1937–1956

In November 1955, with the launch of the men's fashion and life-style magazine *Señor: La Revista del Hombre* (Sir: The men's magazine), founder and editor-in-chief Segismundo de Anta, who was also director of the Spanish National Fashion Show, declared in an introductory editorial, "Our publication does not intend to fill any kind of gap, nor to create anything new. The editors wish [only] to do profound and practical constructive work in the field of menswear and complementary industries."[1] Notwithstanding this perhaps insincere humility, *Señor* was in actuality a radically new publication: Francoist Spain's first consumer magazine aimed primarily toward men, and quite possibly the first ever conceived and produced domestically.[2] It also formed part of a larger and similarly novel transformation, a rapid expansion in the Spanish consumer press during the Franco dictatorship's first two decades that contributed to the cultivation of a mass consumer culture in mid-century Spain.

Like its department stores, Spain's consumer press expanded rapidly during the early dictatorship. Beginning in 1940, the number of periodicals published in Spain shot upward, so much so that advertising pioneer Francisco García Ruescas later deemed this the beginning of Spain's most prolific period in magazine publishing. He calculated that four times as many new magazines were launched in the 1940s as during the previous decade, and their numbers grew even more in the 1950s, when some of Francoist Spain's most familiar titles first appeared.[3]

At first, these magazines offered little that seemed new, retaining the bourgeois and elite character typical of their nineteenth-century forebears, even as most of the Spanish populace struggled for subsistence.[4] In the "Hunger Years" of the late 1940s, food shortages, soaring black market prices on staple foods, and plummeting wages together raised the cost of living fourfold. Meanwhile, new magazines, including *Alta Costura* (Haute couture), another Anta imprint; the especially long-lived *Mujer: Revista Mensual del Hogar y de la Moda* (Woman: Monthly home and fashion magazine, published 1937–1977); and the Sección Femenina's own journal, *Medina*, continued to cater mainly to economically privileged readers, reporting on new work from foreign designers, or, in *Medina*'s case, to politically elite women. Some also charged as much as 5 to 10 ptas per issue at a time when some day laborers earned a mere 300 ptas per month—half of the necessary amount to support a family.[5]

Yet despite their elite alignment, these magazines also sold fantasies of consumption to a larger and less wealthy public, for whom a journal like *Mujer* or *Medina* could serve as escapist or aspirational literature.[6] As the decade advanced, these periodicals also began to diversify their content to include copy that appealed directly to thrift-minded working-class women, such as ads for courses to become seamstresses that promised readers savings and supplementary incomes.[7]

This strategy worked: by the late 1950s, the consumer press had so grown that titles ran the gamut of content and audiences permitted under Francoist law. There were fashion magazines, cultural and society journals (often featuring fashion columns), and targeted imprints that catered, for example, to women in general, or, like *Funcionarias: Revista para la Mujer* (Civil servant: Magazine for women, launched in 1952), served a narrower readership. Several prewar periodicals meanwhile relaunched, as the three-decade-old *El Hogar y la Moda*

(Home and fashion) did in 1941. As noted previously, department store and trade journals catering to Spain's new mass retailing professionals also appeared. And, of course, there was *Señor*.

These new magazines shaped Spain's embryonic consumer society in several ways. They drove the formation of a Spanish mass consumer society by selling visions of prosperous, upwardly mobile, bourgeois lifestyles defined by the possession of products like fashionable clothing to which all could aspire, regardless of social standing. They promoted the act of consuming and, through it, performance of middle-class identity—an impulse that underpinned Spain's mass consumer revolution of the 1950s and 1960s as much as its American counterpart.[8] And they did so en masse, suggesting that, in this instance, these periodicals should be taken seriously as reliable reflections of mainstream opinion.[9] Meanwhile, the trade journals then professionalizing the retailing sector likewise extended this professional ideal to the domestic sphere. Increasingly, these publications (and society more generally) likened homemaking to a profession, and expected the nation's housewives to show a commensurate commitment to self-improvement and technical mastery.

These various new periodicals also influenced Spanish society in other ways. In the late 1930s and early 1940s, they were vocally supportive of the Franco regime. They remained so into the 1950s, reorienting their efforts toward reconciling mainstays of Francoism's conservative social project with changes in social practices precipitated by Spain's transition to mass consumption, and at times by these magazines themselves. For the products and popular culture featured therein were often American and Western European imports and they reinforced an affinity for foreign ways that was already evident in the nation's nascent consumer culture. Magazines like *Mujer*, for instance, frequently featured content that built upon and naturalized longstanding local interest in American fashions and the Hollywood star system. As the Spanish women's press in particular grew during the 1950s, some journals also began to introduce new messages concerning the personal and professional expectations that Spanish women could harbor. A few even suggested that women were their husbands' equals, with equally important needs, and should be able to freely secure work even after marriage, which the law did not yet allow.

Circumstances, however, soon vitiated these claims, as did the very same magazines that made them. Spanish readers desired what they saw in these periodicals' pages, but as in the United States, a growing reliance on credit that made consuming more affordable also strained existing gender norms, prompting a social marginalization of women as consumers and threatening the existing marital division of labor.[10] Some magazines encouraged married women to pursue extra-domestic work, but most also underscored that a woman's principal place was in the home. Ads for foreign products like Pond's Cold Cream gave readers leave to consume for their own pleasure, which ran counter to the self-abnegating feminine ideal promoted by the Sección Femenina, but many others shifted agency as consumers back to husbands and families, warning readers to use a particular brand of hair dye, for example, or risk their spouses' anger.

In the end, however, the arrival of an American-style consumerism via the Spanish press helped integrate local journalists, retailers, and readers into a larger international community of commercial professionals and consumers. Spain's consumer magazines featured content that preserved, built upon, and naturalized an existing interest in American fashions and the Hollywood stars who wore them, which wore away at early Franco-era discourses emphasizing Spanish national exceptionalism and isolation. Later, particularly after *Señor*'s launch, these periodicals also began to suggest that Spaniards could be more than passive members of this international network. No longer merely enthralled by the latest clothing from Paris or New York, the Spanish fashion press now argued that Spain too produced worthwhile designs—claims that would only multiply in later decades. To be sure, these publications experienced the late 1940s and 1950s as a time of tension as well as growth and reorientation toward the masses, just as the nation's department stores did. The nascent consumer society they helped build still remained largely imagined and aspirational. Nevertheless, these aspirations to consumer prosperity were real, and in cultivating familiarity among the Spanish public with foreign products and lifestyles, these magazines rendered America and Western Europe less foreign, and sold Spaniards on the idea that they were part of that same consumer-capitalist world.

Politics, Class, and Consumer Messaging in Early Franco-Era Women's Magazines

Among the earliest and most influential consumer periodicals launched during the Franco era were a series of women's magazines. They included possibly the first new consumer publication to appear under Francoism, the women's home and fashion monthly *Mujer*, which first circulated out of the Basque city of San Sebastián in June 1937—that is, less than a year into the Civil War and just nine months after Franco's forces took the city in September 1936.[11] *Mujer* was soon joined by other such journals, some with direct ties to the regime. The Sección Femenina alone published two such magazines between 1938 and 1946: *Y: Revista de la Mujer Nacional-Sindicalista* (Y: The National-Syndicalist woman's magazine, 1938–1946) and *Medina* (1941–1946), followed by yet another journal, *Ventanal* (Window), in 1946.[12] And while some of these magazines focused primarily on promoting Francoist ideology rather than on consumption, many were strongly consumer-oriented, including *Mujer*; the similarly long-lived *Alta Costura*, founded by the politically connected brothers Santiago and Segismundo de Anta in 1943; *El Hogar y la Moda*; and, to a degree, *Medina* as well.[13]

Such early forays into a Franco-era women's consumer press were usually traditional in content, and these publications were no exception. They offered conservative models of femininity compatible with (when not purposely advancing) official National-Catholic notions of proper womanly behavior.[14] Like (much) older women's illustrated magazines such as the nineteenth-century *La Moda Elegante* (Elegant fashion), these new magazines reported primarily on subjects that Spanish society coded feminine, including coverage of the latest Parisian fashions and tips on home décor as well as short stories that focused on love and marriage.[15] In 1937, for instance, *Mujer* published "La Tapia" (The wall), the tale of a woman named Margarita, who rejected her handsome military pilot suitor Alberto, deeming herself unworthy, only to accept him after he returned as a blind Civil War veteran.[16] *Medina* and *Alta Costura* offered similar content; the latter also featured outfits by Spanish fashion designers like Asunción Bastida, which it presented as elegant, sober, and respectable, rather than frivolous or immoral.[17]

Indeed, the well-dressed women in these magazines were more specifically well-dressed brides, wives, and properly submissive daughters. Stories like "La Tapia" both catered to existing interest in marriage and reinforced its place in Francoist society as the supreme feminine goal, as did other columns such as "Women's Hands in History's Threads," which celebrated historical women like King Louis XVI's daughter Marie Thérèse for their adherence to normative femininity. In its 1946 biographical sketch of Marie Thérèse, for example, *Alta Costura* offered the princess, who had escaped imprisonment in Revolutionary France, as a model of femininity both for greeting her uncle, the future Louis XVIII, with the plea, "Be my father!," and for her subsequent quick marriage to the Duke of Angouleme. In other words, the article praised her for assuming the roles of wife and daughter with all haste.[18] Other articles focused on similarly domestic subjects like home décor or how to be a properly meek wife.[19] All reinforced some form of the thesis, voiced explicitly by *Mujer* in 1939, that "in Spain, a woman has one great part to play, that of creating inviting homes."[20]

These publications also presented a series of more specific characteristics that the proper Spanish woman was to have, which again conformed to the National Movement's dicta.[21] This woman was religious: *Mujer's* second issue featured a poem in which a woman called on the Virgin Mary to help her "be always good, as she wishes to be . . . and never offend . . . [Jesus]"—a display of religious fervor that was at once characteristic of Francoist femininity and a far cry from Republican-era secularism.[22] And she was submissive. In another, more subtle text published in November 1938, "La Mujer y los libros" (Woman and books), *Mujer* took readers on a guided tour of a woman's personal library and especially recommended Fray Luís de León's *La Perfecta Casada* (The perfect married lady), a women's manual first published in 1583 that called on wives to submit completely to male authorities. This book was one of the ideological cornerstones of Francoist gender politics and became a traditional bridal gift after 1939.[23] *Mujer's* recommendation, then, represented an early step toward what Morcillo has termed a "recovery of tradition" in the realm of religion, authoritative texts, and gender politics, and was a symptom of the regime's stance on religion and gender.[24] And, to reiterate, this stance in turn had significant repercussions. Under Franco, women lost a host of Republican-era advances, including access to divorce, to the vote, to the right to run for elected office, and to myriad opportunities in careers like architecture, from which they were now largely or wholly banned.[25]

At the same time, the regime's views on women's place in society left them some room to act in the public sphere, mainly in the Sección Femenina and its Auxilio Social (Social Aid) program, which was modeled after the Nazi Frauenschaft women's organization and its Winterhilfe aid program.[26] To be sure, the Falangist feminine ideal as typified by the Sección Femenina's female leadership embraced subservient domesticity. Founder Pilar Primo de Rivera declared, for instance, that creating a family was a woman's "only goal to achieve in life."[27] Yet, through initiatives like Auxilio Social, the Women's Section also provided members with what Stanley Payne has termed "a conservative social and moral framework for female activism"— that is, venues in which women could access an otherwise inaccessible public sphere, albeit in normatively feminine areas like charity and homemaking. Indeed, wartime legislation made such domesticity-infused public service compulsory for unmarried Spanish women.[28]

The female editors at many women's periodicals of the early Franco era, including *Mujer* and the illustrated women's magazine *La Ilustración Femenina*, took this opportunity for public action a step further. They carved out long careers that included prominent turns writing for a women's press that otherwise promoted marriage and domesticity as women's proper destiny. Author Carmen Nonell, for example, regularly published in magazines like *Mujer* and the Sección Femenina women's journal *Teresa* in the 1940s and 1950s, before becoming the Berlin correspondent for the newspaper *Pueblo* and the first Spanish journalist to earn press credentials from the postwar German *Presserverband* in 1957.[29] Sección Femenina publications in particular served as public platforms for many of mid-century Spain's most prominent female writers. Perhaps most notably, after a stint as *Medina*'s editor, jurist and long-standing Falange member Mercedes Formica began writing for *A.B.C.* There she penned a watershed domestic abuse exposé in 1953 that so devastated Spanish illusions of widespread marital bliss it elicited hundreds of reader responses and catalyzed a push to reform women's legal status that culminated in the 1958 revision of the Spanish Civil Code, the first expansion of women's rights under Franco.[30]

This cautious admission of women into a closely circumscribed public life and the early Franco-era politicization of daily life that underpinned it found an echo in a series of parallel discourses on femininity that emerged in *Mujer*'s and other Spanish women's magazines' pages during the early 1940s. *Medina*, for instance, which identified publicly as a "mouthpiece" for Falangist thought with a mission to form the new Spanish woman politically, offered a model of feminine behavior that was both nationalist and service-oriented but also conservative and traditionally domestic. This model woman engaged in gender-appropriate public service, such as participating in the Women's Section's folkloric song and dance troupe, the Coros y Danzas, but was ultimately grooming herself to be a housewife and mother.[31] Similarly, early issues of *Mujer* declared the periodical "a thoroughly national magazine able to compete with counterparts abroad ... one conceived and created for women [who are] the ornament and hope of the new Spain ... [and a journal that would] afford Spanish fashion the attention that this excellent and patriotic issue merite[d]."[32]

These were strategic claims: by claiming the ability to compete with foreign counterparts, a "thoroughly national" editorial philosophy, and engagement in "patriotic" work, *Mujer*'s editors aligned themselves with the Franco regime's cultural and imperial project, which rejected foreign influences and sought to reestablish Spanish global prominence.[33] Articles in *Mujer*'s wartime issues likewise positioned the magazine in support of the Falange and the public feminine roles that the Sección Femenina promoted. In 1937, for example, *Mujer* lauded a children's soup kitchen run by the Auxilio Social for safeguarding the "seed of the New Spain," and exemplifying "every Spanish woman's duty" as maternal caregiver. A series of articles from 1938 likewise praised Italian Fascist women for engaging in a domesticity-infused mode of feminine public action, particularly their work raising Italy's next generation of fascists.[34]

Mujer was not just an early example of a politicized consumer magazine; rather, it blended consumption and politics in ways that would grow common in later decades. On the one hand, *Mujer* mobilized consumption—readers' consumption of the publication itself, as well as the spectacle of consumer lifestyles depicted in its pages—for political ends. Hence, the magazine's profiles of the Auxilio Social kitchens, intended to sow public support for the Sección Femenina's work, as well as its more explicitly political articles on Italian Fascist women. As in *Medina*, these articles disseminated gender norms consistent with National-Catholic doctrine.[35] Indeed, *Mujer*'s quick appearance after the Nationalist capture of San Sebastián, combined with its stated mission of guiding women as "Spain . . . renew[ed] its traditional essence," suggest that the magazine launched when it did to help the regime and church indoctrinate the city's women (and Spanish women more generally) with National-Catholic models of femininity and consumption.[36] The magazine similarly supported the Franco regime's postwar campaign to promote patriotic, economy-stimulating domestic tourism by publishing travel itineraries, which, "[like] all of Spain's [tourist] routes, c[ould] compete [with foreign counterparts] in all types of beauty and evocative stimuli."[37]

At the same time, *Mujer* and other Civil War–era commercial entities also exploited the war, Franco's movement, and Nationalist wartime rhetoric for commercial ends by using the conflict as a source of material by which to engage readers and so sell more magazine issues and advertised products. In *Mujer*, this figured principally in its fiction and feature articles. Stories like "La Tapia" used the drama of the Civil War to grip readers, as did the magazine's serialized publication of what it claimed was a young woman's wartime diary that soldiers had found abandoned in a house on Madrid's outskirts.[38] Advertisers, meanwhile, also used *Mujer* as a venue to conduct war-related trade, as when San Sebastián haberdasher Casa Vilar ran an ad in October 1937 announcing that it specialized in Falangist, Requeté (Carlist), and Army uniform shirts.[39]

Socioeconomically, the latter half of the 1940s represented a turning point for Spain's consumer magazines. Earlier in the decade, *Mujer* and *Alta Costura* had often depicted upper-class scenes in which fashionably dressed women played golf or sailed and articles casually referenced luxuries like wet nurses or cosmetics suitable for operago-ing.[40] *Alta Costura*'s steep ten-peseta price made the magazine a luxury item in itself.[41] However, as Spanish economic fortunes plummeted, *Mujer* began to court women who, though still relatively well-off, felt the effects of the struggling economy. Ads printed in the late 1940s, for example, reflected this more socioeconomically diverse readership: alongside its usual reports on Parisian fashion, by 1947

Mujer also ran ads courting thrift-minded women with promises of savings, suggesting that such women now numbered among its readers. These ads were commonly for seamstressing correspondence courses, as in the case of one from February 1947 that featured the image of a woman mending a girl's dress against the backdrop of a giant one-hundred-peseta bill and read: "Be Practical and Modern and you will save much money. Besides [being] a joy, the thrift it represents for your household, madam, [and] the possibility of creating your little ones' dresses, perfecting your innate ability with technical instruction . . . is a factor to consider."[42]

Another ad instead targeted single women, offering them the chance to "quickly credential themselves as [sewing] teachers, earning 300 pesetas per month."[43] Such promises were no doubt appealing to, and advertisers likely intended them for, postwar Spain's financially struggling wives and daughters, rather than for *Mujer's* traditional wealthier readers, who were more likely to hire a seamstress than become one. Haute-bourgeois Barcelona housewife María Freixas i Bru, for example, frequently hired a seamstress in those years, occasionally for large commissions like a brown suit she ordered in April 1947 for 207 ptas.[44] By contrast, the allure of being able to cheaply make a wardrobe for oneself was likely only heightened by the pressure to dress well that Gerald Brenan observed urban Spaniards faced, even as wages remained so low that many lived on a single daily meal.[45]

Improbably, when *Mujer's* editors raised the magazine's price from 3.5 to a sizeable 5 ptas in August 1947, *Mujer* used this to further present itself as a thrift-oriented publication for frugal women. That month, a special editorial apologized for the price hike, promised to reverse it as soon as possible, and stressed both that *Mujer* had kept its price low long after competitors' had raised theirs, and that it had only followed suit when rising graphic design costs and a national paper shortage forced its hand.[46] Thereby, the magazine claimed a long history of sensitivity toward readers' need for thrift and accused competitors of being less friendly to thrifty readers, because they had raised prices before it was necessary. Most of all, this also framed the price hike as proof not just that *Mujer* was a journal for frugal women, but that it was itself similarly frugal because it could make hard financial choices—raising prices—when its budget demanded.

This shift was not universal. *Alta Costura* gave no evidence of thrift-mindedness or of having many readers as interested in saving money as they were in the latest foreign fashions. To the contrary, articles devoted to elite lifestyles abounded in the magazine, including columns on decorating one's country house, and ads for luxury goods like champagne and Parisian perfumes were also prominent, to the exclusion of the sort of thrift-oriented content that *Mujer* printed.[47] Nor was *Alta Costura* alone. Both the interior design magazine *Arte en el Hogar* and the women's journal *Astra: Revista moderna para la mujer*, launched in 1943 and 1950, respectively, shared this haute-bourgeois pricing and content. *Arte en el Hogar* mostly profiled villas, artist studios, and other upper-class spaces, while *Astra* featured articles on English furniture and Parisian bolero jackets, as well as ads for perfumes, nail polish, and radios, rather than the sewing courses advertised in *Mujer*.[48]

Still, *Mujer*'s apparent service to a cross-class audience was not unique. Its claims regarding competitors' higher prices overlooked the fact that the pricier but also more specialized *Arte en el Hogar* was a different kind of publication from *Mujer*, much as the American women's home décor magazine *Better Homes and Gardens* differed from a more literary and fashion-oriented journal like *McCall's Magazine*.[49] It also ignored the many women's magazines that remained cheaper than *Mujer*. *Ventanal*, the successor to Sección Femenina's *Medina*, for example, cost just 1.50 ptas in 1946, while the popular celebrity gossip magazines *Lecturas* and *¡Hola!*, the women's digest *Meridiano Femenino*, and the adolescent girls' magazine *Chicas* all cost 3.5 ptas or less.[50]

That put these magazines within the financial reach of still more women. Like *Mujer*, the women's journal *Para Nosotras*, published by the Catholic lay organization Acción Católica (Catholic Action, founded in the 1920s), also tailored its content to a broader and less wealthy audience. Tellingly, Acción Católica's Women's Press Secretariat would reject a proposal in 1958 to merge *Para Nosotras* with the more exclusive *Senda*, citing the former's ability to reach a culturally and materially poorer "popular" readership.[51] Meanwhile, other women's magazines that continued to offer largely patrician content, but at plebeian prices—including *Mujer*, before 1947—could serve as aspirational literature for readers who could occasionally afford an issue, if not the items shown therein. Publication figures suggest that these magazines circulated broadly: in the mid-1940s, *Mujer* and *El Hogar y la Moda* both printed an average of 45,000 copies of each issue, and, a decade later, such magazines still typically ran editions of 25,000 or more copies. *El Hogar y la Moda* even reported an edition of 80,000 copies in 1954. In practice, this meant that in Spain's urban and semi-urban areas, where these magazines were mostly consumed, at least one in one hundred women bought a copy.[52] The real rate was likely higher still.[53]

Echoes and Harbingers of Spain's Initial Rapprochement with the West, 1946–1950

Meanwhile, and despite the Franco regime's slowly improving but still-frosty relationship with the United States and its allies, the dawn of the 1950s brought another shift in the content that these magazines offered their growing audiences, content that increasingly catered to rising popular interest in foreign and especially American fashions and lifestyles. Fascination with Hollywood and its star system was one form this took. In itself, such interest was nothing new: *Mujer* had covered Hollywood fashion since the late 1930s, profiling stylish Hollywood leading ladies such as Ann Rutherford and offering male idols like Clark Gable as models of the confidence and sobriety that women sought in a man.[54] But notably, this interest in Hollywood and American fashion persisted in the late 1940s, despite Spain's trade and diplomatic pariah status. In 1946, *Alta Costura* regularly ran photo spreads of Hollywood's famous women and their outfits under the title "*Alta Costura* en Hollywood." Between 1948 and 1950, issues featured interviews with heartthrobs like Gregory Peck or famous recent brides such as actress Lana Turner, columns that were themselves often translations of articles originally published in the United States. Meanwhile, in 1947 alone, *Mujer* turned to stars, including Lucille Ball for guidance on loungewear, touted actress Marguerite Chapman as an example of a woman who found fulfillment in housework, and even covered a special fashion show that took place aboard a yacht in Florida.[55]

Though seemingly innocuous, this content held real subversive potential. Victoria de Grazia has noted that Hollywood fashion appealed to Italian Fascists because it vitiated Italy's traditional class system, yet also sparked concern that it might undercut both domestic gender roles and autarkic calls to only buy Italian products. Spanish magazines' portrayals of Hollywood and Franco's visions for his new Spain were similarly in tension.[56] Such coverage humanized stars, rendering Hollywood's glamour at once enticingly exotic and familiar, and, despite the Franco regime's official national exceptionalism, treated Spain as part of rather than separate from the rest of fashion-producing Western Europe. Thus, though *Alta Costura*'s photo spreads often highlighted Spanish designers' work, many also showcased the latest from London and Paris, while *Mujer* devoted a special issue in 1947 to foreign couturiers like Paris's Alice Belier.[57] Indeed, an editorial in *Mujer* already defended this focus in October 1938, reasoning that Spanish interest in—or as author Vera de Alzate phrased it, "servile obedience to"—foreign fashions was long-standing, natural, and not worth challenging. At the same time, de Alzate's article also showed the tensions already brewing between this interest in foreign fashion and early Francoism's vigorous Spanish nationalism, with which the Nationalist-aligned *Mujer* sympathized. De Alzate's acceptance of what she termed sartorial servility was grudging and quickly tempered with patriotic boasts about Spain's own national aesthetic prowess.[58] The result was that, as for patrons of Spain's leading department stores, foreign fashions and popular culture retained currency among readers of these women's magazines, and when they ran stories on new, subversive Western European and American fashions later in the 1950s and 1960s, these did not appear ex nihilo, but followed in earlier journalists' footsteps.

A few of these magazines also echoed the disregard that Italian consumers had shown toward Fascist attempts to restrict their consumption of foreign goods. They regularly printed ads for imported Philips radios or beauty products like French perfumes that showed similar indifference toward Francoist import restrictions and calls for feminine modesty.[59] Class privilege helped make this possible. The Italian women who flouted Mussolini's autarky by seeking out Hollywood fashions had been wealthy and bourgeois; just so, it was the pricey and unapologetically upper-class *Alta Costura* that ran many of these ads.[60] A single issue of *Alta Costura* from 1947, for instance, advertised Vitamol Revitalising Skin Crème, manufactured by a subsidiary of Switzerland's Hamol Company; French Bardinet liqueur and Legrain perfumes; and American-made Bella Aurora facial soap.[61]

By their very presence, these ads and the products they promoted challenged the regime's official import restrictions. *Alta Costura*'s ads also reveal how some foreign firms were able to circumvent those restrictions by manufacturing locally through domestic subsidiaries or selling through Spanish concessionaires. Hamol, which produced Vitamol locally through Hamol-Spain, took the former approach, while the Stillman Company, makers of Bella Aurora, chose the latter.[62] Notably, the reverse was also possible: Galerías Preciados likewise bypassed Francoist import restrictions from within Spain by securing foreign fabric swatches through the Cuban department store El Encanto, from which it produced local versions of fashionable but scarce French- and American-style printed textiles.[63] And when they were imported, products like Bella Aurora soaps sometimes bore a particular label whose popularity was growing rapidly—"Product of the USA"—and that commanded special prestige in later decades.[64] Indeed, some entirely Spanish products like the skin cream Lacto-crema Gran Dama or the hair tonic Marinalba sought to capitalize on this American vogue by invoking Hollywood stars like Marilyn Maxwell, promising consumers similarly smooth skin and lustrous hair (see fig. 5). This type of ad not only courted readers by appealing to their taste for things American, but reinforced this appeal. More generally, such advertising kept Spanish consumers attuned to foreign products and lifestyles.

Such advertising also posed an immediate, albeit still narrowly elite, challenge to National-Catholicism's modest feminine ideal, given that ecclesiastical authorities like Cardinals Segura and Plá y Deniel condemned such beauty products as vain and sinful. Consequently, these ads anticipated a more widespread subversion of orthodox Francoist feminine norms that Aurora Morcillo has argued took place as

> Spanish women were exposed to ... advertisements for makeup, perfume, fashion, and luxury products . . . the consumption of luxury articles such as watches, Chanel perfume, and high-fashion clothing became more common by the end of the 1950s . . . [and] colorful ads appealed to women's search for eternal youth and beauty ... [which] contradicted the treatises from the 1500s that had been promoted by Franco's regime . . . and urged Spanish women to remake themselves . . . [to] purchase a new identity, a sense of self-worth based on physical appearance rather than spiritual value.[65]

Many of *Alta Costura*'s ads for beauty products offered similar messages as early as the mid-1940s. In 1957, makeup producer Dermiluz declared, "Being young and pretty is marvelous!," and in 1958, an ad for Pond's Cold Cream showed a beautiful woman who had "enhanced her charms [with Pond's]." Both ads, Morcillo asserts, promised not

FIG. 5. "To make your hair look like Marilyn Maxwell does . . . always use Marinalba." *Alta Costura*, no. 61, Year VI (December 1948). Courtesy of the Biblioteca Francesca Bonnemaison, Ajuntament de Barcelona.

just makeup, but youth, beauty, and, most importantly, the ability to remake oneself—to reconfigure one's subjectivity.[66] Similarly, in 1946, ads for Dana perfumes, Bella Aurora beauty products, and Tintolax-brand hair products promised readers "grace and success in perfume form," or told them to "ask for this quality brand if [they] want[ed] youth, beauty, and freshness."[67] Like latter-day counterparts, then, these ads offered women youth, beauty, and social approval, and, more importantly, normalized shopping for their own pleasure, not just their families' benefit.

With that said, if *Alta Costura* was hardly unique in encouraging women to use beauty products, its ads were unusual for encouraging women to consume for themselves so soon into the Franco era. *Mujer*, by contrast, consistently championed the self-abnegating ideal that women should beautify themselves solely to make their families happier, a notion rooted in the Sección Femenina's tenet of self-sacrifice for the sake of the family.[68] Thus, a February 1947 article on dressing gowns declared, "Being beautiful for one's family is at all times a woman's primordial duty! The home will seem to smile and will sustain your loved ones if you are its principal adornment."[69] Another column in the same issue encouraged readers to treat themselves by setting aside space for a small vanity table, from which they could better manage their households and cultivate the sunny dispositions their families merited.[70] Indeed, the magazine had already advised readers nearly a decade earlier, in 1939, that true vanity was neglecting one's appearance, because this willfully denied one's family the "delight ... [of] life beside a creature who cultivates her beauty like a garden."[71] By contrast, ads like *Alta Costura*'s marked a change in discourse regarding feminine beauty precisely because they broke from this other-centered rationale for cultivation of the feminine self.

Moreover, these magazines' interest in American consumer culture, and their contribution to Spain's own nascent consumerism, ranged beyond simple attention to Hollywood fashions. As the 1940s drew to a close, *Mujer* and other Spanish women's journals began to predict that their nation would soon achieve an American standard of living built upon mass consumption. And this, they hoped, would in turn free housewives from household drudgery, reduce middle-class reliance on domestic help, and so more generally vitiate traditional European class hierarchies.[72] *Mujer*, for instance, displayed such thinking in a 1947 column titled "Una sonrisa para ir a la compra" (A smile when going shopping), which championed a cornerstone of the prosperous and modern American way of life: home appliances, especially the refrigerator.[73] Here, the magazine contrasted the stress that middle-class European housewives faced when their servants were away and so were forced to prepare dinner themselves with the convenience American women enjoyed by turning to canned and prepackaged refrigerated foods. This reliance on refrigerators, the article argued, kept these women free from Europeans' premature wrinkles and gray hair, and left their husbands skinny and "ready to be Hollywood stars." The fault for this sad state of affairs, the article added, belonged to European men, self-styled "gourmets" who were unwilling to accept the "can-and-refrigerator" meals that American husbands routinely ate. The solution, *Mujer*'s column then concluded, was for European women to emulate American housewives and turn to refrigerators, canned vegetables, and cold cuts for culinary help.[74]

This advocacy boldly foreshadowed impending changes to gender norms in Spain and Europe as a whole, yet also highlighted limits to discourse on gender that remained widespread as Spain moved from the material hardships and conservatism of the early Franco period to the economic dynamism and shifting gender relations of the regime's later years. On the one hand, to suggest that housewives were unhappy with their domestic lot and to blame husbands for it was unusual this early into the Franco era. In 1947, the Sección Femenina still wielded considerable influence over millions of Spanish women, and Spanish society still assumed, as Carmen Martín Gaite has noted, "that no woman could cherish a more beautiful dream than submission to a man; if she said otherwise, she was lying."[75] The marital advice that

Mujer itself offered even decades later likewise stressed wifely stoicism and forgiveness of indiscretions far greater than an epicurean bent.[76] Its column on American "can-and-refrigerator" dining, by contrast, ran counter to this feminine model inasmuch as it called for men to instead think of their wives' convenience and treated women's household toil not as a badge of honor to be borne in noble silence but as a problem in need of solving. With that said, the article referred vaguely to "Europeans," not Spaniards, blunting both the article's critique and its potential to offend. It offered no challenge to the notion that a woman's place was exclusively in the home—the push for married women's right to work outside the home was still several years away.[77] Even the problem that *Mujer* addressed was more traditionally bourgeois European than mass-oriented and American in character. While an upper-class woman like María Freixas i Bru may have nodded when reading the column, thinking of her family's summer retreats to nearby Reus or times when the maid was away, most late 1940s Spanish households could hardly afford servants, or indeed a refrigerator.[78]

Despite its limitations, *Mujer*'s championing of the American kitchen, and with it American modernity, was part of an emerging watershed moment in European consumption. At the time, various parties from the United States used this appliance-filled kitchen to promote notions of a modern and democratic way of life laden with promises of futuristic household convenience and national progress. During the late 1940s and 1950s, American exhibitors at Paris's annual Salon of Household Arts exhibition gradually made their nation's standard battery of kitchen appliances equally essential in France, aided by a French women's press that stoked demand and a growing availability of consumer credit.[79] The U.S. State Department meanwhile showcased model American kitchens at the 1950 West Berlin Industrial Fair and the 1959 American National Exhibition in Moscow. And, in 1957, the Department of Commerce mounted its own "Supermarket USA" exhibit in communist Zagreb—all meant to convince visitors of the advantages of the American way of life and especially the modern conveniences it offered.[80]

Alongside such promises of convenience, still more ambitious notions of achieving a more prosperous national future by rationalizing Spanish diets and household management also moved regime officials and private citizens alike to embrace American home technology. Responding to the postwar era's many shortages, the Franco regime and food retailing trade took steps to streamline the nation's food distribution network. Among the earliest was the creation of a government agency devoted to this issue, the Commissary-General for Supply and Transport, in 1939. Another was the launch in 1945 of a private-sector professional journal for the food distribution and grocery trade, *ICA: Industria y Comercio de Alimentación* (Food industry and commerce, henceforth, *ICA*), which soon became one of the industry's leading forums where Spaniards debated issues like the need for a uniform code regulating food quality.[81]

ICA was also symptomatic of a broader shift that encompassed the arrival of American marvels like the Frigidaire: a push toward technical sophistication in every discipline—homemaking included—that Castilian Spanish termed *técnica*. As noted previously, this focus on achieving technical mastery unfolded in various commercial trade journals, many of them newly founded products of the professionalizing moment. In 1945 alone, *ICA* arrived, along with the window dresser's magazine *Escaparate* and the advertising journal *Arte Comercial*, while Galerías Preciados's similarly minded internal bulletin launched soon after, in 1948. For Spanish housewives, the new value placed on *técnica* manifested in magazine articles that encouraged them to pursue greater technical proficiency in the kitchen, home decoration, and even their beauty routines, as they believed American women had. *Mujer*'s report on refrigerators was one example of this; others appeared in publications like *Funcionarias: Revista para la mujer* (Civil servants: Women's magazine), which launched in 1952. *Funcionarias* offered readers various recurring instructional columns on beauty, dancing, cooking, and home décor, penned by contributors boasting professional titles like "Doctor" and "Professor" and pervaded with the aim of cultivating readers' technical mastery. Among these was Dr. S. Vanó's "Beauty Course," whose second installment purported to classify and analyze beauty's physical and "psychic" components and offered a detailed table of "harmonious," and thus beautiful, body proportions.[82] Another article, devoted to home décor, lauded an American country house's harmonious aesthetic as well as its furnishings' clean lines, and, underlining the larger social and perhaps political implications of homemakers' domestic expertise, concluded: "once more it is clear how the home reflects and synthesizes the culture, customs, and well-being of a people."[83]

By the end of the decade, these shifts so influenced Spanish officials' views regarding food distribution that in 1959, two years after visiting Zagreb, "Supermarket USA" reopened in Barcelona. There, it received a warm welcome from a Spanish Ministry of Commerce convinced that the supermarket and the efficient American household management methods they believed it would promote among housewives held the key to Spain's national progress.[84] The supermarket's spread across Spain, which followed soon after, would only reinforce this conviction and fuel calls by officials, trade journals, and women's magazines for housewives to manage their homes with greater technical proficiency.

To be sure, as of the mid-1950s these upheavals still remained years away, but the series of changes that would build to them had begun. Spanish women's magazines' coverage of American kitchen technology and of publicly prominent women who still embraced conventional domesticity buttressed this Spanish (and American) domestic ideal in the short term. But such content also further entrenched cities like London, Paris, and Hollywood as cultural reference points for a growing number of Spanish subjects, particularly vis-à-vis the consumer lifestyles they coveted. These articles likewise ran counter to the early Franco regime's moral and autarkic economic projects by encouraging women to consume for themselves and by preserving interest in foreign consumer ways despite official efforts to restrict imports and encourage strictly domestic consumption. In particular, American appliance culture, an important vector for the ideological package of modernity, prosperity, and democracy that the United States was then exporting across Europe, began to make inroads in Spain. These magazines also gave early hints of an incipient Spanish version of the "Model Mrs. Consumer," who, as consumption became increasingly gendered and appliances became de rigueur, managed the family's consumer choices while caring for her household and battery of kitchen gadgets.[85] And, more generally, such content helped bridge the chasm of national difference that early Francoist doctrine had claimed distinguished Spain from the West's decadent democracies, at a time when the Franco regime was itself working to cultivate diplomatic ties and international trade.

Consumer Magazines and Messaging during Spain's First Recovery, 1950–1956

The landscape of Spain's consumer press continued to shift as the Franco regime's second decade in power dawned. Growth continued. As Francisco García Ruescas later pointed out, the number of magazines launched in 1950s Spain outstripped those introduced during the 1940s even more dramatically than that figure had exceeded previous decades' totals.[86] Among this flood of new periodicals were some that introduced new notions about consumption as well as the changing values and range of lifestyles acceptable in Spain.

Many of these belonged to the women's press, particularly the women's fashion and lifestyle press, which saw a diverse array of new magazines covering a widening range of possible activities for women join established titles like *Mujer*. In 1950, *Astra* launched; its subtitle, "Revista moderna de la Mujer," or "Modern magazine for women," was symptomatic of growing Spanish acceptance of an affluent, cosmopolitan, and fashionable, if also still domestic and family-minded, "modern woman." A mere decade earlier, *Mujer* and its competitors had ridiculed such women as flighty and shallow.[87] *Funcionarias*, founded in 1952, catered to female workers and, remarkably, focused on the legal and practical problems of the married workingwoman—still an unorthodox figure under Francoist gender norms. Almacenes Jorba's self-published customer magazine *Revista Jorba*, aimed mainly at married women, appeared in 1953. And, in 1954, Sección Femenina launched its latest women's journal, *Teresa: Revista para todas las mujeres* (Teresa: Magazine for all women).[88]

During the 1950s, such women-oriented consumer magazines began to give notice of an expanded range of possibilities for women, particularly regarding consumption of goods like makeup and soft drinks for personal pleasure, as well as ambitions to extradomestic work. The Sección Femenina was thoroughly party to this shift. Beginning in 1954, *Teresa* included a section titled "Las Mujeres Quieren Trabajar" (Women want to work), which covered careers suitably consonant with traditional notions of the feminine character, including nursing and journalism.[89] Some precedent for this existed, including columns that *Mujer* ran in 1939 profiling Hollywood script girls and other jobs for women.[90] However, such articles had been careful to note that in Spain these were jobs for single rather than married women, part of their spiritual development on the way to their true conjugal destiny. *Teresa* made no such distinction. This, then, marked a subtle step toward fuller inclusion of women in public life and the workplace, and echoed the ongoing shift in discourse on women's rights that Mercedes Formica's domestic abuse exposé had helped catalyze a year earlier.[91]

Funcionarias went still further. Its content aimed to legitimize married women's careers not as stopgap measures for shoring up family budgets, but as a licit means to professional fulfillment. In addition to the consumption- and domesticity-oriented fare typical of other women's magazines of the time, each issue of *Funcionarias* featured an interview with a working woman, often married, that centered on whether she considered extra-domestic work an obstacle to marriage—the response usually some version of "no." The first interviewee, married government functionary Ernestina Caldevilla, responded pointedly: "Not in the least," she told the magazine, adding, "to the contrary, because we already have our finances sorted, we are free to marry exclusively for true love. So too, I consider housework and office work perfectly compatible."[92] In other columns, *Funcionarias* analyzed and explained Spanish legislation that affected women, especially concerning property ownership and working rights, again in order to help women secure legal work outside the home.[93] These articles, like the rest of the material in the magazine, were moreover not the work of fringe figures, as their unorthodox content might suggest. Rather, contributors included well-placed government officials like Ignacio Zarzalejos Altares, a secretary for Judicial Affairs at the Ministry of Labor, and respected journalists like José Luis Barceló, founder of the successful financial daily *El Mundo Financiero*.[94]

More generally, *Funcionarias* adopted a position on women's abilities and rightful place in society that could cautiously be termed feminist, but for the fact that in Francoist Spain this word often connoted the wholesale destruction of family values. Under the headline "Science Proclaims Women Superior to Men," one article reported on an emerging school of biologists who considered women to be biologically and evolutionarily superior to men due to their supposed greater resistance to pain and disease, coupled with the "feminization" that modern urban males' physical features allegedly underwent as they grew more civilized. And importantly, the article did so without parlaying this into traditional biological-determinist arguments for a female predisposition for motherhood and domesticity.[95] Another told the story of a woman who, raised to rely on male gallantry and believe herself part of a supposed weaker sex, rose above her upbringing during wartime, discovering that she was as strong as her erstwhile male guardians and could support herself by working as an auxiliary firefighter or in a gas-mask factory.[96] This tale ran in *Funcionarias*'s humor pages, but it was no joke—under a thin mask of levity, the periodical was serious.

Such content sounded claims similar to ones that avowed radical Spanish feminists such as María Aurelia Capmany later voiced once Spanish feminisms began to gain strength in the 1970s.[97] *Funcionarias*'s story about the woman who became strong in wartime was a thinly veiled critique of patriarchal portrayals of women as intrinsically weak and instead argued that women had no need for male aid if allowed to develop their own abilities. This foreshadowed an early 1970s tract in which Capmany, adopting the persona of a fictional bourgeois lady, decried having been stripped of economic agency by a patriarchy that denied women the right to work and so to earn their own money and forge their own relationship to the means of production.[98] It was precisely this agency that the woman in *Funcionarias*'s wartime story meanwhile recovered through employment and physical empowerment. Significantly, the magazine touted this message, as well as its other content serving would-be career women, two years before *Teresa*'s launch and a decade before such columns became common in other Spanish women's magazines.[99]

Still, *Funcionarias* was an unusual case of limited scope. No issues survive past 1953, though the magazine remained on the government's official press registry in 1954. Its circulation also remained at just 4,000 copies per issue, nearly half of which went to subscribers, not newsstands—in total, slightly less than *Senda*'s print runs and about what society magazine *Garbo* (total circulation: 65,000 copies per issue) sold by subscription alone.[100] Also, while 1950s Spanish women's magazines fostered spaces for feminine agency, women's roles in society as well as the family remained highly gendered and located within a patriarchal hierarchy, a state of affairs that these periodicals, like some department stores' discriminatory views on saleswomen, typically reinforced. If cautiously emancipating ads circulated, many also ran that reinforced the idea that a woman's efforts and purchases—whether focused on beautifying herself with cosmetics

FIG. 6. "Your Husband Does Not Dare Tell You . . ." *Mujer*, no. 199 (January 1954), 28. Biblioteca de Catalunya, Barcelona.

or cleaning more efficiently by using a dishwasher—should be for her family's and especially her husband's benefit, not her own. In January 1954, for example, *Mujer* ran an ad for Carasa Laboratorios's hair dye Komol that appealed to readers by suggesting that their husbands found their hair unattractive because it was poorly colored, which Komol could fix. The ad in no way acknowledged that women might want to color their hair of their own accord (see fig. 6).[101] Similarly, another ad for a seamstressing correspondence course led by declaring, "Men prefer women . . . elegant!," and added that such elegance (and resulting male regard) required keeping up with changing fashions, which their training could make cheaper.[102]

Mujer was hardly unique in this respect. *Revista Jorba* featured a large volume of ads for products intended not for its readers, who were mainly women, but for their families—items like children's clothes and toys, or men's suits. It likewise ran several Nestlé Company–

sponsored sweepstakes, with prizes meant for family members or the home, such as coffeemakers, radios, and footballs.[103] To some extent, such content likely reflected the fact that, as managers of the household, women in 1950s Spain were responsible for making their families' necessary purchases, not just their own, so companies pushed products like Pelele Kid children's pajamas and Fosfatina Falieres baby food in response to demand.[104] Yet a message of self-abnegation may also be found in this uneven distribution of advertising space, particularly given the magazine's largely female readership—a message that echoed the Sección Femenina's self-denying doctrine, and was reinforced by juxtaposition with articles that stressed a woman's duty to her family. These included several editions of a recurring column on child-rearing that a Dr. José Roig Raventós penned for *Revista Jorba*. Therein, Roig argued that mothers "belong[ed] to [their] child[ren]," used fearmongering rhetoric to browbeat readers into acquiescence, and heaped special scorn on women who, for reasons he assumed were nefarious, did not breastfeed.[105] In a similar vein, an article-cum-advertisement for Almacenes Jorba's low prices, which narrated a fictional couple's discussion of where and how to afford to send their children to school, concluded with the wife, who had bought school supplies cheaply at Jorba, handing her husband the receipt, both so that he could approve the purchases and to show off what a good housewife she was.[106] Again, consumption appeared gendered feminine and more specifically as an act through which women could find fulfillment by efficiently meeting the family's needs, their own notwithstanding—a Model Mrs. Consumer with a Franco-era Spanish inflection.

Even the otherwise radical *Funcionarias* accommodated traditional female domesticity. As it marked out a model of womanhood that provided for the possibility and even the right of married as well as single women to work outside the home, the magazine nevertheless also assumed that, once married, these women would remain their families' and households' primary caretakers—the same "double burden" that married workingwomen in the postwar United States endured.[107] Thus, alongside columns analyzing the legal hurdles women faced in securing work, *Funcionarias* offered recipes that readers could follow to prepare their families' dinners, and columns, like its profile of an American country home, on the similarly traditional feminine duty of decorating the home.[108] Thus too, the magazine's interview subjects most favorable toward women's right to work, like Ernestina Caldevilla, still considered employment "perfectly compatible" with housework, and assumed that readers would shoulder both.[109] Still, the journal did not quite reach *Mujer* and *Revista Jorba*'s self-abnegatory lengths. Ads for Komol hair dye and Almacenes Jorba's low prices emphasized feminine consumption as an other-centered act; by contrast, Dr. Vanó's beauty course in *Funcionarias*, like *Alta Costura*'s earlier ads for Bella Aurora soaps, offered to beautify women for their own pleasure as well as others', and also to help them make a good impression as they ventured into the male-dominated workplace.[110]

As such, these magazines—*Mujer* included—had by the mid-1950s entered a state of tension that lasted into the following decade and was symptomatic of what Morcillo, following Homi Bhabha, has termed an "in between moment" during which the Franco regime sought to shore up its conservative Catholic moral codes against the liberalizing effects of Spain's nascent foreign-influenced consumerism.[111] On the one hand, these periodicals were, as *Funcionarias* described itself, "a little bit classic and a little bit modern," seeking to reconcile Francoist norms with changes in gender relations that Spain's increasingly foreign-oriented consumer culture had helped catalyze, rather than fully embracing these new feminine paradigms.[112] Indeed, as historian María del Carmen Muñoz Ruiz has noted, many such magazines fought this battle in their relationship-advice columns, which, for example, counseled women to stop declaring their feelings to their love interests, who were the ones meant to make such gestures, and to likewise stop viewing summer vacations, an increasingly popular luxury, as opportunities for romance.[113] In some cases, too, these opinions not only aligned with Francoist dictates, but, as at *Teresa*, came from an editorial staff in the regime's actual employ.[114]

Yet the times were changing: the fascination with foreign lifestyles that had quickened in Spain during the late 1940s now intensified in the mid-1950s, and women's magazines responded with a wide range of new content. *Mujer* in particular adapted, dropping both its politicized postwar tone and the reputation for thriftmindedness it had cultivated in the 1940s. In its place, and no doubt facilitated by Spain's diplomatic rehabilitation, *Mujer* offered a profusion of content featuring foreign products that represented consumption as a right accessible to the masses; touted a specifically American consumerism—and its totem, the modern home appliance—with novel force; and predicted that, through this consumerism, prosperity would soon come to Spain. In April 1954, for example, Shirley's Institute of Barcelona advertised its bustline-firming cream as "[a] new and safe AMERICAN procedure [emphasis original]" that was "patented throughout the world." Two months earlier, makeup company Danamask had similarly appealed to readers with the slogan "make yourself up like they do in North America!"[115] And if the seamstressing courses whose ads had peppered *Mujer* in the 1940s now promised trendiness rather than savings, and especially greater ability to attract a man, this was also not just any man—one ad for Curso Fémina CCC's courses included a picture of the sort of husband that graduates could hope to land: American film star Robert Taylor.[116] More generally, both *Mujer* and *Alta Costura*'s coverage of foreign fashion remained extensive. *Mujer*'s many reports on European and American fashions in 1954, for instance, included a February photo spread on the work of six British designers.[117]

Most of all, *Mujer* and other Spanish women's magazines printed ever more content about home goods, especially appliances that were often of American make, which they linked to promises of convenience, modernity, and prosperity. Such items included state-of-the-art spring mattresses ("mattresses like in America! . . . Adopted in half the world and by all social classes . . . [they] are more hygienic . . . [and] permit absolute repose," one ad boasted); Hispano-Suiza brand electric blenders that promised to make housewives' kitchen worries disappear; and dishwashers, which *Revista Jorba* fought to convince readers were a genuine, time-saving, modern marvel, rather than a recipe for broken dishes. In fact, as she sang the dishwasher's praises in 1955, *Revista Jorba* contributor Graciela Elizalde echoed *Mujer's* take on another appliance, the refrigerator, a decade earlier. The dishwasher, she argued, was the secret behind American housewives' superior household management, even when hosting company and despite lacking the domestic help their European counterparts enjoyed.[118]

This and Hispano-Suiza's claim were of a piece with contemporary American discourse that declared the modern kitchen the secret to an easier workload and happier life for European as well as American housewives. Though most visibly championed by American corporate and government figures, especially Vice President Richard Nixon in the much-publicized "Kitchen Debate" he had with Soviet premier Nikita Khrushchev at the 1959 American National Exhibition, the American public also embraced this elision of domestic consumption and marital bliss.[119] In Europe, it met with more mixed success. West Germans enthused over the model home—especially its refrigerator, a much sought-after item in Germany—at the Marshall Plan–funded *Wir bauen ein besseres Leben* (We're building a better life) exhibition held in West Berlin in 1952, but in the Netherlands and Finland, similar showcases sparked comparatively short-lived interest. Within the pages of Spanish women's magazines, however, this fascination appeared more sustained, even if, as in Germany, average real purchasing power remained so low that in 1960, only 4 percent of the population actually had a refrigerator.[120]

For, as the slogan "mattresses like in America! . . . Adopted in half the world *and by all social classes* [emphasis added]," suggests, Spanish women's magazines in the 1950s continued to signal a shift in how they understood and wished the public to understand consumption, despite the only gradual rise in ownership of consumer products. They increasingly defined consumption as an act not restricted to a traditional bourgeoisie but also available to the masses.[121] In the 1940s, these magazines asked readers to identify with either images of affluent individuals pursuing elite hobbies like sailing or hunting for sport, as in *Alta Costura*, or instead with images of thrifty and hardworking housewives, as in Curso Fémina CCC's early ads in *Mujer*. As Spain's diplomatic and economic fortunes improved during the 1950s, the typical Spanish family these magazines portrayed took on a new, prosperously middle-class, yet also accessible and mass character. *Revista Jorba*, for example, ran an ad for its credit service in 1953 that showed a scene from a purportedly average family's life, in which a wife just returning from a pleasant shopping trip to Almacenes Jorba told her husband, who was stressfully trying to balance the family budget: "Stop worrying and doing numbers, darling: with Almacenes Jorba's credit service, I've bought everything we need this winter and we'll pay the regular price in comfortable installments" (see fig. 7). Neither rich nor poor, able to consume freely with a little help from a credit service, and, in the husband's case, wearing the businessman's uniform of white shirt and tie, this average family was unmistakably middle class.[122]

They were also debtors—for good and ill. For much of the still largely rural and poor Spanish populace, Spain's new mass consumption still existed in the form of aspirations and expectations that magazines like *Revista Jorba* had helped cultivate, rather than as real purchases; in Spain's urban centers, however, consumption of goods like televisions, washing machines, and fashionable clothing was much higher, and credit was partly responsible.[123] At the same time, not every result of this spread in consumer credit was as salutary. In nineteenth-century Britain, use of traditional forms of store credit by increasingly anonymous female shoppers generated a host of lawsuits when these women's husbands refused to pay for purchases that they claimed not to have authorized. In the short term, these

FIG. 7. Advertisement for Almacenes Jorba's Installment Credit Service, 1953. *Revista Jorba*, no. 37, Year VI (February 1953). Biblioteca de Catalunya, Barcelona.

suits presented a challenge to husbands' authority as heads of household, and in the long term they left women stigmatized as profligate spenders.[124] In similar vein, *Revista Jorba* referenced the seemingly widespread problem of husbands refusing to pay their wives' store debts nearly a year before Jorba introduced its own credit system in late 1955. This problem, the magazine repeatedly hinted, not only had possible legal consequences, but also threatened the traditional Spanish gendered division of labor and marital harmony between consumer-housewife and breadwinner-husband. Thus, in one article, *Revista Jorba* fashion contributor Lisette joked, with some sharpness, that "husbands . . . who look bitter when it is time to pay" were not a fashionable accessory.[125] In another, a Jorba shopper being interviewed quipped that the store's annual white sale each February did not just drive bargain-hunting women mad, but also their husbands, because, "With store bills [and husbands], you know how it is. . . ."[126] And, in still another, Lisette warned husbands to pay their bills, lest they run afoul of the courts and end up "dethroned"—though it is unclear whether this meant an emasculating loss of financial agency to free-spending wives, the humiliation of legal penalties, or both.[127]

Either way, the rising presence of consumer credit in Spain exposed points of tension between the increasingly prevalent model of the consumer-housewife who purchased on behalf of her household and the primacy of husbandly authority over the family's finances. Convention dictated that husbands should entrust their wives with the running of the household, including its daily finances, while at the same time underscoring that in the end male authority trumped everything. Such trust fit well with the concept of the consumer-housewife. But as *Revista Jorba*'s columns show, with credit growing more available it could also lead to situations where consumer-housewives shopped licitly for the household yet produced debts that challenged the financial agency of husbands who were reticent but obligated to pay.[128]

Finally, *Revista Jorba*'s average Spanish family of the mid-1950s was one thing more: self-consciously not American and liable to harbor remnants of an early twentieth-century European (and Falangist) disdain for a supposed materialist, parvenu American temperament. This was true, despite the stock that magazines like *Revista Jorba* and *Mujer*—and their readers—had placed in American appliance and celebrity culture. It remained so even as longstanding Spanish interest in America gained strength in the wake of Spain's 1953 treaty with the United States, after which, as Alessandro Seregni has shown, public anti-American sentiment also subsided for over a decade.[129]

The lingering notion that American values remained foreign and were not always better than Spanish counterparts appeared with special clarity in *Revista Jorba* contributor C. A. Mantua's serialized story, "María Teresa dice . . . ," where it could reach the magazine's 25,000 monthly readers and their families. Mantua's story was written from the perspective of María Teresa, a fictional fifteen-year-old haute-bourgeois Madrid girl who, over the course of a year-and-a-half's story installments, fell for twenty-four-year-old American tourist Dick Davidson while vacationing with her family on the coast. Through this summer romance, Mantua communicated the sense of difference Spaniards felt toward America, for if there was one trait about Dick and his family on which the tale consistently harped, it was his foreignness. A language barrier existed between Dick and "Mari-Tere," one so thick that she learned his last name only much later, and he in turn only called her "Darling," finding himself unable to pronounce her name.[130]

But Dick's—and by extension, America's—foreign nature extended well beyond language: a gulf in fundamental values also separated the couple as well as their respective societies. Early on, María Teresa's friend Montse warned her that "Yankee boys just want to have fun."[131] This danger was borne out in Mantua's next installment, in which Dick casually kissed María Teresa, which she found shocking, since she had been taught to believe kissing meant love and commitment. The disconnect between her Spanish values and his American ones only became more apparent to María Teresa after a short-lived engagement to Dick that she ended upon learning early in the new year that while she had taken care not to flirt or socialize inappropriately since the summer, Dick had spent Christmas in Havana having fun and neglecting to answer her letters.[132]

Mantua highlighted the national nature of this difference in values through the presence of a second love interest, Jorge, who, like Dick, hailed from a respectable family and lived in the United States, but, unlike Dick, was Spanish and was presented as virtuous and Mari-Tere's ideal future husband. Dick, by contrast, was, in the words of María Teresa's younger brother Nacho, "a second-rate Gregory Peck," and was in "everything... pretty superficial," characterized by a gallantry that, though appealing, left little real imprint on María Teresa. In the end, Dick himself confirmed the national difference that separated them, suggesting that María Teresa's romantic notions of marriage differed from his own because of their Spanish origin.[133]

By the close of the 1950s, the United States had become in the Spanish popular-cultural imaginary a place at once exotic, home to Hollywood's stars and marvels of home technology, but also familiar and enticingly accessible. Thus, in Mantua's story, Dick Davidson's American origin made him not a genuine rarity but merely unusual and even predictable, per Montse's warning, yet the United States still retained enough foreign glamour to fill younger sister María Rosa's head with Hollywood-fueled visions of fairy-tale trips to New York following María Teresa's engagement to Dick.[134]

Yet, no amount of accessibility combined with foreign appeal could conceal the shortcomings that some Spanish observers also found in American ways. In Mantua's narrative this took the form of Montse's warning and Dick's charming but superficial gallantry—easily read as a metaphor for the materially promising but spiritually hollow American way of life. Elsewhere in the Spanish women's press, similar critiques circulated, albeit not always directed specifically at the United States, but more generally at morally vacant modern lifestyles of foreign origin. In a 1953 short story by *Revista Jorba* writer Lina

Font, for instance, protagonist Pepa split with her highly cultured beau, Pablo, against her mother's wishes because of his lack of interest in modern pastimes like tennis and dancing. She then fell for Blackeney, a gallant foreign diplomat who embodied the modern aesthetic. Like Dick Davidson with María Teresa, he turned out to be only casually interested in her—he was, in fact, married—and broke her heart.[135]

Taken in sum, the trajectory that Spanish attitudes toward the United States followed over the course of the early and mid-1950s, as reflected in the women's consumer press, was one that continued shifts begun during the previous decade. Interest in American appliances and the modernity they promised intensified. Long-standing Spanish interest in Hollywood stars and fashion continued unabated and, if anything, also grew. At the same time, a discourse characteristic of the early dictatorship that found the North American republic spiritually lacking survived, if in diminished and at times allegorical form.

This was also true for the other messages, lifestyles, and social realities that these magazines engaged with during the early to mid-1950s. Just as the Spanish press's evolving depiction of the United States kept pace with Spain's warming diplomatic relationship with the North American superpower, *Funcionarias*'s novel choice to cater to married working women, not just the single women who were the traditional audience for such job-related content, kept pace with an incipient push to secure labor rights for Spanish women. Yet, for all of that, *Funcionarias*'s ideas remained an isolated phenomenon, and, while the 1950s brought increased latitude for women to consume for their own rather than just their families' pleasure, ads that peddled beauty products by invoking family members' sensibilities remained common. Most importantly, the arrival of American consumerism in mid-1950s Spain brought with it similarly American expectations of mass access to consumption, along with consumer credit that helped facilitate this access while simultaneously straining the Spanish marital division of labor and gendered social order. As they unfolded in

Spain's women's magazines, then, the 1950s represented a moment of uneasy transition, when a nascent Spanish mass consumer society took form primarily in the guise of expectations and discourse, but not yet material consumption, and magazine editors and readers embraced the promise of American consumer modernity, but not always without reservations.

The Spanish Men's Magazine Quietly Arrives

During the Franco regime's earliest years menswear and male consumption had not figured greatly in circulating discourse concerning consumption. Shifts in Spanish consumer culture took place mainly in female-oriented consumer periodicals like *Mujer* and *Revista Jorba*. In the realm of fashion, as *Revista Jorba* opined in 1953, "it is uncommon, to be sure, to speak of men's fashion. The word 'fashion' seems to have been created to describe a quintessentially feminine thing."[136] Beginning in the mid-1950s, however, a nascent men's consumer press began to take shape and offered its own contribution to the process by which foreign and especially American consumer practices and products made their way into Spain and were adopted and appropriated by Spaniards.

Modern Spain's first men's fashion and lifestyle magazine, *Señor: Revista del Hombre* (Sir: The man's magazine), appeared in Barcelona in 1955 under the editorial direction of Santiago and Segismundo de Anta of *Alta Costura*. The Anta brothers' involvement proved indicative of the new magazine's content. Both men were openly Francoist in allegiance—Santiago, the elder sibling, had been given a death sentence in Civil War–era Barcelona for being a Francoist fifth columnist—as well as publicly prominent and almost certainly wealthy, with Segismundo having by 1956 become secretary general of the Spanish Haute Couture Cooperative. Unsurprisingly, the pair created a periodical that was similarly haute-bourgeois and loyal to the regime.[137]

Like *Alta Costura*, *Señor* was both expensive—it cost twenty-five to thirty ptas per quarterly issue, or about the market price for a whole chicken in 1958—and featured content that reflected socioeconomically elite lifestyles, such as photographic spreads showing the latest fashions for skiing, boating, and other traditionally aristocratic activities.[138] The magazine made its political allegiances as clear as any privately published periodical had since *Mujer*'s postwar years, opening its first issue with an austere full-page image of a bust of General Franco, simply titled "S. E. El Jefe de Estado Generalísimo Franco" (His Excellency the Head of State Generalissimo Franco).[139] And, when *Señor* began printing profiles of Spain's most elegant men, the individuals chosen were as a rule wealthy and possessed either a noble title or a powerful office.[140] The Anta brothers' magazine may have had less-wealthy readers who read it aspirationally, like *Alta Costura* before it, but, like its sibling, *Señor* was neither mass oriented nor progressively minded—this was no *Funcionarias*, nor even a *Mujer* or a *Revista Jorba*.

Señor did, however, stress the social importance of male dress, and like the women's magazines of the previous decades, focused its gaze abroad. Neither action seemed pathbreaking: in the former case, the magazine merely stressed that clothing was as important a factor in achieving personal and professional success as one's intelligence or professional acumen, a point that myriad Spanish etiquette books had already made and would continue to make.[141] In one 1958 short story, for example, *Señor* contributor María Pilar de Molina underlined this point by narrating how she initially rejected her future husband Miguel due to his shabby appearance (which she associated with poor character), after which he saw the error of his ways, embraced fashion, and won her heart.[142] Meanwhile, *Señor*, like *Mujer* before it, featured regular reports on the latest London and Parisian fashions alongside a steady stream of ads for desirable imported products, including the Legrain perfumes and Philips radios that *Alta Costura* had previously advertised, as well as American Camel-brand cigarettes and Swiss Certina watches.[143]

In both cases, the magazine's actions set changes in motion. Albeit unintentionally, *Señor* established a precedent in the new men's consumer press for treating menswear as a symbolically highly charged area for a reassertion of, and later, challenge to, normative Spanish masculine identity. In 1958, *Señor* stressed that "one thing that d[id] make the man . . . [was] dressing well"; five years later, in 1963, a second, recently founded Spanish men's magazine would extend this claim, boasting that following its counsel would reshape the reader's inner self, for instance, making him more socially adroit. This symbolic investment in men's fashion was not yet notably subversive. If anything, these claims dovetailed with the Falangist masculine ideal of the "Man-Warrior" who fought for personal success in peacetime as he fought for Spain in time of war.[144] It would, however, present a challenge to the Francoist status quo once journalists turned their attention to mod, unisex, and the new popular culture of London's Carnaby Street in the late 1960s. Menswear then became a cultural battleground, as these fashions had strong ties to countercultural movements in Spain's American and British reference points and brought subversive social and political ideas with them across the Pyrenees.[145]

Señor, finally, established men's fashion and its representation in the Spanish consumer press as a site for the assertion of national aspirations to a prosperity and modernity that the magazine measured against foreign standards, a measure that Spain's department stores, grocery trade, and advertising sector were increasingly employing, too. Thus, contributor "Petronius" triumphantly proclaimed in 1956 that, at long last, the Spanish textile industry had progressed to such a level of sophistication—one already reached abroad—that it was now possible to buy well-tailored clothes off the rack in Spain, and not just from a custom tailor.[146] The magazine's ads also gave evidence of this way of thinking: in 1955, textile manufacturer Mestre y Ballbé displayed its newest MEYBA-brand clothing lines, which it described as the product of "select[ion] from traditional [Spanish] clothing items [and] *compari[son] with those of other countries* [emphasis added]."[147] In both instances, the message was that Spain was "arriving" in the world of European menswear, to which it could now contribute ideas, not just receive them. Such references to national sartorial accomplishment remained relatively subtle at that moment. Nevertheless, they underlined Spain's growing integration into a larger international community, not just of nations but of fashion professionals and consumers connected across national borders by a shared commitment to elegance.

Over the course of the 1940s and 1950s, the consumer press in Spain expanded dramatically, keeping pace with a burgeoning national retailing infrastructure epitomized by the spread of department stores like Galerías Preciados and El Corte Inglés. While in 1943 there were only fifteen magazines classified as *literatura femenina*—"women's magazines," not all of them devoted to consumption-related subjects such as fashion or home décor—by 1954 the number of women's magazines published in Spain had swelled to more than forty.[148] This growth in the Spanish consumer press saw a variety of new women's magazines join *Mujer* and fellow early arrivals *Alta Costura* and *Medina*: the self-declared but in reality only cautiously modern *Astra*; *Revista Jorba*, the first mass-oriented consumer magazine published by a Spanish department store; and the working women's journal *Funcionarias*. It also witnessed the arrival of the first men's fashion and lifestyle journal, *Señor* (1955), as well as a series of professional journals that advanced consumption-related professions like the advertising and department store retail trades.

As these periodicals filled Spanish newsstands, the content and messages that they offered readers grew more diverse, a change that roughly followed the contours of contemporaneous economic and diplomatic shifts in Francoist Spain's fortunes. Initially elite in both their content and price, some of postwar Spain's new women's magazines—*Mujer* especially—began to display a perhaps cynical sensitivity to housewives' hardships as the nation's economy sank during the mid-to-late 1940s under the weight of the Franco regime's post–World War II diplomatic isolation.

However, with the advance of a diplomatic and trade rapprochement between Spain and the United States as well as Western Europe during the late 1940s and early 1950s, the first germ of a mass consumer society began to take form in Spain—at this point more aspirational than reflected in real consumption—filtering into the country primarily from the United States. Both the now well-established magazines launched during the Spanish postwar era as well as new titles like *Astra* and *Funcionarias* shifted their tone to match, participating in the construction of this new imagined mass consumer society. Building on coverage of foreign lifestyles and products that had remained steady in the largely privileged (and therefore, politically sheltered) consumer press of the early postwar period, these magazines began to devote more content to Hollywood stars' lives as well as American and Western European fashions. They also offered early hints of an American appliance culture that was on the brink of arriving in Spain and came accompanied by visions of modern households effortlessly run by increasingly technically proficient consumer-housewives.

Even as they embraced these new foreign consumer ways, Spain's women's magazines also made a concerted effort to shore up the gendered social order that the regime had enforced since the Civil War against the challenges that these new ideas could pose. As times changed, Spanish women increasingly sought the right to work, not just to supplement their families' incomes, but also to stock their own pocketbooks with the necessary pesetas to consume for their own pleasure.[149] Some magazines, like *Mujer*, reacted by catering to this interest among unmarried readers while making clear that only single women could legitimately pursue employment outside the home. Others remained silent on the subject. Only *Funcionarias* defended married women's work. Like the rest of these magazines, it nevertheless retained the expectation that employed housewives care just as assiduously for their households and families as they had before securing extradomestic work.

These trends intensified as the 1950s progressed, especially after the normalization of relations between the United States and Spain in 1953. Magazines like *Revista Jorba* and *Mujer* began to feature an ever-greater profusion of ads and articles that treated appliances and other new technological innovations for the home as normal, desirable staples of a modern middle-class lifestyle to which all Spanish households could aspire, a way of life that these articles often noted was of American origin. Thoroughly politicized in the wake of the Civil War's end—the regime's most explicitly Falangist and fascist, or "blue" period—several of these women's magazines now redirected their efforts toward a rearguard political agenda. They used devices such as advice columns to combat unwanted changes in gender relations accelerated by the advent of Spanish mass consumption, including a destabilization of the traditional Spanish marital division of labor provoked by the spread of consumer credit. This was, paradoxically, the very development that made consumption increasingly accessible to the Spanish masses. After 1955, *Señor* added to these efforts its own editorial attempts to situate Spain as an increasingly equal and valuable member of an international community of fashion-producing nations.

Another new women's magazine that began to circulate out of Madrid in 1958, titled *Ana María*, neatly encapsulated these changes. It bore the fingerprints of the transformations and new features that the consumer press had experienced and acquired over the previous fifteen years. Like *Teresa* and *Funcionarias*, *Ana María* offered a recurring column, "Caminos Para La Mujer" ([Life] Paths for women), which profiled long-term careers—not just jobs—available to women. Though it did not proclaim outright support for married women's right to work, at least it did not explicitly cast such employment as purely a single woman's pursuit, as *Mujer* had. True to the transitional nature of the 1950s, the magazine emphasized the primacy of domestic life as a woman's principal path to fulfillment. To this end it offered columns devoted to cooking, entertaining, and other domestic subjects, and it featured profiles of stars like Spanish actress and singer Carmen Sevilla or Lucille Ball that focused on how these otherwise career-minded women considered themselves housewives first.[150] That *Ana María* used an American star like Lucille Ball only underscores the centrality of the United States in the Spanish popular-cultural landscape, as well as magazines' continued willingness to use this interest, along with the bully pulpit they enjoyed as purveyors of consumer news, in the service of larger sociopolitical aims.

Most of all, *Ana María* and other Spanish consumer magazines bore witness to a 1950s-era reorientation of Spanish consumption toward the masses, and with it a transformation in what and how ordinary Spaniards bought. *Ana María* published a column in 1958 that neatly encapsulated this change—and how self-aware both the Spanish press and its readers were about it—under the title, "Today's Needs Are Not the Same as Yesterday's." Spaniards of the late 1950s, the article argued, dressed better, buying new clothes more often thanks to the increasing prevalence of store sales. Installment credit and the belief that the latest appliances were available to all meant that Spanish women strove to stock their homes with such devices, even at the cost of breaking the family budget. These women were more publicly active: they flirted, joined clubs, and worked outside the home. Even Spanish diets had changed, as science revolutionized the field of nutrition.[151] In fact, as *Ana María*'s first issue hit newsstands in 1958, another consumer revolution was beginning, one that would further alter Spanish diets and advance a foreign-born mass mode of consumption in Spain's cities as well as its hinterland, potentially reaching every housewife who bought groceries—the supermarket.

CHAPTER 3

(Super)Marketing Western Modernity

Self-Service, Sociocultural Change, and
the Professionalization of Food Retailing
during Spain's Miracle Years

In 1961, Álvaro Ortíz de Zárate, president of SPAR Española, the new Spanish division of SPAR, an international network of affiliated grocery stores and warehouses, exulted over the bright future he foresaw for his organization, his trade, and his country. "Spain's distributive commerce has awakened from its centuries-long lethargy," he wrote. "We are going to advance more in the next DECADE than in the whole of the past CENTURY." Once "the province of small, disorganized, and antiquated investors," Ortíz de Zárate continued, food distribution in Spain was now increasingly falling into the far more capable hands of "the powerful banks [and] the distribution and sales experts." He concluded, "The winds [of change] are coming to Spain."[1]

Ortíz de Zárate's boast was no exaggeration—winds of change were indeed sweeping through Spain. The late 1950s and early 1960s represented a moment of rapid upheaval for the Spanish consumer sector, and especially so for Spain's food retailing trade. Between 1956 and 1966, this industry saw many of its core institutions, leading figures, and the terms of subsequent professional debates emerge, while officials, grocers, and other food industry professionals together integrated Spain with unprecedented speed into international professional circles, meanwhile exposing consumers to new foods and foodways.

This transformation rose out of the arrival of a new American and Northern European commercial model that spread through Spain from late 1957 onward: the *autoservicio*, or "self-service" grocery store, and especially the physically largest variety of this store, the supermarket.[2] In small towns like Yecla (Murcia) as well as Spain's major cities, new autoservicios sprang up, and existing neighborhood grocers converted to self-service. These shops featured innovations including carefully staged lighting, open floor plans with shelves that customers could freely browse—the essence of the self-service model—and rationalized management of everything from inventory to signage. And, in turn, these innovations, which broke sharply with traditional practices, arrived laden with notions of a coming Spanish rise to modernity.[3]

The scope of this change and its effects on the daily experiences of ordinary grocers and shoppers were immense. Shopping in an autoservicio bore little resemblance to buying from a traditional grocer. The latter dispatched goods upon request from behind an often dimly lit shop counter, with few attempts at customer service or marketing. By contrast, an autoservicio's sole counter was often the one supporting the cash register.[4] The pace of expansion was quick, too: by February 1963, five years after its first self-service grocery opened in late 1957, Spain possessed the third-largest number of SPAR autoservicios in Europe—nearly twice as many as the Netherlands, the chain's homeland.[5] Most of all, these stores accelerated changes in Spanish commerce and consumption set in motion during the late 1940s and 1950s by retailers like Galerías Preciados and magazines like *Señor*. Well suited to reach poor and rural Spaniards, autoservicios introduced customers to foreign shopping experiences, products, and lifestyles that promised increased prosperity, convenience, and modernity. These same promises led Spanish food retailing professionals to turn abroad for news and guidance, as Galerías, *Señor*, and others had done. They lured grocers to affiliate with foreign chains like SPAR, and encouraged the grocery trade as a whole, as well as the regime officials who regulated it, to treat these foreign ways of buying and selling as the measure of Spanish modernization. Most of all, food retailers' turn abroad drove not only a radical transformation of their industry but also a shift in their own and their customers' perceptions of Spain's place in Europe that extended the changes that Galerías Preciados and *Señor* had set in motion during the 1940s and 1950s. The foreign foodways these grocers and trade professionals began to introduce added fuel to a Europeanization and Americanization of Spanish consumer lifestyles that was already underway, and meanwhile undermined the Franco regime's discourses of national exceptionalism by normalizing the belief that Spain was European and that its future lay in integrating into a consumer-capitalist Western Europe.

At the same time, the case of the autoservicio's arrival to Spain is singularly remarkable because it happened not via private enterprise, as elsewhere in Western Europe, but through the state. The Franco regime spearheaded the introduction of self-service and remained a constant regulatory presence even after the supermarket's privatization in the early 1960s. Far more so than in the case of the nation's department stores, the regime was thoroughly and even principally implicated in Spain's mass consumer revolution, and, ironically, in the erosion of the very exceptionalist myths that it had long championed.

American Origins, By Way of Europe

Though all had champions who played crucial parts in introducing these concepts to Spain, the innovations adopted by Spanish admen and food retailers—public relations and the supermarket—were not native to the Iberian Peninsula. All arrived from abroad via the same general path: initial development in the United States, filtration during the middle of the twentieth century to Western Europe, followed finally by adoption in Spain through a combination of private interest and state intervention that took reference from both Western Europe and the United States.

For the supermarket, this global process began in the 1920s.[6] Grocery chains such as Kroger emerged after World War I due to a combination of social pressures and an inflation-fueled rise in food prices. They quickly transformed the grocer's trade, introducing innovations such as centralized management, standardized customer service, mass-produced goods, and economies of scale that let them undercut independent grocers.[7] In response, these grocers banded together into new, voluntary store chains of their own, in which they shared a common warehouse store brand, and advertising—and, in so doing, established the model for SPAR.[8] Finally, chains like Piggly Wiggly pioneered the self-service method for selling groceries, in which customers themselves selected purchases from openly accessible store shelves. From the founding of the first supermarkets, New York City's King Kullen (opened 1930) and New Jersey's Big Bear markets (opened 1932), self-service was how supermarkets sold.[9]

Both stores experienced what supermarket advocate Max Mandell Zimmerman termed "phenomenal" success, driven by their promises of extreme customer savings, which Depression-era shoppers welcomed. These stores were so successful that alarmed traditional grocers printed pamphlets attacking them—to little effect, for the supermarket spread rapidly, growing from 94 stores in twenty-four U.S. cities in 1934 to 1,200 groceries in eighty-five cities in 1936.[10] As they spread, these stores evolved, shedding their early emphasis on bargain pricing and carnivalesque spectacle. They instead adopted features such as a focus on customer service, middle-class appeal, and the chain structure from the nation's more upscale chain stores, which they increasingly resembled and replaced. By 1936, supermarkets had largely taken over the American grocery trade.[11]

Self-service and the supermarket arrived in Europe in the late 1940s, after World War II. Voluntary chains of traditional groceries—not yet self-service stores—had first appeared in the Netherlands in the 1930s, most notably SPAR, which Dutch businessman Adriaan van Well founded in 1932, inspired by America's chains.[12] At war's end, SPAR and other Dutch chains like Verkoops Gemeenschaap (VéGé) began to spread abroad, beginning with Belgium in 1947; delegations from European retailing groups such as Migros of Zurich toured American supermarkets and adopted the innovations they witnessed; and, by 1948, two of Europe's most powerful nations, Britain and France, both had self-service grocery stores. The next decade brought still more growth: beginning in 1951, SPAR spread to Germany, Denmark, Austria, France, and Britain, while in 1955, the Rockefeller-funded International Basic Economy Corporation (IBEC) launched Italy's first supermarket, Supermarkets Italiani, in Rome.[13] By the end of the decade, self-service grocery stores—most not large enough to be termed supermarkets in the strictest sense—operated in much of Western Europe.[14] And, in late 1957, they came to Spain.

Spain's adoption of self-service stands out for three reasons. First, there has been little historical scholarship on the subject, unlike the British, French, and American cases. Second, this introduction took place a decade after self-service first arrived in Europe, and the Spanish retailers and officials who drove it forward acted with an awareness of self-service's previous trajectory in Europe and the United States. Therefore the Spanish story illuminates the impact of intra-European developments and exchanges on consumer culture. And, finally, the adoption of the supermarket in Spain happened not through entrepreneurial action, as with Big Bear, King Kullen, SPAR, and other American and Western European stores, but through the direct action of a dictatorship, the Francoist state. So, what impact did state action have on this consumer institution, and how did the supermarket's arrival influence subsequent regime policy?

This process of adoption began on 26 June 1956, when José Ruíz Morales, a diplomatic attaché at the Spanish embassy in Washington, requested technical literature on American supermarkets from the U.S. Department of Commerce. From the outset, Spanish officials thought of the supermarket very much as an *American* phenomenon, though they did tacitly acknowledge Europe's embrace of and contributions to self-service when they wrote of its expansion as taking place "abroad" rather than specifically in the United States.[15] Intrigued by this spread, the Comisaría de Abastecimientos y Transportes (CAT), which had managed postwar Spain's food rationing program, began to monitor the American press for news about foreign supermarkets.[16]

Then, in October 1957, at the behest of Minister of Commerce Alberto Ullastres, the CAT opened Spain's first self-service grocery store inside Madrid's Barceló market. Underscoring the foreign and specifically European influence that remained at play, the diminutive test store sold only frozen meats produced by Danish frozen foods company Danegoods, CAT's partner in the venture. The Barceló experiment was a resounding success, and, within months, the Comisaría set Operación Supermercados, or "Operation Supermarkets," in motion. It opened new test stores in Bilbao, San Sebastián, Gijón, and La Coruña. It founded two subagencies to regulate Spain's autoservicios, the Compañia Auxiliar de Abastecimientos and the Organización Supermercados. And it drafted an ambitious plan to create a national network of 496 state-run self-service stores. Finally, after Ullastres relented on this plan in March 1958, promising that self-service would not become a state monopoly, the agency developed an official regulatory structure for privately owned autoservicios— and it did all of the above by the summer of 1959.[17] Self-service had begun to secure a place in the Spanish grocery trade, and it had done so by the government's own hand.

The Supermarket's State-Led Spread:
Meanings Sought and Measures Taken

Despite the inroads the supermarket had made into Spain by 1959, much still remained undecided. If self-service had achieved near-ubiquity in the United States, in Spain it remained a limited phenomenon, still open to challenge by defenders of the older way of selling groceries. And, perhaps more importantly, the meaning of self-service—what it represented, promised, or even threatened, depending on the observer—remained ambiguous, unfixed. Over the next few years, as this new commercial model expanded across Spain, such a struggle for meaning would remain a constant theme.

First of all, in the CAT's eyes, the supermarket remained an area that legitimately and even primarily belonged to the state. Prima facie, during the last two years of the 1950s, private enterprise appeared to be taking over the Spanish self-service grocery trade. In May 1958—six months after the opening the first autoservicio—the CAT abandoned its plan for a national network of state-run supermarkets, preserving only the twelve stores already in operation or being built. And Antonio Pérez-Ruiz Salcedo, the agency's newly appointed head, spent the rest of 1958 giving interviews in which he reiterated his agency's commitment to this new plan and to a privately owned self-service sector.

Yet, in keeping with the CAT's original postwar mission, the policies and regulations that this agency and the Spanish Ministry of the Interior established between May 1958 and December 1959 formalized the CAT's authority to credential and police Spain's privately owned self-service grocery stores.[18] Between July 1958 and early 1959, the CAT developed a program whereby private self-service grocers could affiliate with the Organización Supermercados, gaining powerful privileges like a 50 percent tax rate reduction. In exchange, they had to adhere to the agency's stringent product quality standards, agree to public health inspections, and purchase their wares from (cheap) government suppliers. Contemporaneously, the Comisaría promised to not build any new autoservicios, but in the same breath reasserted its authority, reserving the right to open new ones when private enterprise failed to do so, in order to ensure "lower prices, [better] food quality, and [serve] the nation's neediest classes, the middle class and workers."[19] Finally, a May 1959 Interior Ministry decree required that all private parties seeking a license to open an autoservicio had to first secure CAT approval.[20]

Public reaction to the newly arrived autoservicio model and the CAT's efforts to spread it was largely favorable, with a few exceptions.

For myriad ordinary Spanish businessmen and grocers, the autoservicio's spread was cause for excitement, speaking to a range of individual hopes and desires, particularly once the CAT put its affiliate program in motion. By early 1959, letters filled with requests were pouring into the agency's Madrid offices from across the country. Their pleas are revealing: for ordinary working- and middle-class Spaniards, CAT autoservicios most especially represented the chance at a job—and a government job at that. Thus, in September 1958, Civil War Veterans Delegation member Tomás García Rebull successfully requested, "[for] Miss Rogelia Astorga Alda, [a] veteran of our War of Liberation . . . an Administrative Assistant position in the Comisaría General de Abastecimientos y Transportes, since it seems that new personnel are being hired to manage those Services [the Organización Supermercados] that this Organization has recently created."[21] As a single woman, the eldest of three siblings, the primary caretaker for her blind father, and an unemployed, former CAT employee between 1949 and 1952, Astorga leapt at the chance to return to the security of government work. Meanwhile, for others, supermarkets were a business opportunity. In April 1959, attorney Enrique Ribalta wrote Antonio Pérez-Ruiz to request affiliate status for the supermarket that self-service grocer SURESA planned to build.[22] And for still others it represented a new field where a little ingenuity could lead to personal advancement. Such was the case for industrial engineer Antonio García Fernández, who in April 1958 sent Alberto Ullastres a proposal for a privately run, vertically integrated store that would sell produce at below-market price.[23] In each instance, the common thread was a belief that the supermarket would soon transform Spaniards' lives, and the writer's in particular.

This was just as true of the supermarket's opponents, for in Spain as in the United States, the new commercial model immediately gained bitter enemies as well as friends. King Kullen and Big Bear had in early 1930s America faced opposition from the chain stores they threatened to replace. Similarly, in late 1950s and early 1960s Spain the CAT encountered resistance and attacks from Spanish grocers' official government syndicates. The National Food Warehousers' Federation (Federación Nacional de Almacenistas de Alimentación), for instance, condemned the CAT's intention to keep running any stores whatsoever, deeming anything but complete privatization a "completely unacceptable" state of affairs. Francisco Olmedo, head of the Madrid Grocers' Guild, took a more extreme position in a bravado-filled September 1960 editorial. Boasting that Madrid's traditional grocers had nothing to fear or learn from the supermarket, Olmedo nevertheless also warned that Spain's autoservicios enjoyed unfair advantages that would allow them to undercut traditional Spanish grocers' prices and drive them out of business. King Kullen, Big Bear, and other store chains before them had faced similar complaints during the early twentieth century.[24] In Spain, these complaints were likewise already so common in 1960 that Pérez-Ruiz Salcedo described this griping as "an inveterate custom." Olmedo's own unease about the supermarket's transformative potential was so great that, even as he penned his boast that all was well, he had already begun looking into adapting his store to self-service.[25]

Olmedo could hardly be faulted for his fears and attempts to discredit self-service, given the speed with which the autoservicio spread through Spain and the hopes that officials, grocers, and the Spanish public attached to the new commercial model.[26] Though the CAT had kept its word and halted further moves to open more state-run autoservicios, the number of privately owned self-service stores still shot upward in 1959. This growth included both currently still-familiar names such as Barcelona's Caprabo as well as long-forgotten ones like Superma and Minimax. By June 1960, Spain boasted 145 autoservicios large enough to be considered supermarkets even in technical terms, with another 194 CAT-affiliated ones planned. The total number of autoservicios was double the former figure, and while most still serviced Spain's more prosperous areas, especially Madrid and Barcelona, poorer areas like Granada had some and were scheduled to receive more.[27] Meanwhile, the CAT and private chains like SPAR stoked Spaniards' high hopes for the supermarket by frequently declaring that self-service would soon transform Spain's grocery trade and standard of living—a future from which traditional grocers were absent. In 1961, SPAR head Ortíz de Zárate gloated that self-service would soon cause "thousands [of] antiquated . . . traditional . . . 'know-it-all' . . . [and] inefficient grocers [to] disappear."[28] The CAT similarly asserted that self-service would do no less than "dignify the grocer's trade," would "totally change [Spain's] nutritional panorama," and would raise the Spanish grocery trade to heights reached abroad. And the agency made these claims where thousands of Spanish housewives saw them, in an early 1960 issue of the women's magazine *AMA*.[29] Faced with this, Olmedo naturally worried.

The Comisaría's dissemination of these claims in *AMA* was part of a larger, concerted campaign to boost sales while disseminating the CAT's vision of what self-service meant for Spain and its citizens. This campaign, rolled out between 1960 and 1962, was designed to reach Spanish women through press like *AMA* as well as radio and television.[30] *AMA*'s very existence bore witness to this ambition: the CAT launched the magazine in December 1959 with Pilar Salcedo, the CAT head's own sister, as a prominent member of its editorial staff.[31] This agenda was likewise evident in the magazine's primary editorial mission, which was to provide Spain's housewives with the dedicated periodical they had never before had, and that for the first time treated their job with the professionalism it merited. Indeed, *AMA*, the magazine proclaimed in its first issue, aimed to foment a professional esprit de corps among Spain's housewives—a sentiment that echoed the growing emphasis on technical sophistication at department stores like Galerías Preciados and at ad agencies like Ruescas and DANIS.[32] The magazine also had a second, tacit, related purpose: to promote CAT policies and to familiarize readers with and encourage them to shop at Spain's growing number of autoservicios. *AMA* considered these stores and readers' own kitchens to be the home venues for the housewife's newly defined profession and the exercise of her technical expertise.[33]

This second mission and its centrality to the new magazine were in evidence from the time of *AMA*'s first issue. When, on 19 December 1959, the CAT announced the launch of its new magazine in the press, the government agency promised readers that *AMA* would provide "the most complete information about SUPERMARKETS [emphasis original]."[34] It then distributed 100,000 free copies of the first issue through Madrid autoservicios and supermarkets, including the five stores that the CAT—that is, the Franco regime—itself operated.[35] Finally, *AMA* featured several recurring and prominently placed columns during its first year of publication that familiarized readers with, and encouraged them to shop in, supermarkets. Foremost among these was an article series "Los Supermercados a Rayos X" (Supermarkets X-rayed), which promised to equip readers with "everything . . . [they] . . . need[ed] to know about the supermarket."[36] Since supermarkets were a new phenomenon in Spain, such columns outlined supermarkets' prior history abroad and highlighted the advantages and conveniences they offered. In particular, these articles worked to promote self-service's most off-putting features, such as a seeming lack of personal attention from store staff or the sale of meat in frozen, pre-packaged form. *AMA* explained the reasons for these changes, and how they actually helped housewives by making them savvier shoppers, by forcing grocers to improve product quality and lower prices, and, in the case of frozen foods, by eliminating wasteful spoilage.[37]

Professionalizing Housewives

More than just promoting self-service, the CAT used *AMA* to advance its original and overarching motive for introducing the supermarket: namely, to improve food distribution in Spain through its rationalization. The agency retained the right to open supermarkets when private parties failed to, as well as to regulate those private markets that did open, in order to ensure self-service's controlled and systematic spread. It also wanted to ensure that shoppers made the best use of the supermarket, promoting a more coordinated, rational purchase and use of groceries by the nation's housewives.

AMA worked toward these ends through three regular columns: "Prognóstico para la Despensa" (Pantry forecast), "Charla de Don Antonio" (Don Antonio's chat), and "Con La Historieta del Día, Aprenda Usted Economía" (Learn economics with the story of the day). The first of these, the Prognóstico, featured a fifteen-day calendar that offered housewives notice of changing food prices, and provided preplanned grocery lists for family meals based around foods going on sale. The second column, penned by Antonio Pérez-Ruiz himself, explained these price fluctuations, which were a subject of frequent reader complaint.[38] Together, these articles sought to reconfigure Spanish diets along rational scientific lines and so improve nutrition standards and optimize family budgets. In this same vein, they sought to convince housewives that they belonged to an important profession and had a duty to carry it out correctly by following *AMA*'s guidelines, which existed to serve the CAT's historical mission of "assuring an adequate supply [of food] for the nation."[39]

The magazine's third column, "Con La Historieta Del Día, Aprenda Usted Economía," represented another attempt to professionalize Spanish housewives through technical education. Using a combination of text and cartoons (see fig. 8), each "Historieta" told housewives a story that illustrated a technical point in economics, home economics, or how food distribution systems worked. Over time, the columns aimed to cultivate in the magazine's readers a more technical and professional understanding of these subjects, with which they could then make better use of tools like the "Prognóstico" to improve their families' diets. For example, a series of "Historietas" from July and August 1960 offered a detailed description of how and why food distributors froze certain products, including an explanation of the cellular effects of freezing on meat and the scientific reasons why improperly defrosted meat suffered a sharp drop in quality. This aimed to produce informed housewives who understood the importance of following CAT instructions on how to defrost frozen goods. These articles also sought to reassure housewives wary of frozen meat, and thus to promote their use of Spain's autoservicios and their cooperation in streamlining Spanish food distribution.[40]

This push to train Spanish housewives to be professionalized household managers and to persuade them to make use of Spain's supermarkets also reveals the effect that the arrival of the autoservicio and the CAT's push to streamline food distribution had on the place of women in Spain, imbuing the role of the housewife with increased importance. The CAT's discourse cast housewives as key contributors to boom-era Spanish prosperity. In part, this rested on the notion that by feeding their families, housewives also fed the nation as a whole. Thus, in a June 1960 editorial *AMA* termed the housewife her family's "minister of finance," and two months later, Pérez-Ruiz Salcedo declared housewives, "the pillar on which Spain's most valuable asset, the Spanish family, rests."[41] The CAT also considered them a pillar of Spanish financial health, for by cutting expenses, *AMA* asserted, housewives could render the nation more solvent, and, similarly, by following CAT directives to buy more or less of a given product, they could bolster struggling sectors of Spanish agriculture or support CAT export campaigns. The Comisaría frequently issued such calls to action: in February 1960, "Don Antonio" called on housewives to patriotically consume more rice, eggs, and chicken, as overproduction of these staples had caused prices to plummet and threatened Spanish farmers' livelihoods. And the following November, in response to housewives' dissatisfaction with olive oil shortages caused by a government oil export campaign, Pérez-Ruiz reminded readers: "It is through shared effort that . . . we will achieve the maximum level of welfare. . . . When you get on the tram, or go to the movies, or buy a medicine . . . know that [they] contain something imported, and thanks to our exports the country will progress. And when this progress is achieved . . . our buying power will be greater, and we will not have to export goods like oil."[42]

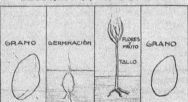

FIG. 8. "Learn Economics with the Story of the Day." *AMA*, no. 12 (1 July 1960), 7.

With that said, these messages did not present a challenge to the domesticity- and motherhood-centered feminine gender roles that Francoism imposed. Rather, as it emphasized the importance of Spanish homemakers becoming better informed and technically proficient at budgeting, shopping, and cooking, the CAT asked these women to perform their normatively feminine roles in a more sophisticated way. Pérez-Ruiz Salcedo's frequent condescension in his columns—sarcastically telling readers to stop complaining about pasteurization, "unless [they] like[d] the flavor of bacteria"—evoked the patriarchal power imbalance that existed between the male CAT head and his female readers.[43] So too, his calls to a patriotic feminine volunteerism had precedent in postwar Spanish pronatalist policies and, indeed, the Sección Femenina itself.[44] Like the women's magazines of the 1950s, *AMA* used interviews with well-known Spanish actresses to underscore how these publicly prominent women were actually more fulfilled by their lives as homemakers than by their careers. It also actively encouraged women toward values like meekness, obedience to one's spouse, and sacrifice, which the Sección Femenina coded feminine. In a December 1960 editorial, for example, the magazine counseled, "happiness is born almost always of sacrifice . . . live[d] in a thousand small details: the roast that is never done, enduring relatives' impertinent comments . . . you will feel [our acclaim] when you can still smile at everyone."[45]

Even so, the importance that officials, food retailing authorities, and ordinary Spaniards began ascribing to homemakers in the late 1950s represented a shift in thinking that was both widespread and reached the highest levels of the regime. Underscoring the widespread nature of the shift, SPAR valued housewives highly enough that in January 1960 it too launched a homemakers' magazine, *La Familia SPAR* (The SPAR family). Like *AMA*, this new journal sought to enlist housewives' help in serving Spain's families and making special sales successful, and also argued that these women actually worked harder than their husbands. By May 1963 the regime's own regard was obvious: Minister of Commerce Ullastres so valued housewives' cooperation that he delivered a televised address in which he answered homemakers' concerns about fluctuating food prices, warned about further changes likely to result from the influence of the European Common Market, and, most especially, asked women yet again to heed the CAT's guidance. His speech was subsequently printed in *AMA* as well as the trade journal *ICA*; the importance he granted housewives was so enduring that it could be found in *ICA* a decade later.[46]

Self-service, finally, contributed to a larger redefinition of women's status in Franco's Spain. In 1961, as legal reforms made it easier for Spanish women to secure employment, *La Familia SPAR* became accepting of married women working in naturalizing if also grudging terms, and the CAT facilitated the ability to hold jobs in the public sphere—at its supermarkets—to women like Rogelia Astorga.[47] Meanwhile *AMA*, which was a women's magazine rather than just a grocery buyer's guide, featured content that encouraged women to shop for pleasure. This continued the social shift that Aurora Morcillo finds in the 1950s emergence of the Spanish consumer-housewife who bought fashionable clothes not for her family's pleasure, as National-Catholic norms demanded, but for herself.[48] Thus, in 1960, *AMA* fashion columnist Pilar Amillo reported on the latest trends in sporty clothing and furs, while ads from stocking maker Sanllehi or for the elasticized "Gom" bathing suit promised attractiveness and, in the latter case, a rare foreign innovation.[49] Such advertising grew so common that, in 1962, *Club AMA*, a televised version of the magazine, fell afoul of Spanish National Television officials for inadvertently promoting several brands, like the Dior fashion label, that had not paid the requisite fees for such publicity.[50]

The Autoservicio and Francoist Spain's Rise to Modernity

Perhaps most of all, though, and especially after 1960, the autoservicio fundamentally represented a Spanish modernity and national progress to be measured against other nations' socioeconomic achievements.

Comparisons between Spain, its neighbors, and trading partners like the United States arose early on in the process of introducing self-service, reaching near-ubiquity in CAT files relating to the autoservicio's initial spread between 1958 and 1960. In these years, CAT officials were fixated on winning Spain prestige abroad by using supermarkets to raise the nation to a foreign standard of living. Indeed, an August 1958 CAT report, titled "Report on Impressions from Trip to U.S.A., Concerning Food Distribution and the Formula for Spain's Future," argued exactly this: that the key to this future lay in achieving an American standard of living via the supermarket.[51] Similarly, in one "Supermarkets X-Rayed" column, AMA declared that, by adopting the autoservicio, "Spain ha[d] taken—and [was] taking—a great step toward reaching the same heights that food commerce has abroad."[52]

Yet it was the autoservicios themselves that were most implicated in this constant referencing of foreign practices. They, along with the agencies that opened them, were by 1960 beginning to function as pathways for exposing traditional grocers who had converted to self-service, as well as housewives who shopped there, to unfamiliar foreign grocery practices that were shot through with notions of modernity. For consumers, such experiences included the aforementioned purchase of frozen, pre-packaged meat, or the comparatively impersonal treatment that they received in an autoservicio. Of the latter, AMA assured its readers this treatment was not actually impersonal, simply more efficient for both shopper and store clerk. Letters to AMA's "Pregunte Usted Lo Que Quiera" (Ask what you like) column reveal other ways in which self-service exposed shoppers to foreign, often confusing practices. In March 1960, for example, reader Adelaida Cebrián wrote to express shock at finding shoes being sold by self-service in her neighborhood supermarket; AMA responded by lauding German supermarkets' similar, efficient sale of men's shirts using standardized measurements.[53] For readers of AMA, these experiences did not exist in isolation. Instead, they took place against the common backdrop of the CAT's insistence that "Spanish autoservicios still need to improve greatly with relation to other countries."[54] In other words, Spaniards were continually reminded of their nation's need to modernize and reach a foreign standard of self-service and prosperity. The overall message was clear—what shoppers experienced when they went to their new neighborhood supermarkets was Spain's future, a convergence with Europe.

This message reached grocers as well, who similarly experienced the spread of self-service as an at times uncomfortable, foreign-seeming, but modernity-tinged change. In 1959, for example, the CAT reached an agreement with the U.S. National Association of Food Chains (NAFC), which had just run a "Supermarket USA" pavilion at Barcelona's International Trade Fair, to acquire the display's supermarket equipment—scarce in Spain—which the CAT then donated to Spanish grocers. The text of this agreement was triumphant, declaring that the supermarket would bring "innumerable benefits ... to the Spanish economy" and strengthen ties between Spain and the United States.[55] Yet grocers did not always know what to do with these new machines or even how to run their still-unfamiliar stores. The CAT-NAFC agreement seemingly recognized this, providing for a six-week supermarket management program in the United States for Spanish store managers.[56] And, at the CAT's supermarkets, inexperience generated a host of problems as store personnel struggled to adopt new, rationalized methods. These problems included inconsistencies in price marking; issues with new machines such as one Madrid store's broken automatic olive oil dispenser; a lack of trained administrative personnel; and, at the CAT's pilot store, space constraints and stymied business stemming from the originally experimental store's intentionally small size.[57]

By 1960, CAT stores accounted for just one-quarter of Spain's approximately fifty autoservicios, yet Spain's privately owned self-service grocery stores and store chains—the other 75 percent—were if anything still more extreme examples of this push toward a foreign commercial modernity.[58] They were fast becoming quasi-foreign commercial outposts, and some were actually foreign stores.[59] With Spain's economy opened to foreign investment as a result of the 1959 Stabilization Plan, the Dutch voluntary cooperative grocery chains SPAR and VéGé entered Spain between 1959 and 1961, and, as Spanish grocers flocked to affiliate with them, they quickly became the country's largest food retailers. These chains imported modern business practices that advanced the CAT's aim to professionalize food retailing. They also altered how Spaniards perceived their, and their nation's, place within a larger international community.[60]

Nowhere was this more the case than at SPAR's Spanish division (SPAR Española), which, according to historian Joan Carles Maixé-Altés, "revolutionized the [Spanish] small business market."[61] SPAR Española founder and president Álvaro Ortíz de Zárate embraced the cause of bringing self-service to Spain well before joining SPAR, after encountering American supermarkets while studying at the Yale School of Drama in the early 1950s. Convinced that he could best serve Spain by introducing the supermarket there, he studied the self-service model in Germany, where he discovered SPAR. By 1958, he was lecturing in Spain on the advantages of the autoservicio, and, in late 1959, he spearheaded SPAR's arrival to Spain, which became the chain's ninth host country.[62] SPAR Española's subsequent growth was meteoric. By January 1961, Spain's SPAR network boasted 100 self-service grocers, by August it had 201, and, by year's end, 300—half of Spain's total number of autoservicios. One and a half years later, in May 1963, SPAR Española possessed 810 affiliated autoservicios, organized into distribution zones that covered most of the country.[63] VéGé expanded with similar speed, and both chains did so in smaller towns like Yecla (Murcia) and Amorebieta (Vizcaya) as well as cities like Barcelona.[64]

As it expanded, SPAR advanced the introduction of foreign foodways and commercial practices to Spain, as well as the idea that Spain was part of rather than outside of the Western international community.[65] Even more so than at CAT supermarkets, the opening of a new

SPAR or the conversion of a traditional grocer into a SPAR offered customers new, foreign shopping experiences. In towns with newly opened SPARs, these stores transformed the urban landscape with branded signs and large window displays (see fig. 9).[66] Inside, the chain obsessed over best practices in lighting, hygiene, background music selection, and myriad other issues. Indeed, in the March 1961 issue of *SPARCO*, Spanish SPAR's member bulletin, one article preached that "to light is to sell"; SPAR head Ortíz de Zárate challenged readers to find "a[ny] truly modern establishment [that was] cloaked in darkness"; and another article even specified the right music to play during the Christmas shopping season.[67] Finally, SPAR sought to introduce a more modern and efficient way of shopping that maximized customer flow through stores by eliminating the bottleneck of traditional Spanish marketplace socializing.[68]

These same commercial and social traditions also helped advance the autoservicio's penetration of the Spanish market. For instance, the CAT's choice to launch Spain's first autoservicio inside a Madrid neighborhood market and to limit that store's inventory to one kind of product—frozen meats—meant that early customers continued to shop and socialize at surrounding market stalls as they had for decades, mitigating the shock of self-service's novel methods. Tellingly, mere months after the pilot autoservicio's launch, Spanish illustrated magazine *Blanco y Negro* observed that the store's narrow product range "reduced shoppers' burden to [simply] picking a desired cut of meat and paying at the register."[69] Self-service, in other words, eliminated the nuisance of haggling and pressure from market vendors to buy—the latter a particularly popular change among Spanish supermarket-goers—but, perhaps unwittingly, this comment also underlined that self-service left patrons free to keep making their remaining purchases in the market.[70] Thus, in 1964, economist Joseph Guerin observed that Spanish shoppers still bought most of their perishables at municipal markets, rather than using supermarkets as "one-stop shops."[71]

Autoservicio Spar-Amancio Ortuña-Oviedo

FIG. 9. Autoservicio SPAR-Amancio Ortuña, Oviedo, 1962. "Spar por dentro—Zona de Oviedo—un poquito de historia," *SPARCO*, no. 32 (September 1962), 11.

As such, neighborhood markets represented a potential source of competition for Spain's autoservicios, but in practice, as historian Montserrat Miller has shown, the two frequently functioned symbiotically instead. Small autoservicios specialized in prepackaged and canned goods, largely complementing rather than competing with nearby neighborhood market meat and vegetable stalls. Indeed, in one admittedly exceptional case, the Totoliu family, who were longtime owners of several stalls in Barcelona's Concepció market, opened a small but successful autoservicio across the street from the market under the name Superestalvi (Super Savings).[72]

Even so, exposing Spanish shoppers to self-service's new methods was not always a smooth process. The experiences on offer, particularly at SPAR, could be disconcertingly foreign, though the chain worked actively to render its foreignness familiar and even appealing rather than off-putting. Shoppers struggled with the unfamiliar burden of finding their purchases themselves, of choosing between prepackaged product sizes they did not always trust, and of having to buy SPAR-brand products, which had displaced the brands they knew—a substitution typical throughout Europe, but unusual in Spain. SPAR responded by instructing chain members on how to reassure customers about the store brand's quality and affordability.[73] This was in contrast with CAT grocery stores, which embraced self-service, but at least still sold familiar Spanish products like Artiach cookies and Chistu marmalade.[74] Meanwhile, the word "SPAR" itself was sufficiently foreign sounding that *La Familia SPAR* made a point of translating the name into Spanish (*abeto*, or "fir tree") to build customer familiarity.[75]

The modernization of Spanish food retailing was also something that SPAR never meant to pursue alone. Rather, the chain consistently sought to partner with the CAT, for, like other Spanish grocers, SPAR expected that self-service's transformation of life in Spain would ultimately happen at the hands of the Franco regime. To this end, between 1959 and 1962, Ortíz de Zárate steadily courted the CAT's favor. He lobbied the agency concerning SPAR's initial struggles to secure a license to sell frozen goods. He sought to cultivate goodwill by sending the agency complimentary copies of *SPARCO* and company pamphlets. And later, Ortíz de Zárate lobbied the CAT again to secure a special Finance Ministry grant for the modernization of local grocery stores.[76]

Most especially, SPAR as well as other grocers and industry professionals looked to the CAT to resolve a series of legal and infrastructural obstacles that they believed stood in the way of the supermarket's spread and the Spanish grocery trade's rise from Ortíz de Zárate's "centuries-long lethargy" to a foreign standard of modernity. These hurdles included Spain's inadequate network for storing and transporting frozen goods, which SPAR Española's president warned could lead to the "tragic" spoilage of more than half of Spain's fruits and vegetable crops.[77] More pernicious and lasting were the legal obstacles that self-service faced throughout the 1960s, which Ortíz de Zárate and his colleagues again looked to the CAT to fix. Among these were Spain's *economatos*, low-price company stores that Ortíz de Zárate and others argued were relics of Spain's autarkic "Hunger Years," and now only served to undercut free enterprise and hinder the supermarket's spread.[78] These obstacles also included laws that allowed municipalities to set their own tax rates on food products or raise property taxes on renovated rented spaces such as newly converted autoservicios. Such codes, per a 1963 *SPARCO* editorial, represented "significant barrier[s] to the progress of Spanish food distribution" by pricing grocers out of converting to self-service—barriers that SPAR looked to the CAT to remove.[79]

Meanwhile, the SPAR chain itself also worked to professionalize the grocers or "SPARistas" who affiliated with it, for SPAR Española's leadership believed that the spread of self-service and the modernity that Ortíz de Zárate sought to bring to Spain required a professionalization of the trade as a whole. Years after SPAR's arrival in Spain, Ortíz de Zárate recalled its early strategy: "We chose retailers and wholesalers and modernized them. We began with the head: a change in mentality [through] courses [and] 'formación.' That was first of all." Through these courses (including early ones held in Germany) and this emphasis on *formación*—systematic, technical, professional education rather than simple training—SPAR sought to disseminate rationalized, modern commercial techniques among its affiliates, including visual point-of-sale marketing methods rarely seen at the time at Spanish groceries.[80] *SPARCO* shared this didactic mission. It offered diagrams showing how to plan store layouts to streamline customer traffic flow and a succession of long technical articles replete with detailed figures that promoted modern bookkeeping practices and inventory rotation, in addition to its detailed guidance on store lighting and music. The bulletin also advised SPARistas on how best to sell to their primary, female customer base, whose budgetary clout *SPARCO* repeatedly underlined.[81] Profit was one desired result of these measures, but, as with *AMA*'s work to professionalize homemakers, improvement of Spanish food distribution and nutritional levels was another.[82]

SPARistas enthusiastically shared in this work. They wrote letters and participated in interviews that *SPARCO* regularly printed in dedicated recurring columns. Therein, they called on their fellow affiliates to embrace the professional knowledge transmitted in *SPARCO* and, most especially, to take the plunge and convert to self-service. In a December 1961 interview with the bulletin, Agustín Muñoz, manager of a recently converted SPAR affiliate in Madrid, reassured readers that the commonly feared problem of shoplifting had not materialized for him after the switch to self-service. Rather, he concluded, "It's a shame we didn't do this a year earlier! We've almost doubled sales!" SPAR member Manuel Blasco Zaldívar's February 1962 letter to the bulletin told the same story, while another from SPARista Jesus Sánchez Ramiro underlined the chain's calls to make store hygiene a priority, to read *SPARCO*, and to make productive use of SPAR product signage.[83] These accounts and others like them mattered. *SPARCO*'s influence as one of the few grocery trade publications circulating in Spain was such that, according to Maixé-Altés, "it in a way explains the dynamism that part of the [grocery] sector displayed in those years," suggesting that affiliates' testimonies had an impact that extended well beyond SPAR itself.[84]

Letters and interviews like Zaldívar's and Agustín Muñoz's, moreover, formed part of an emerging epistolary culture among *SPARCO*'s readers. They offered a kind of secular, self-service conversion narrative, not just of a physical conversion of a store to self-service, but a conversion of their own thinking to zealous belief in the self-service principle. In March 1963, SPAR affiliate José Caballé told readers the story of how joining SPAR and converting to self-service had saved the initially small, struggling grocery store he had opened three years earlier in an outlying, working-class neighborhood of Barcelona. Now it was a nearby competitor who had closed. "[A]utoservicio" had become to him "a marvelous word [that] I can't stop thinking about."

All of this success, Caballé concluded, "[he] owe[d] entirely to SPAR." SPARCO, in those same terms, titled him, "Don José Caballé, a man who saved himself with SPAR." Another SPARista, Diego Martínez, recounted how SPAR's administrative help saved his store during a long illness he suffered, and ended his account with a fervent: "I owe SPAR everything." Not always so forceful, such letters nevertheless appeared regularly in columns like "¿Quieres Colaborar?" (Do you want to collaborate?) and "SPARISTA 100%."[85] The bulletin supplemented these tales of personal conversion with other morality tales. In May 1961, SPARCO contributor P. P. offered the parable of a traveling merchant named Tendel. Initially, he struggled to sell the rich fabrics in which he traded because of his own shabby appearance. After allowing a young lady to clean him up and help him better present his wares, he did a brisk business. Caballé could have written the moral of the story: "SPAR is the young lady who wants to transform you. Pay attention. There may lie your salvation."[86]

And, to its core, this was a salvation defined in foreign terms. SPAR, the CAT, and the Spanish grocery trade measured the national prosperity and modernity that they hoped to produce through the autoservicio against the achievements of Spain's neighbors and the United States—a club of prosperous nations they wanted Spain to join. In 1961, SPARCO cautioned affiliates against complacency: "In Spain modern distribution techniques are unknown; American 'merchandising' . . . is taking its first steps among us. . . . Now what we need is that extra push that elevates us to the respectable heights we deserve to occupy among the European concert of nations."[87] When early critics suggested that adopting self-service was unwise because "Spain [was] not America," SPAR countered that the trend toward self-service was both global and inexorable. Myriad columns in SPARCO profiled the successes of Austrian and English SPARistas, closely followed the trajectory of self-service in America, or, often, stressed the modernizing challenge posed by the newly formed European Economic Community (EEC).[88] The CAT's files on SPAR reflected these same comparisons, containing not just the early *SPARCO*s that Ortíz de Zárate mailed the agency, but also copies of French, English, and German SPAR bulletins, likely also sent by the SPAR president.[89]

Not all of these comparisons revealed anxiety at Spain's perceived backwardness. Encouraged by the autoservicio's at times storied but on the whole rapid spread across the nation, an article printed in *ICA* one year after *SPARCO*'s call for an "extra push" predicted that "[Spain's] next generations will live in a country with high salaries and European consumption levels." *CONAUTA*, the eponymously titled journal of Spain's state-run national self-service grocers' cooperative, followed this two years later with the boast that, though the need to monitor foreign innovations remained, "Spain's self-service grocers [we]re up at the level of foreign ones."[90]

Both SPAR's and the CAT's embrace of these comparisons led them to move beyond improving the distribution and use of Spanish food-stuffs. Instead, in mid-1963 they began direct attempts to reengineer Spanish diets. They pushed ordinary Spaniards to not just shop like other Europeans but to adopt foreign diets that these authorities judged more nutritionally efficient. A 1964 article in *CONAUTA* pressed Spaniards to stop eating homemade soup noodles, unpopular abroad, and instead conform to the international norm of eating more nutritious, Italian-style semolina pasta dishes, whose benefits the magazine revisited throughout the remainder of the decade.[91] The magazine also regularly profiled foreign products like new wheat strains being introduced into Spain and Japan's counterpart to Spanish wine, sake.[92] SPAR, meanwhile, promoted a diet heavier in meat and vegetables, like that of England, arguing in a May 1963 *SPARCO* article that, as things stood, "Spaniards [ate] much in quantity but of poor quality."[93]

Though seemingly limited measures, such advocacy contributed to the Europeanization and Americanization of Spain through the assimilation of foreign foodways. By 1966, according to *CONAUTA* contributor R. C. Cañaveral, Spanish housewives had begun to incorporate foreign products like pineapple, bacon, and paté into their families' diets as Spain more generally adopted a Western European identity and other foreign mores such as a more hurried pace of life.[94] And, as the 1960s advanced, this internationally oriented, modernizing mindset prompted organizations like *CONAUTA* and VéGé to project their hopes for a prosperous national future beyond the everyday consumer items available in autoservicios, beyond mere adoption of foreign products, and onto an image of Spain as innovator. This is evident in their fascination with the as-yet unrealized products of foreign as well as Spanish food research, including instant coffee, a high-protein rice flour developed in Valencia for an international competition in 1969, and contemporaneous American attempts to conserve meat via irradiation.[95] Similarly, *CONAUTA* repeatedly warned that to not pursue such research meant surrendering Spain's best hope of becoming internationally competitive and condemning the nation to "technological [and] economic colonialism."[96]

Perhaps ironically, and notwithstanding the later ubiquity of chain supermarkets, this early period of growth amid uncertainty was arguably the autoservicio's high point in Spain, during which these stores represented the vanguard of the nation's food distribution industry. For these halcyon days were soon to end with the coming in 1973 of a powerful new competitor, the *hipermercado*, or "hypermarket," superstores imported into Spain by the French store chain Pryca (1973) and the Dutch chain Makro Cash and Carry (1974).[97] Still, by the mid-1960s, the arrival and spread of the self-service grocery store in Spain had brought about a sea change in the nation's food distribution and grocery trade as well as myriad ordinary consumers' shopping experiences and perception of Spain's place within the Western world.

For the transformation that Spain's food distribution industry underwent was markedly international and internationalizing in character. In 1956, despite having already spread through Europe in previous decades, the supermarket had yet to cross the Pyrenees. Yet ten years later, in great part through the work of the Comisaría de Abastecimientos, autoservicios were a familiar staple in Spanish cities and towns both great and small. With their new, large window displays, prominent signage, and bright lighting, self-service chains like SPAR and VéGé transformed the visual landscape. Autoservicios offered the possibility of making food distribution in Spain more efficient, and thus increasing national prosperity, to degrees never before possible. Consequently, the CAT and SPAR worked through women's magazines like *AMA* to secure the cooperation of the nation's housewives, whose place in Spanish society now took on an additional, if ultimately unsubversive, importance. At the same time, CAT and SPAR worked to instill a sense of professionalism and raise the level of technical proficiency among Spanish grocers through publication of technical journals like *CONAUTA* and *SPARCO* as well as the creation of new training programs.

To be sure, these changes were often rocky and surrounded by controversy. In particular, the dirigiste path by which the supermarket came to Spain produced early clashes and ongoing tensions between the CAT and private grocers over the extent of the regime's involvement in running Spain's autoservicios. So too, the early years of the Spanish supermarket can be read as a form of what philosopher Homi Bhabha has termed an "in-between moment," during which some older forms of food retailing that reflected the customs and needs of earlier times—most especially the low-cost *economato*, a vestige of the hardscrabble early Franco period—competed with the "futuristic" self-service model. And meanwhile, this new model in turn existed in an ultimately symbiotic tension with the perennial Spanish neighborhood market hall.[98] Taken together, these clashes reveal the practical limits and choices the regime faced in trying to harness self-service to its own project of national socioeconomic progress, such as Comisaría efforts to reengineer Spanish diets to be more nutritionally and financially efficient.

Most of all, the coming of self-service to Spain during the early 1960s continued the erosion of early Francoist discourses of Spanish national difference and sociopolitical separation from Western Europe that the department stores and consumer magazines of the 1950s had set in motion. These notions had already grown increasingly untenable in the face of Spain's ever-greater diplomatic, economic, but also social convergence with its neighbors and the United States. They became more so as the many grocers who became SPAR and VéGé affiliates during these years and their local customers encountered foreign lifestyles, business practices, and new professional colleagues and trade associations. Each of these experiences inserted these Spaniards into an international community of which many of them increasingly considered their nation to be a member, helping to pave the way for a social transition to democracy that preceded and provided a base of popular support for Spain's later political democratization.

CHAPTER 4

"You Can Achieve Anything Nowadays
If You Have Good Publicity"

The Spanish Advertising Industry and Consumer Media
in the International Integration of Late Franco-Era Spain

On the morning of 25 May 1966, at a reception in Barcelona's City
Hall, public relations executive Joaquín Maestre Morata opened the
annual meeting of the International Public Relations Association
(IPRA) with an address marked by the cosmopolitan spirit then
sweeping through mid-century Spain's emergent mass consumer society.[1] As chair of that year's meeting, he praised his colleagues for being
"pioneers, like those adventurous people who crossed America"—
only in this case, theirs was not a westward venture, but rather one
to establish the field of public relations in Spain. If it was to keep
pace with the demands of the decade's vibrant economies, Maestre
warned, his country "must—as the young people say—be WITH
IT [emphasis original]" or better yet, "[be] WAY OUT AHEAD in
public relations in a relatively short time." And for that, he stressed,
his colleagues' expertise would be indispensable.[2]

Phrased as a call to action—and an urgent one—Maestre's appraisal
of Spain's commercial circumstances and need for foreign "know-
how" was as much a symptom of the course his profession had taken
in recent years as it was an vision for the future. Like the food distribution sector, Spain's consumer media and the advertising industry
that helped shape it experienced a professional, social, and cultural

sea change during the period of the Spanish economic miracle (1959–1973), particularly the early 1960s. New ad agencies, trade organizations, and journals sprang up in the space of just a few years. The advertising industry received its first professional charter from the Spanish government, something that the nation's journalists and grocers had long possessed. The early 1960s, finally, saw admen like Maestre embrace another, specifically American novelty: the discipline of public relations. Echoing contemporary hopes among Francoist officials that the recently imported supermarket would "dignify the [Spanish] grocer's trade," these shifts likewise transformed advertising in Spain from a mere business into a profession, a craft practiced exclusively by dedicated professionals who possessed a vocation and sought to advance their industry, not just their bottom line.[3]

And, as among the nation's food retailers, this process of professionalization was moreover marked by a pronounced foreign orientation, one that had consequences far beyond a single profession's history. While Spanish ad agencies multiplied, and regulation gave shape to the advertising profession, the nation's admen, agencies, and trade organizations began to affiliate internationally. During the early 1960s some of Spain's most important agencies built ties with internationally renowned North American firms like McCann-Erickson. And, by 1963, public relations pioneer Maestre became the first Spaniard to join both the Public Relations Society of America (PRSA) and the IPRA, paving the way for his countrymen. Influenced by their colleagues abroad, Spain's admen began to adopt foreign practices and professional views. More dangerously for the Franco regime, their behavior betrayed the same shift taking place among the nation's grocers: a growing belief that Spain was in many ways more alike than different from its Western European neighbors, and that Spain's future lay in becoming a member of a prosperous, Western capitalist, international community.

Similarly dramatic changes were meanwhile taking place in the Spanish consumer press, particularly the nation's fashion and lifestyle magazines. The number of such periodicals circulating in Spain, which had skyrocketed during the 1950s, only continued to rise as the economic boom of 1959–1973 dawned. These magazines, alongside a diverse array of fashion trade journals and new department store bulletins that joined the well-established *Boletín de Galerías Preciados* and *Revista Jorba,* also continued to shape Spain's emergent mass consumer society. More specifically, they publicly pushed the same cosmopolitan focus on foreign ways and pursuit of imported technical expertise that admen like Maestre, supermarket advocates like Álvaro Ortíz de Zárate, or indeed retailing pioneers such as Pepín Fernández all espoused. As in the 1940s and 1950s, Spanish consumer periodicals continued to closely follow the latest sartorial innovations out of Paris and Hollywood. They profiled, and so exposed Spanish readers to, the foreign fashions of London's Bond and Carnaby Streets. And, with increasing frequency, they both feted and fretted over Spain's place among Europe's aesthetic heavyweights.

Finally, though the social messaging in magazines like the pioneering *Señor* initially remained conservative, as the 1960s advanced, Spain's consumer press increasingly featured not just radically new imported fashions but a host of associated subversive ideas, particularly on issues of gender, that further undercut National-Catholicism's patriarchal social doctrine and could even challenge the regime's authority directly. In particular, periodicals like the vanguardist men's journal *Don* popularized a new kind of male consumer, one whose ready embrace of the innovative fashions and popular culture sweeping through 1960s Europe reconciled poorly with the sober, pious, yet also competitive and virile National-Catholic masculine ideal. These publications' fixation on international fashion, pop culture, and Spain's place therein, meanwhile, also normalized the same notion of an internationally oriented Spain then spreading among Maestre and his colleagues. And the upshot of these many changes was that, in yet another part of Spain's burgeoning mass consumer society, the ground was increasingly prepared for Spanish social, economic, and political convergence with Western Europe during the 1970s.

From Walter Dill Scott to Joaquín Maestre: A Long and International Pedigree

Like Spain's incipient self-service grocery trade, a professionalized, mass-oriented advertising and public relations field advanced most visibly in Spain during the late 1950s and early 1960s, and was similarly influenced by North American practices, but its roots were decades old and spanned Western Europe as well as the Atlantic. The advertising trade began to form with the appearance of the first professional admen and agencies in the United States during the 1850s and 1860s.[4] It came to Europe relatively soon after: Germany's first admen in the 1880s and 1890s embraced Anglo-American advertising methods, which they held in high esteem, while British agencies also emulated their American counterparts. Meanwhile, Spain's first advertising agency, Roldós, S.A., launched in 1857 and remained a presence in the industry there through the 1960s.[5]

But this was not yet modern advertising—even in its North American birthplace, advertising remained an unregulated, abuse-ridden, and mistrusted profession. During the late nineteenth and early twentieth centuries, American and European advertising continued to spread and evolve toward greater mass appeal and more formal structure.[6] Between the 1860s and the 1890s, American pioneers like George P. Rowell won advertising increasing recognition as a legitimate, ethics-bound business. During the early 1900s, the trade gained technical sophistication through psychologist Walter Dill Scott's marketing research. And, in the 1920s, public relations developed as a discipline at the hands of public relations counselors (and bitter rivals) Ivy Ledbetter Lee and Edward R. Bernays.[7] Advertising meanwhile similarly expanded and evolved in Great Britain: by 1914, the first modern British ad agencies had opened, and after World War I, British admen began to adopt Dill Scott's methods and to professionalize with the creation of the Association of British Advertising Agencies in 1917 and the first attempts at legal regulation of ad content.[8]

Early twentieth-century Spanish admen were well aware of these advances and their American pedigree. In 1911, Pedro Prat Gaballi, the father of modern, technical Spanish advertising, first encountered America's new advertising methods through various trade magazines as well as the newly published work of early market researchers like Dill Scott. Inspired, he began to call during the interwar years for measures that, once implemented in the early 1960s, drove the trade's professionalization in Spain.[9] As the first modern ad agencies began to appear in Spain circa 1925, he also founded his own agency, Fama; created Spain's first professional advertisers' association, the Club de Publicidad de Barcelona; and began to steadily publish articles about the new, imported, technically sophisticated advertising he had embraced. This emerging expertise and field gained influence in the 1940s, by which time many of Spain's most important agencies had formed, including Helios (1918), Alas (1931), Cid (1945), Ruescas (1948), and the future cradle of the public relations discipline in Spain, DANIS (1953). Meanwhile, foreign agencies also moved into Spain, including Switzerland's Haasenstein & Volger, which opened a branch in Madrid in 1922 under the name Publicitas and soon established influential relationships with Helios and Prat Gaballi's Fama.[10]

Finally, as Spain's economically lean 1940s came to a close, and material conditions began to slowly improve, Spanish advertising experienced one more change. This was the arrival of a new generation of admen who spent the 1950s working with cutting-edge foreign techniques at innovative agencies like Ruescas—home of Spain's first market-research department—and later oversaw their trade's professionalization in the 1960s. They were young, university-educated, and bourgeois. They also hailed from fields like art, sales, law, and broadcasting, as well as from Spain's wealthiest and most touristy areas—Madrid, the Mediterranean coast, and the Basque North.[11] Manuel de Eléxpuru was one such adman. A native of the

Basque city of Bilbao, Eléxpuru left an architecture degree program in 1954, joined the Clarín ad agency as an ordinary draftsman in 1955, and rose through the ranks, becoming head of the agency in 1962.[12] Another newcomer, Joan Fontcuberta, founded DANIS after being inspired by Pedro Prat Gaballi's technically sophisticated approach to advertising. Then, in 1956, Fontcuberta hired yet another young professional, Joaquín Maestre Morata. Two years later, in 1958, Maestre first encountered the public relations field when he happened upon IPRA's annual meeting while traveling on DANIS business. Two years after that, he introduced the new discipline to Spain, founding the nation's first specialized PR agency.[13]

Spanish Advertising Becomes a Profession

This move toward expansion and professionalization of the Spanish advertising sector accelerated sharply as the decade closed and the 1960s dawned. In those years, an assortment of new advertising agencies, organizations, and technical journals proliferated. Manuel Fraga's Ministry of Information and Tourism granted the ad industry its first regulatory charter, the Estatuto de la Publicidad of 1964. And the field of public relations came to Spain, arriving largely at the hands of Maestre, who, in joining a series of international organizations including IPRA and the PRSA, paved the way for others to do the same. Like the grocery trade, the Spanish advertising profession took on an international character as it professionalized. This manifested in the foreign—specifically, American—pedigree that Maestre's chosen discipline displayed, as well as his decision to join international professional organizations. This internationalization figured similarly clearly in a contemporaneous wave of agency-level affiliations that, within the span of just a few years, partnered or even merged most of Spain's premier advertising firms with foreign advertising giants like the McCann-Erickson advertising agency. These changes further eroded Francoist notions of Spanish difference and advanced perceptions of Spain as European, this time among Spanish advertising professionals. Like the CAT and SPAR, these admen became convinced that the nation's future prosperity lay in becoming a member of a prosperous, Western, and capitalist international community.

If the first rumblings of these changes were to be had in Prat Gaballi's professionalizing proposals and the arrival of a new generation of admen in the 1950s, the early 1960s brought a burst of professionalization in the guise of new credentialing and regulatory structures, as well as a proliferation of professional associations. Sociologists Richard Hall and Harold Wilensky have noted that professionalization usually involves some kind of occupational closure—restriction of entry into the new profession to select qualified candidates, typically trained in special schools and certified by professional associations.[14] Though never truly a closed profession, Spanish advertising gained its first technical school for admen in 1961. A second state-run school and an official (but technically voluntary) credentialing program followed in 1964. These measures came on the heels of two reforms enacted earlier that year by Manuel Fraga's Ministry for Information and Tourism: first, the Spanish ad industry's inaugural and much-debated professional charter, and second, the creation of an official regulatory body for the trade, the National Advertising Institute (INP). The charter's contents are revealing. Under the new system, every Spanish ad agency had until 1 January 1969 to hire at least one government-licensed adman—a lax requirement that, coupled with vague language in the new charter, suggests that authorities were trying to have it both ways, leaving the profession open to flourish while still raising technical standards.[15] Paralleling Europe's alphabet soup of advertising associations, such as the European Community for Advertising Organizations (CEOP), a range of professional organizations formed. These included the Association of Public Relations Technicians (ATRP, founded 1961) as well as the Young Spanish Publicists' Group (AJEP), the Association of Spanish Advertisers (AEA), and the Spanish Center for Public Relations (CENERP), all of the latter established in 1965.[16]

Spain's advertising sector took yet another step toward professionalization when, in 1962, it gained a pair of new trade journals in which Spain's admen could debate over their profession's still-evolving organization. The first of these magazines was the public relations journal *Relaciones Públicas*, which after 1965 operated under CENERP.[17] The second, *I.P.: Información de la Publicidad*, quickly became a central organ of the advertising profession in Spain, serving as a clearinghouse for all news related to the field at home and abroad. Countless *I.P.* articles discussed how the INP, the Estatuto de la Publicidad, and even the reader surveys that *I.P.* occasionally conducted ought to be structured. One 1965 editorial, for instance, dismissed these polls as rife with the "overly self-serving opinions" of agency directors who owed their positions to nepotism, not ability. Meanwhile, a digest section on the latest news about Spain's ad agencies fostered professional awareness and a sense of belonging among Spanish admen.[18]

These changes were underpinned by another shift that took place in Spanish admen's discourse about the state of their trade, as many began to voice a rising and acute concern over the need for Spanish advertising to professionalize—what Richard Hall has termed an "attitudinal" professionalization. Though they often disagreed on the right course of action, these admen greeted new policies and longed for other as-yet unrealized measures with a sense of urgency that helped drive many of the period's banner reforms. In April 1963, for instance, ad executive Julio Campos called for his colleagues and their clients to force periodicals to adhere to official circulation figures, warning that "to do otherwise is to play at being serious." In the lead-up to the 1964 charter, controversy raged in *I.P.* concerning a grandfather clause that would grant professional licenses to trade veterans who lacked the otherwise required technical training. And, in 1964, agency director Roberto Arce spoke out against excessive government meddling, arguing that only advertisers' own hard work could truly sort out agencies' problems.[19]

The sheer number and density of agencies operating in Spain, finally, also expanded—as one editorial put it in 1962, "extraordinarily" so. Ad agencies were nothing new to Spain, many of the boom era's foremost names had been in operation for over a decade. These included Alas, with clients like Trans World Airlines, and Ruescas, which by 1960 was arguably the nation's most innovative and important ad firm. But from this base, the number of ad agencies in Spain swelled during the 1960s. This figure reached a total of 1,040 independent agencies in 1963, roughly one for every 30,000 Spaniards, and by mid-1970 rose to 2,531, or one for every 13,000 citizens.[20]

One of these new agencies was SAE de RP (Sociedad Anónima Española de Relaciones Públicas, or Spanish Public Relations Corporation). It was the first dedicated public relations firm in Spain, which Joaquín Maestre and Juan Viñas Bona, another young DANIS talent, founded in a small Barcelona office in July 1960.[21] Maestre and the agency quickly became archetypal contributors to the professionalization and growth of Spanish advertising. The agency took on ambitious projects like a meticulously coordinated, over-the-top weeklong fiftieth-anniversary celebration for Almacenes Jorba, the city's most beloved department store.[22] Maestre meanwhile contributed to *I.P.* and by December 1964 had also served as the Spanish correspondent for *Public Relations Review* for at least a year. Most importantly, he was an especially active participant in his industry's embrace of professional affiliation: by December 1963, he had joined the Advertising Club of Barcelona, the ATRP, the Public Relations Committee of the city's Sales Managers' Club, and even the Spanish Psychological Society.[23]

As in the grocery trade, these changes occurred amid acute concern among both members of the profession and regime officials over Spain's perceived second-tier status in global advertising circles, and, more broadly, over the state of Spain's international prestige and prospects for joining the EEC. These concerns helped drive policy change during this period both within and beyond the advertising sector.[24]

The crop of reformist officials and technocrats who rose to power within the Franco regime during the late 1950s and early 1960s, including Alberto Ullastres and Manuel Fraga, responded to this concern by working to render Spanish exports more competitive and to promote tourism to Spain.[25] As subsequently shown in this chapter, in other commercial areas like fashion, Spanish industry professionals and regime officials organized events and interpreted their nation's participation in foreign shows through an ongoing comparison between Spanish and foreign levels of achievement. In the advertising trade, such concern lay behind most of the professionalizing measures of the day. *I.P.*, for instance, served as a vehicle for the entry of foreign methods and notions. These included the use of direct mailers as well as the opinions of prominent foreign admen such as Belgian agency director Fernand Hourez.[26] From the start, these ideas arrived laden with notions of prosperous modernity whose pursuit was *I.P.*'s self-proclaimed raison d'être. Thus, the magazine's first issue declared, "[*I.P.* appears] . . . under [a] European sign, [with the mission of] inform[ing] Spanish admen . . . about news, events, and measures having to do with Advertising . . . throughout the world," having recognized that "the Common Market is an unquestionable fact that offers our best hope for success, [that] we are nothing without Europe."[27]

This fixation on Spain's ability to operate as an equal within the international community similarly marked the creation and reception of the Estatuto de la Publicidad in 1962. The charter, Fraga declared in his first public statement on the subject, was being created because modern advertising wielded "more money, and thus more influence [on a newspaper], than d[id] its readers."[28] The reaction in *I.P.* was immediate, and rooted in the question of Spanish international prestige. "Really," one anonymous editorialist wrote, "In a country that is trying to integrate itself into Europe, this kind of regulation is long overdue, if what we want is to be able to establish an effective, constructive dialogue with the various [advertising] . . . organizations of the Old World. If we admit—and it is indisputable—that advertising is another facet of the global economic game, this is self-evident. This is nothing more than an initial, but indispensible step."[29] Overdue or not, such commentary did not stop Alejandro Fernández Soto, the new president of the National Advertisers' Syndicate, from invoking the question of Spain's international status in a more triumphal vein in October 1964. The recently passed charter, he boasted, did not just achieve the goal of placing Spanish advertising at foreign levels, but, "like so many other achievements during the last twenty-five years," surpassed them.[30]

In this spirit of European and global integration, Spain's agencies invested considerable energy into cultivating connections abroad, taking work with foreign clients and then publicizing it. SAE de RP, for example, included a list of past clients as part of every project proposal packet it prepared for a potential client; this list prominently featured the agency's international accounts, which in 1963 included the Japan External Trade Organization, two separate Spain-based campaigns for the U.S. Department of Agriculture, H. J. Heinz Ltd. of London, and the International Wool Secretariat, a key player in Spanish efforts to break into global fashion circles.[31] This was again about more than simple trade. It was about a discursive as well as monetary investment in a new model of Spanish greatness—about a new national identity, under which Spain belonged to and counted within the Western capitalist community of nations. And, on a smaller scale, it was about the re-identification of Spanish advertising and specific Spanish agencies as members of, not just participants in, the international advertising industry—a subtle but important distinction. Thus, SAE de RP's promotional literature did not just list the agency's international clients, it also underlined that SAE de RP was an agency with considerable international experience, an extensive network of highly accomplished foreign contacts and references (often listed as well), and a dedication to executing international as well as domestic campaigns.[32] SAE de RP, in other words, cast itself as an organization of international rather than strictly national scope. This was fitting, given that even the domestic enterprises whose business the agency solicited, including Almacenes Jorba, often showed marked interest in foreign commercial and consumer ways.[33]

The integration of SAE de RP and other Spanish advertising and PR agencies into the broader international advertising community unfolded most dramatically through the affiliations they pursued as part of the professionalization of their trade. These included domestic organizations such as the AEA or CENERP as well as international groups like IPRA. Coincidentally, some of the first admen to affiliate thusly worked for Galerías Preciados rather than an ad agency, and became linked to the Intercontinental Group of Department Stores when the store joined that group several years before SAE de RP's founding. But Spain's ad agencies were not far behind—and Maestre and the SAE de RP were again among the vanguard. As mentioned earlier, Maestre's initial exposure to public relations came in 1958, when a business trip in Belgium coincided with IPRA's annual meeting, and he met Lucien Matrat, the father of European public relations. By 1962, Maestre was taking PR correspondence courses through Italy's Instituzione Superiore Internazionale per lo Studio delle Relazioni Publiche (ISIRP); by 1963, he was a member of both the Institute for Public Relations of London and the PRSA, and, after a yearlong application process, joined IPRA in 1964.[34]

All of these memberships benefitted and indirectly included SAE de RP, but this last affiliation in particular advanced SAE de RP's status and work in several ways. First, membership in IPRA, which styled itself as an association of the world's elite PR specialists, carried with it a code of conduct—a staple of Hall and Wilensky's model of professionalization—that Maestre was obliged to impose at his agency. SAE de RP literature touted this fact as a "label of guarantee[d quality]."[35] IPRA membership also furthered the agency's ability to represent itself as part of an extensive international network with headquarters in a host of world capitals. Indeed, late 1960s and early 1970s correspondence between Maestre, IPRA leadership, and various Spanish admen reveals that by this time Maestre had assumed a leadership role as IPRA's liaison with its Spanish members, which involved him in decisions on membership and sundry other items of association business.[36]

Maestre and SAE de RP's integration into IPRA's international network only grew as a result of his (and SAE de RP's) work coordinating IRPA's annual meeting in 1966, which Maestre hosted in Barcelona.[37] Over the course of almost a year's time, Maestre corresponded extensively with top IPRA leadership, with whom he worked closely to organize the meeting, as well as with members as far away as India.[38] He collaborated with Georges Serrell, a past president of IPRA and one of Europe's most important admen. He traded barbs with former association president John Keyser as well as fellow member Francis Shuster over the conference's promotional literature. He flirted with Mrs. Denny Griswold of the New York–based *Public Relations News*. And via a steady stream of conference-related correspondence, he cultivated a friendship with Connecticut state senator Robert Bliss, who was IPRA's sitting president, highly placed in the PRSA, and director of the Robert L. Bliss & Co. ad agency.[39]

The meeting itself illustrated the hopes that Spanish admen hung on this push to affiliate internationally. Spanish Development Plan deputy secretary Vicente Mortes delivered one of the inaugural speeches on "Spain's position, past, present and future in the world of affairs; the importance of meetings of this type to the development of world understanding, and the stake that Spain has in a fuller understanding of its development potential in the congress of nations for a peaceful world with greater enjoyment of the potential that is in the soul of man."[40] This was a loaded claim. Mortes's speech reveals that, in the regime's eyes, the IPRA conference, like other international conferences that Spain hosted during this period, represented an opportunity to claim for the country more ties of greater importance to Europe and the wider world. It also was an opportunity to sell a new version of Spanish national identity, one rooted in global political and economic influence, to the conference's prominent foreign attendees. Mortes lingered on Spain's recent industrial and commercial achievements and its growing levels of investment from abroad. He also noted public relations' role in aiding economic growth throughout the world through the dissemination of information and stressed especially its service to Spain's economic development. Lastly, Mortes closed by underlining the importance that the meeting, as a result of being held on Spanish soil, had "for the development of [mutual] international understanding."[41]

These ambitions toward a greater Spanish prominence abroad as well as Maestre's increased foreign involvement gained added force by virtue of coming at a moment when IPRA's own international profile was growing substantially. In September 1964, after three years of lobbying, the association had won consulting status with the UN Economic and Social Council (UNESCO).[42] IPRA's mission had already been grandly international in scope—namely, to set an international standard for public relations and establish a global network for the exchange of professional knowledge.[43] Now, the organization began to consult with the UN Commission on Human Rights concerning aid to underdeveloped and developing countries, and in 1966 issued a report recommending measures like the creation of talent-identification and public relations professional development programs for candidates in such nations.[44]

This new form of outreach represented another opportunity for Spanish involvement abroad, and indeed, Maestre joined IPRA's humanitarian work in May 1966, submitting a proposal for IPRA-organized public relations campaigns to support UNESCO's efforts to fight global illiteracy.[45] As Vicente Mortes did for Spain, IPRA made claims to global influence and moral authority, in this case the ambition of making public relations and IPRA itself "a force for human betterment, for world progress, and for the elimination of those elements which threaten our civilization and, indeed, our very existence."[46] Maestre himself aspired through IPRA to nothing less than "expan[ding] . . . consumer markets all over the world, rais[ing] the level of education, and [helping people] attain . . . a higher standard of living."[47]

Finally, as historian Núria Puig has noted, Spain's admen and agencies also pursued ties abroad through mergers and contracts to represent foreign agencies locally, while other European and American agencies opened offices in Spain directly.[48] In 1963, Alas proudly became the J. Walter Thompson ad agency's sole Spanish representative. J. Walter Thompson later opened its own office in 1966, reestablishing a presence the agency had not had in Spain since 1936.[49] In December 1964, France's Synergie agency took over Publicidad Tiempo of Barcelona, becoming Tiempo-Synergie, which *I.P.* interpreted as an indication of "the interest being garnered by the business possibilities on offer in Spain."[50] By 1965, too, the American multinational ad agencies Colman, Prentis & Varley, and Kenyon & Eckhardt had established branches in Spain.[51] But most notable was the late 1963 merger of the Ruescas ad agency with North American advertising juggernaut McCann-Erickson, becoming Ruescas-McCann-Erickson, S.A.[52]

The new agency's literature and ads announcing the merger spoke eloquently to what the firm either truly believed about the fusion, or otherwise to what it considered a plausible and advantageous way to publicly frame its choice to forge such ties to the American business world. In a two-page special announcement from June 1963, the agency referred to the hyphen connecting the Ruescas and McCann-Erickson names as "the most significant . . . to have ever been placed in Spanish advertising," because it was "like a bridge [connecting] the Spanish prestige and ability of Ruescas" with the world-class McCann-Erickson agency.[53] Per the ad, this was a watershed moment for Spain. Over this bridge, a mass of personnel would flow between Spain and the wider world, and foreign expertise arriving from the United States would benefit the firm's clients, the Spanish media, local admen with newfound opportunities to cultivate their talents,

PERSPECTIVA DE UNA DE LAS NAVES PARA SECRETARIAS.   HALL DE ENTRADA

RUESCAS–M_cCANN-ERICKSON.S.A.
LA AGENCIA MAS PROFESIONAL Y PROGRESIVA
PASEO DE ROSALES, 34 · Teléfono 247 46.00 · Madrid · 8 ·
TUSET. 26 · Teléf. 254 14 70 · 254 16 90 · Barcelona · 6 ·

FIG. 10. Agency logo and entrance, Ruescas-McCann-Erickson, S.A. *I.P.*,
no. 13 (December 1964).

and, most especially, consumers.[54] The spacious and modern new
offices that the agency occupied offered another, this time visual, representation of its self-proclaimed international identity: an entryway
that featured a relief map of the world—the agency's new sphere of
action—and echoed the firm's new logo, which incorporated a pair
of globes (see fig. 10).

The result of these types of affiliation as well as the rhetoric coming
out of *I.P.* was an erosion of boundaries. This was at times a subtle
rather than spectacular process, manifesting not in direct declarations like Sears's claim that on the day it launched a new Spanish
branch in 1975, "borders did not exist," but gradually, through an
elevation of Spanish advertising to international respectability.[55] It
proceeded via articles like *I.P.*'s celebratory May 1963 coverage of
Spain's participation in the Lyon International Products Show. It
advanced through the stops that motivational research pioneer Dr.

Ernest Dichter made in Spain during his European lecture tours, stops that *I.P.* contributor Jaime Puig termed "obligatory . . . [because Spain's] ad and businessmen are up-to-date on everything having to do with good motivational research." And it revealed itself in Maestre's speech before the 1966 IPRA assembly, which stressed that Spanish public relations might not yet be "with it," but would soon be "not just . . . with it but way out ahead."[56] Through the connections that Maestre and others like him fostered, the advertising communities of Western Europe and the United States converged with Spain's. This contributed to Spain's larger integration into the Western European and American capitalist-democratic commercial community and chiseled away at remaining notions of Spanish difference. As *I.P.* reader Roldán Martínez asserted in an article, "NO to 'Spain is Different,'" in which he responded to the tourist slogan that Manuel Fraga famously revived in 1964,

> [While] there is no doubt about the quality of the phrase "Spain is different" . . . [as] a strong phrase that, in a moment in which the flow of tourists [into Spain] has already begun, awakens interest without the need to explain what Spain was and is . . . unfortunately, due to a number of factors that do not require discussion here, Spain does not currently enjoy "good press" internationally. Europe (and I refer to this continent in particular because it produces the majority of our tourists), does not know us, interprets us wrongly. Europe without a doubt has preconceived notions concerning Spain.
>
> Spain is different, to be sure; but not by the average European's measure. Spain has cars, radio, TV, industry and many other things besides flamenco, bulls, and donkeys with drinking jugs [*botijos*].[57]

Martínez's editorial offers a necessary qualification to Justin Crumbaugh's argument that "normalization does not exclude difference." As Francoist Spain modernized, Crumbaugh argues, discourses of a folkloric, touristic national difference such as the "Spain is Different" slogan were not conservative holdovers, but a display behind which the regime could obscure its increasingly obvious political exceptionality. And because it was "overtly hollow" in content—because those who mattered were aware of the ploy—this display of difference did not impinge on the nation's growing self-congratulatory belief in its successful achievement of modernity.[58] Such a trick, though, could only work when onlookers accepted that modernity and this touristy cultural difference could coexist. Martínez's editorial reveals two ways in which this strategy could and did go awry, both of which sparked the adman's indignation. First, Fraga's narrative of Spanish difference could be mistaken as sincere, undermining Spanish claims to having become a modern Western European state. And, secondly and relatedly, foreign consumers ignorant of Spain's modernizing achievements could, under the combined effects of Fraga's redeployed slogan and the "preconceived notions" Martínez cited, conclude that Spain was indeed "different"—that is, not fully developed, not modern.

The affiliative trend that produced Ruescas-McCann-Erickson could draw similarly critical responses from the nation's smaller agencies. Their concern was justified, as these firms did not typically command comparable foreign interest and, left out of this process, saw the one advantage they had once enjoyed—competitive pricing—disappear in the face of rising demand for multinational agencies' cutting-edge methods.[59] Perhaps more unexpectedly, Francisco García Ruescas himself voiced similar hostility to foreign investment in a 1967 speech, though his critique did focus on industrial rather than commercial investment. Now retired from the firm he had built, the advertising pioneer condemned American investors' excessive influence in Spain, as well as the shortsightedness of the local businessmen and officials who had permitted this "financial colonization." Indeed, inspired by French journalist Jean-Jacques Servan-Schreiber's then recently published book, *Le Défi Américain* (The American challenge), Ruescas went on to equate a worldwide

American economic imperialism, of which Spain was just the latest victim, with the militarily and ideologically fueled conquests of the Soviet Union, the great villain of the Cold War. The adman likewise rejected the Franco regime's efforts to join the European Common Market, as he considered it an ineffective shield against American dominance and its abolition of tariffs a threat to fledgling Spanish industries still in need of protection.[60]

With that said, many of Ruescas's onetime colleagues, and Maestre especially, welcomed and actively pursued such international ties, and as they did so deployed the kinds of discourses of national difference that Martínez decried. They represented Spain to the foreign gaze—to the visiting colleagues with whom they sought those ties—in precisely the culturally reductionist ways that Information and Tourism Minister Fraga and ambassadorial groups like the Sección Femenina's folkloric song and dance troupes employed.[61] Thus, as they planned the 1966 IPRA conference, Maestre and his team at SAE de RP scheduled a program of events filled with supposedly typical cultural experiences. Notable among these was the chance to participate in a bullfight (featuring goat-sized calves rather than full-grown bulls) that was staged in a ramshackle, purpose-built ring outside of Barcelona—a part of Spain where bullfights were not the staple of local culture that they were in regions like Andalucía. Participants received a joking rulebook-cum-waiver titled "Bullfighting without Toil" that digested the affair into cultural kitsch: the booklet stressed that the calves only spoke Spanish, glibly (and for safety's sake, wisely) jettisoned whole portions of the traditional bullfight such as the matador's sword, and asked if the would-be bullfighters wanted a "smashing blonde, mysterious brunette, [or] fiery redhead[ed]" nurse in the event of an injury.[62] At one planning meeting in January 1966, Maestre and his staff mulled over a list of potential conference souvenirs dominated by similarly stereotypical products such as castanets, Toledo-forged letter-openers, and bullfighting programs inscribed with attendees' names.[63] And they promoted the conference with flyers featuring flamenco dancers and beach scenes that sold well to these business travelers-cum-tourists, but which represented a largely flattened, uniform vision of Spanish culture and national identity (see fig. 11). This was exacerbated by Maestre's choice of the quintessentially Spanish figure of Miguel de Cervantes's Don Quixote as the cartoon logo for the conference (see fig. 12), which Maestre followed up on by commissioning wooden Quixote statuettes—one of the options discussed the previous January—as souvenirs.[64]

Fashion and the Erosion of Spanish Difference

This focus on raising Spain to a foreign standard of modernity and prosperity emerged with similar force in the Spanish consumer press and more specifically the nation's coverage of Spain's participation in the world of international fashion. Over the course of the 1960s, the number of consumer magazines circulating in Spain multiplied still more sharply than during the previous decade. Among the new titles that appeared on Spanish newsstands were the haute-bourgeois and avant-garde men's fashion journal *Don: La Moda Masculina Española* (Don: Spanish men's fashion, founded 1962); Catalan textile manufacturer PK's bulletin-cum-fashion newspaper *PK Press* (founded 1966); and the widely circulating seminal cultural and political journal (and regular target for government censors) *Triunfo* (Triumph, launched 1962).[65] Like their predecessors, these magazines displayed a marked penchant for foreign fashion. In these magazines' pages, too, Spanish journalists boasted or otherwise fretted over the Spanish fashion industry's place within the international community of fashion-producing nations, and thereby, over Spain's place within a prosperous postwar West—the same concern that contemporaneously fueled the arrival of the supermarket. And, like the grocers who exposed Spanish customers to European shopping experiences, journalists voiced these concerns, which naturalized the notion that their nation was as much a part of Western Europe as any other, in a medium where readers could see them and internalize this concept of a European Spain.

International Public Relations Association

JOAQUIN MAESTRE
CHAIRMAN OF THE
ANNUAL ASSEMBLY

184, BALMES STREET – BARCELONA, 6
T. 227 25 29 – Cable: PUBLICRELATIONS

Dear Friend and IPRA Member,

Here at last is your passport to joy! . . . the privilege to attend the
star event of the year, to be celebrated this time in Barcelona. Don't
miss your chance to be present at IPRA's Council Meeting and Annual Assembly!

Your days are marked, the omens are propitious, everything points to May
23-24 for the Council Meeting, and May 25-27 for the Annual Assembly. All
IPRA members are welcome. It has become a custom for the Council to vote
to extend invitation to all members present to attend the Council meeting
as observers. Please watch your own agenda so your commitments will permit
you to be with us in Barcelona in May.

If an added weekend appeals to you, please note that our final session will
be completed May 27, which is a Friday. The omens are eager to extend their
protecting wings and help you enjoy the added time, either in Madrid, or –
remaining in Barcelona with your IPRA colleagues and their ladies.

Please fill in the enclosed card today and mail it.

Your hotel reservation will be inmediately protected.

Your name will be printed in the Delegates official list inmediately.

Your Diploma, designating that you are an official Delegate, will be sent to
you. (Frequently useful for company travel expense and tax purposes).

Our meetings will be held at:
        Hotel Ritz (Luxe), Avenue Jose Antonio, 668

        Double room and breakfast . . . . 850 pesetas
        Single room and breakfast . . . , 647 pesetas
but considering the flood of participants expected, we hold an allotment
also at:
        Hotel Avenida Palace (Luxe), Avenue Jose Antonio, 605

        Double room and breakfast . . . . 1.120 pesetas
and at:
        Hotel Majestic (First Class "A"), Paseo de Gracia, 70

        Double room and breakfast . . . . 600 pesetas

        Hotel Arycasa (First Class "A"), Ausias March, 13

        Single room and breakfast . . . . 385 pesetas
Everyone here is anxious to offer hospitality to our honorable IPRA guests.

Your choice is our duty, send it earliest . . . so we may carry a happy
burden!

                        Hasta la vista

                        Joaquín Maestre

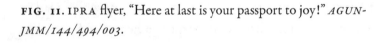

FIG. 11. IPRA flyer, "Here at last is your passport to joy!" *AGUN-JMM/144/494/003.*

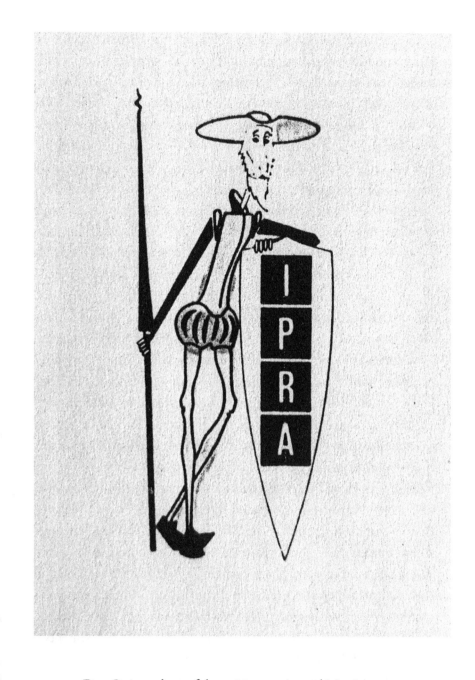

FIG. 12. Don Quixote, logo of the 1966 IPRA Annual Meeting.
Circular—"To Be or Not to Be ... That Was the Question!," n.d., AGUN-
JMM/144/494/003.

International fashion was as constant a presence in Spain's newest fashion journals as it had been in *Mujer* and *Alta Costura* a decade earlier. *Señor* printed reviews of Belgian, German, and Italian fashion shows and lines, as well as surveys detailing what the French were wearing. *Triunfo* profiled French designer Pierre Cardin. And *PK Press* noted Hollywood's sartorial influence in Spain, predicting that Spanish retailers would soon copy foreign counterparts in marketing James Bond's shirts and ties.[66] Most of all, leading into the 1960s these magazines admiringly followed English men's fashion, with even the regime-sponsored homemaking journal *AMA* praising its classicism, elegance, and aesthetic hegemony as the global menswear standard. As the 1960s progressed and new styles from London's Carnaby Street— dynamic, daring, and youthful—began to make their way into Spain, this originally conservative Anglophilia expanded to include them.[67] *Don*, for instance, went from hailing England's sartorial conservatism during the early 1960s to declaring Carnaby Street "the World Mecca of men's fashion" in 1967.[68] PK, meanwhile, named its "Terlenka YOUNG" collection in English and peppered its publicity with English buzzwords, describing the line as its latest "hit," in an attempt to capitalize on the rising popularity of British popular culture in the 1960s, as exemplified by The Beatles.[69] So too, it was this enduring fondness for Bond Street's traditional elegance as well as the novelty of Carnaby Street that motivated El Corte Inglés's newly founded Bilbao branch to launch a special "English Men's Shop" in 1970, which offered every male-gendered English product the store sold in a single boutique-like space designed to convey the high quality and exclusivity popularly associated with Albion. In fact, the entire section, which rested atop a twenty-five-centimeter-tall platform, stood literally as well as figuratively above neighboring departments.[70]

Driving this international focus was a desire for Spain to become part of the select international "club" of trend-setting nations, coupled with ongoing anxiety over Spain's perceived backwardness within an increasingly prosperous Western Europe. Like *CONAUTA* in the grocery trade or *I.P.* in advertising, around 1960 Spanish fashion professionals and consumer magazines began to worry whether Spain's fashion industry would reach European aesthetic, production, and quality standards, or conversely boasted (with suspicious force) about the nation's growing status as a fashion heavyweight. In 1960, for instance, *Señor* hoped that the next meeting of the Assembly of European Fashion Industries would see Spain poised to match its colleagues' achievements. Three years later, *Don* boasted that Spain's technical prowess had "fully integrated [its fashion industry] into [the world of] European fashion design." And by contrast, in a move that ran counter to the easy cultural stereotyping on which Maestre's team had relied as it crafted the mailers for that year's IPRA meeting, *Men's Modes* warned Spanish tailors in 1966 that their continued love of the cape—a traditionally Spanish garment, but now hopelessly passé abroad—could derail this progress.[71]

These concerns crystallized especially around the Salón Nacional de la Confección (the Spanish National Fashion Show), which debuted in Barcelona in April 1961 and represented one of the Spanish fashion industry's signal efforts to achieve their longed-for European standard. Officially, the show's aim was to promote the national fashion industry, yet the shadow of Spain's past shortcomings vis-à-vis Europe remained fixed in the background of *Señor's* coverage. It lurked in praise such as, "the national fashion industry ha[s] never [before] held an event of which it could be truly proud." It also lay behind the unflattering comparisons implied in canvas manufacturer José de Calasanz Martí's declaration that the inaugural *salón's* use of a historic venue was a European break with a traditional (and by implication, irrational) Spanish reverence for old objects like historic buildings that precluded such practical use, or *Señor* columnist Sempronio's description of the show as central to winning the respect of Europe's sartorial hegemons.[72]

The result was that Spanish clothiers, menswear press, and other industry professionals increasingly participated in, hosted, and paid ever-closer attention to international as well as domestic fashion shows, product launches, and trade conferences. All of this only bolstered the hopes of those advocating for Spanish integration into the world of international couture. Domestically, the National Fashion Show was so successful that it expanded to include women's wear and became an annual fixture.[73] The second and third shows even prompted *Señor*'s Manuel Vigil and Jaime Huguet to boast—betraying their hopes for the event—that "Spain's fashion industrial firms ha[d] set their watches to the European hour," and that as a result Spain was no longer "isolated to this side of the Pyrenees . . . [the] limit of Chateaubriand's Europe."[74] Abroad, various Spanish designers presented the Menhir line at Italy's 1963 XII Festival of Men's Fashion, to what *Don* triumphantly declared a warm and surprised reception. Spanish barbers likewise entered the 1961 Hairstyling World Cup and 1962 European Hairstyling Championship, garnering similar acclaim from *Señor*. And, in February 1962, Barcelona became the third city to host the International Industrial Measurements Congress.[75]

Unisex and Youth Culture

The Spanish fashion industry and consumer press turn abroad during the nation's economic boom had a similarly profound effect on the gender discourses that these magazines circulated among the Spanish public, and most especially impacted the models of masculinity they depicted. Like their predecessors in the 1950s, *Don, Triunfo, PK Press*, and 1960s Spain's other new consumer and fashion journals focused an increasing amount of attention on developments in foreign clothing trends, especially menswear. As the 1960s dawned, the gender roles on display in this content remained conservative and seemed innocuous to Francoist eyes. Yet, as the decade advanced, the range of content and social ideas that Spanish readers encountered in these magazines expanded. The cross-cultural connections that the Spanish press's interest in foreign designs had built during the 1950s and early 1960s now served as points of entry for new fashions that arrived, accompanied by sociopolitical ideas that subverted the Franco regime's ordering of Spanish society. In particular, incoming trends like youth and unisex fashion advanced gendered discourses—youth-centered models of gender relations built on a greater equality between the sexes—that undercut early Francoism's patriarchal social order and came dangerously close to challenging the regime's authority directly. This further contributed to advancing Spain's gradual transition to a more open society—and eventually, a democratic one.

Struggles over clothing could have such a profound effect because Spaniards of the boom era, as in the 1950s, believed that sartorial choices were capable of exerting a profoundly constitutive effect on male identity, that clothes could indeed "make the man," as *Señor* had noted in 1958.[76] Indeed, the transformative power of dress was if anything greater in the 1960s because the stakes that *Don* and other new members of the Spanish consumer press associated with clothing were similarly higher. In the 1950s, *Señor* established dress as an external performance or self-(mis)representation to achieve social acceptance, or, as scholar Alison Lurie has put it, merely "dressing for success."[77] *Don* went further and saw outward appearance as a means to cultivate the inner self, arguing that it was not fine clothes but the refined sensibility necessary to appreciate them that marked a man as successful, and that such sensibility and success could be attained by heeding the magazine's sartorial advice.[78] Over time, *Don* refined this relationship between appearance and self into a dialogue, in which cultivation of external appearance ennobled internal sensibilities reflected by exquisite attire. Hence, in 1964 the magazine promised readers that by joining "Club *Don*"—*Don*'s exclusivity-laden moniker for its readership—they could become part of a sophisticated elite who understood the 1960s new aesthetic; always chose the right drink, music, and clothes; and made contacts easily due to an awareness of others' unexpressed, even unconscious, desires.[79] Similarly, journalist Vicente Verdú would argue in a 1971 retrospective on 1960s Spanish fashion that dress had not only become Spaniards' primary form of public self-representation, but that it could also influence wearers' behavior.[80]

Into the early 1960s, the sartorially defined masculine identity championed by magazines like *Señor*, *Triunfo*, and *Don* remained conservative and shot through with strains of the otherwise increasingly marginalized Falange's "Man-Warrior" ideal. Central to this masculinity were two interrelated virtues that achieved near-ubiquity in these magazines as well as Spanish etiquette manuals. These were *distinción* (distinction), or social prominence born of publicly recognized respectability, which one achieved through *elegancia* (elegance), the selfsame sartorial taste and social mastery that "Club *Don*" promised.[81] Consisting at their core of a desire to distinguish oneself from the masses, these concepts were of a piece with the "Man-Warrior's" peacetime struggle for social and professional triumph. And they were embraced by regime officials like MIT provincial delegate Jaime Delgado, who invoked them during his keynote address at *Don's* 1963 launch, which attested to their currency. Moreover, Delgado was only the latest in a long line of prominent Franco supporters linked to these concepts.[82] In this same vein, and continuing the mass-oriented tone they had adopted in the 1950s, Spanish consumer magazines presented these values as unbounded by class privilege and as attainable without need for a noble title or wealth, though in practice the lifestyles that *Don* promoted—and *Don* itself—were not cheap.[83]

More broadly, the fashions and lifestyles that these magazines promoted during the late 1950s and early 1960s reinforced orthodox Francoist masculinity's socially stable character, as well as the dominant patriarchal gender hierarchy into which this masculinity fit. A reassuring sense of stable understatement was central to *Señor's* concept of elegance, which, the magazine advised in 1961, "[consisted of] dressing well and without calling attention to oneself." Jaime Delgado echoed this view in 1963, as did Spanish designer Loewe in a 1964 special feature that praised modern male elegance for eschewing "novelty" in favor of sober timelessness, a conservatism that *Triunfo's*

Ignacio Agustí took as a mark of Spanish superiority and a source of national pride.[84]

For these magazines, this stability was indicative of a broader male superiority over women, who were morally as well as sartorially unstable and in consequent need of male tutelage.[85] *Don's* María Luz Morales lauded England's classic style, quipping that for men even a return to wigs and cassocks was preferable to the chaos of women's wear. Meanwhile, *Triunfo* contrasted the sobriety of 1963's Menhir (Megalith) menswear collection with the stigma of feminine weakness that fashion often bore, while *Señor* protested, "Women designing men's suits? No! No!," and argued that wives could not be trusted to buy their husbands tasteful clothing.[86] This dovetailed with Spanish department stores' disciplining of saleswomen's bodies through store uniforms, which also visually reproduced gender difference, as did some television commercials of the time. One late 1960s spot for the Spanish cognac Soberano, for example, compared the liqueur to the army, labeling each "a man thing"—a privilege reserved for virile Francoist "Man-Warriors."[87]

As the 1960s advanced, however, these and other Spanish consumer magazines began to champion new masculinities whose contours did not conform to, and sometimes even ran counter to, Francoist orthodoxy. In Spain as in the United States and much of Europe, the 1960s were a countercultural period: new music by foreign bands like The Beatles crossed the Pyrenees; Catalonia produced the dissident Nova Cançó (New Song) music movement; 1968 saw student protests erupt in Madrid and Barcelona as well as worldwide. And, as Spain became "a nation of youths," with half of its population under thirty years old, which the El Corte Inglés employee magazine *Cortty* noted in 1971, a new youth-oriented popular culture flourished in Spain, finding a voice in magazines like the popular-music-oriented *Quid* (launched 1966).[88]

Scholar Detlef Siegfried has pointed to the broad appeal and impact that such demographic "juvenilization" and resulting youth cultures had in the United States and much of Western Europe at this time.[89] Similarly, under the aegis of this youth culture and its celebration of youthful exuberance, Spanish menswear began to change more rapidly and in ways that had till then been only barely tolerated of young men's fashion. In 1959, *Señor* warned that Spanish youths' flamboyant tastes were only proper among the young; grown men, at "the pinnacle of [male] existence," rejected such "extravangance."[90] Yet, by the mid-1960s, innovation was not just for women or the young. As early as 1962, *Triunfo* praised designer Pierre Cardin for rendering menswear as adventurous as women's fashions.[91] By 1967, *la moda joven*—"youth fashion"—was inescapable. That year, the Spanish tailoring journal *Men's Modes* declared the trend to be no less than the will of Spain's youth, and called on tailors to "break old molds . . . and fearlessly launch new models," for the young would never again merely accept their parents' clothes.[92] PK eagerly incorporated the value of youth into the design and marketing of menswear lines like 1967's Terlenka YOUNG collection, which *PK Press* declared, "youthful, dynamic, daring, sensational, agitated," and, most importantly, aimed at "modern men" of all ages, who had now converted to the sartorial iconoclasm of the young.[93]

As this previously feminized and stigmatized dynamism won male acceptance, it lost its effectiveness as a category of gender difference, became decoupled from the narratives of feminine capriciousness and social instability that helped support Francoist patriarchy, and contributed to its deterioration. Thus, even as it emphasized Menhir's sobriety, *Triunfo* also welcomed the wardrobe updates that the menswear line would produce, which the magazine predicted would help women defend their own legitimate desire to shop.[94] In 1967, *Don* went further, explicitly declaring the new men's fashion a step toward gender equality. And conversely, Vicente Verdú argued in 1971, Spanish advances in gender equality, coupled with an embryonic but growing feminist sentiment, encouraged a view of clothing as a form of personal expression rather than a means to assert power, inspiring a "masculinist" movement that sought an end to male sartorial asceticism.[95] Youth fashion's creators and promoters could also attack the political status quo directly, particularly when, as in *Don*'s invocation of gender equality, they drew or seemed to draw inspiration from surrounding social changes. In 1968, PK ran an ad in the popular women's magazine *Telva* under the suggestive title "The rebellion of today's man for an 'ImPKble' future." In it, the brand identified itself with socially conscious students of the kind protesting against the Franco regime in Madrid and Barcelona, students who rejected their elders' sociopolitical immobilism and springtime "stupid grand spectacles." These were all jabs at the regime, the last at its military parades, granting a radical tone to the scenario of a future society that PK all but endorsed.[96]

Meanwhile, a second, related, and similarly subversive trend also made inroads in Spain: unisex fashion, which rejected traditional gendering of clothing, calling instead for neutral outfits that would free individuals from the constraints of gender and focus attention instead on the virtues of youthfulness.[97] Internationally, the trend first emerged in the 1950s, and it flourished in the mid-1960s when the boutiques and youth culture of London's Carnaby Street, designers like Halston, and the New York department store Alexander's all embraced it. In Spain, meanwhile, the consumer press also took notice of unisex by the early 1960s, as in a 1962 *Triunfo* article about women appropriating menswear, a new and increasingly popular trend that had found a champion in the Danish model Maud.[98] And coverage in Spain only increased once Carnaby Street took up the cause. During the late 1960s and early 1970s, content devoted to Spanish as well as foreign unisex fashion became common in PK *Press*, *Cortty*, and *Don*, as did depictions of the unisex ideal of identically dressed men and women. In 1967, for example, *Don* ran an account of the Carnaby Street phenomenon written by its chief figure, boutique owner John Stephen, in which he termed the convergence of male and female fashion "inexorable," citing the pantsuit.[99] A photo editorial in this

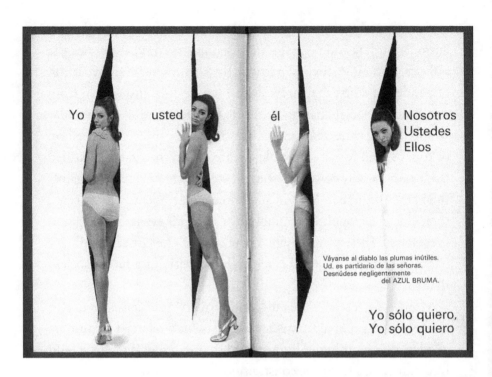

Yo   usted   él   Nosotros
Ustedes
Ellos

Váyanse al diablo las plumas inútiles.
Ud. es partidario de las señoras.
Desnúdese negligentemente
del AZUL BRUMA.

Yo sólo quiero,
Yo sólo quiero

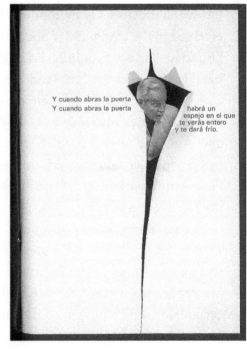

Y cuando abras la puerta
Y cuando abras la puerta   habrá un
espejo en el que
te verás entero
y te dará frío.

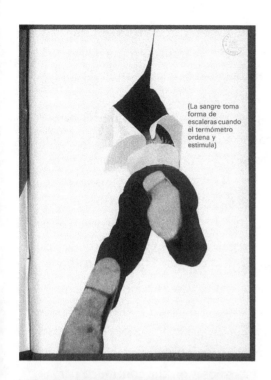

(La sangre toma
forma de
escaleras cuando
el termómetro
ordena y
estimula)

FIG. 13. *Don* magazine model
steals reader's suit, emasculating
him. "*Don*: ¿Es para usted? ¿Para
él? Para ellos? Para mi? Es para
quien? El azul bruma y complementarios *Don*," *Don*, no. 7
(1966). © 2019 Estate of Eugeni
Forcano Andreu/Artists Rights
Society (ARS), New York/
VEGAP, Madrid.

same issue featured a woman not only wearing a man's suit but first seducing its owner (the reader, whom she pulls into the magazine) and stealing it, leaving him in shirttails and helpless—an act of appropriation, but also emasculation (see fig. 13).

As *Don*'s editorial might suggest, unisex represented a direct challenge to the Francoist gender order. National-Catholic moral authorities had abolished coeducation for fear of excess socialization and consequent sin, and had assigned the sexes different social roles. Unisex clothes sent a contrary message of gender equality, female ability, and the admissibility of casual social interaction between men and women. In particular, Verdú argued, these simple "sporty" styles promoted easier mixed-sex friendships between Spanish teenagers, rendered their personalities more similar, and undermined a long-standing misogynistic culture of sexual conquest.[100] This last claim was admittedly optimistic: years later, in the ostensibly more progressive late 1970s, magazines like couples lifestyle journal *Vivir a Dos* (Living as two, founded 1976) would run exposés on the continued pervasiveness of sexism in post-Francoist Spanish society.[101] Yet unisex also subverted Francoist gender separation simply by bringing the sexes together physically. Between 1969 and 1972, Galerías Preciados, El Corte Inglés, and Sears all built consolidated youth sections where teenaged boys and girls could purchase—and mingle over—both traditionally gendered and unisex garments.[102] On the whole, the irreconcilability of unisex with the regime's gender canon was so clear that, as Verdú penned his essay in 1971, PK *Press* meanwhile worried that unisex was ultimately doomed in Southern Europe, which would never accept women having the same rights as men, much less the same attire.[103]

This bleak assessment had some merit, inasmuch as neither youth fashion nor unisex lacked for obstacles to their spread. PK still marketed Terlenka YOUNG using the traditional goal of *elegancia*, and in 1969 concluded that a lack of hippies in Spain pointed to a conservative national character inhospitable toward the counterculture of the 1960s.[104] Unisex's elision of gender differences, meanwhile, faced a challenge in the early 1970s from a resurgence of gendering in both foreign and Spanish fashion spearheaded by the popular maxi skirt, which *Cortty* proclaimed a harbinger of the end of women's attempts to "eclipse man [by] resembling him."[105] And, as scholar Fred Davis has noted, unisex's own androgynous credentials are questionable, since designers have historically tended simply to dress women like preadolescent boys, leaving male wardrobes untouched and defanging any threat to male social power.[106]

Still, both trends had by the early 1970s made a notable impact on Spanish society. In 1971, an advertising executive assured Verdú that youth fashion had grown so broadly influential during the previous decade that while adolescents had once worn versions of their parents' clothes, now the converse was true.[107] So too, if most unisex wear in Spain was patterned on traditional male garb, it was hardly infantilizing (see fig. 14). Meanwhile, gender-bending fashions for men such as male handbags and floral prints rose in popularity alongside the maxi skirt. And, this last garment, though coded feminine, did not necessarily imply subjugation but could instead represent (and merchants tried to sell it as) a new way for women to rebel against patriarchy by denying one's legs to the male gaze, just as the miniskirt had done by baring them.[108] Official censors responded sharply to the daring new sartorial context, underscoring the moral danger they believed it to pose: in 1966, for instance, the otherwise conformist *Mujer* was nearly suspended for showing two bikini-clad models being body-painted.[109] And, the next year, censor Félix Rodríguez Madiedo fined the deliberately subversive *Don* for its "degenerate sensuality" and use of "sadist symbols." One ad for Copan brand pants, for instance, featured a dominatrix-like woman holding a phallically positioned chain wrapped sadomasochistically around a supine half-naked man, and the suggestive caption, "Copan Satisfies" (see fig. 15).[110]

Over the course of the 1960s and 1970s, then, Spain's consumer magazines helped fuel a sociopolitically significant shift in gender

FIG. 14. "Terlenka Proclaims Freedom of Fashion." *PK Press*, no. 5 (n.d. [1968]).

FIG. 15. "Copan Satisfies." *Don*, no. 7 (1966). © 2019 Estate of Eugeni Forcano Andreu/Artists Rights Society (ARS), New York/VEGAP, Madrid.

discourse. As the nation's department stores moved consumers away from notions of national difference and toward a view of Spain as a peer of its European neighbors, magazine copy that championed youth and unisex fashions—aided by retailers' "youth" sections that sold those clothes—similarly shifted Spaniards away from patriarchal National-Catholic gender hierarchies and toward a fledgling support for exercise of individual political conscience and gender equality. Circa 1960, fashions and models of masculinity that crossed the Pyrenees were largely conservative and capable of reinforcing Francoist patriarchal ideals. But even then, social danger loomed. For instance, in 1960, *Señor* responded with hostility to a seemingly innocuous American ad campaign that encouraged women to buy their husbands ties as a way of bonding emotionally. Far from harmless, the magazine considered such actions an insidious effort by the weaker sex to dominate men.[111] As the 1970s dawned, the threat posed by foreign fashion trends and the social ideas they carried with them only grew as unisex and youth fashion arrived and challenged the Franco regime's patriarchal authority. Indeed, journalist Verdú argued in 1971 that as Spain became a socially mobile society with increasingly blurred class and gender distinctions, such fashions functioned as intermediaries that allowed Spaniards to express not just ever-narrower social differences but growing ideological ones—a progressively democratic state of affairs. The resulting change, Verdú concluded, was total, from "zero to one thousand."[112]

Notwithstanding the transformations that the Spanish ad industry and consumer media experienced during the late 1950s and 1960s, more changes awaited. Maestre's particular field of public relations underwent another wave of international affiliation by the mid-1970s, one that swept up DANIS, among other agencies. And the industry as a whole eventually experienced a homegrown creative revolution, as adman Julián Bravo would later recall, but not till the 1980s.[113] Yet the sea change that Spain's admen witnessed during the early years of their nation's economic boom were indeed so great as to be from "zero to one thousand." And like the transformation of Spanish retailing and consumer culture as a whole, the professionalization of Spanish advertising, the introduction of public relations, and the intensified international orientation of the Spanish consumer press and fashion industry were rooted in a concern with achieving technical and, by extension, social and cultural parity with foreign counterparts.

This motivation stretched back decades, to Pedro Prat Gaballi's pioneering work in advertising during the early twentieth century. By the dawn of the economic boom, it dovetailed with a broader anxiety shared by the Franco regime and Spanish society concerning the country's ability to deal as an equal with its trading partners in Western Europe and North America. Spanish advertising had begun to take shape as a profession with the arrival of a crop of young innovators in the late 1940s and 1950s. During the early 1960s, this professionalization accelerated with the creation of technical schools, trade journals, and a regulatory charter for the industry. Maestre founded the nation's first public relations agency in 1960, and quickly began building his new field's reputation in Spain by taking on prominent international and domestic clients. Looking beyond the Pyrenees, Maestre and his Spanish colleagues increasingly also sought ties with international associations like IPRA and forged partnerships with foreign advertising agencies. By the time of the 1966 IPRA annual meeting that Maestre hosted in Barcelona, Spanish advertising, like the nation's grocery trade, boasted extensive links to commerce abroad, so much so that in a letter to Manuel Fraga one year earlier, IPRA president Robert Bliss could already describe Maestre as "a leader in our field, not only in Spain but in professional circles in Europe."[114]

As with the changes that other Spanish commercial sectors and the nation's society as a whole were experiencing, this process was hardly smooth. The Ministry of Information and Tourism encountered resistance from Spanish admen as it shaped the profession's charter. Some were similarly concerned about a growing number of partnerships and mergers between leading national firms such as Publicidad Ruescas or Alas and multinational giants like McCann-Erickson and J. Walter Thompson, with which they feared they simply could not compete. During the late 1960s, while Maestre and IPRA pursued international protagonism through consultative work with the United Nations, no less a figure than Francisco García Ruescas instead decried what American policymakers called consumer diplomacy, but which he considered a form of global economic colonization; he similarly rejected the notion of Spain joining the EEC. And, in much the same vein as the CAT's contemporary insistence on its authority over Spain's supermarkets, regime press censors worked to suppress potentially subversive notions on a range of social issues that were entering the country alongside foreign products with which the fashion industry and consumer press saturated Spanish society.

Yet a destabilizing discursive shift in society was increasingly evident, particularly so in its popular embrace of youth and social progress over conservative authority, as well as changes in gender relations, which the Spanish consumer press widely disseminated. Initially conservative with regard to the gender norms and especially the masculinities they promoted, as the countercultural 1960s progressed new Spanish men's magazines like *Don* and industry publications like *PK Press* and El Corte Inglés's *Cortty* embraced and imported the socially destabilizing foreign trends of unisex and youth fashion. Such fashions entered the country along the very pathways for the transmission of consumer practices and associated social notions that periodicals like *Mujer* and *Alta Costura* had built in the 1950s. Once present, they began to undercut Francoist patriarchal mores. And, meanwhile, as they imported these new fashions, Spanish consumer magazines like *Señor*, *Don*, and *PK Press* continued another process begun in the 1950s, one that echoed concerns contemporaneously at play within Spain's department stores as well as the Franco regime. That is, they increasingly described Spain as part of, worried over its place within, or boasted of its rise to a modernity proper to a prosperous capitalist West in which they maintained Spain's future lay. In the 1968 musical comedy *Relaciones Casi Públicas*, in which film stars Conchita Velasco and Manolo Escobar play a female public relations agent and the local folk singer she clumsily tries to promote, Velasco at one point promises Escobar's Pepe de Jaén that "you can achieve anything nowadays if you have good publicity."[115] Though it was not the line's intended meaning, for Spain's admen, its consumer press, and, as we see in chapter 5, for the nation's retailers, this included integration into Western European and North American professional, social, and even political circles.

"On That Day, Borders Did Not Exist"

Department Stores and Social
Liberalization in Spain, 1960–1975

In late 1975, Spain's youngest department store chain, a division of a multinational retailing giant, marked the launch of its newest branch on Barcelona's Avenida Meridiana by flying in top executives from its Spanish, European, and world headquarters, which were located in Madrid, Brussels, and Chicago, respectively. Reflecting on the international diversity of this audience, the store's employee bulletin subsequently boasted, "on that day, borders did not exist."[1] Two years later, the new branch's managers could again celebrate, having just bested their Madrid sister store in a sales competition. This time, the company's journal printed a photograph of the remarkable way that these Spanish businessmen chose to mark their victory: dubbed Meridiana's "Confederate high command" by the bulletin, they posed before an American flag, costumed as U.S. Civil War–era Union Army soldiers (see fig. 16).[2]

Incongruous at first glance, this choice to celebrate a Spanish sales victory with a display of Americana in fact made sense. And while the bulletin's 1975 boast specifically referenced the distances traveled by executives like Chicago-based Vice President for International Operations John Gallagher, its claims about Spain's borders rang true. For the bulletin's name was *Noti-Sears*, and the department store, though by then a fixture in Madrid and Barcelona, was the quintessentially American retailer Sears, Roebuck and Co. Sears's Spanish division,

BARCELONA GANO LA GRAN BATALLA DE LOS SATELITES

FIG. 16. Sears-Barcelona's "Confederate High Command." "Barcelona ganó la gran batalla de los satélites," *Noti-Sears*, no. 36, Year VI (January–February 1977), n.p. Galerías Preciados Collection, ARCM.

or Sears Roebuck de España, founded in 1964, arrived as part of a sharp rise in foreign investment during the nation's economic boom of 1959–1973, and, to an even greater degree than Galerías Preciados and SPAR, this store introduced local patrons to new, sophisticated, and modernity-laden foreign products and commerce. An integral part of a multinational organization that transcended Spain's political and cultural borders, Sears de España functioned as a hybrid Spanish-American space, the kind that could produce a tableau of Spaniards in American Civil War uniforms.

More broadly, Sears joined established local retailers like Galerías Preciados and El Corte Inglés in further developing Spain's emergent mass consumer society as well as Spain's commercial and social integration into the capitalist First World, the latter particularly manifest in an ongoing Americanization and Europeanization of Spanish consumer lifestyles. The international bent of 1960s Spanish consumption is well documented; Sears de España represented an acute but also symptomatic case of a department store fueling this foreign interest. As they grew, Galerías Preciados, Sears, and their competitors all built new branches across the country, often in areas that lacked such modern commercial venues. Thereby, they transformed the urban landscape and provided sites for the era's new consumption to take place.[3] Though naturally less international than a multinational like Sears, homegrown counterparts like Galerías Preciados nonetheless built upon the cosmopolitan interest in foreign consumer ways that they had already embraced in the 1950s. In particular, they publicized themselves as world-class commercial landmarks with international clienteles and offered local patrons new foreign products and commercial innovations. Among these were gender-bending unisex fashions sold in novel "youth" departments, in which Spain's formerly sex-segregated teenagers could mingle over clothes that subverted patriarchal National-Catholic gender norms. Meanwhile, a flood of new consumer magazines promoted these same imported fashions and alternative ideas, as well as a more generally socially progressive spirit that further undercut Francoist patriarchy and at times challenged the regime's authority directly.

The result was just such a destabilization of existing mechanisms of social and political control. Indeed, the very same department stores that imported these subversive consumer ways were themselves threatened by them. The era's growing focus on consumption led Spanish department store clerks to abandon their employers' traditional calls to corporatist self-sacrifice and complete identification with the store, degrading the totalizing work cultures that these retailers had long ago patterned after the early Franco regime's social politics. Almacenes Siro Gay and Galerías Preciados in particular also struggled to adapt to changing gender norms in the wake of several tepid social and labor reforms enacted in the early 1960s to appease foreign diplomatic and trading partners that even Franco himself courted.[4]

As for Franco's regime, the boom years' intensified cosmopolitanism subverted not just Francoism's gender paradigm but also profoundly and ultimately fatally undermined Francoism's founding discourse of national difference, a change first set in motion by retailers and media in the 1950s and early 1960s. Sears introduced American products, Galerías Preciados ran employee exchanges with their foreign counterparts, while magazine articles worried over the national fashion industry's status within Western Europe, shifting readers' professional, social, and cultural reference points beyond the Pyrenees to the Continent and the United States. All of these actions helped to disseminate a new, alternative, and internationally oriented Spanish national identity. And the consequences to Francoism's sociopolitical project were far ranging, more so than scholars like Luis Enrique Alonso and Fernando Conde acknowledge. They limit themselves to noting how this mid-century Spanish conflation of notions like "Europe" and "freedom," which the nation's nascent consumerism encouraged, anticipated a similar modern-day conflation of these concepts.[5] But if early Francoism's concept of Spain was exceptionalist, positioning it a countermodel to the First World's decadent democracies and the regime as custodian of this spiritual strength, the international Spain of the boom era aspired to be an equal (if also especially economically vibrant and cosmopolitan) nation within capitalist Western Europe—a marked shift in how Franco-era Spain understood itself and its place in the world.

Becoming World-Class Stores, Imagining a Cosmopolitan Spain

The consummation of this international integration began with a second wave of expansion at Spain's premier department stores that was fueled by Western Europe's booming postwar economies and built on the growth these retailers had achieved in the 1950s. Retailers like Galerías Preciados and El Corte Inglés built new branches in which an increasingly prosperous public and rising number of affluent tourists could consume. They introduced foreign innovations such as a system that shortened production of made-to-measure suits from a matter of weeks to just four days.[6] They pursued initiatives such as calls for greater mastery of (mainly foreign) retailing methods and imported product exhibitions that turned shop floors into international spaces. And, crucially, these stores acted thusly both to win public recognition as world-class retailers and also to raise Spanish retailing and the nation as a whole to a perceived Western standard of professionalism and modernity. As they laid claim to these cosmopolitan, modern, and European identities and performed them for local as well as foreign patrons, these retailers also claimed a similarly modern and European identity for Spain.

Between 1958 and 1975, the number and geographic reach of major department store branches in Spain rose sharply. Galerías Preciados quickened its spread. The chain opened stores in provincial capitals such as Cádiz (1958) and Bilbao (1959 and 1971); launched Nuevas Galerías (1968), a cutting-edge concept store, in a new building next to its Madrid flagship; and absorbed Barcelona's Almacenes Jorba, relaunched as Jorba-Preciados, between 1963 and 1965.[7] Galerías's competitors also flourished. Jorba's takeover was a direct response to the opening of an El Corte Inglés at a prime spot on Barcelona's central Plaza de Cataluña. Siro Gay built a bargain-priced outlet in Ávila in 1960 and two regular branches in Valencia in 1961 and 1962. And in 1964 Botas built an annex, the Nueva Tienda (New Store), featuring a café that the retailer, reflecting the contemporary mania for foreign ways, described as a European-style "snack bar."[8] Lastly, Sears, Roebuck launched its Spanish corporation ("corporation" being Sears's in-house term for the national subsidiaries that made up its multinational network) in September 1964 and opened its first branch on Barcelona's Plaza de Calvo Sotelo in 1967, a second on Madrid's upscale Calle Serrano in 1971, and the Meridiana store in 1975, each complemented by a cluster of smaller affiliated neighborhood "satellite stores."[9]

These retailers also grew organizationally, offering customers new services like in-store supermarkets and adding new layers to the workplace cultures their employees experienced.[10] Siro Gay launched the monthly internal bulletin *"Gay"* in 1957, followed by Almacenes Botas (*Boletín de Botas*, launched 1962); Sears (*Noti-Sears*, 1968); and El Corte Inglés (*Cortty*, 1969).[11] As at Galerías Preciados, these magazines soon became central to their stores' institutional cultures, serving as clearinghouses for messages from management, company news, and social announcements.[12] *Cortty* moreover shared some of the *Boletín de Galerías Preciados*'s paternalistic streak, regularly running official advice columns that sought to influence employees' romantic and private medical choices, as well as their professional lives.[13]

Newly heightened concern among store executives over their firms' prestige abroad and ability to meet the expectations of Spain's growing flood of foreign tourists fueled this unprecedented latest wave of expansion. The stakes—what these retailers had to lose—were significant. As the 1960s dawned and amid the nation's improving economic fortunes, Spain's department stores, and as various scholars have noted, the nation's emerging internationally influenced mass commerce as a whole, commanded notable prestige as a growth sector, with potential for further success abroad. This stood in contrast with the distrust some Spaniards retained toward small-scale local shops that they considered dens of haggling and fraud.[14] Indeed, by the late 1950s, these reputations were already such that Galerías saleswomen of the time broke their employer's rules by choosing to wear their uniforms—thereby showing off their professional ties—while on their lunch breaks about the city. By 1961, the allure of achieving personal success in the commercial sector was so great that rumors of several former comrades' lucrative new business careers led a marine infantry officer named Alfonso Buisán Pérez to resign after over a decade of naval service and seek his fortunes in the private sector. He later became chief of personnel at the first Spanish branch of an American retailing multinational.[15]

Store managers consequently placed new stress on the need for workers to constantly seek professional self-improvement, particularly through mastery of *técnica*, the technically sophisticated professional knowledge that had meanwhile become a concern for Spain's admen and supermarket advocates. During the early 1960s, Botas and Galerías Preciados executives like Galerías legal counsel Blas Sandalio Rueda harped on the importance of *formación*, or "professional development," warning that a continued lack of such technical mastery would leave the nation's retailers uncompetitive abroad. When not voiced so bluntly—a 1963 *Boletín de Botas* article went so far as to liken Spanish underdevelopment to impoverished postcolonial Africa's—this fixation could instead fuel suspiciously strident boasts about these stores' international accomplishments and the world-class status they implied.[16] Thus, in mid-1964, Botas staged a series of window displays publicizing the public relations work done by the commission (headed by Galerías's José Manuel Fernández) that was managing the popular Spanish pavilion at the 1964 World's Fair.[17]

Galerías Preciados courted this kind of cosmopolitan reputation most of all. There was ample precedent for this in the retailer's frequently publicized official memory, which had always stressed its ties to commerce abroad—especially Havana's El Encanto department store—and their place at the heart of a larger transatlantic relationship between Spain and Cuba.[18] These claims only multiplied after the Cuban Revolution and a subsequent counterrevolutionary arson attack—one of many at the time—that razed El Encanto in 1961.[19] They were particularly evident in bulletin articles eulogizing the Cuban store's influence on Galerías, as well as Pepín Fernández's own actions: he joined a newly formed Spanish aid society for Latin American immigrants, hired Cubans and returning Spanish émigrés fleeing Castro, and took the opportunity when several were promoted to *interesado* in 1964 to publicly remember Galerías's departed "sister across the sea and . . . spiritual womb."[20]

Prompted by the newly common sight of foreign tourists, businessmen, and American military personnel in the early 1960s, Galerías redoubled its efforts to attract this potential foreign clientele and to proclaim itself a modern, cosmopolitan establishment—and in the process, advanced both Spanish and U.S. efforts at consumer diplomacy.[21] The store published testimonials from American customers like U.S. Air Force colonel Raymond Buckwalter, former commander of the airbase established at Torrejón de Ardóz (Madrid) under the 1953 treaty. It hosted special events for these foreign patrons, including special fashion shows for the ladies of another American base near Sevilla.[22] Thereby, Galerías represented itself as a world-class store with cross-cultural appeal, and so a key figure in the warming Spanish-American relationship, a discourse that Colonel Buckwalter echoed as he wrote, "I'd dare say that 'Galerías Preciados' plays a large role in bettering the relationship between our two countries."[23]

This cosmopolitan impulse similarly found expression in personnel policies such as employing the store's oft-referenced corps of interpreters, in which Spaniards such as Carmen Tarrazo—described by Buckwalter as "the American woman's best friend in Spain"—mingled with foreign-born colleagues like Dutch student Jetty Kentie, who worked at Callao in 1960, as well as their internationally diverse clientele. These measures also included employee exchanges with sister stores abroad like Selfridges, where Galerías sent telephone operator Paquita Almazán in 1964.[24] Much as in the case of tourism, the cultural encounters that resulted between Spanish customers, clerks, and counterparts from often more sociopolitically open societies eroded Francoist notions of Spanish difference. Thus, Galerías's Ramón Hernández, who worked at Stockholm's Åhlén & Holm department store in December 1961, reported finding the weather and urban layout strange, but not the people. Almazán was still more direct: "Not for a moment did I feel as if in a foreign country, for everyone gave me a wonderful welcome." Like Hernández, she missed Spain's sunshine and Galerías's quirks, but did not see Londoners themselves as alien.[25]

Finally, capitalizing on its status as Spain's premier department store, Galerías Preciados also began pursuing organizational ties abroad. Galerías's 1958 readmission to the Intercontinental Group of Department Stores (IGDS) linked the Spanish store to august names such as Selfridges and Japan's Takashimaya, both fellow members.[26] Of the well-publicized foreign delegations that visited Galerías, many came from these stores.[27] And, in 1964, Galerías's relationship to North American retailing developed financial ties akin to the mergers taking place in Spain's ad industry, as the store sold a 10 percent share to Federated Department Stores, Inc., Macy's parent company. Tellingly, the sale was announced at a joint Spanish-American colloquium on Spanish industry held entirely in English.[28]

Occasionally, even these stores' physical interiors became international spaces, as Galerías and its competitors hosted special foreign product exhibitions such as 1962's "París en 'Galerías,'" 1966's "Norteamérica en 'Galerías,'" as well as three "Extremo Oriente" (Far East) events held at Botas and Galerías Preciados between 1964 and 1973.[29] Perhaps most notably, in 1970, El Corte Inglés's Bilbao branch responded to a contemporary Spanish craze for British fashion by launching its "English Men's Shop" (as referenced in chapter 4), a space in which the store consolidated all of its men's items of English make in a space distinguished by walls of dark wood, columns shaped like Big Ben, and a dedicated staff in special English-style livery.[30]

Spain's foremost department stores, then, displayed a pronounced cosmopolitan bent. Botas pushed employees to professionalize and fretted over the nation's perceived commercial backwardness, all while self-consciously insisting on its own world-class status. Galerías did too, and with its Cuban roots, offered ordinary Spaniards the ability to buy products from across the globe while surrounded by similarly diverse shoppers and clerks, the latter of whom enjoyed a support network that facilitated travel abroad. Certainly, these stores' aims differed. Almacenes Botas, as the CAT had done with the supermarket, aspired to achieve a European standard of service and modernity that its own discourse deemed still beyond reach. Galerías Preciados and El Corte Inglés, by contrast, already considered themselves beacons of modernity, and in the former case, the equal of its IGDS colleagues. Meanwhile, *Cortty* boasted in 1970 that Spanish merchants and consumers felt "neither inferior, nor provincial, nor backwards," and store executive Cesar Conde quipped, "From Japan I would only bring . . . the customers."[31]

Department Stores, the Built Environment, and Spanish International Integration

As Galerías and El Corte Inglés grew into international spaces, they and other such establishments also transformed the urban areas surrounding them. In so doing, they altered the daily experiences of an urban populace beyond those who could actually afford to shop there, and provided them opportunities to encounter new foreign consumer ways. Autoservicios had begun to alter Spanish urban landscapes with their sleek storefronts; Spain's spreading department stores accelerated this change. They helped remake urban spaces like Madrid's Puerta del Sol, over which the architecturally incongruous white structure of El Corte Inglés's flagship store loomed; the capital's Plaza de Callao,

FIG. 17. Hotel Florida, 1959. Juan Miguel Pando Barrero, Archivo Pando, IPCE, Ministerio de Educación, Cultura y Deporte.

where Nuevas Galerías's featureless concrete storefront replaced the historic Hotel Florida in 1966 (see figs. 17 and 18); and Granada's downtown, after a Galerías opened there in 1975.[32] This last store—second only to the flagship in size—offered passersby the spectacle of a massive storefront the likes of which the city had never seen before, ringed with the most display windows of any store in the country. Its construction was moreover contingent on an agreement between Galerías Preciados and the mayor's office under which the chain paid to install streetlights along the two avenues bordering its new branch, transforming the district's evening landscape.[33] Finally, Galerías-Granada's arrival touched off a debate over the existing legal closure of businesses on Saturday afternoons, which the retailer got repealed, altering the city's daily rhythms and producing new scenes of weekend shoppers strolling into Galerías, past its many windows, and through the downtown.[34]

Meanwhile, the growing popularity of the automobile in Spain also began to influence store locations. The number of cars in Spain rose from just 257,000 in 1953 to 2 million by 1964; indeed, the traffic in Barcelona was so dense by 1961 that the city eliminated its venerable streetcar network to accommodate the automotive flood.[35] As in the United States previously, this embrace of the automobile spurred the development of new commercial areas—shopping centers—well outside traditional downtown commercial districts, to which customers drove rather than walked.[36] Surely inspired by Vizcaya province's automotive density, which was among the nation's highest, Galerías Preciados built its second Bilbao branch in 1969 at just such a location: Spain's first shopping center, which had recently opened on the city's peripheral Plaza de Zabálburu. As at Galerías's other recently constructed locations, the shopping center's architecture, which included a subterranean parking garage with space for one thousand cars, betrayed the store's (and the public's) growing expectation that life in Spain would soon be thoroughly motorized.[37] Galerías Preciados itself fueled this advancing car culture both by hosting

FIG. 18. Nuevas Galerías and Galerías Preciados -Callao, 1972. Juan Miguel Pando Barrero, Archivo Pando, IPCE, Ministerio de Educación, Cultura y Deporte.

events such as the 1969 launch for Spanish car maker Barreiros's new Simca 1200 model, as well as through club and store initiatives that offered employees cars at discount prices and placed them in contact with driving schools, which directly increased the number of cars and drivers on Spanish roads.[38] By 1970, the automobile was so common a part of the Spanish shopping experience that *Cortty* declared the American adage of "No parking, No business" an imperative in future store planning in Spain.[39]

The Zabálburu shopping center's advertising reflected an expectation that now Bilbao would rise to a specifically foreign modernity. One late 1969 newspaper ad commissioned by the developers, Construcciones Alcorta, boasted that, as result of this project, Bilbao had now joined a "Shopping Center Common Market"—a reference to the European Common Market that had become synonymous in Spain with cosmopolitanism, international integration, and prosperity.[40] Another listed Bilbao among the European pioneers of the shopping center, which included world cities like Paris and Frankfurt. And Galerías similarly boasted that its new store, which Pepín Fernández declared to be Spain's prettiest, was located in the nation's "most modern commercial zone."[41]

The Challenges of Cosmopolitanism

Unrest accompanied this apparent progress. As store chains like Galerías Preciados transformed Spain's urban landscapes and rendered Spanish consumer life more international, at Almacenes Botas and Jorba-Preciados the changing times also fostered (tame) reassertions of Spain's minority Asturian and Catalan cultures and languages.[42] At Botas, this fueled cultural events such as *bolos* (Asturian-style bowling) matches and Asturian Cultural Circles as well as columns in the *Boletín de Botas* celebrating Asturias's natural beauty and national character, lent extra folkloric charm by fragments of Bable (the Asturian language) scattered throughout.[43] In one 1963 editorial, too, bulletin contributor "Julio" chastised Asturias's youth for no longer possessing even basic knowledge of their own culture, Bable and *bolos* included.[44] Comparatively muted performances of Catalan identity—especially subtle given the muscular expressions of Catalanism then taking shape—similarly began to develop at Jorba-Preciados during the 1960s. For instance, Jorba-Preciados began to honor exemplary employees with a pin shaped like a Phrygian cap, or *barretina*, one of Catalonia's national symbols, and also participated in local Catalan cultural events.[45]

Still, these particular expressions of regionalism did not pose much of a challenge to the regime or its unitary and centralist conception of Spanish identity. Jorba-Preciados and Botas both reduced regional practices and culture to folkloric curios, stripping them of the ability to describe true alternatives to Francoist Spain's approved Castilian cultural identity. Jorba-Preciados's Catalanism simply extended Almacenes Jorba's participation in regional festivals and its inclusion of Catalan in *Revista Jorba* and other printed materials; Asturian culture, from which the Franco regime appropriated what it wished and stigmatized the rest as low culture, presented even less of a threat.[46] Thus Botas's own "Julio" classified the Asturian language and *bolos* as "old," "local color," and "tradition," by contrast with a vibrant, modern (and Castilian) popular culture. And, in 1965, when Jorba-Preciados hosted a Spanish cultural exhibition that included the Catalan *sardana* dance, the store presented it as safely part of a unitary Spain's national patrimony, reinforced by a massive image of Don Quixote— the Castilian symbol par excellence—which dominated the store's façade and the proceedings.[47]

If this regionalism failed to present a substantive challenge to the regime as Galerías and other Spanish stores continued to expand, these stores nevertheless did find themselves navigating more serious challenges. Some of these challenges were new, linked to the changing times and these stores' intensified expansionary pace, while others were an enduring legacy from their earlier growth in the 1950s.

As in that decade, Spain's premier department stores faced the danger that their increasingly far-flung personnel would lose a sense of connection with one another, of belonging to a single organization. This was especially true at Galerías Preciados, which remained heavily invested in viewing its employees as a professional "family" joined together by genuine bonds of affection born of daily teamwork toward a shared goal—affective ties that were possibly at risk should the chain become overly atomized. Galerías consequently continued to make aggressive and even heightened use of its social structures, including the *Boletín de Galerías Preciados* and the Club de Galerías, to foster interbranch communication and preserve the chain's traditional shared esprit de corps. As the Madrid-based chain added branches, these began to report local news and to profile particularly popular branch employees within an ever-expanding section of the *Boletín* devoted to goings-on at the store's provincial locations and most especially their local club chapters. While the 1957 *Boletín* featured only a motley assortment of such columns scattered throughout its pages, by the mid-1970s well-defined recurring sections on the club and other storewide social activities could take up as much as half of each issue.[48]

These activities included one of Galerías's primary methods for preserving its internal cohesion, particularly as social unrest began to grow in Spain: interstore tourism. This consisted of sending sales clerks from branches in the Spanish periphery on visits to other Galerías host cities (especially Madrid), where they toured the local Galerías Preciados and befriended colleagues—their extended Galerías "family"—whom they had never before met, building camaraderie across the store chain. Such trips were not an entirely new invention. In 1958, for instance, a pair of distinguished employees at Galerías's Valencia and Barcelona buying offices won trips to Madrid and the Callao branch, where they were awed by the store's size, inventory, and density of customer traffic.[49] Yet, by the late 1960s, these visits were both more frequent and different in tone. Once just welcome side-effects, the store pride, collegiality, and interbranch unity that these trips inspired had become their point—and the club's reason for organizing them, as the *Boletín de Galerías* eventually acknowledged in 1975.[50] Thus, in 1969–1970 alone, groups from Valencia, Murcia, Córdoba, Seville, Bilbao, Eibar, and Don Benito all traveled to Madrid with the purpose of at last seeing "their" flagship store and the much-remarked Nuevas Galerías, visits that Pepín Fernández then cited in a *Boletín* interview to underline that every Galerías branch and employee formed part of a single "Great Galerías Family."[51]

The social context for this new interstore tourism was also much changed, for, by then, Justin Crumbaugh has argued, tourism had become a "model of thought, a way to frame . . . [the] experience" of Spain's boom-era rise to modernity, as well as a primary symbol of that modernity. In the 1967 comedy film *El Turismo es un Gran Invento* (Tourism is a grand invention), the mayor and town secretary of the village of Valdemorillo travel to the beach resort town of Torremolinos to observe—as tourists—the spectacle of boom-era tourism.[52] Just so, the club's trips turned employees into tourists of distant Galerías branches, where they took in the "natives"—local store clerks—as well as "attractions" like the Madrid flagship store's cafeteria and underground garage, all through the same tourist's gaze used by the Valdemorillo duo. A group visiting the flagship from Murcia even responded like their filmic counterparts: they resolved to bring home the modernity they witnessed, in this case retailing innovations rather than mass tourist methods. Tourism, then, served here both as a lens through which to view Spanish modernity and also as a means to reproduce it.[53]

Store soccer clubs were another community-building strategy used by nearly every major Spanish department store, as well as other kinds of commercial enterprises. They were so common that whole tournaments and leagues formed around these company teams.[54] By 1963, the Club de Galerías Preciados, which continued to work to insert the store into employees' leisure activities, had organized such teams at the store's Las Palmas, Bilbao, Córdoba, and Sevilla branches, as well as at the flagship Callao store. As new store and club branches opened over the course of the next decade, more teams formed, such that by 1974, it was rare for a branch *not* to have one—between them, the Madrid stores alone had eight.[55] Again, seemingly in imitation of Galerías, Almacenes Botas's own club formed an employee soccer club in 1965, which that same year faced a squad representing American soft drink–maker Pepsi-Cola's local office.[56] By 1971, Sears's Spanish corporation too had a team; the following year, they placed third in an international tournament for company teams, with Parisian retailer Prisunic coming fourth and last, and El Corte Inglés taking top honors.[57] And these were only the stores' tournament squads. Both the Club de Galerías and Sears frequently organized morale-boosting intramural games that pitted a branch's married salesmen against its bachelors, for example, or its executives versus the shop floor. They held interstore matches, too, including one in 1976 between "Meridiana F.C." and "Real Calvo Sotelo"—representing the two branches that Sears then operated in Barcelona—and a 1974 game between Galerías-Zaragoza and Jorba-Preciados.[58] Finally, they also organized teams and tournaments in other sports, such as basketball.[59]

Galerías and Sears were both open about the community-building motive behind these sports clubs. In a 1974 article titled "Sport as a Tie of Unity," the *Boletín de Galerías Preciados* proclaimed "the fomenting and development of human relations between the [store's] personnel . . . [to be] one of the principal tasks and goals of the clubs." After citing examples of various soccer and basketball matches, the store underscored, "We will achieve the task we have pursued of fostering fellowship and understanding between all of the Company's personnel via different means, but sport is one of the principal ones."[60] Similarly, an early issue of *Noti-Sears* lauded Sears's own sports initiatives, citing their role in cultivating "true conviviality and dialogue among all of us [Sears employees], who should spend most of our days united by a common goal and [shared] labor."[61] More broadly, these sports clubs constituted attempts by managers to manipulate and represent their respective stores' identities to the employees they oversaw. They were, in other words, what Spanish public relations pioneer (and contemporary of Joaquín Maestre) Jaime de Urzaiz termed "internal public relations," or the act of representing a company to itself.[62] At Galerías, these efforts consequently formed part of the store's longer-term discursive construction of a "Galerías family"—a kind of "imagined community," whose contours were marked by store employment "citizenship" and by shared values of productivity and self-sacrifice as well as Pepín Fernández's cult of personality. Football matches contributed to the construction of this family through performance of the same fictive ties of brotherhood, intimacy, and mutual affection that underpinned *Boletín* articles a decade earlier.[63]

The crucial role that such initiatives played in preserving the esprit de corps that various department stores worked to cultivate within their ranks is highlighted by the outlying case of El Corte Inglés, which expanded quickly during the 1960s but possessed no club-style social structure to bind it together. By contrast, after the founding of the seemingly Galerías-inspired Club de Botas in 1959, both Galerías and Botas possessed social clubs; at Botas, moreover, the lack of a national store network saved its club from Galerías's burden of preserving a sense of familiarity between distant employees. Sears de España, though it lacked such a formally constituted social division (the store would finally found one in 1979), was nevertheless active socially, organizing morale-boosting contests, day trips to places like Catalonia's scenic Sau Valley, and of course the store's sports teams. In addition, the chain used *Noti-Sears* to publicize employees' personal achievements, like Barcelona department head Francisco Ballbé's successes as a competitive chess player.[64] Siro Gay possessed a store network and lacked a club, but was, as of the early 1960s, more concerned with the more basic problem of declining sales and the resulting overstock than issues of morale.[65] At El Corte Inglés, meanwhile, warehouse worker Jesús Benito Sánchez complained in 1970 that for want of a physical space where employees from different departments could mingle—a staple of every Club de Galerías chapter—the store's warehouse staff had become demoralizingly isolated from the rest of the El Corte Inglés's "family."[66]

Raising the underlying stakes for El Corte Ingles was the fact that these unifying measures responded to not one but two separate challenges that emerged as the 1960s progressed. Alongside the atomization that threatened chains like Galerías, disenchantment with these stores' cultures of loyal self-sacrifice began to spread among their workers—and both emerged in step with a growing disaffection in Spain with the politically stagnant Franco regime.[67] From the mid-1960s on, Galerías began to steadily lose company veterans like Jorba-Preciados's director general over the store's efforts to meet the growing technical demands of modern mass commerce by hiring and rapidly promoting recent university graduates, who took positions that these disaffected veterans considered theirs by right of seniority.[68] A loss of investment in Galerías's official set of values among the store's remaining ranks meanwhile caused employee volunteerism to plummet in the early 1970s. The decline was so severe in 1971 that the store's employee retirement fund had to delay elections for its representative to the Ministry of Labor due to a lack of candidates (ultimately one person volunteered). It also drove a sharp drop in attention paid to both official memoranda and the *Boletín*, the latter a traditional vehicle for the store's official values and the cultivating of interbranch community. Indeed, readership of the bulletin had so dwindled by 1971 that the ordinarily sanitized journal noted it bitterly.[69] A critical reading of early 1970s *Boletín* insistence on the importance of the Club de Galerías suggests that its membership too was falling.[70] Meanwhile, at Botas, employee contributions to the store bulletin had grown so lackluster in 1969 that the magazine had to repeatedly delay publication, and later complained about the lack of employee volunteerism and declining sense of duty this betrayed.[71]

Such protestations, issued in magazines that had historically been managerial mouthpieces, themselves represented one attempt by store executives to right their company ships; other attempts included awards for seniority and excellence that began to proliferate at these retailers just as discontent did. In 1959, Galerías introduced its Gold Insignia program, which the *Boletín de Galerías Preciados* quickly mobilized didactically. It used 1960 insignia recipient Crisanto Ortega both as a model of the store's embattled culture of loyalty and, because he was well known across the store chain, as a source of the same unifying sense of familiarity the bulletin had sought to elicit in its 1953 article on Tangier branch head Luis García. To these ends, the *Boletín* lingered especially on Ortega's raw emotions at receiving Galerías's highest honor after twenty-five years of giving everything—even his son, Fabio—to the store, painting an intimate and endearing picture of the visibly shaking veteran's nerves and attempts to calm himself with a smoke.[72] In 1968, as social unrest and the commercial threat posed by El Corte Inglés both grew, the *Boletín*'s editors turned to another award, Galerías's Gold Keychain for twenty-five years of service, to underscore the need for "continuity, healthy tradition, and fidelity to [the store's] normative principles," especially an unflagging service ethic and sense of duty.[73] A series of award statuettes, insignia lapel pins, and medals similarly proliferated at Botas, typically accompanied by speeches that, in keeping with the store's aspirations to modernity, stressed the need for employees to work hard and improve themselves in order for Botas to succeed in the new mass consumer age.[74]

Finally, these stores struggled to adapt to Spain's slowly shifting gender politics. This shift began with the 1958 and 1961 reforms to women's legal status and continued through the end of the decade, as Spanish feminists, housewives' associations, and the Sección Femenina itself demanded greater public agency for Spanish women, efforts only strengthened by similar campaigns and the rise of second-wave feminism unfolding abroad, as well as the Franco regime's own attempts to appear moderate internationally.[75]

Initially, Spanish department stores met the mild egalitarianism of these reforms with palpably grudging acquiescence and by questioning their own saleswomen's professional commitment. In a 1960 interview, for instance, Pepín Fernández doubted younger, supposedly marriage-crazed saleswomen's professionalism. Two years later, *"Gay"* warned its shopgirls that now that they would be paid like men, they would have to also work as hard as them—implying that this had hitherto not been the case, a claim that store executive José Luis Gay voiced explicitly soon after.[76] In this same vein, Galerías Preciados's 1959 revision of its internal regulatory code preserved termination as the default for new brides, even as it incorporated pay equality, and *Galerías*, a short-lived women's magazine that the store launched that year, stressed the need to raise properly feminine girls while tepidly defending the modern working woman.[77]

As the decade progressed, and particularly by the early 1970s, more charitable views concerning women's work gained ground at Spain's department stores, but skepticism and a continued loyalty to the traditional gendered division of labor also persisted. Thus, *Boletín de Galerías Preciados* contributor "Manises" declared in 1963 that women were if anything more productive than men. In 1969, Botas executive Marisol Llerandi González similarly argued that being female had no bearing on one's professional abilities—statements that moved beyond the paternalistic and perhaps not even sincere affirmations of women's equal professional potential that had characterized post-1958/1961 responses like José Luis Gay's.[78] Just so, in 1970, the editors of *Cortty* made a point of noting that the store's convivial work culture hinged upon respect for colleagues of the opposite sex. And if the magazine continued to portray women as flighty shoppers, it increasingly described men as equally biddable, and comparatively ill informed to boot.[79] Finally, during the International Women's Year of 1975, both El Corte Inglés's and Galerías Preciados's bulletins periodically celebrated the global event. *Cortty*, the more active of the two, ran columns that detailed the Women's Year as well as the activities of the UN Commission on the Status of Women, and chronicled the long struggle for women's legal rights. Other columns also surveyed Spanish women's contemporary social and legal status (accompanied by detailed supporting sociological data) and, in one instance, profiled feminist Betty Friedan without the hostility that feminism had historically garnered in Franco-era Spain.[80]

Yet the more progressive views of bulletin writers like Llerandi and Manises remained far from universally shared. To the contrary, both their stores' track records on women's equality suggest that gestures of the sort that Galerías Preciados later made in 1975 were not necessarily of substance or sincere. In November 1963, for instance, Sederías Carretas salesman Luis Molina Romero echoed Pepín Fernández in declaring men better workers than their marriage-obsessed female colleagues. In 1970, *Boletín de Botas* contributor "Conchita" echoed José Luis Gay in blaming saleswomen's lack of professional advancement on their own supposed poor performance.[81] And indeed, Galerías's participation in the International Women's Year proved paltry when compared to El Corte Inglés's; the store also remained conservative on women's rights, much like the Sección Femenina, whose own ostensibly evolving stance on this issue had become passé and even retrograde by the mid-1970s.[82] Thus, while reporting on an event recognizing Galerías's saleswomen, the *Boletín de Galerías Preciados* specially praised women's divinely ordained work as mothers, helpmeets, and homemakers, sentiments that Spanish feminist Maria Aurelia Capmany contemporaneously decried as toxic to women's advancement in the public sphere.[83]

Sears, Roebuck and the Internationalization of Spanish Retail Commerce

Spain's consumption-mediated international integration and the concomitant Americanization and Europeanization of Spanish consumer lifestyles and social norms are especially well illustrated by the case of Sears. During its eighteen years in Spain, from its founding in 1964 through its 1982 sale to the Spanish holding company RUMASA,

Sears, Roebuck de España epitomized the role that mass retailing played in late Franco-era Spain's foreign turn. More than Galerías Preciados, Sears de España boasted extensive international ties, simply by virtue of belonging to the international division of a U.S.-based multinational corporation, initially managed from Chicago, and later, after 1974, out of a new European head office in Brussels. Among its employees, the store cultivated a growing cognizance of their place within this multinational chain. This, like the Spanish advertising industry's and Galerías Preciados's efforts at international outreach, in turn advanced a shift in public perception of Spain's place within a larger interconnected community of nations, and so undermined Francoist notions of Spanish national difference. As did Spain's supermarkets (most notably SPAR), department stores, and magazines like *Don* and *Señor*, Sears also exposed its Spanish clientele to foreign consumer products and practices that similarly eroded this sense of difference, and, as in the case of unisex fashions, engaged with a series of contemporary social changes that helped prepare the way for the Spanish transition to democracy after 1975.

The global Sears chain fostered this sense of connection between Spanish retailing and international commerce in part through its hiring practices. Since its first foray into Mexico in the late 1940s, Sears's stated policy had been to fill its foreign ranks with locals, believing them best equipped to sell to their countrymen.[84] Before opening its first Barcelona branch in 1967, Sears de España placed classifieds in the city's leading daily, *La Vanguardia Española*, seeking to fill positions ranging from department heads to merchandise buyers to spots in the company's accounting offices.[85] Locals flocked to apply, and, at the store's opening, the new Sears–Calvo Sotelo boasted managers with typically Catalan surnames like Castells, Ferrer, and Cavestany, as well as Barcelona native Alfonso Buisán Pérez as its first head of personnel.[86] Again, per standard practice, but also due to a dearth of job candidates with experience in department stores, Sears de España supplemented these Spanish hires with veteran managers from its American and International divisions, including Cuban-born director of personnel Ramiro Fernández, and American Ted Hujar, who became Sears–Calvo Sotelo's first store manager.[87] This resulted in a markedly international work environment, in which Spaniards worked alongside North and Latin American colleagues who had often already worked for Sears in multiple countries, a cosmopolitan state of affairs akin to that of Galerías Preciados's interpreter corps. This quickly became permanent, because Sears never realized its goal of eventually replacing this foreign contingent with local talent.[88]

Sears's hiring practices also produced a supporting, steady flow of personnel, professional knowledge, and cultural experiences between Sears's branches in the Americas, Spain, and, after 1972, a newly acquired network of Belgian stores, which underscored the links that tied Sears de España to its parent multinational chain. Alfonso Buisán, for instance, joined Sears in 1966 and spent two months training at branches in Chicago, Mexico City, and Puerto Rico, where he encountered American retail work cultures, but also colleagues whose varied backgrounds underlined Sears's international character, including Cuban Gustavo Fernández of Sears–San Juan (formerly of El Corte Inglés), and more than one Spaniard, such as Mexico City security chief Athenógenes Sánchez. When Buisán returned to Spain, he arrived armed with training materials to facilitate Spain's incorporation into the multinational Sears network as well as valuable firsthand experience traveling the length of those ties.[89] Meanwhile, American and International Division Sears employees made this journey in reverse, their careers mapping the global Sears network into which Spain now fit. Catalan native Assistant Manager Ramón Tintoré returned to help launch the Barcelona store after eight years at Sears in Venezuela, where he had joined the chain in 1959 as a recent émigré. Ramiro Fernández similarly worked at branches in Havana, Miami, and Colombia before arriving in Barcelona, as did subsequent arrivals like Barcelona store manager (and later, Sears de España president) John Riney, who came to Spain in 1969 by way of

Tennessee, Brazil, and Peru; and John Gardner, the Spanish corporation's president in the early 1970s, who had previously worked for Sears in the United States, Venezuela, and Peru, and went on to lead its European operations in Brussels before retiring in 1976.[90]

The effect of these frequent comings and goings across national borders was a deemphasizing of these borders' significance and of Francoism's sense of Spanish national difference. As Galerías Preciados and Almacenes Botas carved out temporarily foreign spaces within their stores via exhibitions like the 1966 "Norteamérica en Galerías," this movement of personnel went further, turning Sears's Spanish branches into internationalized, hybrid Spanish-American spaces linked to counterparts abroad via a larger transnational network of relationships. The store termed this "La Gran Familia Sears," or the "Great Sears Family," which the store's well-traveled managers physically embodied.[91] Hence, in 1975 *Noti-Sears* marked the arrival of foreign Sears executives for the launch of the chain's new Avenida Meridiana branch by declaring, "on that day . . . borders did not exist."[92]

Calvo Sotelo display artist and *Noti-Sears* regular Eduardo "Edy" Llorens both reproduced this notion of belonging to a "Great Sears Family" and gave special evidence of how fully ordinary employees had already internalized it, through a series of articles about his international travels. Llorens was a well-known figure at Sears, partly due to his growing success as a pen-and-ink artist, which was a point of pride in *Noti-Sears* and so emboldened the designer that in one instance he dared to dismiss Pablo Picasso as bad for art. Yet he was still better known for his globe-spanning vacations, which included visits to local Sears branches and often received detailed coverage in *Noti-Sears*.[93] These travel articles—like Galerías's own "store tourism"—represented a tourism-mediated consumption of Sears's global identity and Sears de España's place therein, a use of tourism as a lens through which Llorens and his readers could experience the Spanish corporation's ties to a larger community of stores and individuals abroad. The bulletin's account of Llorens's 1976 trip to Brazil made special note of how he toured the Rio de Janeiro branch's many departments, and bonded with the store's staff over their shared experience of working under John Riney.[94] And, in a second piece on his 1977 trip to Lake Titicaca, Llorens himself declared, "I could not help but be transported by the mild climate and sweet voices to Barcelona, to rush hour and the metro. ANTI-NATURE! I imagine that few of us, unlike Titicaca's inhabitants, will reach ninety years old."[95] This was an indictment, but also an assertion, of Spain's achievement of a specifically European and American modernity, much as adman Roldán Martínez had argued in his 1964 critique of Manuel Fraga's tourist slogan: "Spain is different, to be sure; but not by the average European's measure. Spain has cars, radio, TV, industry, and many other things besides flamenco, bulls, and donkeys with drinking jugs."[96]

Institutionally, a broad assortment of policies and programs implemented by the global Sears Corporation further cultivated ties between the chain's Spanish branches and its multinational network as well as changed perceptions of Spain's place in the world. Some, in fact, produced the same transatlantic movement and interpersonal encounters that Alfonso Buisán and Eduardo Llorens experienced. In 1971, for instance, Sears brought executives from its many international divisions to Chicago for an "International Advanced Management Conference," and, in 1973, it sent Spanish repair service manager Luis Díaz to the Puerto Rican corporation for a specialized professional seminar.[97] And this was just a fraction of Sears's efforts. Sears de España operated only semi-independently of its American parent. By contrast with the chain's highly decentralized structure within the United States, management at Sears's Spanish branches reported simultaneously to a central office in Madrid and the International Division headquarters in Chicago, and, after 1974, also reported to a new Brussels-based European head office.[98] Training materials and daily operating procedures were largely standardized across the Sears network, so much so that executives transferred abroad could take up their new positions while still learning the local language.[99]

The Sears Extension Institute (SEI), a professional development program that offered ongoing specialized correspondence courses for employees, continued this standardized training and ran contests for most completed courses between Sears de España and its sisters abroad. The parent company similarly offered sales competitions that pitted Sears store departments worldwide against each other. All of these contests met with considerable staff buy-in: Spain at one point placed third in the SEI's 1971 contest for most completed courses, ahead of well-established national corporations like Sears–Mexico, while *Noti-Sears* brimmed with pride when the Spanish branches won top honors worldwide for appliance warranty sales in March 1973 and furniture sales two years later.[100]

Indeed, *Noti-Sears* itself represented one of Sears de España's most potent ties to its brethren abroad. It was part of "the *Noti-Sears* chain": eight bulletins that circulated under that name at different Sears corporations worldwide, which together made up a microcosmic international Sears network of their own.[101] The magazine linked the Spanish corporation to its American parent through articles that advanced the store's official pedagogy. A March 1977 column historicized and stressed Sears's policy of "Satisfaction Guaranteed or your Money Back," which was not a commercial tradition in Spain.[102] It placed employee contributors like *Noti-Sears* regular África Galeras in contact with foreign colleagues such as Roderick Kevend of the International Division, whom she interviewed in 1974 and 1977.[103] But, most of all, as employees' main source for news about Sears's activities worldwide, *Noti-Sears* lent a sense of immediacy to those activities, the global Sears chain, and the Spanish corporation's place within it. In its December 1972 article "Sears en el Mundo," for example, the bulletin offered a detailed overview of the chain's international presence, its Spanish branches carefully situated therein.[104] The article took pride in the fact that Sears—"our company," it repeatedly stressed—"is the largest commercial organization in the world." In other columns, the bulletin's editors (all employee volunteers) celebrated the company's latest accomplishments as their own, including the construction of the Sears Tower in Chicago in 1973 and Sears's winning bid to outfit the 1972 U.S. Olympic Team.[105] *Noti-Sears*, in other words, worked at the discursive level to build the Sears network into a single, international, and interconnected place—a commercially and corporately mediated imagined community—and to populate it with employees shaped into, as Alfonso Buisán put it in 1968, "Sears citizens."[106] By the early 1970s, this sense of citizenship was well-enough entrenched among Sears de España's ranks that not only does it seem to have prompted some to spend valuable vacation time visiting members of their commercial "family" abroad, as in the case of Edy Llorens, but when an earthquake devastated Nicaragua in 1972, Spanish corporation employees donated en masse to help their comrades in Managua, prompting a heartfelt note in which Sears–Central America personnel head Vasilie Crisán thanked the "Spanish Sears Family," which *Noti-Sears* eagerly published in March 1973.[107]

Sears stressed this international character just as actively to the Spanish public. Much as Pepín Fernández had done in 1934, Sears bought a full-page ad in *La Vanguardia Española* two months before opening its first branch. In this ad, the store introduced itself as both a leading American retailer and also as an international organization with millions of customers in ten countries, one that was now poised to improve life in Spain by offering the same modern conveniences, low prices, and fair business practices that its other host nations enjoyed.[108] Like SPAR, Sears exposed its clientele to new, foreign consumer practices and experiences. This began with the branches' physical structures: Sears's inaugural store featured a windowless façade that an internal Galerías Preciados memo on this new competitor considered "a relative novelty in Spain."[109] Anticipating Bilbao's Zabálburu shopping center, Sears also built its Calvo Sotelo branch unusually far from Barcelona's city center, where both Jorba-Preciados and El Corte Inglés stood—so much so, that at first some locals believed that it more properly served the city's suburban periphery rather than its urban core.[110] Again anticipating Zabálburu as well as Nuevas Galerías (then under construction), Sears's new store featured an unprecedented four-hundred-car underground parking garage, suggesting that the choice of location was influenced by the same American automotive culture and expectations of a largely motorized clientele that later shaped the Zabálburu project.[111]

This foreignness extended to the store's products. Though roughly 80 percent of them were manufactured domestically per standard Sears's policy, these were also items that were not commonly stocked in Spain, such as unusually large spring mattresses and dress shirts that came in different sleeve lengths. Indeed, the chain reportedly faced considerable trouble securing contracts with local manufacturers, who were skeptical about these products' salability.[112] Appliances like refrigerators and washing machines—mainstays of Sears's business— were similarly a novelty for many Spaniards, who associated such items, as well as the futuristic diet of frozen foods that the refrigerator and Spain's proliferating supermarkets made possible, with notions of a Spanish rise to a specifically foreign modernity.[113] Even the way customers bought these products—using Sears's own charge card system—was different. While store credit was hardly new in Spain, the novelty of Sears's system was such that the store had to distribute 20,000 Sears Cards prior to the Calvo Sotelo store's opening.[114] One year later, this credit system remained foreign enough to even the store's own workers that *Noti-Sears* printed a comic strip explaining how the service functioned, and moreover did so in such inexpertly undiplomatic terms, painting customers as defaulting cheats, that store officials took exception to it.[115]

Sears de España made several other such missteps as it worked to import foreign consumer ways. Some arose from the fact that, notwithstanding the store's commitment to local employment, the Spanish corporation's leadership was from the start mostly American. The resulting lack of local knowledge showed when the retailer decided in 1967 to build brand recognition by selling its products in

Spain under a single Sears label rather than using traditional brands like Kenmore. Management failed to note that, in Spanish, "Sears" sounded almost exactly like SEAT, which ignited a dispute that only ended after the store agreed to add "Roebuck" to the branding on its automotive products.[116] More seriously, the chain may have had trouble attracting patrons. On the one hand, Sears garnered praise from Madrid city councilman Ezequiel Puig Maestro-Amado on at least one occasion for having revitalized commerce in peripheral and semi-peripheral districts like the Salamanca neighborhood that adjoined Sears-Madrid. Not only had the store granted local residents access to a fully stocked department store without having to travel to the city center, he asserted, but it also encouraged commercial activity indirectly by promoting greater patronage of other area businesses. Notwithstanding, historian Pilar Toboso has argued that Sears de España ultimately folded because it never quite caught on with customers.[117]

Yet, as Maestro-Amado's testimony suggests, Sears's tenure in Spain from 1964 to 1982 was no mere footnote. Particularly in its last years—the years of resurgent sociopolitical dissidence, Franco's death, and the transition to democracy—the store reflected and contributed to the same social shifts that were then destabilizing Galerías Preciados's totalizing work culture and that formed part of Spain's larger transition to a postauthoritarian society. In 1972, Sears built its own "Youth Boutique" to match the youth sections at Galerías Preciados and El Corte Inglés, further fueling youth fashion's and unisex's spread and the undermining of Francoist patriarchy.[118] The store's introduction of a special credit card for young adults between the ages of eighteen and twenty-five underscored how seriously Sears took Spanish youths' growing economic as well as social impact. And, the year before, *Noti-Sears* profiled the daring new women's fashion of pairing shorts with long coats left open to display one's legs, declaring, in seeming challenge to the moralism of National-Catholic authorities like Cardinals Pla y Deniel and Segura: "No one was confused, no one smiled, no one was scandalized. Civilization continues advancing. Because civilization comes from sociability, affability, courtesy . . . and all of that without the need for the intervention of a group of pedagogues."[119] Meanwhile, as Francoism collapsed and a climate of political, social, and, in particular, sexual liberation advanced—famously, in the embrace of toplessness known as the Destape (top removal)—Sears workers acted through their employer's institutional structures in ways that let them participate in and reproduce the changes that Spanish society as a whole was experiencing.[120] In 1977–1978, for example, Sears cartoonist José García peppered *Noti-Sears* with cartoons that reveled in raunchy humor unusual in a store bulletin. One such strip, set at a nudist beach, showed a group of naked women haranguing an "immoral" passerby for "shameless[ly]" daring to dress in immaculate formalwear, a charivariesque inversion of the Franco-era prudery that Destape filmmakers were similarly overturning. Another instead condemned Spanish police's violent response to protests, showing them chasing down innocent cherubs guilty only of wishing for peace at Christmastime (see figs. 19 and 20).[121] Shortly thereafter, in 1978 and 1979, Sears department heads Jaime Marbá and Jorge López declared their support for sexual freedom, including free access to pornography, abortion, and divorce.[122] And in 1976, secretary María Presentación González Honrado had given more subtle evidence of how changing gender norms had penetrated Sears's ranks when she proclaimed herself, "married but by the Grace of God childless," and, after stating that she would not mind a promotion if it did not hurt her marriage, added the aside, "Spanish Husband" to explain her spouse's chauvinism.[123]

The 1960s and 1970s witnessed Spain's economic boom, the Franco Regime's decline, and the first years of the nation's transition to democracy. They also saw the consummation of the internationally oriented expansion of retail commerce and the development of a new mass consumer society that had tentatively begun in Spain during

FIG. 19. *Noti-Sears* cartoon, "Nudist Beach." *Noti-Sears*, no. 37, Year VI (March–April 1977), n.p. Galeries Preciados Collection, ARCM.

the 1950s, with the grocery and advertising professions at the front line of these changes during the early 1960s.

During the 1940s and 1950s, new department stores like Galerías Preciados had established conduits by which professional knowledge and new notions of Western Europe–centric Spanish national identity gained traction in Spain. Fueled by the same concern that moved Spain's admen, grocers, and their regime liaisons to look beyond the Pyrenees, Spain's department stores turned even more fully abroad. As they spread across Spain, these retailers built store branches filled with foreign innovations like underground parking garages. Like SPAR supermarkets' sleek façades, these garages transformed the Spanish urban landscape along European and American lines, particularly in dialogue with an American culture of automobility contemporaneously on the rise in Spain. Through initiatives like foreign product exhibitions that turned shop floors into temporary

FIG. 20. *Noti-Sears* cartoon, "Christmas 1976." *Noti-Sears*, no. 35, Year V (November–December 1976), n.p. Galerías Preciados Collection, ARCM.

international spaces and employee exchanges with sister stores abroad, they courted world-class cosmopolitan reputations. And, when this very same expansion as well as rising social tensions that marked Francoist Spain's 1960s and 1970s threatened these retailers' institutional cultures, they responded with further initiatives like store tourism programs and soccer clubs meant to shore up cohesion and loyalty within their ranks.

Finally, as part of a multinational American retailing chain, Sears, Roebuck de España epitomized this influx of American and European commercial influences. Certainly, Spanish stores like Galerías Preciados ran employee exchanges with foreign counterparts, held foreign product exhibitions, and affiliated with the IGDS. Sears de España, however, was actually part of a foreign chain, one that shuttled managers between its American and Spanish branches; trained all of its hires in Spain in highly standardized American commercial methods; and filled its inventory with products that were so alien that local manufacturers balked, but which also promised an equally foreign modernity. In so doing, the store fostered personal connections between employees across its multinational network, and, across the shop counter, introduced its Spanish clientele to foreign consumer mores. In both cases, this highlighted Spain's growing connection to a broader international community, and, at Sears specifically, underscored that there was not a Spanish Sears and an American Sears, but a single "Great Sears Family," of which both divisions were members.

More generally, these changes further eroded Francoism's already beset foundational discourse of Spanish national difference, which had set Spain—supposed bastion of the West's core Christian values— above Western Europe's parliamentary-liberal decadence. By courting foreign investment and products, as well as pursuing Spanish integration into Europe, these stores, magazines, and their patrons turned that earlier discourse on its head. Increasingly, they looked abroad for sociocultural guidance rather than expecting the reverse, and emphasized the commonalities between rather than the differences separating Spain and its American and European trading partners. Thus, *Señor* boasted as early as 1961, "fashion being a font of progress, nothing stands in the way of believing in the imminence of a great Federal Europe of which Charlemagne first dreamed," suggesting a future political as well as social convergence of Spain with Europe.[124] Indeed, inasmuch as a discourse of exceptionalism retained currency, it boasted not so much of national difference (save culturally, and to tourists) but rather of Spain's precocious rise to a European professional and living standard, as in advertisements for the Zabálburu shopping center that listed Bilbao among Europe's commercial capitals.

More broadly, this shift to an other-centered system of references and embrace of foreign lifestyles undermined the integrity of the late Franco regime's sociopolitical project. As ordinary Spaniards increasingly consumed like their European neighbors, this threw the regime's political exceptionality into the kind of harsh relief evidenced in José García's 1976 comic strip. And that in turn drove forward what Walter Bernecker has described as a shift in Spanish mentalities toward support for democratization, sounding the death knell for Francoist domination of Spanish society.[125]

Epilogue

In 1980, Spaniards who tuned in to the radio were likely to be greeted by the heavily distorted opening riff to "Enamorado de la Moda Juvenil" (In love with youth fashion), the first hit song by Radio Futura, one of the leading bands participating in the early 1980s Spanish countercultural movement known as La Movida.[1] Forty years before, Pepín Fernández had ordered Sederías Carretas's storefront decorated in honor of Generalissimo Franco, whose newly established dictatorship soon distinguished itself by its embrace of an exceptionalist Spanish nationalism, its legal imposition of conservative Catholic morality on the populace, and, relatedly, a socially imposed reverence for adult paternal authority that found maximum expression in the person of Franco himself as paterfamilias of the Spanish people. Now, by contrast, the Paris-educated brothers Luis and Santiago Auserón, Radio Futura's frontmen, sang of a revelation they had as they walked through the Puerta del Sol in Madrid and witnessed the self-assured air with which the city's youth circulated across the plaza:

I fell
In love with youth fashion
With the prices and sales that I saw . . .
With the guys, with the girls, with the models
In love with you . . .[2]

Radio Futura's lyrics crystallized the radical sociopolitical changes that Spain experienced during the four decades separating Pepín's 1939 decree from the band's countercultural moment. In the song's bridge section, for instance, the Auserón brothers seemingly proposition the listener, hinting at and celebrating casual afternoon sex, as they belt:

New shoes (they're for special occasions!)
Oh, what a tie! (What pants!)
Come on, take off your belt
And the afternoon's for the two of us . . .

This was a far cry from the prudery of the Franco era. It also illustrated
how thoroughly the growth of a Spanish mass consumer society under
Francoism was implicated in these shifts. As the Auserón brothers
belt the song's chorus ("I fell in love . . ."), they make clear just whose
fashions, prices, sales, and models so captivate them. The scene they
describe takes place in the Puerta del Sol, home to El Corte Inglés's
massive white flagship branch and within eyeshot of both Galerías-
Callao and Nuevas Galerías. This scene was only possible because of
the wave of department store expansions that launched these and
myriad other branches throughout Spain from the 1940s onward, as
well as the mid-century development of the Spanish mass consumer
society in which Radio Futura's parade of consuming urban youth
participated.

As this book's first chapter shows, Galerías Preciados and El Corte
Inglés, along with Almacenes Botas, Jorba, Siro Gay, and other smaller
retailers began to expand as of the late 1940s, even as Franco's Spain
remained mired in postwar food and goods shortages, rationing, and
a diplomatic isolation that compounded these problems. These stores
built new branches in Spain and Spanish Morocco. Galerías and El
Corte Inglés both developed domestic manufacturing divisions to
supplement the inventory they were able to secure through postwar
Spain's rationing system. And—though unmentioned in Radio Futura's radio hit—all of these retailers constructed the workplace cultures
through which their employees experienced the initial emergence of
a Spanish mass consumer society during the 1950s.

At Galerías and El Corte Inglés, these institutional cultures were
all-encompassing, featuring employee codes of conduct and welfare
work initiatives that sought to colonize every aspect of employees'

lives. This, on the one hand, functioned as part of the early Franco regime's efforts to assert control over Spaniards' daily lives through proxies such as Spanish Catholic moral authorities, a style of governance that one Civil War–era thinker termed "subjective totalitarianism."[3] On the other hand, this paternalism was also a legacy of El Encanto, early twentieth-century Havana's premier department store. It was there that Pepín Fernández and Ramón Areces had learned their trade during the 1910s and 1920s, and both men retained its controlling management style upon launching their own department stores in 1930s Madrid.

These stores' early adoption of foreign commercial methods— management methods, in this instance—hinted at the foreign character that Spain's developing mass consumer society would acquire as it began to take shape in the 1950s. Initially, this shape was insubstantial and imaginary. Chapter 2 of this volume reveals how, just as department stores like Galerías Preciados and Almacenes Siro Gay began to spread across Spain, so did a flood of newly launched consumer periodicals like the women's magazine *Mujer* and the men's journal *Señor*. These publications, which increasingly courted a cross-class audience, invited readers to imagine themselves inhabiting a society in which all could freely consume products such as automobiles, home appliances that promised convenience and modernity, and the latest fashions. They sold, in other words, an imagined and aspirational Spanish mass consumer society, oriented strongly around foreign products, consumer notions, and commercial methods. Galerías Preciados embraced not just El Encanto's management methods but also foreign sales techniques, and the fashions that Spain's magazines promoted were those of Paris, London, and Hollywood.

Radio Futura's youth fashion arrived from just such foreign fashion capitals, particularly London, during the 1960s. As the Spanish economic "miracle" of 1959–1973 unfolded, foreign products and advertising flowed into Spain to an unprecedented degree, Spaniards' buying power rose, and the nation's formerly imagined mass consumer society became a material reality. Early 1960s Spain's new foreign-inspired supermarkets contributed notably to this influx as they quickly spread across the country and placed small-town as well as urban housewives in daily contact with new, modernity-laden frozen foods and ways of grocery shopping. These methods were just as novel and foreign to the Spanish grocers who adopted them, particularly those who did so as new members of the handful of foreign self-service grocery chains that rapidly came to dominate food retailing in Spain. Both newly arrived foreign chains like the Dutch grocer SPAR, as well as a Spanish government agency, the Comisaría de Abastecimientos y Transportes (CAT), worked to disseminate such foreign techniques and so professionalize Spanish food retailing along foreign lines. They did so in the belief that this was the key to Spain's future prosperity. And, in so doing, they echoed similar professionalizing efforts that Spain's department stores had made during the 1950s.

Meanwhile, the Spanish advertising trade had also begun to professionalize. Innovating Spanish admen like public relations pioneer Joaquín Maestre and trailblazing agencies like Publicidad Ruescas embraced foreign methods and pursued affiliations with international trade organizations. Sometimes, as at Ruescas, they established partnerships or even merged outright with multinational agencies like McCann-Erickson. In tandem with the regime's Ministry of Information and Tourism, Spanish ad executives gave their trade the trappings of a true profession—technical schools, credentialing programs, and a legal charter that established it as a profession— always looking abroad for guidance, just as Spain's grocers and the CAT did. And, as foreign cultural influences flowed into Spain during the countercultural 1960s, these advertising professionals integrated these cultural imports into their ads and commercials.

Among the nation's admen, grocers, and thousands of ordinary consumers, these changes together advanced a new perception of Spain as properly part of Europe rather than separate, unique, and exceptional as early Francoist discourse had proclaimed it. Membership in multinational chains like the SPAR network of grocery stores and international organizations like IPRA accustomed Spanish grocers and admen to thinking of their counterparts abroad as professional colleagues rather than foreigners, and to considering Spain simply one more nation among the many linked by these groups. In Spain's new SPAR supermarkets, local housewives had daily encounters with new foreign products and ways of shopping that underscored their nation's growing integration into Western Europe and assimilation of other European societies' patterns of daily life. This new hybrid identity found expression in media such as a famous television commercial that Spain's Publidis agency created in 1965 for Dutch appliance maker Philips, in which Spanish singer and actress Carmen Sevilla declared herself a "*flamenca yé-yé*," while literally singing the brand's praises.[4] In so doing, she performed just such a composite identity, one that fused traditional Spanish cultural elements like flamenco-inspired melodies and guitar flourishes with references to the hip popular culture of the British Invasion. These included the figure of the young, cosmopolitan, and stylish *yé-yé* who embraced this new pop culture—whose moniker itself referenced the shouts of "yeah, yeah" typical of bands like The Beatles—as well as a backing soundtrack stylistically in line with the era's rock and roll.[5]

Meanwhile, it is telling that Radio Futura's song was about youth fashion. During the 1960s and early 1970s a series of important shifts in Spanish beliefs and practices, including the emergence of new alternatives to Francoism's conservative gender norms, unfolded with special force in the youth culture and fashions that were among the period's most symbolically powerful and subversive imports. Those fashions, as this book's penultimate and final chapters show, arrived partly via Spain's department stores. These stores added new branches still more quickly than in the 1950s and contributed to the Europeanization of Spanish life through measures like foreign employee exchanges, which they embraced in pursuit of cosmopolitan reputations. In the aisles of new "youth" departments selling unisex garments that deemphasized the gender differences that had been central to National-Catholicism's moralistic ordering of society, Spanish adolescents could freely mingle with members of the opposite sex. This was a remarkable opportunity in a society that had until recently proscribed such unsupervised interaction, and in which overfamiliarity with men could still taint women with disrepute.[6] Spanish consumers also encountered these fashions in Spain's similarly proliferating consumer magazines, including some, like the avant-garde men's journal *Don*, that offered risqué content that tested the limits of regime censors' conservative sense of sexual propriety.

The lyrics of "Enamorado de la Moda Juvenil" underscore the lasting impact that youth culture, unisex fashion, and their subversion of Francoism's conservative gender norms had in Spain. By 1980, Spain's youth had some cause to walk with an "air of self-assuredness," despite the political and economic uncertainties of the transition era and the country's growing number of *pasotas*—disillusioned young Spaniards who "passed" on any kind of political involvement or social engagement.[7] They and the youth culture that first emerged in Spain during the 1960s had become socially and culturally significant. Now, they influenced the fashions their elders wore. Spain's youth continued to grow in number and economic importance over the course of the 1970s, so much so that Spanish-American department store chain Sears, Roebuck de España sought to capitalize on this demographic shift by launching a special "youth" credit card. And with all of this youth culture had come a rejection of Francoist prudery that, as noted previously, found expression in Radio Futura's proposition, "come on take off your belt, and the afternoon's for the two of us." In this, Radio Futura echoed both the Destape and late 1970s "S-rated" Spanish soft-core pornographic films, which historian Daniel Kowalsky has argued performed Spain's emergence from Francoism through allegories of young protagonists' sexual liberation.[8]

These many and broadly disseminated claims—that Spain had fully integrated into postwar Western European culture and society, and that the new, youth-oriented, and socially progressive popular culture of the 1960s and 1970s offered a way forward for Spanish society—were politically charged statements. And, again, this book takes the development of a Spanish mass consumer society seriously as a politically as well as socially and culturally transformative event. Officials within the Franco regime and prominent supporters like Pepín Fernández politicized consumption and retail commerce from the dictatorship's earliest years. During the Spanish Civil War, *Mujer* ran columns that promoted the Francoist camp's preferred conservative model of femininity—the very purpose of the magazine's founding—as well as the social work of the Falange's women's organizations. In the 1940s and 1950s, Galerías Preciados became an extension of National-Catholic efforts to control ordinary Spaniards' private lives and morality, while Pepín Fernández himself collaborated directly with the regime in its work to parlay Spain's cultural legacies in Latin America into economic ties, and new politically tied consumer magazines like *Medina* continued to disseminate Francoist notions of femininity. Finally, in the 1960s, the Franco regime spearheaded the introduction of the supermarket to Spain and collaborated closely with the Spanish advertising industry in its professionalization, in both cases with the political goal of raising Spanish prestige abroad, and with it the regime's own international reputation.

Ultimately, however, the foreign-oriented mass consumer society that developed under the Franco regime played a profound role in undermining the Franco dictatorship's sociopolitical project. This was a longer-term and more gradual social and cultural transition to a democratic Spanish society that scholars have also found in the activities of Spanish civic associations and in the influence of foreign tourism to Spain, and which created a context conducive to political democratization.[9] During the late 1960s and 1970s, for instance, American multinational retailing giant Sears, Roebuck operated a chain of store branches and satellite outlets that epitomized both the cosmopolitanism to which local chains like Galerías Preciados aspired and their integration of Spain into international commercial and consumer networks. Sears's multinational network of national corporations across the Americas, in Spain, and, as of the early 1970s, in Belgium, itself represented such a set of relationships. This was an international network, moreover, that intersected with others into which Spain had ventured, for, in 1965, Sears de España was a client of the Ruescas-McCann-Erickson ad agency, the product of the Ruescas ad agency's recent merger with McCann-Erickson.[10]

Importantly, not the rise of mass consumption nor the spread of department stores, nor the coming of the supermarket, nor even subversive foreign fashions like unisex directly brought about Spain's political transition to democracy. Indeed, it would be dangerous to simply equate modernization with liberalization in Spain, for, again, consumption under Franco was at its core politically neutral, available to CAT officials seeking to improve the regime's image by raising Spanish living standards even as *Don* and its contemporaries began to test MIT censors' prudish sensibilities. Scholarship on the development of mass consumption in other illiberal twentieth-century settings has underlined that the interactions between emerging mass consumer cultures and authoritarian regimes have often been complex and ambiguous rather than simply conflicting. Sometimes, as in the case of Coca-Cola in Nazi Germany or mass-produced plastic consumer goods in socialist East Germany (at first glance, a monument to the hated capitalist foe's innovative modernity), newly arrived foreign products ostensibly laden with counterhegemonic social and cultural potential could, when properly repurposed by authorities, instead reproduce official biopolitical or Marxist ideologies.[11] The Franco regime was no different. And yet, even as the CAT and MIT further integrated Spain into European professional and consumer life by introducing foreign-style supermarkets and professionalizing the ad industry in ways that similarly took cues from abroad—measures that in some ways strengthened the regime, as they were meant to—this nevertheless also helped subvert Francoism's own discourse of Spanish national difference.

The causes of the transition to democracy, then, were multiple and contingent—as were the factors underpinning the development of a mass consumer society in Spain. As historians Pablo Martín Aceña and Elena Martínez Ruiz have noted, Spain's mass consumer revolution would not have been possible had the European and world economies not then experienced an "extremely expansionary phase," on which Spanish economic progress relied.[12] The Spanish tourist industry (and thus, the Spanish economy) in particular depended on this foreign prosperity. By 1973 Spain was receiving more than thirty-one million foreign tourists annually, generating $3 billion in revenues, or more than three-quarters of its total foreign trade deficit.[13] Meanwhile, other narratives focused on activities of civil associations, trade unionism, the clandestine political opposition, and the high-political machinations of Prince (later King) Juan Carlos account more directly for the political contours of Spain's process of democratization in the late 1970s.[14]

Together, these many explanatory threads make up what Pamela Radcliff has recently described as a multicausal model for the Spanish transition to democracy,[15] to which this book contributes its own analysis of how the development of mass consumption under Franco helped drive social, and to a more limited degree political, democratization in Spain. In his study of the Franco-era tourist industry, Sasha Pack has shown that tourism-mediated cross-cultural contacts fostered a Europeanization of Spanish identity that generated a will to democratize within the Spanish populace.[16] This book goes further, showing how the Europeanization of Spanish mores and national self-perception, as well as Spaniards' development of a democratizing will, unfolded on a daily and constant basis. Myriad MIT and CAT policy decisions drove this process forward, as did *SPARCO*'s monthly didactic efforts, and SAE de RP morning meetings in which Maestre's team organized the 1966 IPRA meeting.[17] Spanish Europeanization was fueled by the quotidian acts of shopping—for food, or, less frequently, for clothes and other noncomestibles—and reading magazines, which placed Spanish consumers and salespersons into daily contact with foreign products and commercial methods that underscored for them Spain's growing integration into Western European society. Finally, as Spanish shoppers, retailers, and officials increasingly measured Spain's national progress by European standards, perceptions of a continued Spanish backwardness in fashion and retailing further fueled the nation's consumption-driven push to achieve a European modernity. And this, as Pack has noted, was a goal that ultimately implied democratization. Indeed, as scholar Laura Desfor Edles has observed, an "obsession" with obtaining foreign validation survived through Spain's transition to democracy and influenced the politicians who shaped it.[18]

In fact, at certain points the processes described in this book underpinned the transformations that Pack has found in tourism. Stores like Galerías Preciados served countless tourists—customers whose business was central to that retailer's claims to world-class status—and during Galerías's heyday, its grand flagship store was itself a spectacle for tourists like Spain's "Tourist Number 15,000,000," Mr. Tsegaye Aga of Ethiopia, who visited the branch in 1966.[19] Meanwhile, as they grew and professionalized their trade, Spain's admen promoted and sought to advertise not just products but also the Spanish tourism industry. Thus, in 1965, Maestre's SAE de RP weighed ideas to promote tourist visits to the beach resort town of Playa de Aro, and, in another instance, submitted a pitch to Manuel Fraga's MIT for a public relations campaign promoting tourism to Catalonia's Costa Brava. In this proposal, moreover, Maestre argued that foreign tourism was in a way consumption by another name, inasmuch as sales to tourists were a kind of "export without displacement," by which Spanish goods could reach foreign markets without having to cross borders.[20]

The impact of boom-era Spain's influx of foreign and especially American consumerism was ultimately so great that, beginning in the late 1960s, it provoked a local backlash, much as Richard Kuisel and other scholars have shown was happening elsewhere in Europe.[21]

This backlash focused its concern on rising U.S. economic influence worldwide and the social dysfunctions that unfettered consumerism had begun to foster in Spain. Thus, in 1966 the Catholic charity Caritas Española founded a sociological institute, FOESSA, to study the social effects of the Spanish boom. And, during the next decade, critics like Francisco García Ruescas and dissident journalist Manuel Vázquez Montalbán condemned American investment in Spain as a form of socioeconomic imperialism, accusing the United States of reducing Europe to an economic colony.[22] Indeed, initiatives like Sears, Roebuck's spread to Mexico in the 1940s and the Rockefeller-funded introduction of the supermarket to Italy in the 1950s had formed part of a Cold War "consumer diplomacy" that sought to combat communism by exporting capitalist consumerism, an impulse that Sears de España similarly evidenced when it greeted the Spanish transition with a special *Noti-Sears* column extolling the virtues of the democratic free market.[23] With that said, Sears's Spanish employees could still figure among American cultural imperialism's critics. *Noti-Sears* cartoonist José García, for instance, crystallized local concern over Americanization in a 1979 cartoon in which Spain's traditional Christmastime gift givers, the Three Kings, face off in a Western-style showdown against American consumerism's avatar, Santa Claus, who warns them of the fate that awaits all who resist his advance: "sleep[ing] forgotten in oblivion's darkness" (see fig. 21).

Ironically, the social, economic, and political upheavals that began shaking the foundations of Spain's current democratic polity beginning in the mid-2000s have underscored important flaws in the Spanish transition's nevertheless significant reforms.[24] Over time, it has likewise become clear that some of the same commercial agents of Americanization that in the late 1970s threatened to consign Spanish mores to oblivion simultaneously helped preserve Franco-era power structures in the retailing sector. The transition itself, as noted in this book's introduction and argued especially by historian Cristina Palomares, hinged significantly on carefully limited reformist efforts

FIG. 21. *Noti-Sears* cartoon, "Santa and the Magi at High Noon." José García, [Untitled Cartoon], *Noti-Sears*, no. 50, Year VIII (December 1979), n.p. Galerías Preciados Collection, ARCM.

by moderate Francoist elites seeking their own political survival.[25] Likewise, the late Franco era's rapidly spreading consumerism could at once undermine Francoist social doctrine and contribute to what Tatjana Pavlovic has called "a mood of acceptance that carried over to today's arguably apolitical democracy and a postmodern blend of amnesty and social amnesia gelled in the 'pact of oblivion' (pacto de olvido)."[26] Moreover, this official "disremembering" of Francoism, which lies at the heart of ongoing and recently intensified struggles over how to grapple with the regime's past crimes and modern legacies, was by no means universal. Recent scholarship has underscored the extent to which a need to deal with Francoism's long shadow, whether this meant passing progressive legislation that burnished Spain's postdictatorial credentials or denouncing the transition's unfulfilled promises of true progress, pervaded political conversations on women's rights and gender equality as the democratic era dawned.[27] Yet this period also saw several socially and politically radical subcultures and practices, including the performative nudity of Destape-era cinema, and the queer identities defiantly showcased in director Pedro Almodóvar's earliest films gradually become commodified and their radicalism tempered.[28]

Similarly, while Spain's social and political landscape changed, the workplace conditions experienced by thousands of workers at Spain's leading retailers both did and did not—in many ways, disaffected workers' margin for action expanded greatly, but, in others, the change was more of outward form than substance. Labor advocacy had been a risky affair under Franco, when unionizing and strikes had been illegal and violently suppressed when organized in secret—indeed, at Galerías Preciados and El Corte Inglés, aggrieved workers had during the 1960s and early 1970s turned instead to the Ministry of Labor's official arbitration courts for redress, repeatedly filing suits in the early 1970s, for instance, for wrongful termination.[29] And, to be sure, under the new democratic order these stores' employees could affiliate with powerful national syndicates like Comisiones Obreras (CC.OO.) as staff at El Corte Inglés did in 1977. Yet management at both retailers still worked to suppress such collective action, including through newly founded puppet, or "yellow," store employee unions, whose efforts to tie up proposed measures in endless intersyndical committee deliberations, for example, were a subject of bitter complaint at the first annual meeting of El Corte Inglés's CC.OO. chapter in 1980.[30] On issues of gender equality, too, these stores could and did retain a misogynistic streak reminiscent of Franco-era views and practices: tellingly, as of this writing, El Corte Inglés appears to still follow a gendered policy of dressing many of its saleswomen in store uniforms while merely requiring men to wear (presumably store-bought) suits, and only introduced pants as a uniform option as recently as 2007.[31] More insidiously, leading Spanish retailers' sus-

tained efforts to leverage existing labor regulations have dispropor-
tionately penalized women, as stores, including El Corte Inglés, have
used morning shifts, which working mothers need in order to have
afternoons free for childcare, as leverage to compel them to accept
lower pay or unwanted weekend hours.[32]

El Corte Inglés might act thusly, but, after a time, Galerías could
not: though still remembered by many, oblivion was by contrast
the fate that ultimately awaited the department store that had most
visibly championed late Franco-era Spain's push to integrate into
commercial and consumer Europe. In mid-1995, Galerías was bought
out by its primary competitor, El Corte Inglés, which over the course
of the 1980s had become not just Spain's premier department store,
but the nation's third-largest private company of any kind.[33] This
buyout ended a long process of decline that had begun fifteen years
before, when Pepín Fernández's family had lost control of the store
to its creditors, and which had been brewing since the early 1970s.[34]

The primary cause of the once-mighty retailer's decline was debt.
During the 1940s, 1950s, and much of the 1960s, Galerías had enjoyed
undisputed leadership in the Spanish retail sector. However, Fidel
Castro's Cuban Revolution did more than flood Pepín's payroll
with Cuban exiles; it also brought Cesar Rodríguez back to Spain
in 1960, and with him the fortune he had made decades earlier at El
Encanto, which he subsequently poured into his nephew Ramón
Areces's store.[35] This sudden and dramatic influx of funds fueled
El Corte Inglés's rapid expansion during the Spanish boom, which
yielded new branches in cities like Barcelona and new divisions like
the highly successful travel agency Viajes El Corte Inglés (Voyages
El Corte Inglés, launched in 1969).[36] But it also drove Pepín Fernández to match this growth with store openings of his own—Jorba-
Preciados, for instance—which he financed largely on credit just as
Galerías began to lose market share to El Corte Inglés, whose new
branches were as a rule larger and dealt in more expensive, better-
quality merchandise.[37]

This combination of plummeting business and rising debt worsened once the Spanish economy went into recession in 1973–1974, and after Galerías posted net losses of more than 280,000 ptas in 1978, its principal creditor, Urquijo Bank (*Banco Urquijo*), quickly took over the store's board of directors, beginning with Pepín Fernández's own forced retirement that year. Over the next three years, Urquijo's men managed to balance the store's books, but at the cost of a reduced payroll, inventory, and ability to compete commercially, ending with the store's 1981 sale to RUMASA—the same corporation that one year later bought Sears de España.[38] Thus started the increasingly insolvent store's fifteen-year decline, during which it passed through the hands of various Spanish and foreign investors before its eventual purchase by El Corte Inglés.[39]

In the end, Pepín's store failed to outlast the dictatorship with which its founder had cultivated such close ties, but whose demise Galerías, El Corte Inglés, Almacenes Botas, and other Spanish department stores had helped bring about through their work to develop a foreign-oriented Spanish mass consumer society. Yet these stores did not do this work alone. If such department stores have sometimes been termed "cathedrals of consumption"—Geoffrey Crossick and Serve Jaumain's edited volume on Europe's department stores even taking this phrase as its title—then supermarkets were Spain's parish churches of international consumer modernity. As churches do for the devout, these grocery stores served as visible beacons of virtue—in this instance, the virtue of modernity rather than divine grace—both through the textual claims they issued and as physical symbols of those claims. SPAR knew this: part of a new SPARista's expected work in converting his store to the SPAR way was to festoon it, in predetermined, highly studied ways, with myriad company-issued signs identifying the store as a member of the SPAR network. SPAR and the supermarket more generally had a visual identity with powerful associated meanings: modernity, prosperity, convenience, efficiency, and the future, all of an international character. So too,

Galerías Preciados, El Corte Inglés, Sears, Roebuck de España, and Spain's other modern foreign-influenced department stores stood for a new future for Spain, the future that was "already here," one in which the "great" in "One, Great, and Free" might not mean imperial greatness, but the greatness of economic vibrancy and the prestige of First-World status.

To conclude, while these contributions to the sociopolitical transformation of Spain had tangible dimensions in the form of commercial structures—literal as well as figurative—political decisions, and consumer products, it unfolded most of all in discourse and the meanings encoded in these structures. The processes described above are, ultimately, as or more discursive in nature as they are structural. Galerías Preciados adopted its *Boletín* from Macy's, and sent its clerks to Selfridges; SPAR introduced Spanish housewives to a new way of buying, and the concept of the store brand; and, certainly, buying an appliance from Sears was something much more typical of Virginia than the Madrid neighborhood of Vallecas. But more important was what these enterprises and the consumers they served stated and believed about these measures, themselves, and Spain's place in the world.

NOTES

Abbreviations

AGA-CAT   Archivo General de la Administración (Alcalá de Henares, Spain), Comisaría de Abastecimientos y Transportes Documentation

AGA-MIT   Archivo General de la Administración (Alcalá de Henares, Spain), Ministry of Information and Tourism Records

AGUN-GMM   Archivo General de la Universidad de Navarra (Pamplona, Spain), Gregorio Marañón Moya Personal Papers

AGUN-JMM   Archivo General de la Universidad de Navarra (Pamplona, Spain), Joaquín Maestre Morata Personal Papers

AHT-AS   Archivo de la Historia del Trabajo, Fundación 10 de Mayo–CC.OO (Madrid, Spain), Almeida-Salorio Law Offices Archive Collection

AHT-GP   Archivo de la Historia del Trabajo, Fundación 10 de Mayo–CC.OO (Madrid, Spain), Galerías Preciados Collection

ARCM   Archivo Regional de la Comunidad de Madrid (Madrid, Spain)

BNC-MFIB   National Library of Catalonia (Barcelona, Spain), María Freixas i Bru Family Budget Books Collection

BNE   Spanish National Library

INE   Instituto Nacional de Estadística

Introduction

1. "Sederías Carretas: El comercio, servicio público," *A.B.C.*, 4 October 1934; "Una nueva doctrina y un nuevo estilo en el comercio de Madrid," *A.B.C.*, 21 October 1934; Toboso, *Pepín Fernández*, 122–25; Toboso, *Pepín Fernández (Galerías Preciados), César Rodríguez y Ramón Areces (El Corte Inglés)*, 24–27.

2. For the 1934 strike and the coming of the Spanish Civil War, see Bunk, *Ghosts of Passion*.

3. For a general description of this process of cultural introduction, see Abella, *La vida cotidiana bajo el régimen de Franco*, 174–83.

4. Pack, *Tourism and Dictatorship*; Pack, "Tourism and Political Change in Franco's Spain." For late Franco-era Spanish women's activism, see Nash, *Dones en transició*; Kaplan, "Luchar por la democracia"; and Nielfa Cristóbal, "El debate feminista durante el franquismo." For contemporary feminist tracts, see, for instance, Campmany [*sic*], *Carta Abierta al Macho Ibérico*; and Falcón, *Los dereches civiles de la mujer*.

5. See Toboso, *Pepín Fernández*; Toboso, *Pepín Fernández (Galerías Preciados), César Rodríguez y Ramón Areces (El Corte Inglés)*; Cuartas, *Biografía de El Corte Inglés*; Maixé-Altes, "Interpreting the Early Stages of the Self-Service Revolution in Europe"; Maixé-Altes, "La modernización de la distribución alimentaria en España, 1947–1995"; Grandío and Maixé-Altés, eds., *Vegalsa-Eroski*; and Pavlović, *The Mobile Nation*. By contrast, the historiography of twentieth-century European and American retailing and consumption is extensive. For a small sampling, see de Grazia, *Irresistible Empire*; Oldenziel and Zachmann, *Cold War Kitchen*; Crossick and Jaumain, *Cathedrals of Consumption*; and Strasser, McGovern, and Judt, *Getting and Spending*.

6. For Americanization in postwar Europe, see de Grazia, *Irresistible Empire*; de Grazia, "Changing Consumption Regimes in Europe, 1930–1970"; Kuisel, *Seducing the French*; Poiger, *Jazz, Rock and Rebels*; and Poiger, "A New, 'Western' Hero? Reconstructing German Masculinity in the 1950s."

7. Morcillo, *The Seduction of Modern Spain*, chap. 1. See also Morcillo, *True Catholic Womanhood*; Martín Gaite, *Courtship Customs in Postwar Spain*; Alonso Tejada, *La represión sexual en la España de Franco*; Folguera Crespo, "El Franquismo. El Retorno a la Esfera Privada (1939–1975)"; Nielfa Cristóbal, *Mujeres y Hombres en la España Franquista*; and Benería, *Mujer, economía y patriarcado en la España de Franco*.

8. See Kroes, "Americanisation: What Are We Talking About?"; and Lundin, "Introduction," 1–3.

9. For the somewhat similar case of American consumerism's ideological promiscuity in Eastern Europe, see Nolan, "Negotiating American Modernity in Twentieth-Century Europe," 34–36.

10. For political accounts, see Carr and Fusi Aizpurúa, *Spain: Dictatorship to Democracy*; Preston, *The Triumph of Democracy in Spain*; Maravall, *The Transition to Democracy in Spain*; and Gilmour, *The Transformation*

of Spain. For social and cultural narratives, see Pérez Díaz, *The Return of Civil Society*; Radcliff, *Making Democratic Citizens in Spain*; Pack, *Tourism and Dictatorship*, 14–15. For multicausal approaches, see Radcliff, "La Transición Española: ¿Un Modelo Global?"; and Townson, *Spain Transformed.*

11. Again, scholars have mainly described Franco-era consumption as either apolitical or actively depoliticizing. See Castillo Castillo, *Sociedad de Consumo a la Española*; and Alonso and Conde, *Historia del consumo en España.* Notable exceptions include Pack's *Tourism and Dictatorship*; and Morcillo, *True Catholic Womanhood*, chap. 3.

12. Nigel Townson has suggested, "historians have . . . tended to disregard the social and cultural transformation of the late Franco regime . . . [such that] the 1960s and 1970s have been largely ignored." See Townson, "Introduction," 1. For recent contributions, see especially the work of Pack, Radcliff, Morcillo, and Cazorla Sánchez.

13. See Baudrillard, *Selected Writings*, 21–25.

14. Baudrillard, *Selected Writings*, 19; Debord, *Society of the Spectacle*, 23–25, 34, chap. 2.

15. For the role of credit in promoting consumption, see Morcillo, *True Catholic Womanhood*, 56.

16. For such a comparative Southern European analysis, see Kornetis, Kotsovili, and Papadogiannis, *Gender and Consumption in Southern Europe since the Long 1960s.*

17. Yan, "Of Hamburger and Social Space."

18. For industrial design, urban planning, and social inequality in the Soviet Union, see Reid, "This Is Tomorrow! Becoming a Consumer in the Soviet Sixties"; and Siegelbaum, "Modernity Unbound."

19. Reid, "This Is Tomorrow!"; Siegelbaum, "Modernity Unbound."

20. Yan, "Of Hamburger and Social Space"; Erwin, "Heart-to-Heart, Phone-to-Phone."

21. Gorsuch, *All This Is Your World*, 6–16; Rubin, *Synthetic Socialism.*

22. See chapter 3 of this volume. For a succinct analysis of Michel Foucault's concept of "biopower," see Taylor, "Biopower."

23. Hamilton, "Supermarket USA Confronts State Socialism."

24. For broad analysis of American public—not only consumer—diplomacy to Franco's Spain and the sociopolitical consequences thereof, see Rodríguez

Jiménez, Delgado Gómez-Escalonilla, and Cull, *U.S. Public Diplomacy and Democratization in Spain*.

25. For this model of internal European exchanges, see Lundin, "Introduction."

26. See, for instance, Castillo Castillo, "¿Es España sociedad de consumo de masas?"; Castillo Castillo, *Sociedad de Consumo a la Española*; Alonso and Conde, *Historia del consumo en España*, 80, 86–87, 147–51.

27. Castillo Castillo, *Sociedad de Consumo a la Española*, 54, 101; Ofer, "La Guerra de Agua"; Cazorla Sánchez, *Fear and Progress*, 154.

28. Payne, *The Franco Regime, 1936–1975*, 417–23.

29. See John J. Knezevich to Marquis de Prat de Nantouillet, 20 January 1958, AGUN-GMM, Box/Folder 148/094/001/003; Stanton Griffis to Marquis de Prat de Nantouillet, 14 January 1954, AGUN-GMM 148/094/002; and more in this file.

30. For discussion of American appliances and modernity, see, for instance, de Grazia, *Irresistible Empire*, chap. 9; and Oldenziel and Zachmann, *Cold War Kitchen*.

31. For such popular representation of mass consumption in Spain, see Morcillo, *True Catholic Womanhood*, chap. 3. For the larger European transition from a socially circumscribed bourgeois consumer regime to one in which mass access to consumer products became a universal right, see de Grazia, "Changing Consumption Regimes in Europe, 1930–1970," and Auslander, *Taste and Power*, esp. 20–22, as well as chaps. 1, 7, and epilogue.

32. Serafí del Arco, "El coche que puso a España sobre ruedas," *El País*, 3 June 2007, accessed 17 August 2016, http://elpais.com/diario/2007/06/03/economia /1180821602_850215.html.

33. Crumbaugh, *Destination Dictatorship*; Castillo Castillo, "¿Es España sociedad de consumo de masas?," 7–18; Castillo Castillo, *Sociedad de Consumo a la Española*; Alonso and Conde, *Historia del consumo en España*, 80, 86–87, 147–51.

34. The terms *autoservicio* and "supermarket" were largely interchangeable in early 1960s Spain, and are likewise used interchangeably here. For concise definitions of and the distinctions between *autoservicios* and supermarkets—mainly size—see "Preguntas y respuestas sobre el Autoservicio," *SPARCO: Boletín de Enlace de los Sparistas Españoles* [henceforth, *SPARCO*], no. 9 (November 1960), 6. For the CAT's role in introducing the supermarket to Spain, see Zimmerman, *Los Supermercados*, prologue.

35. See, for instance, Sederías Carretas's store windows in mid-1939, which Pepín ordered decorated with posters, Francoist flags, portraits of the victorious general, and other paraphernalia celebrating his victory and new rule. Toboso, *Pepín Fernández*, 128–30.

36. Linz, "An Authoritarian Regime: The Case of Spain"; and Miley, "Franquism as Authoritarianism: Juan Linz and His Critics." For the Catholic Church's contributions to Francoist authority, see especially Alonso Tejada, *La represión sexual en la España de Franco*, 17–38, 50–61, 72, 101–13; and Callahan, *The Catholic Church in Spain, 1875–1998*.

37. de Grazia, *Irresistible Empire*, 7.

38. Pack, *Tourism and Dictatorship*, 9–10.

39. See Rosendorf, *Franco Sells Spain to America*, esp. chaps. 3 and 6; and also Payne, *The Franco Regime*, 473–74.

40. Indeed, Luis Enrique Alonso and Fernando Conde have noted that Spanish consumer spending in the 1960s rose as incomes did—meaning that Spanish consumers spent rather than saved virtually all of their newfound wealth. See Alonso and Conde, *Historia del consumo en España*, 152–53. For Spain's tourist industry, see Pack, *Tourism and Dictatorship*. For rising Spanish incomes, see Castillo Castillo, "¿Es España sociedad de consumo?," 8; and Fundación FOESSA, *Informe sociológico sobre la situación social de España, 1966*, 82–83, 90.

41. For Maestre and IPRA, see AGUN-JMM, Box/Folder 144/490/001.

42. Crumbaugh, *Destination Dictatorship*; for a more qualified argument, see Cazorla Sánchez, *Fear and Progress*, 150.

43. The term *ye-yé*, which described a participant in 1960s popular youth culture, neatly encapsulated the values of youth (*ye-yés* were typically young), open-mindedness, innovation, and, most especially, rock and roll—indeed, it derived from the "yeah, yeah" exclamations of bands like The Beatles. Otaola González, "La música pop en la España franquista," 6–8.

44. For analysis of European and American youth culture and its rebellious qualities, see Marwick, "Youth Culture and the Cultural Revolution of the Long Sixties"; and, more extensively, Marwick, *The Sixties*. For a brief discussion of youth culture in the Spanish context, see Cazorla Sánchez, *Fear and Progress*, 153–55.

45. Valiente, "An Overview of Research on Gender in Spanish Society," 778–79; and Cabrera, "Developments in Contemporary Spanish Historiography." For such recent work on Franco-era masculinity, see contributions

in Kornetis, Kotsovili, and Papadogiannis, *Gender and Consumption in Southern Europe since the Long 1960s*; and Winchester, "Hombres Normativos: The Creation and Inculcation of Martial Masculinity during the Franco Regime in Spain (1939–1975)." By contrast, the far broader scholarship on consumption and gender includes de Grazia and Furlough, *The Sex of Things: Gender and Consumption in Historical Perspective*; Roberts, "Gender, Consumption, and Commodity Culture"; Shannon, *The Cut of His Coat*; Hollander, *Sex and Suits*; and Breward, *The Hidden Consumer*. On Franco-era femininity, see Muñoz Ruiz, "Mujer Mítica, Mujeres Reales"; and Morcillo, *True Catholic Womanhood*, chap. 3.

46. Cazorla Sánchez, *Fear and Progress*, 145–47; Morcillo, *The Seduction of Modern Spain*, chap. 3.

47. More specifically, this represented a step back from a sartorially conservative, patriarchal status quo comparable to Victorian norms. See Kuchta, "The Making of the Self-Made Man."

48. For sexual liberation during the late 1970s and Francoism's collapse, see Alonso Tejada, *La represión sexual en la España de Franco*, 237–60.

49. For the parallel case of American housewives, see Deutsch, *Building a Housewife's Paradise*.

50. See Seregni, *El Anti-Americanismo Español*, 180–255; García Ruescas, *Problemática de las Inversiones Extranjeras en España*; and Vázquez Montalbán, *La penetración americana en España*. For such fears elsewhere in Europe, see de Grazia, *How Fascism Ruled Women: Italy, 1922–1945*; Kuisel, "Coca-Cola and the Cold War"; and Poiger, "Rock 'n' Roll, Female Sexuality, and the Cold War Battle over German Identities."

51. For the Bon Marché, see Miller, *The Bon Marché*.

52. For the founding of European and American department stores, see Ferry, *A History of the Department Store*; Pasdermadjian, *The Department Store*, chaps. 1–3; and Leach, *Land of Desire*.

53. Zola, *The Ladies' Paradise*, 4–7, 16, 48.

54. Cruz, *The Rise of Middle-Class Culture in Nineteenth-Century Spain*, 126–30; Toboso, *Pepín Fernández*, 35–36; de Sena, "Un Hombre de la Plaza Mayor"; M. P. B., "Por Tierras de Asturias—La Predilección de Ellas y Ellos en lo Magno de Oviedo," *A.B.C.*, 16 September 1945; and, for Almacenes Jorba, see Cabana, *Cien Empresarios Catalanes*, 305–8.

55. Cuartas, *Biografía de El Corte Inglés*, 94–100; Pasdermadjian, *The Department Store*, 5–6.

56. Cruz, *The Rise of Middle-Class Culture in Nineteenth-Century Spain*, 127–28; for Jorba, see "Almacenes Jorba. Dossieres de Prensa, Recortes de publicidad publicados en el diario La Nacion de Buenos Aires sobre empresas de la competencia entre agosto de 1919 y octubre de 1922," in Galerías Preciados Collection, ARCM, 907552/1.

57. Toboso, *Pepín Fernández*, 100.

58. Toboso, *Pepín Fernández*, 122–25.

59. Cuartas, *Biografía de El Corte Inglés*, 103–10; Toboso, *Pepín Fernández*, 86, 90–91, 118–27, 168–72.

60. del Arco Blanco, "Hunger and the Consolidation of the Francoist Regime (1939–1951)."

61. Castillo Castillo, *Sociedad de Consumo a la Española*, 54; Cazorla Sánchez, *Fear and Progress*, 9–12, 61, 72; Abella, *La vida cotidiana bajo el régimen de Franco*, 52, 122–23.

62. Crespo MacLennan, *Spain and the Process of European Integration, 1957–1985*, 14–20; and Payne, *The Franco Regime*, 355–59, 361, 382–83.

63. Abella, *La vida cotidiana bajo el régimen de Franco*, 26; Cazorla Sánchez, *Fear and Progress*, chap. 1, esp. 8, 30–31; and Eslava Galán, *Los Años del Miedo*.

64. For the Falange, see Payne, *Fascism in Spain, 1923–1977*.

65. For National-Catholicism and the Spanish Catholic Church's relationship with the Franco regime, see Morcillo, *True Catholic Womanhood*, 4, 28; Gómez Pérez, *El Franquismo y la iglesia*; and Callahan, *The Catholic Church in Spain, 1875–1998*, chaps. 3–5.

66. Abella, *La vida cotidiana bajo el régimen de Franco*, 213–14.

67. For women's rights under the Republic, see Payne, *Spain's First Democracy: The Second Republic, 1931–36*, 111, 121, 179. For their loss under the Francoist Labor Charter and Law for Family Subsidies of 1938, see "Fuero del Trabajo de 1938," Biblioteca Virtual Miguel de Cervantes, accessed 20 December 2011, http://bib.cervantesvirtual.com/servlet /SirveObras/08149629022036195209079/p0000001.htm; and Alonso Tejada, *La represión sexual en la España de Franco*, 31. For social pressures, see Martín Gaite, *Courtship Customs in Postwar Spain*, 37–41, 44, 46.

68. For pronatalism, see Mary Nash, "Towards a New Moral Order: National Catholicism, Culture and Gender," 299; and Abella, *La vida cotidiana bajo el régimen de Franco*, 161. For women and Catholicism, see Morcillo, *True Catholic Womanhood*, chap. 1, esp. 36–39, 40–41; Abella, *La vida cotidiana*

bajo el régimen de Franco, 160–61; and Alonso Tejada, *La represión sexual en la España de Franco*, 32–34.

69. Morcillo, *True Catholic Womanhood*, 25–26, 102–3.

70. Hooper, *The New Spaniards*, 108–9, 126; Morcillo, *True Catholic Womanhood*, 33, 36, 40–44, 69; Folguera Crespo, "El Franquismo. El Retorno," 529–31. For another example of Francoist male social privilege, see Puertolas, "Masculinity versus Femininity: The Sanfermines: 1939–1978," 99. For prostitution, see Nicolás Lazo, "La reglamentación de la prostitución en el Estado español," 576–78, 675.

71. Abella, *La vida cotidiana bajo el régimen de Franco*, 216; Folguera Crespo, "El Franquismo. El Retorno," 529, 531.

72. For Segura and Plá y Deniel, see Preston, *The Spanish Civil War*, 45–46, 220.

73. Abella, *La vida cotidiana bajo el régimen de Franco*, 106, 111; Alonso Tejada, *La represión sexual en la España de Franco*.

74. This law also required journalists and publications active in Spain to register with the government, which became the gatekeeper of the press. See Fernández Areal, *La Libertad de Prensa en España, 1938–71*, 35–41.

75. As noted previously, while a minority retained much of this wealth, many more could aspire to its trappings thanks to growing access to credit and a vibrant Spanish consumer media. See also Castillo Castillo, *Sociedad de consumo a la Española*, 54; Castillo Castillo, "¿Es España sociedad de consumo de masas?," 14–16; Alonso and Conde, *Historia del consumo en España*, 132–33; Morcillo, *True Catholic Womanhood*, 51–52, 56–64; Payne, *The Franco Regime*, 416–17, 464–66; Pack, *Tourism and Dictatorship*, 39–40, 43, 48, 51, 64–65, 68–76, 80–82; González, *La Economía Política de Franquismo (1940–1970)*, 39–42; and, for a direct use of tourism as Francoist propaganda, see Holguín, "National Spain Invites You."

76. Morcillo, *True Catholic Womanhood*, 55, 66–70; Cazorla Sánchez, *Fear and Progress*, 84, 422–23; Lieberman, *Growth and Crisis in the Spanish Economy: 1940–93*, 44–46; González, *La Economía Política de Franquismo (1940–1970)*, 55–57.

77. Cazorla Sánchez, *Fear and Progress*, 82–84; Payne, *The Franco Regime*, 441–44, 450–51, 467–72; Lieberman, *Growth and Crisis in the Spanish Economy*, 46; For the boom's origins, see also Lieberman, *Growth and Crisis in the Spanish Economy*, chap. 2, esp. 57–86; Martín Aceña and Martínez Ruiz, "The Golden Age of Spanish Capitalism"; Serrano Sanz and Pardos, "Los años de crecimiento del franquismo (1959–1975)." For tourism, see

Harrison, *An Economic History of Modern Spain*, 156; and Pack, *Tourism and Dictatorship*, chap. 4 and 106–9. For the Development Plans, see Lieberman, *Growth and Crisis in the Spanish Economy*, 62–79, 89–94; Payne, *The Franco Regime*, 472–73; Matés Barco, "La economía durante el franquismo"; and del Campo and Navarro, *Crítica de la planificación social española, 1964–1975*, 1976.

78. For examples of this term's use, see Harrison, "Spanish Economic History"; and Domènech Sampere, "La otra cara del milagro español."

79. González, *La Economía Política de Franquismo (1940–1970)*, 306, 309; Pack, *Tourism and Dictatorship*, 86, 108; Payne, *The Franco Regime*, 478; Tusell, *La Transición Española*, 19.

80. Notably, the loyally Francoist Galerías Preciados made certain to celebrate Eisenhower's visit in its store bulletin. See Payne, *The Franco Regime*, 458–59; and Vara Ayuso, "La simpatia de Ike," *Boletín de Galerías Preciados*, no. 98, year XI (January 1960), 7. For efforts to present the regime in a more appealing light, including Fraga's campaigns, see Crespo MacLennan, *Spain and the Process of European Integration*, 51; Pack, *Tourism and Dictatorship*, 68–72, 140, 149–150; Abella, *La vida cotidiana bajo el régimen de Franco*, 191–193; Payne, *The Franco Regime*, 508; and Crumbaugh, *Destination Dictatorship*, 55. For Spain and the EEC, see Crespo MacLennan, *Spain and the Process of European Integration*, chap. 2; and Crespo MacLennan, *España en Europa, 1945–2000*, 112–25.

81. Abella, *La vida cotidiana bajo el régimen de Franco*, chap. 15; Cazorla Sánchez, *Fear and Progress*, 164–65, 170–72.

82. de Grazia, *Irresistible Empire*, chap. 9; Payne, *The Franco Regime*, 485, 488; Fundación FOESSA, *Informe sociológico sobre la situación social de España, 1966*, 74–80.

83. Seregni, *El Anti-Americanismo Español*, 180–82.

84. Between 1966 and 1971, MIT-imposed sanctions rose tenfold. Fernández Areal, *La Libertad de Prensa en España*, 35–41; "Spain," in *Censorship: A World Encyclopedia*; and Crumbaugh, *Destination Dictatorship*, 51. For more on the 1966 Press Law and its effects, see Alferez, *Cuarto poder en España*.

85. Ofer, "La Guerra de Agua," 223; and Cazorla Sánchez, *Fear and Progress*, 95–96, 115–22, 154–55.

86. In 1966, for example, 72 percent of upper-class households owned a television, while only 29 percent of working-class families did. Fundación FOESSA, *Informe sociológico sobre la situación social de España, 1966*, 74–

86. See also Payne, *The Franco Regime*, 491; Cazorla Sánchez, *Fear and Progress*, 127–32; and Fundación FOESSA, *Efectos sociales queridos y no queridos en el desarrollo español*, 54–56.

87. See Molinero, Tébar, and Ysàs, "Comisiones obreras de Cataluña," 75–88; Ibarra Güell and García Marroquín, "De la primavera de 1956 a Lejona 1978. Comisiones Obreras de Euskadi," 111–19; and Gómez Alén, "Las Comisiones Obreras de Galicia y la oposición al franquismo (1962–1978)," 259–73.

88. For Basque terrorism under Franco, see Woodworth, *Dirty War, Clean Hands*, chap. 2. For a second example, Catalonia's Nova Cançó cultural movement, which championed the persecuted Catalan language, see Aragüez Rubio, "La Nova Cançó catalana." See also Carr and Fusi Aizpurúa, *Spain: Dictatorship to Democracy*, 156–61.

89. For a fuller analysis of the Spanish clergy's criticism of the regime during the 1960s, see Callahan, *The Catholic Church in Spain*, chap. 4.

90. During the recession, for instance, inflation briefly climbed as high as 35 percent (1977), and, in 1978, 250,000 individuals found themselves newly unemployed. Payne, *The Franco Regime*, 491; Lieberman, *Growth and Crisis in the Spanish Economy*, 152, 177, 183.

91. Cazorla Sánchez, *Fear and Progress*, 200–201; Carrillo-Linares, "Movimiento estudiantil antifranquista, cultura política y transición política a la democracia"; Radcliff, *Making Democratic Citizens in Spain*; Callahan, *The Catholic Church in Spain*, 508, chap. 20.

92. Cazorla Sánchez, *Fear and Progress*, 210; Payne, *The Franco Regime*, 557–60, 592–98; Carr and Fusi Aizpurúa, *Spain: Dictatorship to Democracy*, 195–206, chap. 10.

93. Carr and Fusi Aizpurúa, *Spain: Dictatorship to Democracy*, chap. 10; Gilmour, *The Transformation of Spain*, chaps. 8–10.

94. For department stores as a telltale of mass consumption, see Williams, *Dream Worlds: Mass Consumption in Late Nineteenth-Century France*, 3.

95. "Gran . . . Inauguracion de la tienda de Meridiana!," *Noti-Sears*, no. 4, October–December 1975, in Galerías Preciados Collection, ARCM.

1. World-Class Stores and (Inter)national Ambassadors

1. Casares, *Conferencia que el secretario de la Asociacion de la Prensa D. Francisco Casares*, 7.

2. Aurora Morcillo, for example, tracks the effects that spreading notions of a desirable and respectable mass consumer prosperity had on gender norms in 1950s Spain. See Morcillo, *True Catholic Womanhood*, chap. 3.

3. Castillo Castillo, "¿Es España sociedad de consumo de masas?," 15–18; Castillo Castillo, *Sociedad de Consumo a la Española*; and Alonso and Conde, *Historia del consumo en España*, 80, 86–87, 147–51.

4. The one exception was advertising in the conservative monarchist Madrid daily *A.B.C.*, one of Spain's largest newspapers, with which Galerías had negotiated special rates. Toboso, *Pepín Fernández*, 140–41, 152.

5. Toboso, *Pepín Fernández*, 138–39. For the kinds of barriers to consumption that the war posed, see Wiesen, *Creating the Nazi Marketplace*, chap. 5.

6. Toboso, *Pepín Fernández*, 152–54, 448.

7. Alonso and Conde, *Historia del consumo en España*, 132–33; Cazorla Sánchez, *Fear and Progress*, 72; Abella, *La vida cotidiana bajo el régimen de Franco*, 52.

8. See, for instance, the example of Catalan bourgeois housewife Maria Freixas i Bru, who, as is noted in chapter 2 of this work, regularly purchased bolts of cloth during the 1940s from which a seamstress made dresses for her and her daughters. Alonso and Conde have noted that such home production of clothing persisted into the 1960s, preserving the sewing machine's importance among more novel appliances like refrigerators. Alonso and Conde, *Historia del consumo en España*, 177–78.

9. Brenan, *The Face of Spain*, 23. For the black market and Spanish nouveau riche, see Molinero and Ysàs, "Las Condiciones de Vida y Laborales durante el Primer Franquismo," 19–20; Eslava Galán, *Los Años del Miedo*, 96–100.

10. Toboso, *Pepín Fernández*, 143–52.

11. Toboso, *Pepín Fernández*, 152; Zafra Aragón, *Méritos, errores, ilusiones y personajes de Galerías Preciados*, 39.

12. Toboso, *Pepín Fernández*, 143–52; Toboso Sánchez, "Grandes Almacenes y Almacenes Populares en España. Una Visión Histórica"; Zafra Aragón, *Méritos, errores, ilusiones y personajes de Galerías Preciados*, 35; and Payne, *The Franco Regime*, 268.

13. Cuartas, *Biografía de El Corte Inglés*, 244–45, Toboso, *Pepín Fernández*, 177–78.

14. O., "Nuestra Agencia de Tánger: Nuevo local en la calle más céntrica," *Boletín de Sederías Carretas y Galerías Preciados*, no. 46, Year V (undated), 11; Finlayson, *Tangier: City of the Dream*, 8, 10, 17.

15. Cuartas, *Biografía de El Corte Inglés*, 240–43, 245–48; Toboso, *Pepín Fernández*, 178–79, 181. Incorporation allowed El Corte Inglés to expand the range of products it could legally sell to include products like furniture and perfume.

16. "Madrid, Trasunto de España," lxix–lxxi.

17. Galerías Preciados, "Ad—Magnífica ropa de hombre en la gran liquidación final de la Venta Posbalance," *A.B.C.*, 10 February 1956; El Corte Inglés, "Ad—La Piscina Ideal para Jardín o Terraza," *A.B.C.*, 28 June 1956; "Salarios—remuneración íntegra por hora y jornada trabajada, Años 1955 y 1956," INE, accessed 18 October 2018, http://www.ine.es/inebaseweb /pdfDispacher.do?td=169916&ext=.pdf.

18. See de Sena, "Un Hombre de la Plaza Mayor"; "Almacenes Siro Gay y Filiales"; M. P. B., "Por Tierras de Asturias—La Predilección de Ellas y Ellos en lo Magno de Oviedo," *A.B.C.*, 16 September 1945; and Rodríguez-Vigil Reguera, "Grandes almacenes, centros comerciales y otros espacios de consumo contemporáneos," 1:796.

19. See, for instance, an ad from El Barato/La Casa de la Economia (The Cheap One/The House of Thrift), which declared: "In the household that does not save, things cannot go well. By contrast, housewives who buy everything at El Barato always come out ahead, [going] from success to success. This week, Progressive Sales. . . . ," "Ad for El Barato, 11 November 1945," Almacenes Jorba—Newspaper Advertisement Clippings, 1945–58, ARCM 296582/2. For retailing in Madrid, see "Madrid, Trasunto de España," lxix–lxxi.

20. "Quién es Quién," *Boletín de Botas*, no. 24, Year III (November 1964), 5.

21. See Zafra Aragón, *Méritos, errores, ilusiones y personajes de Galerías Preciados*, 30, 39; "Editorial: Somos más de mil," *Boletín de Sederías Carretas y Galerías Preciados*, no. 9, Year II (January 1951), 1, reproduced in "Páginas Antológicas," *Boletín de Galerías Preciados*, no. 236, Year XXV (December 1973), 15.

22. Toboso, *Pepín Fernández*, 138, 160, 165; Zafra Aragón, *Méritos, errores, ilusiones y personajes de Galerías Preciados*, 41, 51–52, 58, 61

23. For window displays in the United States, see Benson, *Counter Cultures*, 18, 102; and Whitaker, *Service and Style*, 109–29, esp. 110–13. For pre-1940s

displays, see "Escaparatistas Españoles—Al habla con Aycuens, primer premio en el concurso de Escaparates madrileños 1939," *Escaparate: Revista del arte decorativo comercial* [henceforth, *Escaparate*], no. 2, Year I (May 1945); and, for examples of older-style displays, see "Almacenes Siro Gay y Filiales"; Samuel Venero, "Escaparates Sintéticos," *Escaparate*, no. 3, Year I (June 1945); Toboso, *Pepín Fernández*, 150; and "Dos Escaparates de Arte en Galerías Preciados," *A.B.C.*, 16 October 1943.

24. Specifically, this was Spain's first professional window-draper's journal, as opposed to earlier, nonspecialist commercial literature. See, for comparison, *Butlletí Portaveu Mensual del "Centro de Dependientes del Comercio y de la Industria,"* no. 1, Year 1 (April 1927), Diputació de Barcelona Digitized Local Periodicals Collection, accessed 17 January 2013, http://www.diba.es/xbcr/default.htm.

25. Hosgood, "The Shopkeeper's 'Friend.'" For English window drapers' professional literature, see *Warehousemen and Draper's Trade Journal*, vol. 3 (1874); and *A Guide to Window-Dressing* (1883), 3. For the American case, see Whitaker, *Service and Style*, 110–13; and Benson, *Counter Cultures*, 18, 102.

26. "La necesidad de un buen escaparate," *Escaparate*, no. 2, Year I (May, 1945); "Escaparatistas Españoles," *Escaparate*, no. 2, Year I (May 1945); for the magazine's mission statement, see Arturo Castilla, "Nueva Vision—El Escaparte—Importancia y valor del palco escenico comercial," *Escaparate*, no. 1, Year I (April 1945). For another account of Galerías Preciados's early innovations in window dressing, see Fernández García, "Galerías Preciados (1943–1975)."

27. Similarly telling was the fact that both Galerías and Jorba claimed to have been the first to install the device in Spain. See Toboso, *Pepín Fernández*, 226–27; Zafra Aragón, *Méritos, errores, ilusiones y personajes de Galerías Preciados*, 48; Almacenes Jorba, *1911–1961—Bodas de Oro—Almacenes Jorba*, 9; "El hombre que resuelve 'pegas,'" *"Gay": Revista Mensual de Almacenes Siro Gay* [henceforth, *"Gay"*] (December 1961); "Perspectiva de la escalera mecánica," *"Gay"* (February 1962); "Un modernísimo bazar para Valencia: Gay ha inaugurado su nuevo establecimiento," *"Gay"* (February 1962); "Escaleras mecánicas de la Exposición—Las primeras instaladas en España," *La Vanguardia*, 23 May 1929; and, Patrícia Faciabén Lacorte, "Los Grandes Almacenes en Barcelona," *Scripta Nova: Revista Electrónica de Geografía y Ciencias Sociales* 7, no. 140 (May 2003), accessed 4 February 2012, http://www.ub.edu/geocrit/sn/sn-140.htm.

28. For the earlier store publication *El Siglo*, see, for instance, *El Siglo—Periodico Quincenal, Organo de los Grandes Almacenes de este Titulo*, no. 7, Year I (1 October 1883), held at BNE. For Galerías's bulletin, see Toboso, *Pepín Fernández*, 165–66.

29. For Muñoz Ruiz's analysis, see Muñoz Ruiz, "La construcción de las relaciones de género en el franquismo y sus conflictos."

30. Macrina, "Consultorio Femenino," *Revista Jorba*, no. 12, Year II (December 1954–January 1955); Macrina, "Consultorio Femenino," *Revista Jorba*, no. 15, Year III (April 1955).

31. For *Galerías*, see *Galerías*, no. 2 (Spring 1959); for supermarket-sponsored magazines, see chapters 3 and 4 in this volume; for Galerías's 1980s fashion magazine, see, for example, *Galerías Marcando Estilo*, Spring-Summer issue (March 1986), ARCM 903247/2.

32. "Ad—Por fin esta a su alcance lo que tanto deseaba: Servicio de Crédito S.A.," *Revista Jorba*, no. 17, Year III (June 1955); "Ad—Señoras, Aquí está la solución . . . Compre a plazos a precios de contado," *Revista Jorba*, no. 18, Year III (September-October 1955).

33. For Morcillo and credit, see Morcillo, *True Catholic Womanhood*, chap. 3. For more on Spain's continuing economic struggles, see Cazorla Sánchez, *Fear and Progress*, chaps. 1–3.

34. Cuartas, *Biografía de El Corte Inglés*, 578–79.

35. For credit at Macy's, see Whitaker, *Service and Style*, 233; for credit anxiety, see Cohen, *A Consumer's Republic*, 123–24.

36. See note 15 above.

37. For another, more general analysis of foreign—especially American—modernizing influences on Spanish managerial methods and the role this played in Spain's subsequent economic development, see Puig, "La ayuda económica norteamericana y los empresarios españoles."

38. Toboso, *Pepín Fernández*, 212–17; *El Arte de Vender* (Madrid: El Corte Inglés, 1943), held at the BNE; for the *Normas*, see [No Author], *Sederías Carretas y Galerías Preciados—Normas* (Madrid: Sederías Carretas y Galerías Preciados, 1953), also at the BNE, as well as two other editions in ARCM 124661/8; and for the *Normas de Botas*, see Rodríguez-Vigil Reguera, "Grandes almacenes, centros comerciales y otros espacios de consumo contemporáneos," 2:805; and M., "En el Sitio mas Inverosimil surge la Idea. No la deje Marchar. Dele Forma y Espere Los Resultados.

Habra Servido a la Comunidad y Obtendra un Premio," *Boletín de Botas*, no. 11, Year II (June–July 1963), 10.

39. "Quién es Quién—Hoy: Jesús Méndez González," *Boletín de Botas*, no. 26, Year IV (January 1965), 5; C. J., "Bilbao-Cóloquios Económicos," *Boletín de Galerías Preciados*, no. 106, Year XI (November 1960), 14; Galiana, "Esperanza Aguado dió un cursillo de formación para vendedoras," *Boletín de Galerías Preciados*, no. 106, Year XI (November 1960), 14; Zafra Aragón, *Méritos, errores, ilusiones y personajes de Galerías Preciados*, 59–60, 148.

40. Toboso, *Pepín Fernández*, 165–66; Cuartas, *Biografía de El Corte Inglés*, 595–96.

41. Wilensky, "The Professionalization of Everyone?"; also, Vollmer and Mills, *Professionalization*.

42. Alejandro Soto, "Psicologia de la Compra y Venta," *Boletín de Sederías Carretas y Galerías Preciados*, no. 46, Year V (n.d. [likely 1953]), 5; J. I. M., "La venta es arte y ciencia," *Boletín de Sederías Carretas y Galerías Preciados*, no. 46, Year V (n.d. [likely 1953]), 3; R. B. C., "La Degeneración," *Boletín de Galerías*, no. 63, Year VII (June 1956), 14; Jobaco, "Superación," *Boletín de Galerías*, no. 70, Year VIII (March 1957), 10; reprinted from *Dólar* magazine, "Mal vendedor será," in *Boletín de Galerías*, no. 73, Year VIII (June 1957), 15.

43. "La psicología en la venta," *Boletín de Galerías*, no. 73, Year VIII (June 1957), 3.

44. At Sederías, monthly pay for male warehouse division chiefs, window dressers, and ordinary salesmen of at least twenty-five years of age was 1,200, 1,080, and 750 ptas, respectively, or 25–40 ptas daily for a thirty-day month; cabinetmakers and tailors, by contrast, made 17–21 ptas per day on average. Sederías Carretas, S.L., "Reglamento de Régimen Interior," 1948, ARCM 124661/6; "Salario nominal máximo, por jornada, que corresponde a obreros de tipo profesional corriente, según los distintos grupos de actividad. Cifra media nacional, en pesetas. Años 1936 y 1940 a 1948," INE, accessed 8 August 2018, http://www.ine.es/inebaseweb/pdfDispacher .do?td=29953&ext=.pdf.

45. Boliche (Agustín Mencía Sanz), "Cada Mes—¡¡Veinte al Bote!!," *Boletín de Sederías Carretas y Galerías Preciados*, no. 46, Year V (undated), 12; A. M., "El club abre un paréntesis," *Boletín de Galerías Preciados*, no. 61 Year VI (April 1956), 11; Zafra Aragón, *Méritos, errores, ilusiones y personajes de Galerías Preciados*, 52.

46. Benson, *Counter Cultures*, 124–26, 142–45.

47. Galerías created a dedicated personnel department in 1942 precisely to manage this growth. See Toboso, *Pepín Fernández*, 135.

48. Toboso, *Pepín Fernández*, 208.

49. See *Sederías Carretas y Galerías Preciados—Normas*, 15; Benson, *Counter Cultures*, 130. El Corte Inglés, for instance, required employees to "strictly observe standards of personal hygiene" and "seek maximum elegance in their appearance," which for female employees, who unlike their male colleagues wore uniforms, meant keeping these clean and pressed. See Cuartas, *Biografía de El Corte Inglés*, 752–53.

50. *Sederías Carretas y Galerías Preciados—Normas*, 16, 20–21; For mid-century Spanish bodily and dental hygiene, see Toboso, *Pepín Fernández*, 132, 134; and González Iglesias, *Historia General de la Higiene Bucodentaria*.

51. Camino, "A mis compañeros," *Boletín de Galerías*, no. 93, Year X (June 1958), 12; Luis Estebaranz Sanz, "El Arte Difícil," *Boletín de Galerías*, no. 93, Year X (June 1958), 12.

52. For an example of the club's educational programming, see "Actividades del Club—Cinematografía," *Boletín de Galerías*, no. 90, Year X (March 1958), 12.

53. "Al habla con nuestro presidente—clubs, llaveros y medallas," *Boletín de Galerías Preciados*, no. 213, Year XXIII (June 1971), 3.

54. O., "Nuestra Agencia de Tánger: Nuevo local en la calle más céntrica," *Boletín de Sederías Carretas y Galerías Preciados*, no. 46, Year V (n.d. [likely 1953]), 11. For another example, see Olivera, "Badajoz, la íntima," *Boletín de Galerías*, no. 92, Year X (May 1958), 10–11.

55. Cuartas, *Biografía de El Corte Inglés*, 565–67.

56. Cuartas, *Biografía de El Corte Inglés*, 747–48.

57. *Sederías Carretas y Galerías Preciados—Normas*, 16–18.

58. See, for example, *Galerías Preciados—Normas* (Madrid: Galerías Preciados, n.d., post-1966) in ARCM 124661/8. This black border appears four times in the *Normas*, always around tenets at the heart of Pepín's doctrine of unfailing customer service and jealous protection of the company's reputation: in addition to the treason policy, these included a clause that called for constant moral discipline, and two others stressing the need to warmly welcome customers and to scrupulously keep all promises made to them.

59. "Vigilancia Moral," *Boletín de Galerías Preciados*, no. 90, Year X (March 1958), 7; Cuartas, *Biografía de El Corte Inglés*, 592–93.

60. See *Normas* (Oviedo: Anónima Botas Roldán, n.d.), 23, in personal collection of José María Rodríguez-Vigil Reguera; and *Sederías Carretas y Galerías Preciados—Normas*, 10.

61. [No Author], "Desde el Pakistán," *Boletín de Galerías Preciados*, no. 50, Year VI (n.d. [1954–1955]), 4.

62. Samuel Venero, "Lo que los demás piensan de nosotros—mi punto de vista," *Boletín de Botas*, no. 6, Year I (January 1963), 8.

63. Toboso, *Pepín Fernández*, 213.

64. Toboso, *Pepín Fernández*, 194; Cuartas, *Biografía de El Corte Inglés*, 592.

65. McGovern, "Consumption and Citizenship in the United States, 1900–1940," 41–45, 51–55, 57–58.

66. Galerías Preciados, *Normas* (Madrid: Galerías Preciados, n.d.), 20, 37, in ARCM 124661/8.

67. Galerías Preciados, *Normas*, 5–6, 11.

68. See, for instance, A. F., "4 reclutas, 4, se despiden," *Boletín de Galerías Preciados*, no. 61, Year VII (April 1956), 6; and "Nuestro Legionario," *Boletín de Galerías Preciados*, no. 61, Year VII (April 1956), 10. For more on Spanish military service, see Molina Luque, "Quintas y servicio militar."

69. José Javier Aleixandre, "Fuerzas de Choque," *Boletín de Galerías Preciados*, no. 98, Year XI (January 1960), 4. See also Agustín Olivera's series of vignettes from the launch grouped under the title "Ráfagas Bilbaínas" ([Gunfire] Bursts from Bilbao). Agustín Olivera, "Ráfagas Bilbaínas," *Boletín de Galerías Preciados*, no. 98, Year XI (January 1960), 4–5.

70. See, for example, Cuartas, *Biografía de El Corte Inglés*, 604–6.

71. Payne, *Fascism in Spain*, 128; Carr and Fusi Aizpurúa, *Spain: Dictatorship to Democracy*, 47; Maravall, *Dictatorship and Political Dissent*, 2–3; and Linz, *Totalitarian and Authoritarian Regimes*. For another account that more specifically shows how the bellicose Falangist masculine ideal figured in the establishment of the businessman as a prestigious figure in Franco-era Spain, see Alcalde, "El descanso del guerrero," 189–90, 196.

72. Payne, *Fascism in Spain*, 271–72, 366, 388–89. Totalitarian discourse within the regime was especially prevalent during this, the regime's "blue" period, it is worth noting, in part because it was then that the Francoist state contained the largest number of Falangist ministers it would ever employ

at one time, including Franco's cousin and first minister of propaganda, Ramón Serrano Súñer. For Azpiazu, see Payne, *Fascism in Spain*, 285–86.

73. Amador Carretero, "La mujer es el mensaje," 102. Amador's arguments, notably, draw on the work of Louis Althusser. See Althusser, "Ideology and Ideological State Apparatuses," 15–18.

74. The store, for instance, routinely hosted visits by prominent clergymen, including a Lenten religious lecture series organized by Galerías's employee social services department (Asistencia Social) in 1958, and delivered by a Dominican priest. See R .S. B., "Charlas Cuaresmales," *Boletín de Galerías*, no. 92, Year X (May 1958), 4.

75. Casares, *Conferencia que el secretario de la Asociacion de la Prensa D. Francisco Casares*; *Sederías Carretas y Galerías Preciados—Normas*, Introduction.

76. Casares, *Conferencia que el secretario de la Asociacion de la Prensa D. Francisco Casares*; *Sederías Carretas y Galerías Preciados—Normas*, Introduction.

77. Casares, *Conferencia que el secretario de la Asociacion de la Prensa D. Francisco Casares*; *Sederías Carretas y Galerías Preciados—Normas*, Introduction.

78. In fact, the store handbook even aligned, or could be made to align, with the regime in its indictment of Francoism's great ideological foe, Marxism—in this instance, Casares used the *Normas* to condemn Marxists' misrepresentation of work as a "yoke . . . an infamous servitude," and their materialistic "mechanization" of workers' lives. See Casares, *Conferencia que el secretario de la Asociacion de la Prensa D. Francisco Casares*. For early regime efforts to implement corporatism, see Payne, *Fascism in Spain*, 405–6.

79. Under the Republic, Casares had founded an anti-Marxist press syndicate, was appointed to his secretaryship in Nationalist-controlled wartime San Sebastián, and went on to hold many other regime posts, including four decades as Madrid and National Press Association secretary. See Asociación de la Prensa de Madrid, "Secretarios generales, siglos XIX y XX," accessed 28 November 2012, http://www.apmadrid.es/apm /secretarios-generales/secretarios-generales-siglos-xix-y-xx; "Se han celebrado las elecciones para renovar por mitad las diputaciones provinciales," *A.B.C.*, 22 March 1955, 27–28; "Constitución del III Consejo Nacional de Prensa," *A.B.C. (Sevilla)*, 24 April 1969; and "Memoria de la Diputación Provincial de Madrid, Año 1955," Biblioteca Digital de la Comunidad de Madrid, accessed 17 June 2014, http://www.bibliotecavirtualmadrid.org/bvmadrid _publicacion/i18n/catalogo_imagenes/grupo.cmd?path=1057588.

80. Toboso, *Pepín Fernández*, 166–68, 130. For a comprehensive analysis of Francoist outreach to Latin America, see Delgado Gómez-Escalonilla, *Diplomacia Franquista y Política Cultural Hacia Iberoamérica,*.

81. A., "Actualidad," *Boletín de Botas*, no. 17, Year III (February 1964), 16; "Imposición de la Medalla de Plata al 'Mérito en el Trabajo,' a don Siro Gay," *"Gay,"* no. 9, Year II (August–September 1960), 50–66; "La medalla del mérito al Trabajo, concedida a nuestro Director-Gerente," *Boletín de Galerías Preciados*, no. 123, Year XIII (June 1962), 3; "Don José Recibió la Medalla de Oro al Mérito en el Trabajo," *Boletín de Galerías Preciados*, no. 237 (January–February 1974), 4–13.

82. For expressions of admiration for Galerías and its founder, see, for example, Jesús Val, "Pepín Fernández, creador del más importante complejo comercial de Madrid: Galerías Preciados-Sederías Carretas, habla para 'Gay,'" *"Gay,"* no. 9, Year II (August–September 1960), 27–31; "Galerías Preciados: Ocho Pisos Llenos de 'Muchachas de Azul,'" *"Gay,"* no. 9, Year II (August–September 1960), 32; "Galerías Preciados, Parque de Atracciones," *Boletín de Botas*, no. 8, Year II (March 1963), 15; Manuel Sarmiento and Alberto Delgado, "Grandes Figuras: Pepín Fernández," no. 10, Year II (May 1963). For reverence toward the *Normas*, see, for instance, "Las 'Normas' y su Espiritualidad," *Boletín de Galerías Preciados*, no. 103, Year XI (June 1960), 3; "Las 'Normas' y su Interpretación," *Boletín de Galerías Preciados*, no. 106, Year XI (November 1960), 9; and, at Botas, "A modo de consigna: Servir es mas que Amar," *Boletín de Botas*, no. 16, Year II (January 1964), 16; and "Nuestra fiesta," *Boletín de Botas*, No. 18 Year III (March–April, 1964), 3.

83. For Club de Botas, see "V Aniversario del Botas Club," *Boletín de Botas*, no. 17, Year III (February 1964), 2.

84. Toboso, *Pepín Fernández*, 194–95; Mencía, "Examen de Ingreso," *Boletín de Galerías Preciados*, no. 50, Year VI (n.d. [1954–55]), 7.

85. At Galerías, there were thirty-six distinct positions in 1948 (which grew to eighty-six by 1959), each of which possessed its own base salary, promotion criteria, and pay raise schedule. See Sederías Carretas, S.L., "Reglamento de Régimen Interior," 1948, ARCM 124661/6; "Reglamento de Régimen Interior de Galerías Preciados, S.A.," 1959, AHT-GP, Folder 26/004; *Sederías Carretas y Galerías Preciados—Normas*, 12–13; and Cuartas, *Biografía de El Corte Inglés*, 594.

86. Zafra Aragón, *Méritos, errores, ilusiones y personajes de Galerías Preciados*, 42.

87. By contrast, tips were a common and accepted practice at Siro Gay. See, for instance, "Entrevistas: Nicolas Gil," *"Gay,"* no. 9, Year II (August–September 1958), 15. For discipline at Galerías and El Corte Inglés, see Zafra Aragón, *Méritos, errores, ilusiones y personajes de Galerías Preciados,* 5–6; "Reglamento de Régimen Interior de Galerías Preciados, S.A.," 1959, AHT-GP 26/004; El Corte Inglés, *Reglamento de Régimen Interior,* 57; and Cuartas, *Biografía de El Corte Inglés,* 592–593.

88. Toboso, *Pepín Fernández,* 194; Cuartas, *Biografía de El Corte Inglés,* 592.

89. The first panel reads, "Give me *three* centimeters of that!," while panels three and four read, respectively, "Give me *three hundred* meters of that!!," and, "What did the gentleman say??," by which the salespersons, now interested in doing business, placed themselves at Boliche's service. The unstated moral of the satirical episode, one of the *Normas's* central tenets, is that the customer must always be welcomed regardless of whether or how much they buy. See *Sederías Carretas y Galerías Preciados—Normas,* 19.

90. Other humor page regulars included "Benjamín," who offered short, comically oversimplified truisms, and Agustín Olivera, "El Protestón" (The Moaner), who Manuel Zafra recalled as the *Boletín's* foremost contributor in 1950 for his frequent observations about problems at the store. For Olivera, see Zafra Aragón, *Méritos, errores, ilusiones y personajes de Galerías Preciados,* 41; for an example of "Benjamín"'s work, see B., "Benjaminadas," *Boletín de Galerías,* no. 61, Year VII (April 1956), 6.

91. Boliche (Agustín Mencía Sanz), "Cada Mes–¡¡Veinte al Bote!!," *Boletín de Sederías Carretas y Galerías Preciados,* no. 46, Year V (undated), 12; Dorotea (Agustín Mencía Sanz), "Cada Mes–¡¡Veinte al Bote!!," *Boletín de Galerías,* no. 63, Year VII (June 1956), 16.

92. For devotion to the store and the *Normas,* see "El Interés del Negocio," in *Sederías Carretas y Galerías Preciados—Normas,* 5–6; also Toboso, *Pepín Fernández,* 212–13; and Cuartas, *Biografía de El Corte Inglés,* 600, 604.

93. Zafra Aragón, *Méritos, errores, ilusiones y personajes de Galerías Preciados,* 59.

94. See, for example, "Despedida a José Blanco," *Boletín de Galerías Preciados,* no. 127, Year XIII (December 1962), 8.

95. See note 90 above.

96. Don Nuño, "Otra Inauguración—La Mampara de Jacometrezo," *Boletín de Galerías Preciados,* no. 98, Year XI (January 1960), 7.

97. For an earlier example, see, for instance, Mencía, "Usted 'No' Es Así–El Señor Rojo," *Boletín de Galerías Preciados,* no. 74, Year VIII (July 1957), 8.

98. Indeed, both of the subtitles to the *Boletín*'s humor page, "One can also laugh [while] buying and selling," and, "After work, a joke feels good," spoke to this aim, as did a February 1962 editorial in *"Gay,"* which counseled readers to read the bulletin not only as a means of professional communication but also for "instruct[ion] and distract[ion]." See *Boletín de Galerías Preciados*, no. 74, Year VIII (July 1957), 8–9; and "Como hay que leer nuestra revista," *"Gay"* (February 1962).

99. See "La Mujer, Es Buena Compradora?," *"Gay"* (January 1962); "¡Ay esos niños!," *Revista Jorba*, no. 42, Year VI (September–October 1958); and, "Humor," *Revista Jorba*, no. 11, Year II (November 1954).

100. "No Comment," *"Gay,"* no. 8 (August 1960).

101. Jesús Val, "Pepín Fernández, creador del más importante complejo comercial de Madrid: Galerías Preciados-Sederías Carretas, habla para 'Gay,'" *"Gay,"* no. 9, Year II (August–September 1960), 29.

102. Toboso, *Pepín Fernández*, 202.

103. Sederías Carretas, *Sederías Carretas, S.L.–Reglamento de Régimen Interior* (Madrid: Sederías Carretas), 6, 14, in ARCM 124661/6; "Reglamento de Régimen Interior de Galerías Preciados, S.A.," 1959, AHT-GP 26/004.

104. "Los Dereches de la Mujer . . . y Sus Obligaciones," *"Gay"* (March 1962).

105. Lazaga, *Las Muchachas de Azul*.

106. Lazaga, *Las Muchachas de Azul*.

107. For one version of this poster, see Cartel de Las Muchachas de Azul (1957), available at Centro Virtual Cervantes, accessed 4 February 2013, http://cvc.cervantes.es/actcult/cine/historia/.

108. This assertion of domesticity as women's primary destiny echoed similar missives by departing brides that were commonly printed in the *Boletín de Galerías Preciados*. See María Begoña, "Cara abierta a mis compañeras—un saludo para todas y una despedida a la vez," *"Gay"* (August 1961); and "Una Carta Conmovedora," *Boletín de Sederías Carretas y Galerías Preciados*, no. 46, Year V (undated), 5.

109. "Lo que NO deber ser y lo que SI debe ser," *"Gay"* (August 1960).

110. Paff Ogle and Damhorst, "Dress for Success in the Popular Press," 80–81; donning the suit, Ogle and Damhorst's Foucauldian argument runs, "disciplines" the male body, making it better capable of accomplishing "the serious work of business for modern society" and "reaffirm[s] the hegemony and legitimize[s] the power of its wearers." In this same vein, Alison Lurie argues for fashion's patriarchal potential, pointing to articles

like high heels and heavy Victorian undergarments as hobbling mechanisms that rendered women dependent on men, and, long before either of these interventions (or indeed Foucault's work), James Laver argued that male dress "perpetually crystalliz[es] into a uniform," one that defined men first by their professions, and only then as persons, and set their public roles forth as more important than their domestic ones. See Lurie, *The Language of Clothes*, 220–21, 226–28; and Laver, *Taste and Fashion from the French Revolution until To-day*, 234.

111. Galerías Preciados, *Galerías Preciados—Normas* (Madrid: Galerías Preciados, undated), 15, in ARCM 124661/8; Cuartas, *Biografía de El Corte Inglés*, 752. Notably, Galerías added another such requirement, that saleswomen care for their uniforms, as dirty or damaged ones would reflect badly on the store's reputation, after the *Normas*'s 1953 printing. While a concrete reason for this addition is not known, the lack of a similar ruling on salesmen's attire suggests that it too was motivated by perceptions of a gendered difference in stability of temperament. El Corte Inglés's code made similar demands of its female personnel, while only requiring male employees to maintain "maximum elegance and distinction in their appearance."

112. Galerías Preciados, *Galerías Preciados—Normas*; Boliche, "¡Veinte al Bote!," *Boletín de Galerías Preciados*, no. 99, Year XI (February 1960), 8.

113. Toboso, *Pepín Fernández*, 202–3. Both this assimilation of store pride, and the store's ongoing desire to sartorially discipline female employees' bodies through the imposition of both a uniform and the duty of caring for it, were such that "Os Habla Graciela" (Graciela Speaks), a women's column that debuted in the *Boletín* in 1957, devoted its first edition to commenting on both these phenomena and in particular offered readers detailed instructions on how to care for their uniforms, including methods (brushing and washing, even specifying the recipe for the detergent) and frequency. "Os Habla Graciela," *Boletín de Galerías*, no. 73, Year VIII (June 1957), 13.

114. For reference to such complaints, see, for instance, "Humor—No falla. A uniforme nuevo, critica a 'porrillo,'" *Boletín de Galerías Preciados*, no. 126, Year XIII (November 1962), 8; "Despues . . . ," *Boletín de Galerías Preciados*, no. 126, Year XIII (November 1962), 8; and "Dos Preguntas Nada Mas," *Boletín de Galerías Preciados*, no. 126, Year XIII (November 1962), 9.

115. Sederías Carretas, S.L., "Reglamento de Régimen Interior," 1948, ARCM 124661/6; Brenan, *The Face of Spain*, 23.

116. Toboso, *Pepín Fernández*, 202–3.

117. Notably, the last of these ties, linking Galerías and Botas, was deeply rooted and personal in origin. It derived in part from Asturian pride—Botas celebrated Galerías's accomplishments as the successes of a retailer that through Pepín Fernández shared Botas's regional roots. As Javier Cuartas has shown, the stores' ties to one another also stemmed from the presence of Botas family members' among Galerías's top managers, as well as ties between the Fernández and Botas families that dated back to the turn of the century. See "Gentileza de una casa faterna," *Boletín de Galerías Preciados*, no. 134, Year XIV (July 1963), 8; Diego de Salcedo, "Galerías Preciados, Parque de Atracciones," *Boletín de Botas*, no. 8, Year II (March 1963), 15; Manuel Sarmiento and Alberto Delgado, "Grandes Figuras: Pepín Fernández," no. 10, Year II (May 1963); Cuartas, *Biografía de El Corte Inglés*, 572.

118. Intercontinental Group of Department Stores, *Intercontinental Group of Department Stores, 1946–1996* (Essen: Karstadt, 1996), accessed 30 January 2013, http://www.igds.org/publicarea/aboutigds/IGDS%201946%20%201996.pdf; Toboso, *Pepín Fernández*, 262–64.

119. A. M., "La propaganda en los almacenes *La Rinascente*," *Boletín de Galerías Preciados*, no. 63, Year VII (June 1956), 7; "Nueve Puntos Esenciales," *Boletín de Galerías Preciados*, no. 99, Year XI (February 1960), 7; Francisco Pablos, "De Tiendas por Europa: 1.-Paris," *"Gay,"* no. 9, Year II (August–September 1958), 22–26; "Crónica de Alemania: Un centro de información para resolver todos los problemas de las amas de casa," *"Gay"* (December 1960).

120. "Cartas que alientan y obligan," *Boletín de Galerías Preciados*, no. 98, Year XI (January 1960), 6.

121. A. M., "La propaganda en los almacenes *La Rinascente*."

2. Imagining a New Señora Consumer

1. Segismundo de Anta, "[Untitled Introductory Editorial Article]," *Señor: La Revista del Hombre*, no. 1, Year I (November 1955).

2. Tellingly, while a number of women's fashion journals published in late nineteenth-century Spain are well-known to scholars, among them historian Jesús Cruz, *Señor* is by contrast the earliest such magazine meant for men to appear in the extensive periodicals catalog at the Spanish National

Library. For Cruz and nineteenth-century consumer periodicals, see Cruz, *The Rise of Middle-Class Culture in Nineteenth-Century Spain*, chap. 4.

3. García Ruescas, *Historia de la Publicidad*, 120. Though not all of these magazines were primarily consumer oriented, this does not mean they lacked any consumer content. Religious publications, like a 1924 Almacenes Jorba catalog devoted to religious supplies (*objetos de culto*), for instance, show that Catholicism possessed its own consumer-oriented aspects. See "Catalogo Especial para Objetos de Culto," ARCM 296582/4.

4. For the nineteenth-century women's and fashion press in Spain, see Cruz, *The Rise of Middle-Class Culture in Nineteenth-Century Spain*, chap. 4.

5. Indeed, rationing fell so short that in 1945 the Balearic Islands' monthly allotment of 103,304 rations was only enough to feed one-quarter of the population. See Ginard i Ferón, "Las Condiciones de Vida durante el Primer Franquismo," 1112–17; and, for population figures, "Censo de 1940. Resúmen general por provincias," INE, accessed 26 April 2013, http://www.ine.es/inebaseweb/pdfDispacher.do?td=118239&ext=.pdf; and "Censo de 1950. Clasificaciones de habitantes de Hecho por grupos de edad," INE, accessed 26 April 2013, http://www.ine.es/inebaseweb/pdfDispacher.do?td=125359&ext=.pdf. For the cost of living, see Molinero and Ysàs, "Las Condiciones de Vida y Laborales durante el Primer Franquismo," 7–14; and Abella, *La vida cotidiana durante la guerra civil*, 246, 316. For magazine prices, see "A Nuestras Lectoras," *Mujer*, no. 122 (August 1947); *Medina* (2 December 1945), and *Alta Costura*, no. 26, Year IV (January 1946). For *Medina*, see Carrión Jiménez and Hernando Carrasco, "'Medina,' prototipo de la prensa femenina de postguerra," 166. For Paris fashion, see, for example, Fred, "Crónica de la Moda," *Mujer*, no. 2, Year I (July 1937).

6. For *Medina* as escapist literature, see Pinilla García, "La mujer en la posguerra franquista a través de la revista *Medina* (1940–1945)," 176.

7. For examples, see "Ad for Cursos Femina—Academia CCC: Sea Vd. Practica y Moderna y ahorrara mucho dinero," *Mujer*, no. 116 (February 1947), and "Ad for Instituto Nacional de Corte," *Mujer*, no. 117 (March 1947).

8. For class identity and consumption in Spain, see Alonso and Conde, *Historia del consumo en España*, 137–43, 194–96. The centrality of class performance to mass consumption in the United States has been recognized—not always happily—by scholars of consumption dating back as far as Thorstein Veblen's watershed *The Theory of the Leisure Class* (1899). For a survey of scholarship on this, see Cohen, *A Consumer's Republic*, 10–11,

412–13. For more on perspectives on the rise of mass consumption in the late nineteenth and early twentieth-century United States, see Horowitz, "Consumption and Its Discontents"; and, for its postwar counterpart, see Cohen, *A Consumer's Republic*, 55–56; 101–2; 152–67.

9. This is in response to historian Leonore Davidoff's caution that periodical literature cannot simply be assumed to reflect dominant attitudes. For reference to Davidoff's warning, see Breward, *The Hidden Consumer*, 42.

10. For reliance on consumer credit in the United States, see Cohen, *A Consumer's Republic*, 123–24.

11. See *Mujer*, no. 1, Year I (June 1937). The reader should note that the discussion here concerns specifically *consumer* publications, defined here as primarily focused on consumer products and consumer lifestyles, such as fashion magazines, rather than focused mainly on promoting a particular political ideology.

12. For a more exhaustive catalog of the women's press under the Franco dictatorship, see Sánchez Hernández, "Evolución de las publicaciones femeninas en España."

13. The Anta brothers were already noteworthy figures in the early 1940s: Santiago had worked with the regime's official press syndicates since 1939, while in 1941, Segismundo de Anta founded Spain's National Fashion Show, an annual affair for decades thereafter. For Santiago de Anta, see "Don Ramón Serrano Súñer, caballero del ideal que redime a España, estudia los problemas de trabajo y de economía de las provincias catalanas," *La Vanguardia Española*, 16 June 1939; for Segismundo de Anta, see Manuel del Arco, "Mano a Mano–Segismundo de Anta," *La Vanguardia Española*, 23 February 1939; and "Inauguración del Primer Salón de la Moda Española," *La Vanguardia Española*, 6 March 1941. For other women's magazines, see Gallego Ayala, *Mujeres de papel: De ¡Hola! a Vogue*, 43–44.

14. Muñoz Ruiz, "Mujer Mítica, Mujeres Reales," 177–78, 262–63. See also the introduction to this book, and Morcillo, *True Catholic Womanhood*, chap. 1.

15. For *La Moda Elegante*, see Cruz, *The Rise of Middle-Class Culture in Nineteenth-Century Spain*, chap. 4, and, for an example, see *La Moda Elegante: Periódico de las Familias*, no. 2, Year I (10 January 1961).

16. Javier Machado, "La Tapia," *Mujer: Revista Mensual del Hogar y de la Moda* [henceforth, *Mujer*], no. 2, Year I (July 1937). The story's title comes from an old stone wall where Margarita meets Alberto both times.

17. The linking of fashion to acceptable femininity is evident in plates like two that appeared in this issue of *Alta Costura*, titled "Modelos Juveniles" ([clothing] models for youths) and "Modelos infantiles" (Children's models), which showed sketched designs for outfits for, respectively, young women, presumably the reader's adolescent daughters, and for younger children, invoking the accepted feminine role of motherhood. See "Modelos juveniles" and "Modelos infantiles" in *Alta Costura*, no. 26, Year IV (January 1946). For *Medina*, see Carrión Jiménez and Hernando Carrasco, "'Medina,' prototipo de la prensa femenina de postguerra," 165.

18. V.P., "Manos de Mujer en los Hilos de la Historia–La Huerfana del Temple," *Alta Costura*, no. 28, Year IV (March 1946).

19. See, for instance, "Lo que no os adorna," *Mujer*, no. 27, Year of Victory (August 1939), 67; and "Trajecitos de Niños (Children's outfits)," *Mujer*, no. 7, Year I (December 1937).

20. Elsa Kiepura, "Los 'papeles' de la mujer," *Mujer*, no. 28, Year of Victory (October 1939).

21. As noted in chapter 1, despite its multifarious nature, the National Movement quickly imposed a traditional model of femininity on the Spanish population that became hegemonic. Even the Women's Section of the fascist (and thus, less strictly conservative) Falange, which granted women the opportunity to remain in the public sphere, engaged in public work consonant with the traditional feminine caregiving roles of wife and mother. For example, kitchen aprons featured among the Women's Section uniform items. For the Sección Femenina and femininity, see, for example, Morcillo, *True Catholic Womanhood*, chap. 5, esp. 102–9.

22. M. Fernández Palacios, "Virgen de la Esperanza," *Mujer*, no. 2, Year I (July 1937). The poem's invocation of the Virgin as a female paragon is telling, for according to Aurora Morcillo, the Catholic tracts on which the Franco regime built its gender ideology envisioned the Virgin in this same role. Here too, *Mujer* and the regime's National-Catholicism appear to have been of the same mind. For Francoism and the Virgin Mary, see Morcillo, *True Catholic Womanhood*, 40. For Franco-era femininity and public Catholicism, see Eslava Galán, *Los Años del Miedo*, 59, 63.

23. Morcillo, *True Catholic Womanhood*, 36–39; "La mujer y los libros," *Mujer*, no. 18, Year II (November 1938), 29.

24. See Morcillo, *True Catholic Womanhood*, chap. 2.

25. For women's rights under the Second Republic and the loss thereof under Franco, see Madorrán Ayerra, "The Open Window: Women in Spain's Second Republic and Civil War." See also the introduction in this book, note 7.

26. Morcillo, *True Catholic Womanhood*, 24–26; Payne, *The Franco Regime*, 257, 303; and Rodríguez López, "La Falange Femenina y Construcción de la Identidad de Género durante el Franquismo."

27. Quoted in Payne, *Fascism in Spain*, 324. The creed of the Women's Section enshrined these same principles, referring to the education of one's children as a woman's "mission," and encouraging women to be obedient and to view others—men—as true agents and patriots, eschewing all personal ambition for themselves. See Morcillo, *True Catholic Womanhood*, 25.

28. Payne, *Fascism in Spain*, 301.

29. Roig Castellanos, *La mujer y la prensa*, 123, cited in Muñoz Ruiz, "Mujer Mítica," 202.

30. Roig Castellanos, *La mujer y la prensa*, 124, 118; Muñoz Ruiz, "Mujer Mítica," 207; Marsá Vancells, *La mujer en el periodismo*, 148, cited in Muñoz Ruiz, "Mujer Mítica," 208; Ruiz Franco, "Pequeña historia de ayer," 27–29; Ruiz Franco, "María Telo y la participación de mujeres juristas en la Comisión General de Codificación (1973–1975)," 167.

31. Carrión Jiménez and Hernando Carrasco, "'Medina,' prototipo de la prensa femenina de postguerra," 164–65, 167, 169–73.

32. [Untitled], *Mujer*, no. 6, Year I (November 1937).

33. These aims were codified in Point Three of the Falange's twenty-six fundamental points, another ideological cornerstone of the early dictatorship, which read, "We reclaim for Spain a preeminent place in Europe. We support neither international isolation nor foreign influence," and in declarations Franco himself made, such as, "we do not want a liberal, capitalist, bourgeois, Jewish, protestant, atheist and masonic progress. We prefer Spanish backwardness." See Francisco Franco Salgado-Araujo, *Mis Conversaciones Privadas con Franco*, 99, cited in Eslava Galán, *Los Años del Miedo*, 57–58.

34. "La Nueva España: en los comedores del auxilio social," *Mujer*, no. 6 (November 1937); Carlos de Llorente, "Mujeres Fascistas," *Mujer*, no. 8, Year II (January 1938), 17, 24, and Carlos de Llorente, "Mujeres Fascistas," *Mujer*, no. 9, Year II (February 1938), 20.

35. For Segura's and other National-Catholic moral authorities' moralism, see, for example, Martín Gaite, *Courtship Customs in Postwar Spain*, 118–20; and Alonso Tejada, *La represión sexual en la España de Franco*, especially chaps. 6–7.

36. See Martín Gaite, *Courtship Customs in Postwar Spain*, chaps. 2–3; Alonso Tejada, *La represión sexual en la España de Franco*; Morcillo, *True Catholic Womanhood*, chap. 2.

37. "Itinerario," *Mujer*, no. 27, Year of Victory (August 1939). For the regime and postwar domestic tourism, see Pack, *Tourism and Dictatorship*, 33–34. Pack has noted the economic motivations behind the Spanish government's own tourism push; *Mujer*'s call "¡Viajad por España!" (Travel through Spain!), immediately following the assertion that Spain would achieve "total reconstruction . . . along the path of a strong, potent, and hard-working nation that it ha[d] set for itself," strongly suggests that the magazine had this same objective in mind.

38. "Untitled Article on Diary of Adela-María," *Mujer*, no. 17 (October 1938), 52–53. Whether the diary was real or fictional is ultimately of little importance, as, either way, *Mujer* used the drama of the Civil War to sell issues. For another example of such use of a short story, see P. Vila San-Juan, "Una Mujer Especial," *Mujer*, no. 12 (May 1938), 10–11.

39. "Ad for Casa Vilar," *Mujer*, no. 5 (October 1937).

40. For fashionable dress, see, for example, Fred, "Crónica de la Moda," *Mujer*, no. 2, Year I (July 1937). For sailing, golf, and attire, see "Vestidos de Sport," *Mujer*, no. 2, Year I (July 1937). For class and sailing in Spain, see Méndez de la Muela, "Evolución del turismo náutico en España en los últimos treinta años," chap. 3. For golf's early history in Spain, in which the titled aristocracy figured prominently, see Real Federación Española de Golf, "Historia del Golf en España," accessed 25 April 2013, http://www.rfegolf.es/Noticias/NewsSection.aspx?CatId=28. See also A. Vallejo Nájera, "Agotamiento y vida de negocios," *Arte Comercial: Revista Técnica de Publicidad y Organización* [henceforth, *Arte Comercial*], no. 3, Year I (June 1946), 17–18. For wet nurses, see José Ma. Batllé Miquelerena, "Temario Médico—Alimentación del recién nacido," *Alta Costura*, no. 28, Year IV (March 1946). For evening make-up, see Elena Chavalera, "Charlas de Belleza—En torno al gran maquillaje de noche," *Alta Costura*, no. 28, Year IV (March 1946).

41. See Sánchez Hernández, "Evolución de las publicaciones femeninas en España."

42. "Ad for Cursos Femina–Academia CCC: Sea Vd. Practica y Moderna y ahorrara mucho dinero," *Mujer*, no. 116 (February 1947).

43. "Ad for Instituto Nacional de Corte," *Mujer*, no. 117 (March 1947).

44. "20 September 1943," "27 September 1943," and "19 April 1947," BNC-MFIB. Moreover, though Freixas also frequently bought fabric—perhaps to work with herself, perhaps to send out for seamstressing—these purchases were not thrifty. That same month, she spent over 1,000 ptas on material. Myriad ready-made clothing purchases also peppered her budgets, including 55 ptas spent on 26 March for a belt for herself, and 40 ptas spent on 21 March for two blouses. In short, a woman with Freixas's means did not have to sew her own clothes. See "19 April 1947," "22 April 1947," "2 April 1947," "26 March 1947," and "21 March 1947," BNC-MFIB.

45. Brenan, *The Face of Spain*, 23.

46. In fact, this shortage was so severe that *Ventanal* was temporarily forced to suspend publication as a result. "A Nuestras Lectoras," *Mujer*, no. 122 (August 1947), 5; Roig Castellanos, *La mujer y la prensa*, 107.

47. For such content in *Alta Costura*, see, for example, "Advertisement for Legrain Perfumes," *Alta Costura*, no. 55, Year VI (June 1948); "Ad for Champaña 'Coquet' Mestres," *Alta Costura*, no. 55, Year VI (June 1948); and A y Marinel-lo, "La Casa y Su Estilo–Estufas de Cerámica," *Alta Costura*, no. 55, Year VI (June 1948).

48. See, for instance, "Sumario," *Arte y Hogar*, no. 43 (n.d.); and J., "Paletós, boleros y esclavinas," *Astra: Revista moderna para la mujer*, no. 5, Year I (August 1950).

49. The same was true of the hair and beauty magazine *Creaciones*, which was more expensive but also a more technical publication than *Mujer*. For *Creaciones* as well as a summary of *Arte en el Hogar* and *Mujer*'s different content, see *Anuario de la Prensa Española*, Year II, 482–83, 488. For descriptions of the women's press in the early-to-mid-twentieth-century United States, see Walker, *Shaping Our Mothers' World: American Women's Magazines*.

50. Specifically, *¡Hola!* and *Chicas* sold for 2 ptas per issue, *Meridiano Femenino* for 3, and *Lecturas*, the most expensive, for *Mujer*'s pre-1947 hike price of 3.5 ptas per issue. For *¡Hola!*, see "Tres generaciones al frente de '¡Hola!,'" *A.B.C. (Sevilla)*, 15 July 2010.

51. Montero García, "Las Publicaciones Periódicas de Acción Católica durante el Franquismo," 35–36.

52. This figure assumes an average real distribution rate of 75–80 percent of each edition and a 1950 adult female population of 6,847,000 in the urban and semi-urban areas referenced. For edition figures from the mid-1940s, see *Anuario de la Prensa Española*, Year I, 288–91; *Anuario de la Prensa Española*, Year II, 488. For 1954 figures, see Muñoz Ruiz, "Mujer Mítica," 231; and for other magazines' figures, *Anuario de la Prensa Española*, Year III, Vol. 2. For historic magazine dissemination rates, see Muñoz Ruiz, "Mujer Mítica," 231. For these magazines' largely urban audience, see Muñoz Ruiz, "Mujer Mítica," 49. For the adult female population in Spanish urban and semi-urban areas in 1950, see "Censo de 1950. Clasificaciones de habitantes de Hecho por grupos de edad."

53. The rate of one magazine for every one hundred women corresponds specifically to *El Hogar y la Moda*'s dissemination. Given the likelihood that some women who did not buy this magazine bought others like *¡Hola!* or *Meridiano Femenino*, the portion of the female populace reading a women's magazine of some kind was thus almost certainly higher.

54. See, for instance, "La Moda en Hollywood," *Mujer*, no. 9, Year II (February 1938), 16–17; "La Moda y el Cine," *Mujer*, no. 18, Year II (November 1938), 12–13; and "Ellos . . . como ellas los prefieren," *Mujer*, no. 15, Year II (August 1938).

55. See, for example, "*Alta Costura* en Hollywood," *Alta Costura*, no. 28, Year IV (March 1946); also, Juan del Sarto, "Hablan los ídolos acerca de qué es más agradable en la mujer: Si el talento o la belleza—Opiniones de Cary Grant, Gregory Peck, Tyrone Power y Gary Cooper," *Alta Costura*, no. 55, Year VI (June 1948); "Emociones de Mujer–Merle Oberon, Greer Garson, Lana Turner y Linda Darnell evocan la impresión de su puesta de largo," *Alta Costura*, no. 63, Year VII (February 1949); "El arte del vestido de interior," *Mujer*, no. 116 (February 1947); S.V., "En todo se puede poner un poco de belleza," *Mujer*, no. 121 (July 1947); "La moda viaja," *Mujer*, no. 118 (April 1947).

56. de Grazia, *How Fascism Ruled Women*, 209–10, 221–26.

57. For *Alta Costura* reports on London and Paris, see J. R. B., "Salones de la Moda de Paris . . . el de Alice Belier," *Mujer*, no. 116 (February 1947); "El Proximo Numero, gran Extraordinario de Primavera-Verano," *Mujer*,

no. 117 (March 1947); "Los efectos juveniles constituyen lo esencial de la moda 1947," *Mujer*, no. 119 (May 1947).

58. Vera de Alzate, "Modas españolas," *Mujer*, no. 17 (October 1938).

59. For Italian resistance to Fascist promotion of domestic fashions, see de Grazia, *How Fascism Ruled Women*, 221–22. For ads in Spanish women's magazines, see, for instance, "Ad for Bride au Vent Perfume, Legrain, Paris," *Alta Costura*, no. 61, Year VI (December 1948); "Ad for 'el Perfume de París de Raphael,'" *Astra*, no. 3, Year I (June 1950); and "Ad for Philips Radios," *Astra*, no. 8, Year I (November 1950).

60. Moreover, the magazine's pricing for ad space, 2,000 ptas per page, was among the highest of any Spanish women's magazine, making it an expensive option as well for smaller domestic brands looking to advertise. Only the extensively read *El Hogar y la Moda* charged more, at 2,650 ptas per page. By contrast, *Mujer* as well as several other magazines charged 1,400 ptas per page, and the women's home magazine *Menaje*, which later became *La Ilustración Femenina*, charged just 500 ptas. See *Anuario de la Prensa Española*, Year II, 481–90. For bourgeois Italian women and autarky, see de Grazia, *How Fascism Ruled Women*, 221–22.

61. *Alta Costura*, no. 43, Year V (June 1947).

62. *Alta Costura*, no. 43, Year V (June 1947).

63. This again paralleled the case of Fascist Italy, where, "autarkhic silks"—domestically produced fashions in the Hollywood style—had similarly straddled the line between the nationalized fashion that the Fascist government pursued and the foreign garments that Italian women saw in theaters and coveted. For Galerías, see Toboso, *Pepín Fernández*, 138–39. For Italy, see de Grazia, *How Fascism Ruled Women*, 221–22.

64. The full label in Bella Aurora's ads prominently proclaimed, "Product of the Stillman Co., Aurora, Illinois USA." See "Ad for Bella Aurora," *Alta Costura*, no. 55, Year VI (June 1948).

65. Morcillo, *True Catholic Womanhood*, 40–41, 54; Alonso Tejada, *La represión sexual en la España de Franco*, 51, 58–61.

66. Morcillo, *True Catholic Womanhood*, 55–56.

67. "Ad for Perfumes Dana," "Ad for Bella Aurora," and "Ad for Tintolax," in *Alta Costura*, no. 26, Year IV (January 1946).

68. For examples of this argument as presented in *Medina*, see Pinilla García, "La mujer en la posguerra franquista a través de la revista *Medina* (1940–1945)," 171–74. This stands in contrast to the Sección Femenina's content

from the 1950s, for many of the ads Morcillo cites ran in the Sección Femenina's own *Teresa*. See Morcillo, *True Catholic Womanhood*, 55–56.

69. "Boudoir," *Mujer*, no. 116 (February 1947).

70. "El Arte del Vestido de Interior," *Mujer*, no. 116 (February 1947).

71. Marcelle Auclair, "Entre Nosotras," *Mujer*, no. 20, Year II (January 1939), 9.

72. This represented one of the primary cultural exports from the United States to postwar Europe. For the American standard of living in Europe, see de Grazia, *Irresistible Empire*, chap. 2, esp. 75–78, 93–95. For the arrival of the concept of the "American way of life" to Spain, see Alonso and Conde, *Historia del consumo en España*, 137.

73. *Alta Costura*, meanwhile, ran ads that displayed a similar preoccupation with modern, technologically driven convenience, promoting products like hybrid clothes/dish-washing machines, DDT-infused insect repellants, and special detergents that promised to clean the family's clothes while housewives went to the movies—a genre of goods that Victoria de Grazia has identified as staples of American consumer capitalism's efforts to spread the American model household abroad. As many scholars have noted, the appliance-filled, modern "miracle kitchen" represented the heart of this Cold War–era household and crystallized core postwar capitalist American values such as freedom of consumer choice, modernity, and convenience. The refrigerator, for instance, promised women freedom from daily visits to the butcher and grocer. As such, the modern kitchen occupied a central place in the U.S. political struggle with the Soviet Union and, more specifically, efforts to spread an American, consumerist brand of democracy abroad, culminating with the 1959 American National Exhibition in Moscow, which included a series of model kitchens meant to sell Soviet citizens on the superiority of free enterprise. For *Alta Costura*, see "Ad for máquina de lavar ropa y platos Turmix-Berrens, offered by Casa Edison," *Alta Costura*, no. 77, Year VIII (April 1950); "Ad for Fogo," *Alta Costura*, no. 54, Year VI (May 1948); "Ad for Libel Detergent," *Alta Costura*, no. 69, Year VII (August 1949). For the American kitchen in Europe, see de Grazia, *Irresistible Empire*, 418–19, 425–27; and various contributions in Oldenziel and Zachmann, *Cold War Kitchens*, including Oldenziel and Zachmann, "Kitchens as Technology and Politics," 2–3; Castillo, "The American 'Fat Kitchen' in Europe," 48; Hamilton, "Supermarket USA Confronts State Socialism," 142–43, 147–48; and Cieraad, "The Radiant American Kitchen," 113–36.

74. "Una sonrisa para ir a la compra," *Mujer*, no. 122 (August 1947).

75. Martín Gaite, *Courtship Customs in Postwar Spain*, 44.

76. Muñoz Ruiz, "Los consultorios sentimentales," 229–35.

77. Morcillo, *True Catholic Womanhood*, 73–74.

78. Indeed, over a decade later, in 1960, only 4 percent of the Spanish population owned a refrigerator, with the overwhelming majority of these concentrated in urban centers. For Freixas and servants, see, for example, "6 July 1947," BNC-MFIB. For appliance ownership, see Fundación FOESSA, *Informe sociológico Sobre la Situación Social en España, 1966*, 75–76.

79. de Grazia, *Irresistible Empire*, 425–28, 438–45.

80. Castillo, "The American 'Fat Kitchen' in Europe," 38–40; Hamilton, "Supermarket USA Confronts State Socialism."

81. Whereas other magazines catering to the food distribution industry, such as the CAT's own publication, *Alimentación Nacional: Publicación de la Sección de Información de la Comisaría General de Abastecimientos y Transportes* (1941–1955), eventually disappeared, *ICA*'s importance is attested to by its long print run, which lasted from 1945 through the end of the dictatorship, to 1977. The magazine's prominent position as print organ of the grocery trade would be further borne out once private supermarket chains began appearing in Spain in the early 1960s, as these chains sent copies of their own internal bulletins to the *ICA* for its editors' perusal. See "Hemeroteca," *ICA*, nos. 130-131-132 (July–August–September 1961), 48.

82. Dr. S. Vanó, "Curso de Belleza, Lección 2.a," *Funcionarias: Revista para la mujer*, no. 3, Year I (September 1952), 16. See also Profesor Villa Sory, "Bailes de Sociedad," *Funcionarias: Revista para la mujer*, no. 3, Year I (September 1952), 9.

83. "Decoración," *Funcionarias*, no. 1, Year I (February 1952).

84. See "Documents relating to Supermercado USA pavilion, XXVII International Trade Fair, Barcelona, 1–20 June 1959," AGA-CAT 29607, Folder 2.

85. This hegemonizing impulse bears comparison to how French authorities reconciled fin-de-siècle Frenchwomen's embrace of public shopping with the domestic ideal it violated, which they did by casting these shoppers as traditionally feminine caretakers—caring, in this instance, for French taste. See Tiersten, *Marianne in the Market*. For Model Mrs. Consumer, see de Grazia, *Irresistible Empire*, 419–20, 446–48.

86. García Ruescas, *Historia de la Publicidad*, 120.

87. In a 1939 cartoon by *Mujer* director Baldrich, for instance, the magazine showed one of these modern women grandly proclaiming, in defense of the choice to drive rather than walk, that while walking was better for one's "line"—one's figure—cars had such lovely lines, and also that "Aquatic sports are lovely, but so tiring!" Also pictured were a pair of these women musing about which one of their hats—both of them of ridiculous design—would be fashionable next season; and, most tellingly, an exchange between a modern woman and a bookseller, in which the woman requested "well-edited books, with lots of pictures, wide margins and large print," to which the bookseller witheringly responded, "Might you not prefer one of these that looks like a book but is actually a little box?" See "Horas de la Mujer Moderna, Texto y Dibujos de Baldrich," *Mujer*, no. 27, Year of Victory (August 1939).

88. For *Teresa*, see Morcillo, *True Catholic Womanhood*, chap. 3.

89. Morcillo, *True Catholic Womanhood*, 73–74.

90. For the example of *Mujer* on the script girl as a job opportunity for women, see Elsa Kiepura, "Los 'papeles' de la mujer," *Mujer*, no. 28, Year of Victory (October 1939).

91. Morcillo, *True Catholic Womanhood*, 73–74. For Mercedes Formica, see Ruiz Franco, "Pequeña Historia"; and Ruiz Franco, "María Telo."

92. Funcionaria X, "Nuestras Entrevistas—Ernestina Caldevilla," *Funcionarias: Revista para la mujer*, no. 1, Year I (February 1952).

93. See, for example, Ignacio Zarzalejos Altares, "Panorama Legislativo Español Sobre la Mujer," *Funcionarias*, no. 1, Year I (February 1952); M. Y. N., "Legislación: La mujer, la funcionarias y sus problemas jurídicos, Vestibulo," *Funcionarias*, no. 2, Year I (April 1952).

94. See, for example, Zarzalejos Altares, above, and also José Luis Barceló, "La mujer en el actual sistema de trabajo," *Funcionarias*, no. 2, Year I (April 1952); and José Luis Barceló, "Sacerdotisas Católicas," *Funcionarias*, no. 6, Year I (December 1952).

95. Dr. Luisa Guarnero, "La ciencia dice que la mujer es superior al hombre," *Funcionarias*, no. 2, Year I (April 1952). For reference to early twentieth-century biological determinism in Spain, see Morcillo, *True Catholic Womanhood*, 19.

96. "Pagina de Humor—El Complejo del Sexo Debil," *Funcionarias*, no. 6, Year I (December 1952).

97. For a series of interviews offering firsthand accounts of Spanish feminism as it coalesced in the late 1960s and 1970s, see Gould Levine and Feiman Waldman, *Feminismo ante el Franquismo*.

98. Aurelia Capmany, "Cartas Impertinentes."

99. For the appearance of such columns in the Spanish women's press, which María del Carmen Muñoz Ruiz dates to 1961, see Muñoz Ruiz, "Mujer Mítica, Mujeres Reales," 219–20.

100. *Anuario de la Prensa Española*, Year III, 675–76.

101. Another ad for Komol similarly warned readers that, if they were to allow their gray hair to show, their husbands "wouldn't forgive them for it." See "Ad–Komol," *Mujer*, no. 209 (November 1954), 3.

102. "Ad for Curso Fémina CCC, Corte y Confección–Los Hombres las prefieren . . . elegantes!," *Mujer*, no. 200 (February 1954), 3.

103. That the magazine consciously had a mainly female readership is clear from recurring features such as "Ideas para Ud. Señora" (Ideas for you, Madam) and was acknowledged by the magazine itself on at least one occasion. See "Para Usted, Caballero," *Revista Jorba*, no. 3 (October–November 1953). For examples of sweepstakes, see "Ad for Chocolates Nestlé," *Revista Jorba*, no. 4 (Special Christmas–New Year's–Three King's Issue, 1953–1954); and "Ad—Todavía más de 10.000 premios, Chocolates Nestlé," *Revista Jorba*, no. 7 (March–April 1954).

104. Decades later, feminist Lidia Falcón would note the continued presence of this domestic role. See Falcón, "La Opresión de la Mujer: Una Incógnita." For examples of such ads, see "Ad—Pelele Kid," *Revista Jorba*, no. 5, Year II, (January 1954); and "Ad—Fosfatina Falieres," *Revista Jorba*, no. 13, Year III (February 1955).

105. Notably, Dr. Roig Raventós's opinion on why some women did not breastfeed hinged on socioeconomic class. Roig assumed that it was poor, desperate women who worked as wet nurses, and wealthy women who hired them, accusing the former—whom he described using the socioeconomically loaded insult "gypsies"—of resorting to carrying "false papers" and taking illicit medications to force lactation, and chastising the latter for caring more about buying the latest fashions than about their infants. See José Roig Raventós, "Puericultura," *Revista Jorba*, no. 8 (May 1954).

106. "Problema Resuelto," *Revista Jorba*, no. 2, Year I (September 1953).

107. For more on women in the postwar American workplace, see, in Joanne Jay Meyerowitz's edited volume *Not June Cleaver: Women and Gender in*

Postwar America, 1945–1960: Rimby Leighow, "An 'Obligation to Participate,'" 37–56; Cobble, "Recapturing Working-Class Feminism," 57–83,
esp. 57, 73; and Hartmann, "Women's Employment and the Domestic
Ideal in the Early Cold War Years," 84–100, esp. 96–97.

108. "Cocina por Ella," *Funcionarias*, no. 3, Year I (September 1952); "Decoración," *Funcionarias*, no. 1, Year I (February 1952).

109. Funcionaria X, "Nuestras Entrevistas–Ernestina Caldevilla," *Funcionarias:
Revista para la mujer*, no. 1, Year I (February 1952).

110. This was also a far cry from *Mujer*, which in one issue counseled women
to speak when spoken to, avoid ostentatious dress, make their homes into
sanctuaries for their husbands, and indulge their spouses' whims—values
practically lifted from the Sección Femenina's creed. See S. Vanó, "Curso
de Belleza—Presentación y justificación," *Funcionarias*, no. 2, Year 1 (April
1952); "¡Qué Chino Tan Sabio!," *Mujer*, no. 202 (April 1954), 30; "Al
marido hay que tratarle así . . . ," *Mujer*, no. 202 (April 1954), 41.

111. Morcillo, *The Seduction of Modern Spain*, 14.

112. "Al Abrir," *Funcionarias*, no. 1, Year I (February 1952).

113. The latter of these problems, admittedly, was not addressed in the form
of a *consultorio sentimental*, but in a feature on how to behave while on
vacation by *Mujer*'s advice columnist, Lidia Dupont, and thus bears some
measure of kinship with her regular column. See Lidia Dupont, "Si sales
de vacaciones . . . ," *Mujer*, no. 216 (June 1955); for Muñoz Ruiz, see Muñoz
Ruiz, "Los consultorios sentimentales," 219–39. For an example of such a
column, see Macrina, "Consultorio Femenino," *Revista Jorba*, no. 15, Year
III (April 1955).

114. Muñoz Ruiz argues this very point of both *Teresa* and a growing number of similarly government-aligned and -sponsored women's magazines
that would follow in the 1960s, from groups such as the Catholic lay
organization Opus Dei, or the Comisaría General de Abastecimientos y
Transportes (Commissary-General for Supply and Transport), an agency
within the Ministry of Commerce. See Muñoz Ruiz, "La construcción
de las relaciones de género en el franquismo y sus conflictos," 223.

115. "Ad for SEN-APPEAL," *Mujer*, no. 202 (April 1954), 41; "Ad for Polvo
Maquillador DANAMASK," *Mujer*, no. 200 (February 1954), 2.

116. "Ad for Curso Fémina CCC, Corte y Confección—Los Hombres las
prefieren . . . elegantes!," *Mujer*, no. 200 (February 1954), 3.

117. "La moda británica," *Mujer*, no. 200 (February 1954), 12–13.

118. "Ad for Colchones FLEX," *Mujer*, no. 211 (January 1955), 4; "Ad for Hispano-Suiza Blenders and Electric Razors," *Revista Jorba*, no. 15, Year III (April 1955); and Graciela Elizalde, "El lavaplatos no es un 'rompeplatos,'" *Revista Jorba*, no. 15, Year III (April 1955).
119. May, *Homeward Bound*, chap. 7. For the kitchen debate, see de Grazia, *Irresistible Empire*, 75–78, 93–95.
120. For the 1952 West German exhibition, see Castillo, "The American 'Fat Kitchen' in Europe," 44–49. For other reactions to American mass consumer culture, see Cieraad, "The Radiant American Kitchen," 113–36; and Saarikangas, "What's New? Women Pioneers and the Finnish State Meet the American Kitchen," 285–311. For Spanish appliance ownership figures, see Fundación FOESSA, *Informe Sociológico Sobre la Situación Social en España, 1966*, 74–76.
121. See "Ad for Curso Fémina CCC, Corte y Confección," 3.
122. For the suit, white shirt, and tie as uniform markers of middle-class status as well as masculine stability, see Paff Ogle and Damhorst, "Dress for Success in the Popular Press"; and Lurie, *The Language of Clothes*.
123. Morcillo, *True Catholic Womanhood*, 59.
124. Rappaport, "'A Husband and His Wife's Dresses.'"
125. Lisette, "Ideas," *Revista Jorba*, no. 14, Year III (March 1955).
126. Mauricio Estany, "Ensayo que da en el blanco," *Revista Jorba*, no. 13, Year III (February 1955).
127. Lisette, "Ideas," *Revista Jorba*, no. 16, Year III (May 1955).
128. This stands in contrast with the case of the postwar United States, where, as historian Lizabeth Cohen has shown, the rise of credit and the consumer-housewife unfolded in tandem with social and business practices that underscored both the primacy of male authority and the unreliability of women in the making of family financial decisions. This, according to Cohen, produced the "husband-wife dyad," featuring a male architect of family financial policy paired with a female consumer-housewife who executed rather than developed that plan. See Cohen, *A Consumer's Republic*, 147–48.
129. For Seregni and post-1953 anti-Americanism, see Seregni, *El Anti-Americanismo Español*, 173–82.
130. C. A. Mantua, "María Teresa Dice . . . ¿Mis Felices Vacaciones?," *Mujer*, no. 205 (July 1954), 12.
131. Mantua, "María Teresa Dice . . . ¿Mis Felices Vacaciones?"

132. C. A. Mantua, "María Teresa Dice ... Una fiesta inolvidable," *Mujer*, no. 206 (August 1954), 13; C. A. Mantua, "María Teresa Dice ... ¿Acaso Tengo Novio?," *Mujer*, no. 208 (September 1954), 12; C. A. Mantua, "María Teresa Dice ... Año Nuevo, ¿Vida Nueva?," *Mujer*, no. 211 (January 1955), 13.

133. C. A. Mantua, "María Teresa Dice ... La Respuesta de Dick," *Mujer*, no. 212 (February 1955), 13. Read thusly, Mantua's story becomes a commentary akin to critiques of a materialist early twentieth-century American cultural aesthetic that Victoria de Grazia found circulating at Rotary International's Dresden chapter in the late 1920s. Dresden's Rotarians, de Grazia argues, recognized the promise of American modernism and rejected the pomp of fin-de-siècle bourgeois culture, but at the same time refused to accept the replacement of traditional European aesthetic consumption with the humdrum pragmatism of ordinary American consumer culture. de Grazia, *Irresistible Empire*, 45–47.

134. Mantua, "María Teresa Dice ... ¿Acaso Tengo Novio?"

135. Lina Font, "Cuento de Verano—El Diplomático," *Revista Jorba*, no. 1, Year I (June 1953).

136. "Para Usted, Caballero," *Revista Jorba*, no. 2 (September 1953).

137. For Santiago de Anta, see "Don Ramón Serrano Súñer, caballero del ideal que redime a España, estudia los problemas de trabajo y de economía de las provincias catalanas," *La Vanguardia Española*, 16 June 1939; for Segismundo de Anta, see Manuel del Arco, "Mano a Mano—Segismundo de Anta," *La Vanguardia Española*, 23 February 1939; and "Inauguración del Primer Salón de la Moda Española," *La Vanguardia Española*, 6 March 1941.

138. Such photo spreads were in actuality doubly elite, as examples of what fashion scholar Alison Lurie has termed "conspicuous multiplication," or the acquisition and display of multiple specialized suits of clothing as a marker of wealth and class. See Lurie, *The Language of Clothes*. For the price of a chicken in 1958—specifically, the price for which it sold in the cheaply priced supermarket recently opened in the regional capital of La Coruña—see R. Ventureira and C. Fernández, "'Teles' viejas, a medio millón," *La Voz de Galicia*, 25 February 2001, online database, accessed 22 December 2008, http://www.lavozdegalicia.es/hemeroteca/2001/02/25/440223.shtml.

139. Juan Gyenes, "S. E. El Jefe de Estado Generalísimo Franco," *Señor: La Revista del Hombre* [henceforth, *Señor*], no. 1, Year I (November 1955), 3.

140. See, for instance, Marquesa de [Marquise of] Quintanar, "La Elegancia y la Sencillez de la Casa de Alba," *Señor*, no. 1, Year I (November 1955).

141. See, for instance, Sanchez Moreno, *Distinción y Etiqueta Moderna*, 6; and, López Sainz, *La Cortesía en la Vida Moderna*, 33–34.

142. María Pilar de Molina, "Confidencia," *Señor*, no. 10 (Spring 1958).

143. See, for instance, "Advertisement for Camel Cigarettes," *Señor*, no. 2, Year I (Spring 1956); and "Advertisement for Certina Watches," *Señor*, no. 3, Year II (May 1956).

144. Abella, *La vida cotidiana bajo el régimen de Franco*, 216; Folguera Crespo, "El Franquismo. El Retorno," 529, 531.

145. For more on menswear as Franco-era cultural battleground, see chapter 4 in this volume.

146. "Petronius," "La primera impresión es la que prevalece," *Señor*, no. 3, Year II (May 1956). Similarly, Petronius elsewhere suggested that Spain possessed a particular "temperament" that could help perfect male elegance by moderating the "excesses" of foreign ideas about fashion. See "Petronius," "Comentario," *Señor*, no. 4, Year II (August 1956).

147. Mestre y Ballbé, S. R. C., "Nuevos Atisbos," *Señor*, no. 1, Year I (November 1955).

148. See note 52 above.

149. See, for example, "Nuestras Entrevistas: Interesantes declaraciones de Elena Andaluz Recalde," *Funcionarias*, no. 2, Year I (April 1952).

150. P. L. Campos Tejón, "Las Estrellas en la Intimidad: Carmen Sevilla," *Ana María: Revista para la Mujer* [henceforth, *Ana María*], no. 6 (November 1958); "Pequeña historia de matrimonios felices: Lucile [sic] Ball, 'Cabello rubio' revive en la TV su felicidad hogareña," *Ana María*, no. 2 (October 1958).

151. "Las necesidades de hoy no son las de ayer," *Ana María*, no. 3 (October 1958).

3. (Super)Marketing Western Modernity

1. Antonio Ortíz de Zárate, "Carta del Director-¡Renovarse . . . o morir!," *SPARCO*, no. 12 (February 1961), 8.

2. *Autoservicios* came in three varieties distinguished by square footage, ranging from small *tiendas de autoservicio* (usually abbreviated *autoservicios*), to mid-sized *superettes*, to the still larger *supermercados*—"supermarkets." In practice, however, *autoservicio* and *supermercado* were used interchangeably and as shorthands for the whole genre. For categories of *autoservicios*, see

"Preguntas y respuestas sobre el Autoservicio," *SPARCO*, no. 9 (November 1960), 6.

3. "Establecimientos SPAR de Autoservicio," *SPARCO*, no. 12, (February 1961), 4–5.

4. See, for instance, the floor plans proposed in "Productividad comparativa de tiendas tradicionales y de autoservicio," *SPARCO*, no. 9 (November 1960), 1, 4–5; and Miguel Angel Alonso, "Planificación de Autoservicios," *SPARCO*, no. 47 (December 1963), 9.

5. SPAR of Spain boasted 4,120 locations compared to 2,142 Dutch affiliates. See "SPAR Europa-Los 14 Eslabones de la Cadena SPAR," *SPARCO*, no. 37 (February 1963), 12–13.

6. While similar stores had previously existed, they neither used the moniker "supermarket" nor had any substantially transformative effect on the grocery trade. See Zimmerman, *Los Supermercados*, chap. 2.

7. Deutsch, *Building a Housewife's Paradise*, 50–53. This was also the source of early complaints from independent grocers, who called the chains monopolistic. See Zimmerman, *Los Supermercados*, 21–24.

8. Zimmerman, *Los Supermercados*, 33–35. For SPAR's founding, see notes 12, 13, and 14 below.

9. Deutsch, *Building a Housewife's Paradise*, 53–54; Zimmerman, *Los Supermercados*, 58.

10. Zimmerman, *Los Supermercados*, 61–63.

11. Deutsch, *Building a Housewife's Paradise*, 145; Zimmerman, *Los Supermercados*, 41, 69–70.

12. Maixé-Altes, "Interpreting the Early Stages of the Self-Service Revolution in Europe," 12, 24n33.

13. "Treinta Años de Existencia," *SPARCO*, no. 29 (June 1962), 3–4, 6, 18. For SPAR in Britain, see Maixé-Altes, "Interpreting the Early Stages of the Self-Service Revolution in Europe," 12; de Grazia, *Irresistible Empire*, chap. 8.

14. Zimmerman, *Los Supermercados*, 359; Bowlby, *Carried Away*, 160–61.

15. Letter from Robert J. Bond to José M. Ruiz-Morales, 2 July 1956, AGA-CAT 29605, Folder 1, Subfolder 7. For language on supermarkets, see "El Ministro de Comercio Inaugura, en Nombre del Jefe del Estado, la XXVI Feria Internacional de Muestras de Barcelona," *ABC* (Madrid), 3 June 1958, 34.

16. For instance, "Advertising: Supermarket Buyers are Super," *New York Times*, 6 February 1957; Ben Weberman, "Chain Stores Enlist Own Shop-

ping Center Realtors," *Journal of Commerce*, 16 August 1956; and "The 'American Way' Supermarket in *Italy*," *American Exporter*, September 1956, 25–27; all in AGA-CAT 29605/1, Subfolder 7.

17. Maixé-Altes, "Interpreting the Early Stages of the Self-Service Revolution in Europe," 5; "Experiencia Piloto del Autoservicio de Barcelo," undated, AGA-CAT 29608; Letter from Juan Abril to Ilmo. Sr. Comisario General de Abastecimientos, 27 May 1958, AGA-CAT 29608/2; "Proyecto de Sociedad Auxiliar de Abastecimientos," 5 November 1958, AGA-CAT 29605/1, Subfolder 8; "Plan de Red Nacional de Autoservicios," November 1958, AGA-CAT 29608; "El Desarrollo de los Autoservicios," *ICA*, no. 136 (January–February 1962), 6–8; and, "Informe Relativo a Supermercados, Federación Nacional de Almacenistas de Alimentación," 11 February 1959, AGA-CAT 29607/5, Subfolder 2.

18. Federación Nacional de Almacenistas de Alimentación, "Informe Relativo a Supermercados," 11 February 1959, AGA-CAT 29607/5, Subfolder 2.

19. Federación Nacional de Almacenistas de Alimentación, "Informe Relativo a Supermercados,"; Informe sobre situación de "ORGANIZACION SUPER-MERCADO," 21 July 1958, AGA-CAT 29608/7, p. 5; General, "Propuesta-Plan Supermercados Madrid y Barcelona," 7 April 1959, AGA-CAT 29607/5, Subfolder 1, p. 1; Comisario General, "Propuesta de Estudio Sobre la Situacion al 1 de Marzo de 1960 del Desarrollo de los Autoservicios de Alimentacion," 1 March 1960, AGA-CAT 29605/2. For one such petition for affiliate status, see Antonio Muñoz Chao to Comisario General, 16 March 1959, AGA-CAT 29608/6.

20. Comisario General to Ministro de Comercio, "Informe Relativo a Legislación sobre Supermercados," 8 September 1959, AGA-CAT 29607/1, Subfolder 3, pp. 8–9.

21. Astorga's working or—at best—petit bourgeois status follows from García Rebull's assertion that she "needed to work" and that her subsequent unemployment was neither by choice nor due to marriage. Letter from Tomás García Rebull to Antonio Pérez-Ruiz Salcedo, 30 September 1958, AGA-CAT 29608/6; Comisario General to Secretary of the Minister of Commerce, Solicitud de la Srta Rogelia Astorga Alda, de ser admitida como auxiliar de esta comisaria general, 17 January 1959, AGA-CAT 29608/6; and Rogelia Astorga Alda to Tomás García Rebull, [Unsigned Note], n.d., AGA-CAT 29608/6.

22. Letter from Enrique J. Ribalta to Antonio Pérez-Ruiz Salcedo, 4 April 1959, AGA-CAT 29608/1. For another type of request, see Letter from Manuel Llonís Romero to Personal Secretary to the Comisario General Lázaro Gómez, 16 March 1959, AGA-CAT 29608/6. Plaintiff Antonio Muñoz Chao, previously denied CAT affiliate status because of his store's proximity to an existing affiliate, repeated his request, claiming that the other store was never built.

23. Antonio García Fernández to Excmo. Sr. Ministro de Comercio, Letter and Project Summary for a Private Commercial Organization to Sell Produce, 21 May 1958, AGA-CAT 29608/2. Tellingly, García Fernández self-interestedly offered himself to manage the proposed venture.

24. For Federación Nacional de Almacenistas de Alimentación, see note 19; for Olmedo's article and a response by Antonio Pérez-Ruiz Salcedo, see F.P. de la P, "Tres Mil Establecimientos de Ultramarinos Hay en Madrid," *Ya*, 28 September 1960; Letter from Antonio Pérez-Ruiz Salcedo to Aquilino Morcillo, Director of "Ya," 28 September 1960; and Antonio Pérez-Ruiz Salcedo, "Replica a unas declaraciones de Don Antonio Olmedo, Presidente del Gremio de Detallistas de Ultramarinos," 28 September 1960; all in AGA-CAT 29605/1, Subfolder 2. For a similar complaint, see "La C.A.T., los Supermercados y los Detallistas Madrileños," *ICA*, no. 112 (January 1960), 29–30. For earlier American complaints, see Zimmerman, *Los Supermercados*, 24–31, 69–71.

25. Pérez-Ruiz Salcedo, "Replica a unas declaraciones . . . ," 28 September 1960, AGA-CAT 29605/1, Subfolder 2.

26. Not everyone was so charitable. One CAT affiliate described Olmedo's editorial as little more than a cynical bid to retain his guild presidency. Letter from Autoservicios San Bartolomé to Antonio Pérez-Ruiz Salcedo, 14 October 1960, AGA-CAT 29605/1, Subfolder 2.

27. Supermercados—Tabla Estadística, 17 June 1960, AGA-CAT 29605/1; in January 1960, Spain boasted 1 autoservicio for every 97,000 inhabitants, or an estimate of 309 autoservicios for a national population of roughly 30 million—a ratio certainly reached six months later, given self-service's rapid spread. See "El Autoservicio en Europa: No. de habitantes por cada establecimiento de Autoservicio," *SPARCO*, no. 11 (January 1961), 1. For population figures, see "Estado XI—Reparto de Habitantes de Hecho por Zonas, Tomo I—Cifras Generales de Habitantes. Censo de 1960, Censos de Población," INE, accessed

26 February 2011, http://www.ine.es/inebaseweb/treeNavigation .do?tn=92670&tns=126665#126665. For poverty in Granada, see Cazorla Sánchez, *Fear and Progress*, 73, 131.

28. Ortíz de Zárate, "Carta del Director-¡Renovarse . . . o morir!"

29. "Los Supermercados a Rayos X: Todo los que a las Amas de Casa les Interesa Sobre Este Nuevo Sistema de Venta," *AMA*, no. 1 (15 January 1960), 14–15.

30. "Radio nacional 12-12-1959"; "Antonio Pérez-Ruiz Salcedo to Director of 'PROA' Daily Newspaper [Province of León]," 1 December 1959; "L. Figuerola-Ferreti, Subdirector of Noticiarios y Documentales Cinematograficos to Secretary of the Comisario General," 2 October 1959; and "Cuestionario sobre los temas de Autoservicio y Supermercados para el Excmo. Sr. Comisario General de Abastecimientos y Transportes. Para Radio Nacional de España—Ultima Hora de la Actualidad," 18 September 1958, all in AGA-CAT 29605/2, Subfolder 5.

31. "Antonio Pérez-Ruiz Salcedo to Pilar Salcedo," 30 December 1960, AGA-CAT 29669/1; and "María del Pilar Corvera de Cocero to Antonio Pérez-Ruiz Salcedo," 11 December 1961, AGA-CAT 29669/2, Subfolder 1.

32. Ama de Casa, "Carta al ama de casa," *AMA: La Revista de las Amas de Casa Españolas*, no. 1 (15 January 1960), 3.

33. Ama de Casa, "Carta al ama de casa," 3.

34. Newspaper Ad—"Ama de Casa: Revista de la Familia Española Patrocinada por la Organiazcion Supermercados C.A.T.," 19 December 1959, AGA-CAT 29669.

35. "Distribución de Revistas 'Ama de Casa,'" 19 December 1959, AGA-CAT 29669.

36. "Los Supermercados a Rayos X: Todo los que a las Amas de Casa les Interesa Sobre Este Nuevo Sistema de Venta," *AMA*, no. 1 (15 January 1960), 14–15.

37. "Los Supermercados a Rayos X: Todo los que a las Amas de Casa les Interesa Sobre Este Nuevo Sistema de Venta," *AMA*, no. 1 (15 January 1960), 14–15; "Los Supermercados a Rayos X: Todo los que a las Amas de Casa les Interesa Sobre Este Nuevo Sistema de Venta," *AMA*, no. 2 (1 February 1960), 14–15; "Los Supermercados a Rayos X: Todo lo que tienen que saber las amas de casa," *AMA*, no. 6 (1 April 1960), 12–13.

38. Antonio Pérez-Ruiz Salcedo, "Charla de Don Antonio con las Amas de Casa," *AMA*, no. 4 (1 March 1960), 5; and "Prognóstico para su Despensa

(Vale del 1 al 15 de marzo)," *AMA*, no. 4 (1 March 1960). For reference to such a complaint, see A. Pérez-Ruiz Salcedo, "Charla de DON ANTONIO con las AMAS DE CASA," *AMA*, no. 20 (1 November 1960), 5.

39. Antonio Pérez-Ruiz Salcedo, "Charla de Don Antonio con las Amas de Casa," *AMA*, no. 1 (15 January 1960), 5; and, Antonio Pérez-Ruiz Salcedo, "Charla de D. Antonio con las Amas de Casa," *AMA*, no. 23 (12 December 1960), 6–7.

40. See figure 8; and "Con la Historieta del Día, Aprenda Usted Economía," *AMA*, no. 14 (1 August 1960), 6.

41. "Carta al ama de casa," *AMA*, no. 10 (1 June 1960); A. Pérez-Ruiz Salcedo, "Charla de DON ANTONIO con las AMAS DE CASA," *AMA*, no. 14, (1 August 1960).

42. A. Pérez-Ruiz Salcedo, "Charla de DON ANTONIO con las AMAS DE CASA," *AMA*, no. 3 (15 February 1960), 5; A. Pérez-Ruiz Salcedo, "Charla de DON ANTONIO con las AMAS DE CASA," *AMA*, no. 20 (1 November 1960), 5.

43. A. Pérez-Ruiz Salcedo, "Charla de DON ANTONIO con las AMAS DE CASA," *AMA*, no. 16 (1 September 1960), 5.

44. See the introduction to this volume, notes 61, 63–64, and 66.

45. Josefina Figueras, "Nuria Espert: Somos una familia burguesa y feliz," *AMA*, no. 18 (1 October 1960), 29; "Las Artistas en la Cocina-Maria Mahor y las Tortillas Rellenas," *AMA*, no. 20 (1 November 1960); "Carta al Ama de Casa," *AMA*, no. 23 (15 December 1960), 3; and Morcillo, *True Catholic Womanhood*, 25–26. Similarly Spanish women's growing civic engagement through homemakers' associations in the 1960s gained them only a marginalized voice on traditionally feminine issues. See Radcliff, *Making Democratic Citizens in Spain*, 109–11.

46. "Ullastres, en los hogares españoles," *ICA*, no. 139 (May 1962), 6–7; Antonio Ortíz de Zárate, *La Familia SPAR: Revista para el ama de casa y la familia* [henceforth, *La Familia SPAR*], no. 3 (August 1960), 1; "Mi Mujer No Trabaja," *La Familia SPAR*, no. 6 (November 1960), 6; "El Ama de Casa Puede Adelgazar Fácilmente," *La Familia SPAR*, no. 15 (September 1961), 4; Jorge de la Riva, "Las Buenas Amas de Casa," *ICA*, no. 289 (April 1975), 37.

47. Some positions at CAT autoservicios were indeed reserved for women. See "Unsigned Response to Nicolás Murga Santos," n.d., AGA-CAT 29608/6. For *La Familia SPAR*, see "El éxito puede resultar peligroso para la mujer:

La vida íntima se resiente del exito en los negocios," *La Familia SPAR*, no. 10 (March 1961), 6.

48. For both of these approaches to consumption, see Morcillo, *True Catholic Womanhood*, 35–36, 56–64.

49. Pilar Amillo, "¡Pieles! El sueño de la mujeres, el terror de los maridos," *AMA*, no. 1 (15 January 1960); Pilar Amillo, "¿Prefiere usted los conjuntos sport? Una moda que siempre favorece," *AMA*, no. 2 (1 February 1960), 35–37; "Ad—Destaque . . . las medias Jenny," *AMA*, no. 5 (15 March 1960), 58; "Ad—Super-Bañador Gom," *AMA*, no. 35 (15 June 1961).

50. Hernando Calleja, Televisión Española, to Comisaria General de Abastecimientos y Transportes, 27 January 1962, AGA-CAT 29669/2, Subfolder 1. Notably, viewers also criticized the ads, but only because they could not afford the brands shown, not because they disagreed with the kind of shopping described. See V. A. Cortél de Echevarría (Palencia) to Club Ama, n.d., AGA-CAT 29669/2, Subfolder 1.

51. Abelardo Cervera Martínez, "Informe de la [*sic*] impresiones recogidas con motivo del viaje a los EE.UU. de America, sobre la distribución de alimentos, y fórmula para el futuro en España," August 1958, AGA-CAT 29608/7.

52. "Los Supermercados a Rayos X: Todo los que a las Amas de Casa les Interesa," *AMA*, no. 1 (January 1960), 14–15. Such declarations were common, including in pamphlets by the National Cash Register Company, a fixture in the American grocery trade, which promoted the supermarket in Spain as a prosperity-generating American innovation. See National Cash-Register Company, "Super Market Merchandising: The True Look of the Super Market Industry 1959," AGA-CAT 29605; and, National Cash-Register Company, "El Autoservicio tiene exito en negocios de tipos tan variados como los que aqui se ilustran . . . en todo el mundo!," AGA-CAT 29610.

53. "Pregunte usted lo que quiera: Adelaida G. Cebrián (Madrid)," *AMA*, no. 5 (15 March 1960), 2.

54. "Los supermercados, a Rayos X," *AMA*, no. 2 (1 February 1960), 14.

55. "Agreement between the National Association of Food Chains and the Comisaria de Abastecimientos y Transportes," 16 June 1959, AGA-CAT 29607/2. "Supermarket USA" is notable both as another display of the supermarket's American origin and promise to export prosperity to Europe and because the exhibition had visited communist Yugoslavia in 1957,

where it also attempted to promote the supermarket. See Hamilton, "Supermarket USA Confronts State Socialism," 137–60.

56. Hamilton, "Supermarket USA Confronts State Socialism"; Álvaro Ortíz de Zárate, "Autoservicio y Supermercados," *ICA*, no. 110 (July 1959), 10–12; J. de los Cobos, "Colaboración: Algunos aspectos del libre servicio," *ICA*, no. 111 (August 1959), 24.

57. "Visita Inspección Supermercado del Ejército de Tierra," 6 May 1960; "Visita Inspección Supermercado Núm. 6, Calle de Embajadores," 20 May 1960; "Visita Inspección Supermercado del Ministerio del Aire," 1 April 1960; and "Visita Inspección Supermercado oo," 25 May 1960, all in AGA-CAT 29605/1, Subfolder 1.

58. "Grafico porcentaje CAT y privados (2 colores)," n.d. [three pie graphs appear, labeled August–September 1958, October 1958, and September 1959], AGA-CAT 29605; this estimate is based on the above percentage, and a total of eleven CAT supermarkets on record in July–August 1959. See "Resumen de ventas de todos los supermercados, Meses: Julio–Agosto [1959]," n.d., AGA-CAT 29610/5. For the opening of the CAT's military supermarket, by which this otherwise undated report can be placed in 1959, see "Supermercado Militar," *A.B.C.*, 23 July 1959.

59. Exemplifying the latter, in January 1960 the American supermarket chain Market Basket tried to enter the Spanish market, writing to Pérez-Ruiz Salcedo's agency for leave to open branches in Spain, though the CAT's response to this request leaves its outcome unclear. See Antonio Pérez-Ruiz Salcedo to F. C. Thomas, Inc., 7 March 1960, AGA-CAT 29605/1, Subfolder 4.

60. Indeed, the chain listed "dignifying the [grocer's] profession" as one of the SPAR system's five benefits. See "El Sistema SPAR," *SPARCO,* no. 1 (March 1960), 1, in AGA-CAT 29621/2, Subfolder 1.

61. Maixé-Altes, "Interpreting the Early Stages of the Self-Service Revolution in Europe," 12.

62. Memoro, "Interview with Álvaro Ortíz de Zárate," accessed 10 September 2012, http://www.memoro.org/es-es/video.php?id=4011; Álvaro Ortíz de Zárate to D. Lázaro Gomez, 16 June 1959, AGA-CAT 29605/2, Subfolder 1; and "Curso de Autoservicio de Productos Alimenticios, Dirigido por Álvaro Ortíz de Zárate . . . 15 al 19 de Junio de 1959," n.d., AGA-CAT 29605/2, Subfolder 1.

63. "Establecimientos SPAR de Autoservicio," *SPARCO*, no. 11 (January 1961), 4–5; "20 Aniversario," *SPARCO*, no. 17 (July 1961), 1; Álvaro Ortíz de Zárate, "Inauguración de SPAR Española," *La Familia SPAR*, no. 1 (June 1960), 1; "Establecimientos SPAR de Autoservicio: ¡201!," *SPARCO*, no. 18 (August 1961), 6–7; "Número No-SPAR y SPAR de Autoservicios," *SPARCO*, no. 23 (December 1961), 1; "La organización SPAR cumple su cuarto año en España," *SPARCO*, no. 40 (May 1963), 1; and "Relación de Autoservicios SPAR por Zonas según Marcha del negocio," *SPARCO*, no. 45 (October 1963), 21.

64. For VéGé, see "La planificación del trabajo en una zona VéGé," and "Noticias de las Zonas VéGé," in *Revista VéGé*, no. 24, Year IV (November–December 1965); and José María López Roca, "Editorial: ¿A Dónde Vamos? Programa de desarrollo VéGé 1966," *Revista VéGé*, no. 27, Year V (March 1966). For Yecla and Amorebieta, see "Establecimientos SPAR de Autoservicio," *SPARCO*, no. 11 (January 1961), 4–5; and, "Establecimientos SPAR de Autoservicio: ¡201!," *SPARCO*, no. 18 (August 1961), 6–7.

65. Maixé-Altes, "Interpreting the Early Stages of the Self-Service Revolution in Europe," 12–14.

66. See also "Exteriorización," *SPARCO*, no. 15 (May 1961), 12; "Linea SPAR-Identificacion y Exteriorizacion SPAR," *SPARCO*, no. 42 (July 1963), 6–7; "¡Atención! La nueva exteriorización de las franjas," *SPARCO*, no. 51 (April 1964), 10.

67. Álvaro Ortíz de Zárate, "Carta del Director-¡Más Luz!," *SPARCO*, no. 13 (March 1961), 10; "La Música de Supermercados y Autoservicios," *SPARCO*, no. 38 (March 1963), 17–18.

68. "El buen y el mal sparista (dos dialoguitos)," *SPARCO*, no. 19 (September 1961), 1; and Álvaro Ortíz de Zárate, "Doña Gárrula," *La Familia SPAR*, no. 8 (January 1961), 1.

69. José Medina Gómez, "El autoservicio ha aparecido en Madrid. Dos establecimientos han adoptado la fórmula de 'sírvase usted mismo,'" *Blanco y Negro (Madrid)*, 7 December 1957, 38.

70. Miller, *Feeding Barcleona, 1714–1975*, 229–30.

71. Guerin, "Limitations of Supermarkets in Spain," 24–25.

72. Miller, *Feeding Barcelona*, 231. Since the early 1990s, Barcelona's official Municipal Markets Institute has cultivated this synergistic relationship between autoservicios and market halls, opening supermarket branches inside—rather than simply near—many of the city's new as well as newly

renovated market halls, including Concepció as well as the central Santa Caterina and Fort Pienc markets. See Miller, *Feeding Barcelona*, 251; and "'Mix' Comercial i Institut Municipal de Mercats de Barcelona," *Mercats: L'experiència de Barcelona* (Barcelona: Ajuntament de Barcelona, 2015), accessed 18 February 2017, http://w110.bcn.cat/Mercats/Continguts /Documents/Fitxers/pub_mercats_cat_def.pdf.

73. Ricardo Martín, "Marcaje Perfecto," *SPARCO*, no. 46 (November 1963), 21; "Relaciones Públicas," *SPARCO*, no. 22 (November 1961), 13. For building familiarity with the SPAR brand, see, for instance, "Exhibe—Da Preferencia—Promueve: Chocolate SPAR," *SPARCO*, no. 10 (December 1960), 2; "Articulos de Marca SPAR," *SPARCO*, no. 44 (September 1963), 7; Pedro Manuel Pinzolas, "Una obligada necesidad como Sparistas," *SPARCO*, no. 48 (January 1964), 6–7; A. F., "Cuidado que Somos Cabezones! (o el desprecio de nuestras marcas)," *SPARCO*, no. 56 (September 1964), 20.

74. "Inspección Supermercado Núm 6," AGA-CAT 29605/1; "Inspección Supermercado Núm 10 de Zaragoza," AGA-CAT 29605/1. For the Chistu brand, see Gran Enciclopedia Navarra, "Conservas Chistu, S.A.," accessed 7 September 2012, http://www.enciclopedianavarra.biz/navarra/conservas -chistu-sa/5183/1/.

75. A. O. de Z., "Mensaje para Usted, Señora," *La Familia SPAR*, no. 3 (August 1960), 1. This column went on to explain the history of the chain, placing heavy emphasis—as did other, similar articles—on the store's thirty years of experience and the fact that it was a staple elsewhere in Europe. See, for example, "La Cadena se Fortalece," *La Familia SPAR*, no. 11 (April 1961), 1, which actually spoke of "the familiar fir tree" spreading across Spain.

76. "Álvaro Ortíz de Zárate to Dr. Ramiro Matarranz, Director-General of Domestic Commerce," 7 December 1959, AGA-CAT 29621/2, Subfolder 1; "Álvaro Ortíz de Zárate to Antonio Pérez-Ruiz Salcedo," 20 February 1960; "Álvaro Ortíz de Zárate to Antonio Pérez-Ruiz Salcedo," 13 September 1961, AGA-CAT 29621/2; "Álvaro Ortíz de Zárate to Antonio Pérez-Ruiz Salcedo," 21 January 1960, AGA-CAT 29621/2, Subfolder 1; and "Álvaro Ortíz de Zárate to Antonio Pérez-Ruiz Salcedo," 8 June 1961, AGA-CAT 29621/2, Subfolder 1.

77. Álvaro Ortíz de Zárate, "Autoservicio y Supermercados," *ICA*, no. 110 (July 1959), 10–12.

78. Álvaro Ortíz de Zárate, "Carta del Director–¡Esos Dichosos Economatos!," *SPARCO*, no. 10 (December 1960), 8–9; "De Pluma Ajena—Mas

Sobre Economatos," *ICA*, nos. 120–21 (October 1960), 51; "Punto de vista—La injusta competencia de los economatos," *SEPESA: Revista de la Industria y del Comercio de la Alimentación*, no. 2, Year I (June 1965), 32; "Los economatos y la austeridad," *Boletín Autoservicio COVIC*, no. 1 (II Trimester 1968); "El Ministro de Comercio Clausura en Guadalajara la Asamblea de Camaras de la Zona Centro," *A.B.C.*, 26 March 1972.

79. Álvaro Ortíz de Zárate, "Carta del Director—Arbitrios y Servicios Municipales," *SPARCO*, no. 30 (July 1962), 3–6; and "La Ley de Arrendamientos Urbanos, freno comercial," *SPARCO*, no. 39 (April 1963), 4, 7. It should be noted that the Ministries of the Interior, Commerce, and Finance had by 1963 abolished the first of these two laws, the Ley de Arbitrios Municipales, which took effect 31 December 1962. The other would undergo the first of a series of reforms in 1964, but would remain contentious for at least the next eight years. See "Gracias Gobierno!," *SPARCO*, no. 36 (January 1963), 4; "Decreto 4104/1964—Texto Refundido de la Ley de Arrendamientos Urbanos," *Boletín Oficial de Estado*, no. 312 (29 December 1964), 17387–17405.

80. "Interview with Álvaro Ortíz de Zárate." For the difference between training and what *formación* meant at SPAR, see "Formación," *SPARCO*, no. 11 (January 1961), 6.

81. For *SPARCO* as a medium of professional knowledge, see Álvaro Ortíz de Zárate, "Carta del Director—Crece 'SPARCO,'" *SPARCO*, no. 23 (December 1961), 3, especially the magazine's new subtitle, "Technical-Informative Sales Monthly." For accounting and stock rotation, see "Control Administrativo," *SPARCO*, no. 26 (March 1962), 7. For store layouts, see Miguel Ángel Alonso, "Planificación de Autoservicios," *SPARCO*, no. 47 (December 1963), 9; and "Vista de pájaro de los movimientos de compras de cien clientes en un Supermercado," *SPARCO*, no. 50 (March 1964), 12–13. For female shoppers, see "El hombre gana . . . y la mujer gasta: La importancia de la mujer como compradora," *SPARCO*, no. 15 (May 1961), 8; "¡Arriba las Ventas!: ¿Por qué una cliente entra en tu establecimiento?," *SPARCO*, no. 36 (January 1963), 5–6.

82. See A. O. Z, "Comentarios a un Prólogo," *SPARCO*, no. 18 (August 1961), 1–3; Álvaro Ortíz de Zárate, "Carta del Director—Distribución y costo de vida (Importancia económica y social de la distribución)," *SPARCO*, no. 28 (May 1962), 3–4; and, "La tendencia, a favor de los grandes autoservicios," *SPARCO*, no. 5 (July 1960), 3, in AGA-CAT 29621/2, Subfolder 1.

83. "Autoservicio—Entrevista con los hermanos MUÑOZ, de Madrid," *SPARCO*, no. 23 (December 1961), 6–7; Jesús Sánchez Ramiro, "¿Quieres Colaborar?," *SPARCO*, no. 23 (December 1961), 10–11; Manuel Blasco Zaldívar, "¿Quieres Colaborar?," *SPARCO*, no. 25 (February 1962), 7.

84. Maixé-Altes, "Americanización y consumo de masas, la distribución alimentaria en España, 1947–2007," 14. For other letters, see "Invitaciones a Colaborar," *SPARCO*, no. 41 (June 1963), 23; José Luis Monedero, "Anecdotario SPAR," *SPARCO*, no. 48 (January 1964), 20, which introduced a new magazine column featuring testimonials; and "Teodoro Santiago—Matapozuelos (Valladolid)," *SPARCO*, no. 51 (April 1964), 19–21.

85. José Caballé, "Sparistas cien por cien: Don José Caballé, un hombre que se salvó con SPAR," *SPARCO*, no. 38 (May 1963), 21; Diego Martínez, "Sparistas 100%: A SPAR se lo debo todo," *SPARCO*, no. 33, (October 1962), 9.

86. P. P., "Quien a buen árbol se arrima... (cuento viejo)," *SPARCO*, no. 15 (May 1961), 3. See also "Linea Spar–Los fantasmas de D. Faustino," *SPARCO*, no. 38 (March 1963), 5–6.

87. "El Instituto de la Alimentación," *SPARCO*, no. 15 (May 1961), 1. Other such statements abounded. Two months later, for instance, the bulletin called SPAR "an injection of faith, confidence, mutual cooperation ... when we [the Spanish] are so in need of these ... resources for success." See "20 Aniversario," *SPARCO*, no. 17 (July 1961), 1, and also note 1 above.

88. "La tendencia, a favor de los Grandes autoservicios," *SPARCO*, no. 5 (July 1960), 3, in AGA-CAT 29621/2, Subfolder 1; "El Autoservicio en la Spar austríaca," *SPARCO*, no. 11 (January 1961), 7; "La Clave del Éxito: El SPARista inglés que ha logrado unas ventas de £1.000 a la semana (170.000 ptas) en solo 15 meses," *SPARCO*, no. 19 (September 1961), 4–6; "La industria del supermercado en Estados Unidos en 1962," *SPARCO*, no. 41 (June 1963), 18; and "Central Internacional de Compras," *SPARCO*, no. 19 (September 1961), 9.

89. These included an issue of *Die SPAR Familie*, the German predecessor to and almost certainly the template for *La Familia SPAR*. See *SPAR Magazine: Magazine of the National Guild of Spar Grocers, Ltd.* 2, no. 1, (January 1961); *Le Maillon: Revue d'Information de l'Association Française SPAR*, no. 47 (December 1960); and *Die SPAR Familie: Die Kundenzeitschrift für Heim und Hausfrau*, no. 52 (29 December 1960), all in AGA-CAT 29621/2, Subfolder 1.

90. "Las Nuevas Generaciones Habitarán un Pais con Salarios Elevados y Niveles de Consumo Europeos," *ICA*, no. 137 (March 1962), 11–12; "45

Minutos con Don Francisco de la Caballería: Los autoservicios españoles estan a la altura de los extranjeros," *CONAUTA: Revista Técnica del Autoservicio* [henceforth, *CONAUTA*], no. 1, Year I (December 1963–January 1964), 6–8.

91. A. Navarro Aranda, "Las Pastas Alimenticias," *CONAUTA*, no. 1, Year I (January 1964), 51; and, for other references, see, for example, A. Navarro Aranda, "Las pastas alimenticias conservan la línea," *CONAUTA*, no. 3, Year I (April–May 1964), 44–45; and "Las Pastas Alimenticias: Nutritivas, Agradables, Económicas," *CONAUTA*, no. 35, Year V (July–August 1968), 35.

92. M. C. H., "Nuevos trigos en España," *CONAUTA*, no. 19, Year III (November–December 1966), 42–44; and "El sake, bebida nacional del Japón," *CONAUTA*, no. 13, Year II (December 1965), 49–53.

93. "Los españoles comemos mucho en cantidad y poco en calidad," *SPARCO*, no. 40 (May 1963), 21.

94. R.C. Cañaveral, "Hacia una alimentación española abierta," *CONAUTA*, no. 19, Year III (November–December 1966), 56.

95. A. J. Cruz, "El Café Soluble, ¿Barrera del Mercado al Café en Grano?," *Revista VéGé*, no. 30, Year V (June 1966); Atomus, "Triunfo Científico Español," *CONAUTA*, nos. 41–42, Year VI (March–April 1969), 35; and Manuel Calvo Hernando, "Conservación de carne por esterilización atómica," *CONAUTA*, no. 25, Year IV (July–August 1967), 11–12.

96. Raimundo de los Reyes, "Es necesaria y urgente una mayor colaboración entre el capital y la investigación alimentaria," *CONAUTA*, no. 36, Year V (September 1968), 29–30; Raimundo Algora, "La falta de ayuda oficial igual a colonialismo económico," *CONAUTA*, no. 47, Year VI (October 1969), 5.

97. Maixé-Altés, "Americanization y consumo de masas, la distribución alimentaria en España," 18, 20–21, table 5.

98. Bhabha, *The Location of Culture*, 2–4; for another use of Bhabha's in-between moment as a framework for analysis of Franco-era society, see Morcillo, *The Seduction of Modern Spain*, 14.

4. "You Can Achieve Anything Nowadays"

1. The quotation in the title of this chapter is taken from the film *Relaciones Casi Públicas*, directed by José Luis Sáenz de Heredia.

2. [Untitled Speech Draft], n.d., AGUN-JMM/144/494/001; "Apertura de la Asamblea Internacional de Relaciones Públicas," *La Vanguardia Española*, 26 May 1966.

3. "Los Supermercados a Rayos X: Todo los que a las Amas de Casa les Interesa," *AMA*, no. 1 (January 1960), 14–15; J. García Ibañez et al., "Coloquio Profesional—Momento Actual de Nuestra Publicidad," *I.P.: Información de la Publicidad* [henceforth, *I.P.*], no. 2 (February 1963), 6–7.

4. Lears, *Fables of Abundance*, 88–89.

5. Ciarlo, *Advertising Empire*, 23, 114, 134; Richards, *The Commodity Culture of Victorian England:*, 12; García Ruescas, *Historia de la Publicidad*, 17–18, 255. For the rather different French case, see Tiersten, *Marianne in the Market*, 69–70; and Martin, *Selling Beauty*, chap. 3.

6. Lears, *Fables of Abundance*, 89; Fox, *The Mirror Makers*, 14–15.

7. Fox, *The Mirror Makers*, 20–30; for Walter Dill Scott, see "Biography—Walter Dill Scott Collection Finding Aid," Northwestern University Archives, Evanston IL, accessed 8 August 2012, http://files.library.northwestern.edu/findingaids/walter_d_scott.pdf. Dill Scott's influence reflected a late nineteenth-century shift in advertising from rational slogans to reliance on irrational, emotional appeals. See Strasser, *Satisfaction Guaranteed*, 1989. For public relations, see Tye, *The Father of Spin*, chap. 12.

8. Richards, *The Commodity Culture of Victorian England*, 12; Nevett, *Advertising in Britain*, 78–79, 99, 102–3, 107, 120–21, 126–29, 150–56. French and German advertising was meanwhile similarly in transition. See Ciarlo, *Advertising Empire*; Tiersten, *Marianne in the Market*.

9. These included, for instance, the creation of a national advertisers' syndicate in 1964. Javier María Pascual, "Prat Gaballi, Pionero y Maestro," *I.P.*, no. 2 (February 1963), 10.

10. Javier María Pascual, "Prat Gaballi, Pionero y Maestro"; J. A., "Bibliografía," *I.P.*, no. 2 (February 1963), 11; García Ruescas, *Historia de la Publicidad*, 254, 260–74, 309–10; Rodríguez Salcedo, "Public Relations before 'Public Relations' in Spain," 285–87.

11. For Spanish universities, see Claret Miranda, *El Atroz Desmoche*, 19; Rubio Mayoral, *Disciplina y Rebeldía*, 84–85; and Morcillo, *True Catholic Womanhood*, 82. For comparative regional wealth, see Tamames, *Estructura Económica de España*, 2:890–94; and Ferrer Andreu, "Distribución regional de la renta en España, (1947–1970)." For Spanish tourist spots and regional differences in hotel capacities, see Pack, *Tourism and Dictatorship*, 98–100 and "Map: Major tourist destinations of Spain." For Ruescas, see Francisco García Ruescas, *Historia de la Publicidad*, 273.

12. "Nuestro Consejo Editorial—Manuel de Elexpuru del Valle," *I.P.*, no. 2 (February 1963), 4. See also the similar story of Laperal, one of mid-century Spain's premier commercial poster designers. "Laperal—Arte Publicitario—Concurso permanente dedicado a dibujantes," *I.P.*, no. 7 (December 1963), 10–11.

13. For DANIS, Fontcuberta, and Maestre, see Rodríguez Salcedo, "Public Relations before 'Public Relations' in Spain," 285–86.

14. Hall, "Professionalization and Bureaucratization"; Wilensky, "The Professionalization of Everyone?," 137–58.

15. This tension was also central to debates over the credentialing requirement prior to the charter's release. "Realidades de la Publicidad española: La Escuela de Publicidad y Relaciones Públicas lleva tres años de funcionamiento," *I.P.*, no. 3 (April 1963), 14–15; Centro Español de Nuevas Profesiones, "Historia del CENP," accessed 9 March 2012, http://www.cenp.com/website/historia.htm.

16. "Publicidad en el mercado comun," *I.P.*, no. 2 (February 1963), 44; van Ruler and Verčič, *Public Relations and Communication Management in Europe*, 396–97. For another example of a European-level organization, the European Conference for National Public Relations Associations (CEDAN), see "Nueva Organizacion del Centro Europeo de Relaciones Publicas," *I.P.*, no. 2 (February 1963), 43.

17. Joaquín Maestre Morata to Mr. Roy J. Leffingwell, 5 April 1966, AGUN-JMM/144/490/002.

18. For one such editorial on the organization of advertising in Spain, see "La clasificación de agencias, solución al Articulo 15," *I.P.*, n.n. (September 1964), 5–7; for the 1965 editorial, see Ricardo de Iriondo, "Libre Opinión—Una sección polémica escrita por los lectores—Las opiniones de los Directores de Agencias son muy parciales," *I.P.*, no. 16 (March 1965), 13.

19. Hall, "Professionalization and Bureaucratization," 92–94; Julio Campos, "Bien a Control Si, pero . . . ," *I.P.*, no. 3 (April 1963), 5; Roberto Arce, "Tengo la Palabra: El Sidol Ministerial," *I.P.*, n.n. (November 1964), 7. See also "La Entrevista del Mes: Es muy necesario un *sindicato fuerte*, al que ha de llegarse por la *flexibilidad*, el *dinamismo* y la *diversidad coordinada*, declaraciones de Alejandro Fernández Soto," *I.P.*, no. 12 (October 1964), 18.

20. "Coloquio Profesional—Momento Actual de Nuestra Publicidad," *I.P.*, no. 1 (December 1962), 10–11; "Información Bibliográfica—Anuario Español de la Publicidad," *I.P.*, no. 5 (August 1963), 58; García Ruescas, *Historia*

de la Publicidad, 276. For census data, see INE, accessed 10 March 2012, http://www.ine.es.

21. Rodríguez Salcedo, "Public Relations before 'Public Relations' in Spain," 285–86; "SAE de RP," AGUN-JMM/144/003/008.

22. This experience left SAE de RP agent José Maria Soler Vilá convinced that Jorba's sales and advertising methods were, by contrast, antiquated and unprofessional. For Jorba and SAE de RP, see José Maria Soler Vilá, "Informe Confidencial para la Direccion de SAE Relaciones Publicas Accion Bodas de Oro Almacenes Jorba—Notas Sobre Las Distintas Acciones—Festival en el Zoo," AGUN-JMM/144/024/002; and José Maria Soler Vilá, "Informe Confidencial—Notas al Márgen," AGUN-JMM/144/024/002. For SAE de RP's full list of proposed events, see "Untitled study document–Almacenes Jorba—De acuerdo con sus indicaciones . . . ," 2 February 1961, AGUN-JMM/144/024/001. Notable among the resulting measures was a commemorative volume published a year later for friends of the store. See Almacenes Jorba, *1911–1961—Bodas de Oro*.

23. Joaquín Maestre Morata, "Las Relaciones Publicas: Un Nuevo Concepto Económico Social (II)," *I.P.*, no. 13 (December 1964), 38–39; [Profile of SAE de RP], AGUN-JMM/144/003/008.

24. Thus, in 1965 *I.P.* speculated over Spain's prospects for joining the Common Market, or Mercado Común. See "Puntos de Vista—España y el Mercado Común," *I.P.*, no. 23 (October 1965), 7.

25. For the work of Manuel Fraga and the technocrats, see Payne, *The Franco Regime*, 467–79; and Pack, *Tourism and Dictatorship*, chap. 5.

26. See, for example, Fernand Hourez, "El futuro de la publicidad directa en Europa," *I.P.*, no. 6 (December 1963), 11–12; and Enrique Casas Santasusana, "La Publicidad Olvidada: Publicidad Directa," *I.P.*, no. 6 (December 1963), 12–13.

27. "Untitled Editorial," *I.P.* no. 1 (December 1962), 4.

28. "Editoriales—Estatuto de la Publicidad," *I.P.*, no. 1 (December 1962), 5.

29. "Editoriales—Estatuto de la Publicidad."

30. "La Entrevista del Mes . . . declaraciones de Alejandro Fernández Soto."

31. "SAE de RP," AGUN-JMM/144/003/008.

32. "SAE de RP," AGUN-JMM/144/003/008.

33. Other prospective clients included the MIT and the Barcelona department store Gales. See "Gales, S.A.—Semblanza de la Compañia," 7 December 1963, AGUN-JMM/144/003/004; "Operacion 'Falsa Compra,'" 22 January

1965, AGUN-JMM/144/003/004; "Gales, S.A.—Rapport de Trabajo No. 4," n.d. [1964], AGUN-JMM/144/003/005; and "Ministry of Information and Tourism Campaign Proposal," n.d., AGUN-JMM/144/009/002.

34. Rodríguez Salcedo, "Public Relations before 'Public Relations' in Spain," 287. For ISIRP, see Joaquin Maestre to Dottor Guido de Rossi, 4 January 1962; ISIRP, "Quota partecipaziones Corso ISIRP," 11 January 1962; and Joaquin Maestre Morata to Guido de Rossi del Lion Nero, 20 September 1962, all in AGUN-JMM/144/490/001. For Maestre's memberships in 1963, see "Information for the International Wool Secretariat," 4 July 1963, AGUN-JMM/144/003/001. For Maestre and IPRA, see Correspondence between Joaquín Maestre Morata and Guido de Rossi del Lion Nero, IPRA General Secretary, 8 April 1963–12 July 1963, AGUN-JMM/144/490/001; and John A Keyer, Chariman, IPRA, to Joaquín Maestre Morata, 8 May 1963, AGUN-JMM/144/490/001.

35. Guido de Rossi del Lion Nero to Joaquín Maestre Morata, 12 June 1963, AGUN-JMM/144/490/001; "International Public Relations Association Code of Conduct," in "International Public Relations Association Application for Membership–José Manuel Rico Zorrilla," n.d. [1968–1969], B, AGUN-JMM/144/003/003; "SAE de RP," AGUN-JMM/144/003/008. For Hall and Wilensky, see Hall, "Professionalization and Bureaucratization," 93; and Wilensky, "The Professionalization of Everyone?," 139, 141, 145–46.

36. For Maestre's involvement in membership applications, see Joaquín Maestre Morata to Manos B. Pavlidis, 13 January 1969, AGUN-JMM/144/490/004; and Joaquín Maestre Morata to Jean-Jacques Wyler, 30 April 1971, AGUN-JMM/144/490/005. For Maestre and late dues, see Joaquín Maestre Morata to Keith Kentropp, 3 May 1971, AGUN-JMM/144/490/005; and Memorandum from Keith E. Kentropp, Honorary Treasurer, to Messrs. Traverse-Healy, Pavlidis, Wyler, Buckle, and appropriate corresponding Council members, n.d. [1972], AGUN-JMM/144/490/005. For Maestre as Corresponding Council Member, see Robert L. Bliss to Joaquín Maestre Morata, 7 December 1965, AGUN-JMM/144/494/003; and D. H. Buckle to Jean-Jacques Wyler, 7 November 1972, AGUN-JMM/144/490/005.

37. "SAE de RP—Acta de reunión," 18 May 1965, AGUN-JMM/144/431/002; "SAE de RP–Acta de la reunión," 28 January 1966, AGUN-JMM/144/494/003; and "Informacion Grafica—Barcelona," I.P., no. 18 (May 1965), 75.

38. Such figures included future IPRA secretary Manos Pavlidis, from whom he secured membership lists. For Manos Pavlidis, see Joaquín Maestre Morata to Manos Pavlidis, 15 April 1966, AGUN-JMM/144/490/002. For India, see Joaquín Maestre Morata to Satya Prakash, 29 March 1966, AGUN-JMM/144/490/002.

39. Joaquín Maestre Morata to Georges Serrell, 25 October 1965, AGUN-JMM/144/490/002; Joaquín Maestre Morata to John A. Keyser, 4 April 1966, AGUN-JMM/144/490/002; Joaquín Maestre Morata to Francis E. Shuster, 7 May 1966, AGUN-JMM/144/490/002; Francis E. Shuster to Joaquín Maestre Morata, 17 May 1966, AGUN-JMM/144/490/002; Denny Griswold to Joaquín Maestre Morata, 24 November 1965, AGUN-JMM/144/490/002; Denny Griswold to Joaquín Maestre Morata, 5 January 1965, AGUN-JMM/144/490/002; Joaquín Maestre Morata to Denny Griswold, 11 January 1966, AGUN-JMM/144/490/002; and, for correspondence with Robert Bliss, see Joaquín Maestre Morata to Robert L. Bliss, 5 April 1966, AGUN-JMM/144/490/002; Robert L. Bliss to Joaquín Maestre Morata, 16 September 1966, AGUN-JMM/144/494/001; and Joaquín Maestre Morata to Robert L. Bliss, 29 September 1965, AGUN-JMM/144/494/001.

40. Joaquín Maestre Morata to Laureano López Rodó, 29 April 1966, AGUN-JMM/144/494/004; Joaquín Maestre Morata to Laureano López Rodó, 18 June 1966, AGUN-JMM/144/494/004; and Joaquín Maestre Morata to Vicente Mortes, 18 June 1966, AGUN-JMM/144/494/004.

41. "Información para prensa: Inauguración oficial de la asamblea de la Asociación Internacional de Relaciones Públicas en el salon de ciento del ayuntamiento de Barcelona," n.d. [26 May 1966], AGUN-JMM/144/494/003. For another conference hosted in Spain during the 1960s, see L. G., "El G.I.G.A., en Sevilla," *Boletín de Galerías Preciados*, no. 113, Year XII (June 1961), 6.

42. John A. Keyser, President, "Presidential Letter," 14 September 1964, AGUN-JMM/144/490/003.

43. For IPRA's aims, see "Pamphlet on the IPRA association," November 1971, AGUN-JMM/144/490/004.

44. Untitled Report on IPRA Liaison to the U.N. Activities, n.d. [mid-1966], AGUN-JMM/144/494/004.

45. Joaquín Maestre Morata to Ernst Kottow, May 1966, AGUN-JMM/144/490/002.

46. Untitled Report on IPRA Liaison to the U.N. Activities, n.d. [mid-1966], AGUN-JMM/144/494/004.

47. Joaquín Maestre Morata to Ernst Kottow, May 1966, AGUN-JMM/144/490/002.

48. See Puig, "The Education of a Foreign Market." For another reference to this trend, see Tamames, *Estructura Económica de España*, 2:752.

49. "Noticias de las agencias—Alas, Compañia General de Publicidad, Sociedad Anonima, se ha establecido definitivamente en el Edicifio Lima," *I.P.*, no. 4 (June 1963), 41; Puig, "The Education of a Foreign Market," 2, 14–15. Worth noting too is that earlier, from the postwar through to its partnership with Alas, J. Walter Thompson had worked through another Spanish agent: none other than Ruescas.

50. "Noticias de las Agencias—Asociación de Tiempo con Synergie," *I.P.*, no. 13 (December 1964), 113.

51. "CPV Española entra a Formar Parte de Publinsa, K & E," *I.P.*, no. 21 (August 1965), 76.

52. For a brief account of the negotiations surrounding Ruescas Publicidad's merger with McCann-Erickson, see Puig, "The Education of a Foreign Market," 14–15.

53. "El más significativo guión que se coloca en la publicidad en España, Ruescas-McCann Erickson," *I.P.*, no. 4 (June 1963), 16–17.

54. "El más significativo guión que se coloca en la publicidad en España."

55. "Gran . . . Inauguracion de la tienda de Meridiana!," *Noti-Sears*, no. 29, Year IV (October–December 1975).

56. "España reserva dos galerías en la más internacional de las ferias francesas," *I.P.*, no. 3 (April 1963), 43; Jaime Puig, "Exclusiva—la motivación en pleno desarrollo, una entrevista con el doctor Ernest Dichter," *I.P.*, n.n (November 1964), 19. For Ernest Dichter, see "Sex and Advertising—Retail Therapy: How Ernest Dichter, an Acolyte of Sigmund Freud, Revolutionised Marketing," *The Economist*, Special Holiday Double Issue (17 December 2011), accessed 7 March 2013, http://www.economist.com/node/21541706; "El doctor Ernest Dichter presentado en Madrid por IP," *I.P.*, no. 17 (April 1965), 28–29; and Ernest Dichter, "La creatividad en publicidad: como infundir mayor fuerza a las campañas," *I.P.*, no. 23 (October 1965), 32–36. For Maestre's speech, see "Your Excellency, Mr. Mayor, Mr. Chairman, Mr. President, Ladies and Colleagues . . . ," n.d. [1966], AGUN-JMM/144/494/002.

57. Roldán Martínez, "Libre Opinion—Un no a 'España es diferente,'" *I.P.*, no. 20 (July 1965), 13.

58. Crumbaugh, *Destination Dictatorship*, 38–39.

59. Puig, "The Education of a Foreign Market," 11.

60. García Ruescas, *Problemática de las Inversiones Extranjeras*, 1–4, 12–14. For two other contemporary references to Servan-Schreiber, see "France: The American Challenge," *Time*, 24 November 1967, accessed 27 March 2011, http://www.time.com/time/magazine/article/0,9171,844150-1,00.html; and Carlos Martínez de Campos, "Autarquía," *A.B.C.*, 1 March 1968, 3.

61. For the Sección Femenina and Spanish folklore as diplomacy, see Monés et al., "Between Tradition and Innovation: Two Ways of Understanding the History of Dance in Spain," 152; Eiroa San Francisco, "Relaciones internacionales y estrategias de comunicación de la España de Franco ante la coyuntura de 1956," 20; Stehrenberger, "Folklore, Nation, and Gender in a Colonial Encounter," 231; and Morcillo, *Seduction*, 202–5, 221.

62. Fernando Díaz de San Pedro, "Pamphlet—Bullfighting without Toil," AGUN-JMM/144/494/003; "Photograph—Bullring and *Novillada*," n.d. [1966], AGUN-JMM/144/494/004.

63. Acta de la reunión del comité social de IPRA, 28 January 1966, AGUN-JMM/144/494/003.

64. Joaquín Maestre Morata to Robert L. Bliss, 12 May 1966, AGUN-JMM/144/490/002.

65. *Don: La Moda Masculina Española* [Barcelona, 1962–1967, henceforth, *Don*], like *Alta Costura* and *Señor*, was haute bourgeois in both price and content, costing 150 ptas per issue, more than twice the daily minimum wage, and marketed itself toward an audience wealthy enough to spend thousands of ptas on clothes each season. Mitigating this, however, was the journal's biannual frequency, and, in a new twist on *Alta Costura*'s situation in the 1940s, the affluent lifestyles that the magazine offered drew rather than repulsed the increasingly consumerist Spanish middle class. See "Ud. debe leer DON porque es ...," *Don*, no. 4 (Fall–Winter 1964). For prices, see Paul Hofmann, "After 25 Years, Franco Is Still a Sphinx," *New York Times*, 19 April 1964, SM36; and "Presupuesto DON," *Don*, no. 4 (Fall–Winter 1964). For *Triunfo*'s circulation, see Raquel Maciucci, "Triunfo en Perspectiva," *Olivar* 1 (2000), accessed 14 October 2008, http://www.vespito.net/mvm/triunfo.html; and "Letters to the editor," *Triunfo*, no. 248, Year XXI, (March 1967), 5.

66. Again, in the tradition of earlier Spanish consumer magazines, *Señor* also engaged with Hollywood's popular impact in Spain by interviewing actors and actresses like Cornel Wilde and Joey Heatherton. See "Preferencias de un gran actor internacional en materia de indumentaria: Cornel Wilde," *Señor*, no. 10 (Spring 1958); and "Joey Heatherton," *Señor*, no. 38, Year X (February 1965); Anglo-Spanish Press Bureau, "La Linea "Y" Belga," *Señor*, no. 10 (Spring 1958); "¿Como Vestiran los Franceses en 1962?," *Señor*, no. 27 (Summer 1962); Suzanne, "1963: El Dandy y El Mujik"; H. C. "Las modas que ha popularizado el cine," *PK Press*, no. 2 (September 1966).

67. In the late 1950s, for instance, *Señor* had maintained that Spanish youths' predilection for daring styles was best satisfied by Italian designs, which regular columnist Edgar Neville (a Spanish baron) elsewhere declared categorically inferior to English style. See I. W. S., "Nuevas ideas de elegancia masculina," *Señor*, no. 10 (Spring 1958); Edgar Neville, "Elegancia y Disfraz," *Señor*, no. 5, Year II (November 1956); "Ciudades Europeas y su Moda," *PK Press*, no. 11 (March 1971), 2; "Nueva linea masculina: La moda 'Trapecio,'" *Señor*, no. 12 (Fall 1958); "Linea London 1962," *Señor*, no. 25 (Winter 1961); "Londres Impone La Moda Masculina," *Señor*, no. 21 (Winter 1960); María Luz Morales, "Lo que piensan ellas de nosotros," *Don*, no. 2 (Fall–Winter 1963); and Adriana, "El Punto Flaco de los Caballeros," *AMA*, no. 1 (January 1960), 41.

68. María Luz Morales, "Lo que ellas piensan de nosotros," *Don*, no. 2 (Fall–Winter 1963); "Carnaby Street," *Don*, no. 7 (1967).

69. "Terlenka YOUNG: Una Nueva Moda a Ritmo Joven," *PK Press*, no. 6 (February 1967); "Ciudades Europeas y su Moda." For The Beatles and the British Invasion, see Marwick, *The Sixties*.

70. "Tienda inglesa en la 3a Planta: 'English Men's Shop,' en Bilbao," *Cortty*, no. 3, Year II (January 1970), 4.

71. In 1970, *Triunfo*'s own survey of the state of Spanish fashion would gainsay all of these hopes, concluding that, sartorially, Spain remained "Europe, but less"—that is, aesthetically European, but not yet actually able to provide consumers that level of quality. See "Asamblea General de la Asociacion Euroepa de las Industrias del Vestir," *Señor*, no. 20 (October 1960); Los(?) nte, "La Moda," *Men's Modes: The Custom Tailor's Journal (Edición en Español)* [henceforth, *Men's Modes*], no. 109, Year XXVI (1966), 7; "La Facilidad del Bien Vestir," *Don*, no. 2 (Fall–Winter 1963); and, for *Triunfo*,

José Eduardo Mira, "El sistema de la moda en España," *Triunfo*, no. 440, Year XXV (November 1970), 26.

72. "Creaciones de Confecciones Albert, S.A., Empresa que ha participado en el I Salon Nacional de la Confeccion con su marca Bailet's," *Señor*, no. 23 (Summer 1961).

73. Thus, for reference to the tenth annual show, see "Salon Nacional de la Confeccion, Consagracion de la Maxifalda," *Cortty*, no. 5, Year II (March 1970), 10.

74. "Creaciones de CONFECCIONES FARGAS, S.A. empresa que participó en el II SALON NACIONAL DE LA CONFECCION," *Señor*, no. 27 (Summer 1962); Jaime Huguet, "El III Salon Nacional de la Confeccion. Reflejo de Industria Naciente," *Señor*, no. 31 (Summer 1963). Notably, Vigil credits clothing manufacturer Confecciones Fargas's stylish designs, and the work of Spanish tailors in general, to Spain's rising national prosperity.

75. "XII festival de la moda masculina en San Remo," *Don*, no. 1 (Spring–Summer 1963); "La Moda 1961 en el Peinado Masculino," *Señor*, no. 22 (Spring 1961); "Untitled Hairstyling Photographic Spread," *Señor*, no. 25 (Spring 1962); "III Congreso de la Medida Industrial," *Señor*, no. 26 (Spring 1962).

76. María Pilar de Molina, "Confidencia," *Señor*, no. 10 (Spring 1958).

77. Lurie, *The Language of Clothes*, 118–19.

78. "El Hombre y Su Circunstancia," *Don*, no. 1 (Spring–Summer 1963); see also María Luz Morales, "Lo que ELLAS piensan de ELLOS," *Don*, no. 3 (Spring–Summer 1964), and "Las manecillas del reloj corren implacables para el hombre moderno" *Don*, no. 3 (Spring–Summer 1964).

79. "Club *Don*," *Don*, no. 4 (Fall–Winter 1964).

80. See Vicente Verdú, "La Moda ya no es Frivolidad," *Cortty*, no. 22, Year III (August 1971); for Verdú himself, see Vicente Verdú, "Los Años de la Reconquista," *El País Digital*, 22 November 2000, accessed 22 December 2008, http://www.elpais.com/especiales/2000/rey/rey19a.htm.

81. For distinction and elegance in *Señor*, see I. W. S., "El Guardarropa en cada momento," *Señor*, no. 24 (Fall 1961). For *Triunfo*, see "Vuelve el Dandy," *Triunfo*, no. 213, Year XXI (July 1966), 30. For etiquette manuals, see López Sainz, *La Cortesía en la Vida Moderna*, 33–34; Bauer, *Cortesia y Etiqueta Modernas*; and Sanchez Moreno, *Distinción y Etiqueta Moderna*.

82. See, for example, Sanchez Moreno, *Distinción y Etiqueta Moderna*, which included numerous news clippings from major right-leaning Spanish

newspapers praising the book and its contents. Even foreign handbooks championed—or could be made to champion—these values, as when Spanish book publisher Daimon promoted its Spanish-language edition of Hervé de Peslouan's handbook *El Hombre en Sociedad* (Man in society, 1961) with the same promises of social distinction and success through learned urbanity that "Club *Don*" offered two years later. See "Advertisement for *El Hombre en Sociedad*," *La Vanguardia Española*, 1 January 1961. For Delgado, see "Cocktail en la Terraza Martini," *Don*, no. 2 (Fall–Winter 1963).

83. With that said, *Don*'s accessibility is somewhat unclear. When MIT censors threatened to suspend it, editor-in-chief José María Fabra Carbó defended *Don* by claiming a low readership due to expensive pricing. However, this argument was to his advantage, and, as noted previously, *Don*'s pricing was mitigated by its biannual frequency, which reduced each issue's effective monthly price to a reasonable 25 ptas. See José María Fabra Carbó, "Pliego de Descargos," AGA-MIT, Box 67413, Folder 126. Meanwhile, in 1960 *Señor* compiled a list of Madrid and Barcelona's twelve most elegant men, and while many of them were commoners, they were also wealthy and prominent figures, like Juan Ignacio Luca de Tena, formerly editor-in-chief of *A.B.C.* See "Los Doce Elegantes Españoles," *Señor*, no. 18 (Spring 1960). For a categorical assertion of elegance's availability without regard to wealth, see López Sainz, *La Cortesía en la Vida Moderna*, 33–34.

84. "El ideal de los caballeros: Vestir bien y sin llamar la atención," *Señor*, no. 22 (Spring 1961); Loewe, "Loewe," *Don*, no. 3 (Spring–Summer 1964); Ignacio Agustí, "Los trajes que llevamos," *Triunfo*, no. 42, Year XVIII (March 1963), 25.

85. See Paff Ogle and Damhorst, "Dress for Success in the Popular Press," 80–81; and Lurie, *The Language of Clothes*, 234.

86. María Luz Morales, "Lo que ellas piensan de nosotros"; and Morales, "Lo que ELLAS piensan de ELLOS"; Adelaida, "Linea 'Menhir' para el Hombre de 1963," *Triunfo*, no. 39, Year XVIII (March 1963), 53; "¿Que las mujeres diseñen los trajes masculinos? ¡No! ¡No!," *Señor*, no. 16 (Fall 1959); "Señora, deje que su marido vista a su gusto," *Señor*, no. 19 (Summer 1960).

87. Another TV spot, which featured the cautionary tale of a housewife whose hardworking husband hit her because she failed to welcome him home with a snifter of Soberano, similarly reproduced Francoist patriarchy by

reaffirming husbands' socially as well as legally recognized right to such recourse to violence. See "Soberano Commercial—¡Es Cosa de Hombres!," YouTube, accessed 16 November 2008, http://www.youtube.com/watch?v =qpxutp2jh4e; and "Soberano Commercial—Housewife Visits Fortune-teller," YouTube, accessed 16 November 2008, http://www.youtube.com /watch?v=nj_Soch1ovA.

88. *Quid* offered columns on concerts, hairstyles, and beauty and health issues of interest to adolescent readers, along with photographs of singers like flamenco star Rocío Jurado scantily clad in bikinis, hot pants, and even nightgowns, which ultimately drew censors' ire in August 1966. See "La Importancia de ser joven," *Cortty*, no. 6, Year II (April 1970), 8; José María F. Gaytan, "Pulmón de la Semana–Bonitas Piernas," *Quid: Revista Musical*, no. 5 (15 August 1966), 7; and, for its censorship case, "Expediente de Sanción—Quid," AGA-MIT, Box 72, Folder 67114. For the 1960s cultural revolution in the United States and Europe, see Marwick, *The Sixties*, esp. chaps. 9–12. For the Nova Cançó, see Aragüez Rubio, "La Nova Cançó Catalana." For student protests in Spain and elsewhere, see Carrillo-Linares, *Subversivos y malditos en la Universidad de Sevilla (1965–1977)*; Espuny i Espuny, *El moviment estudiantil a Barcelona (1965–1975)*; Fink, Gassert, and Junker, *1968: The World Transformed*; and Klimke and Scharloth, *1968 in Europe: A History of Protest and Activism, 1956–1977*.

89. Siegfried, "Understanding 1968," 59–81.

90. "La Moda Juvenil Representa un Paso hacia Adelante," *Señor*, no. 15 (Summer 1959); and I. W. S., "Nuevas ideas de elegancia masculina." See also *Señor* Correspondent to Düsseldorf I.W.S., "La Nueva Moda Masculina es Juvenil sin Exageración," *Señor*, no. 13 (Winter 1958); and Bauer, *Cortesia y Etiqueta Modernas*, 36.

91. Suzanne, "1963: El Dandy y El Mujik," *Triunfo*, no. 18, Year XVII (October 1962), 70.

92. Los(?)nte, "Moda Joven," *Men's Modes*, no. 110, Year XXVII (1967), 7. *Men's Modes* was a tailoring journal that began publication in 1961, had correspondents worldwide, and was based in Barcelona and New York. It was directly specifically at custom tailors, and consisted primarily of fashion plates and tailoring diagrams, with a few regularly recurring editorials on the state of fashion, including the above.

93. "Terlenka YOUNG: Una Nueva Moda a Ritmo Joven." Like Cardin's designs, these designs represented radical departures from the traditional

business suit, including Regency tailcoats and Mao suits. For other similar lines aimed at "the man of today" or "modern man," including the brand's "festival of youth fashion," see "Un Verano imPKblemente joven," PK *Press*, no. 6 (February 1967), 1; "Este es el festival de la moda joven," PK *Press*, no. 5 (1967[?]), 4–5; "4 Modelos de la colección PK," PK *Press*, no. 5 (1967[?]).

94. Adelaida, "Linea 'Menhir,'" 53.

95. "Estatuto y Apogeo del Azul Bruma y los complementarios DON," *Don*, no. 7 (1967); Verdú, "La Moda ya no es Frivolidad." For the rise in Spanish women's social roles, see, for instance, Pilar Salcedo, "Una Ley Que No Tuvo Enmiendas" *Telva*, no. 80, (January 1967); and Morcillo, *True Catholic Womanhood*, 66–67.

96. "La rebeldía del hombre de hoy por un futuro imPKble," *Telva*, no. 123 (November 1968).

97. Park, "Unisex Clothing."

98. Park, "Unisex Clothing"; Bernadine Morris, "Halston Tips His Hat To Unisex Fashions," *New York Times*, 4 December 1968; Marylin Bender, "He Calls It 'The Couple Look,'" *New York Times*, 9 November 1968; Angela Taylor, "Some Fashions Are for Boys and Girls, While Others Are Strictly for the Ladies," *New York Times*, 15 August 1968, all accessed 23 December 2008 in ProQuest Database, http://www.proquest.com; "Cuando la mujer se viste de hombre," *Triunfo*, no. 21, Year XVII (October 1962), 70. See also knitwear maker Escorpión's ads for his-and-her items, in which the male and female models wore pants and sweaters whose only gender markers were their collar styles. "Photo spread for Modelos Escorpión," *Señor*, no. 26 (Spring 1962).

99. "Moda Masculina," PK *Press*, no. 6 (February 1967). See also "Camisas y Blusas, Primavera-Verano 1967," PK *Press*, no. 2 (September 1966); "Moda: Seguiran los cuadros y rayas 'Madras,'" PK *Press*, no. 2 (September 1966). For *Cortty*, see, for instance, "Coyuntura Comercial del Cuarto Trimestre del 69," *Cortty*, no. 4, Year II (February 1970), 2, and "La Moda ya no es Frivolidad." For *Don*, see John Stephen, "Carnaby Street," *Don*, no. 7 (1967). See also César Santos Fontenla, "Carnaby Street," *Triunfo*, no. 231, Year XXI (November 1966), 37, 40.

100. Verdú, "La Moda ya no es Frivolidad."

101. "El Plano Moral," *Interviú*, no. 2, Year I (29 May 1976), 45; "La Nueva Moral del Macho," *Vivir a Dos*, no. 16, Year III (February 1978), 46–52.

102. "El Plano Moral"; "La Nueva Moral del Macho"; "Tienda Juvenil: Nueva dependencia," *Boletín de Galerías Preciados*, no. 191, Year XX (April 1969), 11; "Nueva Boutique para Jóvenes," *Noti-Sears*, no. 7, Year I (March 1972). For similar examples of this phenomenon, see Rappaport, *Shopping for Pleasure*, 163–65.

103. "¿Quién es destinatario de la moda unisex?," *PK Press*, no. 11 (March 1971), 3.

104. José Hua[?]te, "¿Tiene Usted Un Hippy En Su Casa?," *PK Press*, no. 8 (September 1969).

105. "La 'Maxi-Midi' o el 'Ocultismo,'" *Cortty*, no. 11, Year II (September 1970), 9.

106. Davis, *Fashion, Culture, and Identity*, 35–37, 41–50.

107. Verdú, "La Moda ya no es Frivolidad." Indeed, the rise of youth fashion was sufficiently widespread that, Verdú claimed, academic sociological categories separating generations into those that dressed à la mode, those that dressed in "yesterday's fashions," and those dressed even more antiquatedly were gradually eroding away. See also "La Importancia de ser joven."

108. "La 'Maxi-Midi' o el 'Ocultismo,'" 9. This rebellious character was only reinforced by the garment's association with counterculture, youth, and, most especially, the hippies. See Connickie, *Fashions of a Decade: The 1960s*, 58; and Piermarco Aroldi and Cristina Ponte, "Adolescents of the 1960s and 1970s: An Italian-Portuguese Comparison between Two Generations of Audiences," *Cyberpsychology: Journal of Psychosocial Research on Cyberspace*, accessed 20 December, 2013, http://www.cyberpsychology .eu/view.php?cisloclanku=2012081004&article=1.

109. In fact, the bikini is perhaps the best-known example of fashion undermining Francoist moralism, for while Spanish police initially arrested bikini-clad beachgoers, this soon ceased for fear of harming the tourist industry. See Alonso Tejada, *La represión sexual en la España de Franco*, 141–42; and Pack, "Tourism and Political Change," 54. See also "Lo que dice la prensa," *Cortty*, no. 6, Year II (April 1970), 15. For *Mujer*, see "Expediente de Sanción, Mujer, No. 368," AGA-MIT 71/12270/39.

110. For the MIT's case against *Don*, see "Expediente de Sanción, Don No. 7," AGA-MIT 67413/126. This was further detailed in direct correspondence this author had with Forcano. Eugeni Forcano, email correspondence with author, 16 September 2008.

111. "Señora, deje que su marido vista a su gusto"; "Y, hablando de corbatas...," *Señor*, no. 19 (Summer 1960).

112. Verdú, "La Moda ya no es Frivolidad."
113. Puig, "The Education of a Foreign Market," 10–11, 23–25.
114. Robert L. Bliss to Manuel Fraga Iribarne, Minister of Information and Tourism, 20 October 1965, AGUN-JMM/144/494/003.
115. Sáenz de Heredia, *Relaciones Casi Públicas*.

5. "On That Day, Borders Did Not Exist"

1. "Gran . . . Inauguracion de la tienda de Meridiana!," *Noti-Sears*, no. 4, Year IV, (October–December 1975).
2. It is unclear whether the article's unnamed author chose the term "Confederate" out of a lack of familiarity with the details of the American conflict or if the choice was intentional and even political, meant to link a culturally rebellious Catalonia with a likewise defiant American South.
3. For the international orientation of 1960s and 1970s Spanish consumption, see Alonso and Conde, *Historia del consumo en España*, 88–90; Crumbaugh, *Destination Dictatorship*, 5; Pack, *Tourism and Dictatorship*, 139–53; Cazorla Sánchez, *Fear and Progress*, 152–55, 162, 171–72; and Rodríguez, *Busque, compare y, si encuentra un libro mejor, ¡cómprelo!*, 34–35. For reference to 1950s precursors, see Alonso and Conde, *Historia del consumo en España*, 137–39.
4. For the regime's limited reforms as diplomatic efforts, see Crespo MacLennan, *Spain and the Process of European Integration*. For Franco's unwillingness to see this outreach generate real social and political change, see Moradiellos, "Franco's Spain and the European Integration Process (1945–1975)."
5. Alonso and Conde, *Historia del consumo en España*, 84–85.
6. Ángel Cruz, "Desde Jaén—Ante una nueva sección . . . Medida Industrial," *Boletín de Galerías Preciados*, no. 167, Year XVII (December 1966), 11.
7. The hybrid name was an attempt to soothe locals irked by the loss of a city icon—and was also why the store preserved its façade. For Jorba, see Toboso, *Pepín Fernández*, 272–76; "La Fusion Comercial de 'Almacenes Jorba' con Nuestra Casa," *Boletín de Galerías Preciados*, no. 133, Year XIV (June 1963), 5; Olivera, "La fusión con 'Jorba'—Nota máxima de la actualidad de 'Galerías,'" *Boletín de Galerías Preciados*, no. 134, Year XIV (July 1963), 3–5. For Galerías Preciados's expansion in the 1960s and early 1970s, see also Jiménez, Pineiro, and Ranedo, *Galerías: Ayer, Hoy y Mañana*, 2:39–47; "Nueva Casa Bilbaina," *Boletín de Galerías Preciados*, no. 215, Year

XXIII (October 1971), 10–11; "La Inauguración de Zabálburu," *Boletín de Galerías Preciados*, no. 216, Year XXIII (November 1971), 3; Toboso, *Pepín Fernández*, 276–88.

8. Cuartas, *Biografía de El Corte Inglés*, 302–4, 310–11. For Siro Gay's expansion, see "Inauguración de Bazar 'Gay' en Ávila," *Gay* (July 1960); "Nuevo Local de Nuestra Cadena, en Valencia," *Gay* (February 1961); "Editorial— Qué Significa 'Gay-Oeste,'" *Gay* (October 1962). For Botas's expansion and the snack bar, see "Un Centro Comercial de Autentico Nivel Europeo: Brillante Inauguracion de la NUEVA TIENDA," *Boletín de Botas*, no. 20, Year III (June–July 1964), 12–13; Miramar, "Un Nuevo Servicio: Snack-Bar en la planta primera de la "Nueva Tienda." ¡Enhorabuena a los maridos!," *Boletín de Botas*, no. 20, Year III (June–July 1964), 6, 9.

9. "Hasta luego, Sr. Clapper," *Noti-Sears*, no. 4, Year I (July 1971); Buisán Pérez, *Memorias*, 2:49–50; "Corporación Informa . . . Nuevo Edificio Sears en Madrid," *Noti-Sears*, no. 2, Year I (December 1968); "La Nueva Tienda Sears en Barcelona," *Noti-Sears*, no. 20, Year IV (March 1974).

10. For Galerías's self-service department and other new services, see Toboso, *Pepín Fernández*, 240–42; Zafra Aragón, *Méritos, errores, ilusiones y personajes de Galerías Preciados*, 53; and "Transcript—Interview with Jorge Fernández Menéndez, Galerías Preciados," as well as "Press clipping— Boletín de Cámara de Comercio," in AGA-CAT 29605/1, Subfolder 4.

11. Besides these magazines, other introductions that added depth to the workplace experience included new summertime vacation packages to the Mediterranean coast, which continued the Club de Galerías Preciados's earlier usurping of clerks' private lives. See "Vacaciones Veraniegas para Nuestro Personal," *Boletín de Galerías Preciados*, no. 130, Year XIV (March 1963), 5.

12. See, for instance, José Luis Gay, "Trágico Descubrimiento," *"Gay,"* no. 9 (September 1960); Moris, "Venta Fin de Balance," *Boletín de Botas*, no. 26, Year IV (January 1965), 7; "Bodas," *Noti-Sears*, no. 10, Year II (August 1972); "Podrá Utilizarse la Tarjeta de Compra en La Agencia de Viajes," *Cortty*, No. 8, Year II (June 1970).

13. For the magazine's professional content, see, for example, "Nuestro Apoyo Publicitario," *Cortty*, no. 6, Year II (April 1970): 10. For its efforts to regulate employees' private choices, see, for instance, "Estimular los deseos— AMOR," *Cortty*, no. 9, Year II (August 1970), 10.

14. Detailed in the previous two chapters as well as below, this general perception of the commercial sector as a growth field is likewise examined in Núria Puig's study of U.S. influence on Spanish management cultures, and also manifested in contemporary press coverage that could, for example, go so far as to equate commercial activity with civilization's progress. See Puig, "La ayuda económica," 122–29; and Luis Moure-Mariño, "Nueva etapa para el comercio," *A.B.C.*, 14 December 1960, 31, 35.

15. Buisán Pérez, *Memorias*, 2:49–50.

16. See, for instance, B. Sandalio Rueda, "Dignidad del Trabajo," *Boletín de Galerías Preciados*, no. 98, Year XI (January 1960), 2; Eduardo A. Tarragona, "Estar a Punto," *Boletín de Botas*, no. 16, Year II (January 1964), 11; and A., "Hacia una nueva mentalidad: ¿Estamos en desarrollo?," *Boletín de Botas*, no. 18, Year III (March–April 1964), 16. For a similar concern voiced by Ramón Areces, see "La hora triunfal del gran almacén," *Cortty*, no. 19, Year III (May 1971).

17. "Correo," *Boletín de Botas*, no. 19, Year III (May 1964), 5.

18. Indeed, in various hagiographic texts on Pepín Fernández, who physically embodied Galerías in the store's official culture, these ties predated the chain's founding to the founder's early career at El Encanto, where he learned the skills he used to build Galerías Preciados. See José Maria Pérez Lozano, "El nombre y el hombre," *Boletín de Galerías Preciados*, no. 192, Year XX (May 1969), 2; Daudet, *Los Empresarios*, 74–76.

19. For El Encanto and arson in mid-century Havana, see Chase, *Revolution within the Revolution*, 135, 158.

20. "Honor y Responsabilidad: Los nuevos interesados, Palabras de nuestro Presidente," *Boletín de Galerías Preciados*, no. 138, Year XV (January 1964), 14–15; Toboso *Pepín Fernández*, 322. Among the the returning Spanish émigrés figured José Suárez Mourelle, who returned to Spain in 1961 and worked in Galerías during the late 1960s as an administrative assistant, before retiring in 1969. See "Jubilados," *Boletín de Galerías Preciados*, no. 191, Year XX (April 1969), 3. Indeed, Pepín even maintained ties with Cuba's ousted ex-president Fulgencio Batista. See Toboso, *Pepín Fernández*, 322.

21. For American business in 1950s Spain, see Rosendorf, "Be El Caudillo's Guest." For American tourism to Spain, see Rosendorf, "Be El Caudillo's Guest," 385; Pack, *Tourism and Dictatorship*, chaps. 4–5.

22. Raymond E. Buckwalter, "Carta Expresiva," *Boletín de Galerías Preciados*, no. 153, Year XVI (June 1965), 4; Joaquín Rodríguez Blasco, "Desde

Sevilla—Pase de Modelos," *Boletín de Galerías Preciados*, no. 157, Year XVI (December 1965), 15.

23. Buckwalter, "Carta Expresiva"; Rodríguez Blasco, "Desde Sevilla—Pase de Modelos."

24. Buckwalter, "Carta Expresiva"; "Jetty Kentie, Interprete de Holandes," *Boletín de Galerías Preciados*, no. 108, Year XII (January 1961), 8; "Seis Meses en Londres: Paquita Martinez Almazan (Centralita Telefonica)," *Boletín de Galerías Preciados*, no. 139, Year XV (February 1964), 5.

25. "Vacaciones en Estocolmo," *Boletín de Galerías Preciados*, no. 117, Year XII (December 1961), 13.

26. Galerías had joined the IGDS in 1951; temporarily left the group in 1957, as the regime's lingering import restrictions denied the chain many of the benefits of IGDS membership; and rejoined after the reforms of 1958–1959. See Toboso, *Pepín Fernández*, 262–64.

27. Perhaps most notable among these visits was the IGDS's XIII Sales Promotion event, which Galerías-Sevilla hosted in 1961, and which the *Boletín* chronicled in detail and with palpable pride. L. G., "El G.I.G.A., en Sevilla," *Boletín de Galerías Preciados*, no. 113, Year XII (June 1961). For others, see Toboso, *Pepín Fernández*, 264–65.

28. José Antonio Flaquer, "'Galerías' agasaja a los analistas financieros norteamericanos," *Boletín de Galerías Preciados*, no. 146, Year XV (November 1964), 3–4.

29. "París en 'Galerías,'" *Boletín de Galerías Preciados*, no. 127, Year XIII (December 1962), 7; "Norteamérica en 'Galerías,'" *Boletín de Galerías Preciados*, no. 161, Year XVII (April 1966), 3; "Desde Sevilla—Promoción Extremo Oriente," *Boletín de Galerías Preciados*, no. 144, Year XV (July 1964), 10; "Extremo Oriente en 'Galerias' de Bilbao," *Boletín de Galerías Preciados*, no. 233, Year XXV (June 1973), 12; Moris, "Nuestras promociones—Exposición de artículos de Extremo Oriente," *Boletín de Botas*, no. 21, Year III (August 1964), 5.

30. "Tienda inglesa en la 3a Planta: 'English Men's Shop,' en Bilbao," *Cortty*, no. 3, Year II (January 1970), 4.

31. "El Grupo Intercontinental y la Asociación Internacinal de Grandes Almacenes," *Boletín de Galerías Preciados*, no. 106, Year XI (November 1960), 4–5; L. G., "El G.I.G.A, en Sevilla"; "Ante las vacaciones: Exito logrado y esperanza de futuro," *Boletín de Galerías Preciados*, no. 194, Year XX (July 1969), 2; "La proprietaria de una 'boutique,'" *Cortty*, no. 9, Year II (July

1970), 3; "Los grandes almacenes japoneses nos superan en superficie— Cesar Conde: 'De japón, solo me traería . . . los clientes,'" *Cortty*, no. 12, Year II (October 1970). For another similar boast, see "Nuestra organización, en la prensa inglesa: La armada española vuelve otra vez," *Cortty*, no. 12, Year II (October 1970).

32. The change wrought by the construction of Nuevas Galerías was so dramatic that urban biographer Ignacio Merino has termed the storefront "an aesthetic aberration built without shame or respect for its surroundings." See Merino, *Biografía de la Gran Vía*, 176; Toboso, *Pepín Fernández*, 278–81.

33. [No Author], "El viernes si inaugurará 'Galerías Preciados,'" *Hoja del Lunes*, 21 April 1975; Juan Bustos, "Más luz para dos avenidas," *Patria*, 13 April 1975; KASTIYO, "Nueva iluminación en Carrera de la Virgen y Avenida José Antonio," *Patria*, 4 April 1975, all in ARCM 133352/4.

34. KASTIYO, "Somos excesivamente pobres para no abrir los sábados," *Patria*, 18 March 1975; José Maria Baviano, "Los comerciantes, en contra de abrir los sábados por la tarde," *Patria*, 27 March 1975; Francisco Pablo Morales Rueda, "Los sábados y el comercio," *Ideal*, 15 April 1975; Mercedes Terreros, "Estudiar una fórmula," *Ideal*, 30 April 1975; "Reunión en la Casa Sindical para estudiar el horario de los sábados en el comercio," *Ideal*, 23 April 1975, all in ARCM 133352/4.

35. Fundación FOESSA, *Informe Sociológico Sobre la Situación Social en España, 1966*, 77–79; Buisán Pérez, *Memorias*, vol. 2. Indeed, photographer Eugeni Forcano's images of daily life in 1960s Barcelona, many of which featured automobiles in the background, bore at times unintentional witness to their centrality to life in the Catalan capital. See, for example, Forcano, Giralt-Miracle, and Martínez Rochina, *Eugeni Forcano: La meva Barcelona*, 24–25, 28–30, 54–55, 168–69, 172–73.

36. For the automobile as a factor in the rise of shopping centers in the United States, see, for example, Cohen, *A Consumer's Republic*, chap. 6; and Jackson, *Crabgrass Frontier: The Suburbanization of the United States*, 258–59.

37. Nuevas Galerías, for instance, featured a parking garage with 250 fixed spaces spread out across three underground levels—in practice, the bulletin underlined, enough space for 400 cars—and tellingly, boasted a new "Parking Packages" service, whereby customers could make their purchases throughout the store and pick them up at a central location in the parking garage. "Visitas a las Obras," *Boletín de Galerías Preciados*, Special Issue, Year XVIII (September 1968), 4–7; "Las últimas fotografías—Planta y

Escalres en Septiembre de 1968," *Boletín de Galerías Preciados*, Special
Issue, Year XVIII (September 1968), 8.

38. This launch, notably, was a markedly international event both due to its
multinational audience, which included companies like Firestone Tires
and the Avis car rental group, and Barreiros's own status as a subsidiary
of Chrysler automobiles. In fact, the SIMCA itself was of French, not
Spanish, design. See "Presentación del 'SIMCA 1.200' en Galerías," *Boletín
de Galerías Preciados*, no. 196, Year XX (November 1969), 9; Thomas,
Eduardo Barreiros and the Recovery of Spain, 186–92, 195, 208–11, 234–
37; "Club—Nueva oferta para el carnet de conducir," *Boletín de Galerías
Preciados*, no. 191, Year XX (April 1969), 8; "Venta de coches al personal,"
Boletín de Galerías Preciados, no. 204, Year XXII (July 1970), 24.

39. "Sin aparcamiento, no hay negocio—el comprador, su coche y el comercio,"
Cortty, no. 8, Year II (June 1970).

40. "Bilbao en el mercado común de los 'Shopping Centres' con su centro
comercial Zabálburu," *A.B.C.*, 2 December 1969. For Spanish perceptions
of the Common Market, see, for instance, note 4 above; chapter 3 in this
volume; and also Julio de Diego, "Comentario: Nuevos Rumbos industri-
ales y comerciales," *ICA*, no. 106 (March 1959), 2–3; as well as José Pedro,
"Agrupación de Detallistas," *SPARCO*, no. 50, Year VI (March 1964).

41. "Ad—En el Mercado Común de los 'Shopping Centres'–Bilbao con
su Centro Comercial Zabálburu," *A.B.C.*, 2 December 1969; "Ad—
Birmingham Rotterdam Francfort Oslo-Paris BILBAO . . . nueva etapa
de la Europa Comercial de nuestro Siglo," *A.B.C.*, 23 November 1969;
"Nueva Casa Bilbaína," *Boletín de Galerías Preciados*, no. 215, Year XXIII
(October 1971), 10–11; "La inauguración de Zabálburu," *Boletín de Galerías
Preciados*, no. 216, Year XXIII (November 1971), 3.

42. There is ample, if often politicized, scholarship on the Franco regime's
relationship with the Catalan language. For a condemnation of the dictatorship's postwar efforts to publicly suppress the language, see Benet,
L'intent franquista de genocidi cultural contra Catalunya. See also Solé i
Sabaté, *La repressió franquista a Catalunya, 1938–1953*; Guibernau, *Catalan
Nationalism*, chaps. 2–3; and, for a general reference, Centre d'Estudis
sobre les Èpoques Franquista i Democràtica (CEFID), *Catalunya durant
el franquisme—Diccionari*.

43. See, for example, "V Aniversario del Botas Club"; T. y P., "Monumentos,"
Boletín de Botas, no. 18, Year III (March–April 1964), 12; Amable, "Un

Juego Sano," *Boletín de Botas*, no. 23, Year III (October 1964), 12; and Carmen, "Carácter Astur," *Boletín de Botas*, no. 28, Year IV (March 1965), 10.

44. Julio, "Asturianismo de carnet de identidad," *Boletín de Botas*, no. 8, Year II (March 1963), 4.

45. "Barretinas de Honor," *Boletín de Galerías Preciados*, no. 174, Year XVIII (July 1967), 14; "'Jorba-Preciados' en la Fiesta de la Merced," *Boletín de Galerías Preciados*, no. 146, Year XV (November 1964), 7.

46. For Jorba's deployment of Catalan, see, for instance, its fiftieth anniversary commemorative volume, Almacenes Jorba, *1911–1961—Bodas de Oro—Almacenes Jorba*. For the regime's neutral relationship with Asturian culture, see Zimmerman, "Faer Asturies: Linguistic Politics and the Frustrated Construction of Asturian Nationalism, 1974–1999," 65–80.

47. Thus too, a 1964 issue of the *Boletín de Botas* featured a traditionally garbed Asturian cultural troupe dancing and playing the bagpipes in front of an old stone church in the mountains, alongside the caption "Asturias is thus!" See [Cover Illustration], *Boletín de Botas*, no. 21, Year III (August 1964); Cerón, "Valencia y Murcia nos visitan," 8–9; and Mencía, "'Jorba-Preciados': El I Salon de la Artesania Española," *Boletín de Galerías Preciados*, no. 154, Year XVI (July 1965), 11.

48. The June–July 1974 edition of the bulletin's "Caminando por los Clubs" (Strolling through the clubs) section, for instance, which surveyed the activities of the club's many local chapters, spanned twenty-eight pages alone. It was much shorter in the previous issue, at five pages, but a separate column dedicated specifically to the club's sports programs spent ten pages on the subject. See "Sumario," *Boletín de Galerías Preciados*, no. 239 (June–July 1974), 2; "Sumario," *Boletín de Galerías Preciados*, no. 238 (April–May 1974), 2. For social coverage in just one issue of the 1957 *Boletín*, see, for example, "Saltos de agua," *Boletín de Galerías Preciados*, no. 74, Year VIII (July 1957), 7; Mencia, "Usted 'No' Es Así—El Señor Rojo," *Boletín de Galerías Preciados*, no. 74, Year VIII (July 1957), 8; "De viaje a las Agencias—Costa nos cuenta sus impresiones," *Boletín de Galerías Preciados*, no. 74, Year VIII (July 1957), 10. See also Toboso, *Pepín Fernández*, 165–66.

49. "Barcelona y Valencia HAN ESTADO EN MADRID," *Boletín de Galerías Preciados*, no. 91, Year X (April 1958), 8.

50. "Los Intercambios entre Clubs," *Boletín de Galerías Preciafdos*, no. 243 (November–December 1975), 40.

51. In similar vein, Jorba-Preciados's male and female basketball teams included a visit to the flagship store while attending a nearby tournament. See "Visita de Jorba," *Boletín de Galerías Preciados*, no. 194, Year XX (July 1969), 13. For visits in 1969–1970, see Amparo, "Valencia y Murcia nos visitan–Un viaje inolvidable," *Boletín de Galerías Preciados*, no. 192, Year XX (May 1969), 8; Cerón, "Valencia y Murcia nos visitan—Una memorable excursión," *Boletín de Galerías Preciados*, no. 192, Year XX (May 1969), 8–9; "Compañeros de Provincias nos Visitan—Bilbao, Eibar, Córdoba y Sevilla, en Madrid," *Boletín de Galerías Preciados*, no. 198, Year XXI (January 1970), 6–7. For Pepín's "Great Galerías Family" comment, see, "Don José habla de un tema entrañable—la visita de los representantes de provincias," *Boletín de Galerías Preciados*, no. 198, Year XXI (January 1970), 1.

52. Crumbaugh, *Destination Dictatorship*, 9, 22–23.

53. Crumbaugh, *Destination Dictatorship*, 9, 22–23; Cerón, "Valencia y Murcia nos visitan," 8–9.

54. See, for instance, "Campeonato de Empresa de Fútbol," *Boletín de Botas*, no. 28, Year IV (March 1965), 2.

55. Olivera, "Club en Plena Actividad: Hablan Colsa y Suria," *Boletín de Galerías Preciados*, no. 133, Year XIV (June 1963), 13; "El Deporte en los Clubs," *Boletín de Galerías Preciados*, no. 238 (March–April 1974), 34–42.

56. FAROAR, "Pepsi-Cola 2, Botas Club 1," *Boletín de Botas*, no. 29, Year IV (April 1965), 3, 15.

57. "Brillante Desarrollo: I Trofeo de futbol internacional San Isidro," *Noti-Sears*, no. 9, Year II (June 1972), ACRM 296583/1.

58. Part of a larger meeting between the two stores staged in the Catalan port town of Salou, which also featured performances by regional dance troupes from both stores, this event blurred the line between sport and store tourism, as did a visit to the flagship store that Jorba-Preciados's men's and women's basketball teams made while en route to a nearby tournament. José Maria Tarrosa, "Arte, Deporte y Hermandad: Barcelona y Zaragoza reunidas en Salou," *Boletín de Galerías Preciados*, no. 239 (June 1974), 74–75; "Visita de Jorba," *Boletín de Galerías Preciados*, no. 194, Year XX (July 1969), 13. For intramural matches at Sears, see, for instance, J. María Rubio, "Fútbol: Partido entre Gerentes y Jefes de Sección" *Noti-Sears*, no. 22, Year IV (July 1974); and "Gran partido de fútbol: Gerentes contra Jefes de División," *Noti-Sears*, no. 38, Year VI (May–June 1977).

59. "El Deporte en los Clubs de 'Galerias,'" *Boletín de Galerías Preciados*, no. 238 (May 1974), 34–42; "Baloncesto," *Noti-Sears*, no. 2, Year I (March 1971); "Tenis: Torneo para empleados de Sears," *Noti-Sears*, no. 20, Year IV (March 1974).

60. "El Deporte Como Lazo de Unión," *Boletín de Galerías Preciados*, no. 239 (June–July 1974), 60.

61. "DEPORTE y Relaciones Humanas," *Noti-Sears*, no. 10, Year II (August 1972).

62. De Urzaiz, *Teoria y Técnica de las Relaciones Públicas*, 97–98.

63. In my use of the concept of the "imagined community," I follow Benedict Anderson, who defined nations as imagined political communities inasmuch as members of a nation are likely to never meet, yet consider themselves tied by national sentiment and shared values to their fellow citizens. This label, I argue, could be applied with little adaptation to Galerías, whose rapidly growing employee ranks encompassed thousands of individuals based at often geographically distant branches, and showed in its discourse pretentions to "nation-like" claims on employees' loyalties and identities. See Anderson, *Imagined Communities*, 6–7. For "citizenship" at Galerías, see chapter 1 of this volume. For ties of affection in earlier *Boletín* discourse, see chapter 1, note 54.

64. "Jefe por 14 días: Promoción días de Barcelona," *Noti-Sears*, no. 1, Year I (November 1968); "Con gran entusiasmo la Tienda de Barcelona eligio su 'Jefe por 9 Dias,'" *Noti-Sears*, no. 8, Year II (May 1972); "Barcelona—Sau," *Noti-Sears*, no. 2, Year I (March 1971); F. M., "Dialogando con un campeón," *Noti-Sears*, no. 12, Year II (December 1972); "Calvo Sotelo—Club de Empleados Sears," *Noti-Sears*, no. 47, Year VIII (January–February–March 1979), 12.

65. See, for instance, "Las Maulas," *"Gay,"* Special Christmas Issue (December 1960); "La terrible enfermedad 'maula ferocis,'" *"Gay"* (July 1961).

66. Cuartas, *Biografía de El Corte Inglés*, 304–5, 308–9, 318–19; Jesús Benito Sánchez, "Puesta en marcha de un 'club' social," *Cortty*, no. 14, Year II (December 1970).

67. This is in contrast to the war-weariness that had originally led many Spaniards to resignedly (if also fearfully) submit to Francoist rule. See Cazorla Sánchez, *Fear and Progress*, 4.

68. Toboso, *Pepín Fernández*, 201–2. See also Zafra Aragón, *Méritos, errores, ilusiones y personajes de Galerías Preciados*, 79.

69. "Mutualidad Laboral," *Boletín de Galerías Preciados*, no. 210, Year XXIII (March 1971), 8; "Pensamientos con Descuento," *Boletín de Galerías Preciados*, no. 210, Year XXIII (March 1971), 18–19.

70. "La importancia de los Clubs," *Boletín de Galerías Preciados*, no. 220, Year XXIII (July 1971), 16; "Club Madrid—Gran labor de los clubs," *Boletín de Galerías Preciados*, no. 220, Year XXIV (March 1972), 25.

71. Examples of such complaints abound, particularly in the recurring humor/gossip column "Y tú que dices" (And what do you have to say?). See, for instance, "Y tú que dices," *Boletín de Botas*, no. 68, Year VII (January 1969), 4; "Y tú que dices," *Boletín de Botas*, no. 69, Year VII (February 1969), 4; "Y tú que dices," *Boletín de Botas*, no. 71, Year VII (April 1969), 4; and "Y tú que dices," *Boletín de Botas*, no. 73, Year VII (June 1969), 4. Thus, too, the *Boletín de Botas* published columns emphasizing the necessity of virtues such as "participation and responsibility," followed up with barbs in "Y tú que dices" challenging readers, "What do you do that is praiseworthy?" After noting that productivity may be measured both by what one does as well as what one leaves undone, such articles also demanded, "In which camp do you belong?" See "Participación y responsabilidad," *Boletín de Botas*, no. 73, Year VII (June 1969), 3; "Y tú que dices," *Boletín de Botas*, no. 74, Year VII (July 1969), 4; and "Y tú que dices," *Boletín de Botas*, no. 75, Year VII (August 1969), 4.

72. José Javier Alexandre, "Nueva insignia de oro: Crisanto Ortega," *Boletín de Galerías Preciados*, no. 104, Year XI (July 1960), 5. For the bulletin's 1953 article on Galerías-Tangier's Luis García, see O., "Nuestra Agencia de Tánger: Nuevo local en la calle más céntrica," *Boletín de Sederías Carretas y Galerías Preciados*, no. 46, Year V (undated), 11.

73. "El símbolo de los llaveros," *Boletín de Galerías Preciados*, no. 180, Year XVIII (March 1968), 2.

74. Sears, by contrast, granted its own lapel pins for seniority without such philosophizing—however, this was not their purpose, as these awards were administered by the Sears, Roebuck and Co. parent chain rather than Sears de España. Thus, Edmund Dusek of the Spanish Corporation central office reached fifteen years' service in 1968, just four years into that corporation's existence. See "La Gran Familia Sears—Aniversarios," *Noti-Sears*, no. 1, Year I (November 1968). For Botas, see, for instance, "Mensaje de nuestro gerente a los colaboradores," *Boletín de Botas*, no. 30, Year IV (May 1965), 11–12, 19; and "'El futuro es de aquellos que se

preparan para él,' manifiesta nuestro gerente," *Boletín de Botas*, no. 42, Year V (May 1966), 12–13, 19.

75. Babiano, "Mujeres, trabajo y militancia laboral bajo el franquismo," 54–56; Radcliff, "Citizens and Housewives"; Ruiz Franco, *¿Eternas menores?: Las mujeres en el franquismo*, 131–53. For a brief survey of feminist-minded groups that formed in the regime's final years, see Toboso Sánchez, "Las mujeres en la transición." For feminist activism under the Franco regime, see Nielfa Cristóbal, "El debate feminista," 269–97.

76. See "Editorial—Los derechos de la mujer . . . y sus obligaciones," *"Gay"* (March 1962); and J. L. Gay, "El Grupo Femenino," *"Gay"* (November 1962). For Pepín Fernández, see Jesus Val, "Pepín Fernández, creador del más importante complejo comercial de Madrid: Galerías Preciados— Sederías Carretas, habla para 'Gay,'" *"Gay,"* no. 9, Year II (August– September 1958), 29.

77. "Reglamento de Régimen Interior de Galerías Preciados, S.A.," 1959, AHT-GP 26/004; [No Author], "¿Niños o Niñas?," *Galerías*, no. 2 (n.d. [1959]), 14–15; "No es nada fácil saber ser mujer-¿Puede la mujer cultuvar otra profesión que . . . "sus labores"?," *Galerías*, no. 2 (n.d. [1959]), 8–9. For the magazine's tepid support for gender equality, see, esp., "Los orientales juzgan la supuesta inferioridad de las MUJERES," *Galerías*, no. 2 (n.d. [1959]), 4–5.

78. More specifically, responses like Gay's affirmed women's equal professional ability, but also their inferior performance to date, by framing the latter as a problem of commitment and motivation, one that in typically paternalist fashion fell upon management to solve through programs and opportu- nities that would teach saleswomen to have ambition. See, for example, "La Propietaria de una Boutique," *Cortty*, no. 9, Year II (July 1970), 3. For more progressive responses, see Manises, "También ellas sirven," *Boletín de Galerías Preciados*, no. 134, Year XIV (July 1963), 2; Valcarcel, "Quién es Quién—Hoy, Marisol Llerandi González," *Boletín de Botas*, no. 70, Year VII (March 1969), 5, 15.

79. "La Propietaria de una Boutique," *Cortty*, no. 9, Year II (July 1970), 3.

80. "Año Internacional de la Mujer," *Boletín de Galerías Preciados*, no. 241 (May 1975), 36–37; "Situación actual de la mujer española," *Cortty*, no. 62 (January–February 1975), 23–29; "Los derechos de la mujer: Un largo camino," *Cortty*, no. 63 (March–April, 1975), 25–26; "La mujer, fuerza de trabajo," *Cortty*, no. 66 (September–October 1975), 11–13; "Betty Friedan:

Una pionera del feminismo," *Cortty*, no. 67 (November–December 1975), 12–13. For antifeminist hostility, see, for instance, Scanlon, *La polémica feminista en la España contemporánea (1868–1974)*, 322–24, 329–31, 345–46, 353–56.

81. "[Interview with Luis Molina Romero]," *Boletín de Galerías Preciados*, no. 136, Year XIV (November 1963), 10; Conchita, "Emancipación y Personalidad," *Boletín de Botas*, no. 68, Year VII (January 1969), 3, 15.

82. Díaz Silva, "El Año Internacional de la Mujer en España: 1975."

83. Campmany [*sic*], *Carta abierta al macho ibérico*, 1974; "Año Internacional de la Mujer," *Boletín de Galerías Preciados*, no. 241 (May 1975), 36–37.

84. Steinbach, "A Comparative Study: Domestic Versus International Personnel Policies and Procedures, Sears of the San Francisco Bay Area versus Sears of Barcelona, Spain," 26–27. For Sears's early hiring in Mexico, see Moreno, *Yankee Don't Go Home*, 197–205.

85. See, for instance, "Demandas—Sears, Roebuck de España, S.A. necesita técnico con experiencia," *La Vanguardia Española*, 28 August 1966; and also "Sears, Roebuck de España, S.A. necesita ejecutivo para almacén de Barna," *La Vanguardia Española*, 13 April 1966.

86. These names belonged to Montserrat Castells, management secretary at the new store; Fernando Ferrer, the store's head of payroll; and Mercedes Cavestany, head of the Women's Handbags Department. See "Estas son las personas más ocupadas . . . preocupadas por presentarle a Vd. lo mejor, en Sears Su Almacén Favorito," *La Vanguardia Española*, 28 March 1967. For Buisán, see "Nombramiento del señor A. Buisán como gerente de personal de Sears," *La Vanguardia Española*, 17 January 1967; and Buisán Pérez, *Memorias*, 2:49–50.

87. This lack of candidates had two likely causes: first, as Edward Steinbach has noted, the small scale of most retailing in Spain, with the clear exception of chains like Galerías Preciados and El Corte Inglés; and second, the competition for qualified personnel that these chains' recently opened Barcelona branches presented. See Steinbach, "A Comparative Study," 26. For international hires at Sears de España, see, for instance, "Estas son las personas más ocupadas . . . preocupadas por presentarle a Vd. lo mejor, en Sears Su Almacén Favorito" and "Ted C. Hujar obituary," *Chicago Sun-Times*, 9 July 1987, accessed 29 March 2014, http://infoweb.newsbank.com.

88. Moreno, *Yankee Don't Go Home*.

89. Buisán Pérez, *Memorias*, 2:49–63.

90. Ramón Tintoré anticipated this move in 1972, when he was transferred to Brussels to manage the recently acquired Belgian department store chain Galeries Anspach, before returning in 1973 to run Sears–Calvo Sotelo. "Estas son las personas más ocupadas"; for Galeries Anspach's purchase, see "Belgica: Nuestra Nueva Frontera," *Noti-Sears*, no. 9, Year II (June 1972).

91. "La gran familia Sears," *Noti-Sears*, no. 1, Year I (January 1971), 11–12; for this same ethos at work within the Mexican Corporation in the late 1940s and early 1950s, see Moreno, *Yankee Don't Go Home*, 185–86.

92. "Gran . . . Inauguracion de la tienda de Meridiana!," *Noti-Sears*, no. 4, Year IV (October–December 1975).

93. For Llorens's artistic work and *Noti-Sears*, see, for instance, Blanca Aguirre, "Trabajan con Nosotros—Eduardo Llorens," *Noti-Sears*, no. 35, Year V (November–December 1976).

94. Blanca de Aguirre, "Eduardo Llorens en Brasil," *Noti-Sears*, no. 34, Year V (September–October 1976).

95. Eduardo Llorens, "A mi aire, por Eduardo Llorens—La Paz y el Lago Titicaca," *Noti-Sears*, no. 41, Year VI (November–December 1977).

96. Martínez, "Libre Opinion—Un no a 'España es diferente.'"

97. "Conferencia Internacional de Gerencia Avanzada," *Noti-Sears*, no. 5, Year I (November 1971); "Nuestros hombres viajan y estudian," *Noti-Sears*, no. 16, Year III (July 1973).

98. Steinbach, "A Comparative Study," 20; Moreno, *Yankee Don't Go Home*, 175–76.

99. Steinbach, "A Comparative Study," 20–22.

100. For the founding of the SEI, see "Mail-Order Education," *TIME* (19 May 1952), 104; for the SEI and Sears de España, see, for example, "Concurso Internacional—Sears Extension Institute, Operaciones Internacionales," *Noti-Sears*, no. 3, Year I (May 1971). For warranty sales, see "Dos Trofeos de Internacional para España," *Noti-Sears*, no. 16, Year III (July 1973); for furniture sales, see "Madrid y Barcelona de Nuevo Campeones de Ventas de Muebles en todo el Mundo Sears," *Noti-Sears*, no. 26, Year IV (March 1975).

101. Rudy Greer, "'Presentacion'—Mensaje del Presidente Sr. Rudy Greer," *Noti-Sears*, no. 1, Year I (November 1968), 1.

102. "Satisfaccion garantizada, un lema que nacio con la Compañia," *Noti-Sears*, no. 37, Year VI (March–April 1977). For the foreign nature of Sears's motto in Spain, see Steinbach, "A Comparative Study," 56–57.

103. África, "Visitas Internacionales—El Dpto. de Display en pleno, con los dos ilustres visitantes," *Noti-Sears*, no. 22, Year IV (July 1974); África, "Mr Roderich Kevend, Director del 730 internacional (Promociones Mercancia de Venta), visita la Tienda de Madrid," *Noti-Sears*, no. 40 Year, VI (September–October 1977), 3.

104. "Sears en el Mundo," *Noti-Sears*, no. 12, Year II (December 1972).

105. "Sears en el Mundo"; "Torre Sears: La escalada de 443 metros ha sido concluida," *Noti-Sears*, no. 17, Year III (October 1973); "Los Departamentos de las Oficinas Centrales empiezan a ocupar la Torre Sears," *Noti-Sears*, no. 17, Year III (October 1973); "La Ceremonia de culminación," *Noti-Sears*, no. 17, Year III (October 1973); "Sears y la Olimpiada de Munich," *Noti-Sears*, no. 9, Year II (June 1972).

106. A. Buisán, "Formación Profesional," *Noti-Sears*, no. 2, Year I (December 1968). This is reminiscent of Galerías Preciados's and El Corte Inglés's efforts to shape employees into store citizens—total citizens, rather than international—which the latter retailer termed "Personas Cortty."

107. "Mensaje de Sears Managua," *Noti-Sears*, no. 14, Year III (March 1973).

108. "Esto es Sears," *La Vanguardia Española*, 22 January 1967, 28.

109. "España—Apertura del Primer Gran Almacen Sears Roebuck," in "Hoja Informativa—GP Dirección de personal—Departamento de Formación Profesional," ARCM 88008/5.

110. "España—Apertura del Primer Gran Almacen Sears Roebuck."

111. "España—Apertura del Primer Gran Almacen Sears Roebuck"; see also notes 34–39 above.

112. "España—Apertura del Primer Gran Almacen Sears Roebuck."

113. For the centrality of appliances to Sears de España's business—the chain's "satellite stores" specialized in these items—see Toboso, *Pepín Fernández*, 375–76. For frozen foods, supermarkets, and modernity, see chapter 3 of this volume.

114. "España—Apertura del Primer Gran Almacen Sears Roebuck."

115. See "Conozca Nuestras Secciones—Departamento de Cuentas Caja Principal," *Noti-Sears*, no. 2, Year I (December 1968); and "Historieta de Cuentas y Crédito," *Noti-Sears*, no. 2, Year I (December 1968).

116. "Sears Drops Usual Labels, but Auto Firm Complains," *Wall Street Journal*, 27 March 1967, http://search.proquest.com/docview/133235758?accountid=13626.

117. Indeed, in the years leading up to its sale, the Spanish corporation posted steady losses, though it merits note that the chain's other foreign divisions did as well and that this period coincided with Spain's post-1973 economic crisis, which had already provoked the sale of a majority stake in Galerías Preciados to RUMASA in 1981. See Toboso, *Pepín Fernández*, 369–78; "Habla don Ezequiel Puig Maestro-Amado, Concejal del Ecmo. Ayuntamiento de Madrid: 'Sears ha revitalizado el comercio de esta zona,'" *Noti-Sears*, no. 7, Year I (March 1972); "Sears, Penney List Sharp Profit Declines for Quarter; Tax Item Helps Woolworth," *Wall Street Journal*, 20 May 20 1980, accessed 25 March, 2013, http://search.proquest.com/docview/134526004?accountid=13626; and "Sears Roebuck to Sell Its Spanish Subsidiary to Galerias Preciados," *Wall Street Journal*, 13 September 13 1982, accessed 25 March 2013, http://search.proquest.com/docview/134725462?accountid=13626.

118. See A. Mateos, "Remodelación de la División 48, Boutique Juvenil," *Noti-Sears*, no. 25, Year IV (January 1975).

119. "Solo para Ellas—De la Falda-Pantalon al 'SHORT,'" *Noti-Sears*, no. 2, Year I (March,1971). Similarly, in 1974, merchandise buyer Ana Riba declared, "The Buyer's Office's work for th[e lingerie] department fills us with satisfaction.... Every day we handle flirty, youthful, sexy, campy pieces, which once in store, allow women to find affordable, quality models." See Ana Izquierdo, "Página del Comprador, Entrevista con Ana Riba: El Atractivo Mundo de la Moda Femenina," *Noti-Sears*, no. 22, Year IV (July 1974).

120. By then, the *Boletín de Galerías Preciados* was out of print, and the outwardly apolitical *Cortty* offered no rival content. For the *Destape* and sexual liberation after Franco, see, for example, Alonso Tejada, *La represión sexual en la España de Franco*, 237–60; and Kowalsky, "Rated S: Softcore Pornography and the Spanish Transition to Democracy, 1977–82."

121. For García, see "El Humor y José García," *Noti-Sears*, no. 33, Year V (July–August 1976).

122. Adolfo Gómez, "Hoy es Noticia: Jaime Marbá, Jefe de la D/21," *Noti-Sears*, no. 45, Year VII (September–October 1978), 15; Adolfo Gómez, "Hoy es Noticia: Jorge López Gómez, Jefe de la D/24," *Noti-Sears*, no. 48, Year VIII (July 1979), 10.

123. África [Galeras], "Personajes Populares: Choni, Secretaria de Gerencia (Serrano)," *Noti-Sears*, no. 35, Year V (November–December 1976).

124. "La Camisa, Prenda Esencial del Hombre Civilizado," *Señor*, no. 22 (Spring 1961).
125. Bernecker, "The Change in Mentalities during the Late Franco Regime," 75–76. See also Pollack and Hunter, *The Paradox of Spanish Foreign Policy*, 136–37.

Epilogue

1. For an analysis of Radio Futura, its historical moment, and the band's body of work, see Tango, *La transición y su doble*. For more on La Movida as it unfolded in its birth city of Madrid, see, for instance, Stappell, *Remaking Madrid*. For La Movida more generally, see Lechado, *La Movida*.
2. A televised performance of the song may be found at "Radio Futura—Enamorado de la Moda Juvenil," YouTube, accessed 27 May 2014, http://www.youtube.com/watch?v=wl3o5eZdvtk.
3. For subjective totalitarianism, see chapter 1, note 72.
4. Notably, in April 1965, or at virtually the same time that this commercial aired, Philips numbered among the top advertisers on Spanish television. "Estadística de la publicidad," *I.P.*, no. 19 (June 1965), 52–53.
5. This cultural hybridity was only further reinforced by a costume change that swapped the short, fashionable dress and 1960s bob haircut that Sevilla initially sported for traditional flamenco attire. See "Philips Commercial—Familia Philips," YouTube, accessed 27 May 2014, http://www.youtube.com/watch?v=hs2loz3vkaq; and Rodríguez, *Busque, compare y, si encuentra un libro mejor, ¡cómprelo!*, 48–49.
6. See Cazorla Sánchez, *Fear and Progress*, 157–58; Abella, *La vida cotidiana bajo el régimen de Franco*, chap. 13.
7. For reference to *pasotas*, see Fouce, "De la agitación a la Movida," 145; Lechado, *La Movida*, 41.
8. Kowalsky, "Rated S," 190, 192–96.
9. See, esp., Pack, *Tourism and Dictatorship*; and Radcliff, *Making Democratic Citizens in Spain*.
10. "Noticias de las agencias," *I.P.*, no. 22 (September 1965), 88–89.
11. See Schutts, "Die Erfrischende Pause: Marketing Coca-Cola in Hitler's Germany"; and Rubin, *Synthetic Socialism*.
12. Martín Aceña and Martínez Ruiz, "The Golden Age of Spanish Capitalism," 45–46.
13. Pack, *Tourism and Dictatorship*, 108, 188.

14. For such narratives, see introduction, note 10; and Preston, *Juan Carlos*.

15. Radcliff, "La Transición Española: ¿Un Modelo Global?"

16. Pack, *Tourism and Dictatorship*.

17. See, for instance, "Acta de la Reunion del Comité Social," 28 January 1966, AGUN-JMM/144/494/004.

18. Edles cites a 1977 editorial in the national newspaper *El País*, which criticized democratic Spain's newly minted politicians for their "obsessi[ve]" need for support and validation from their European socialist, communist, and Christian-democratic peers. See Edles, *Symbol and Ritual in the New Spain*, 57.

19. "El turista 15.000.000, señor Tsegaye Aga, honró 'Galerias' con su visita, acompañado por el secretario de Protocolo del Ministerio de Informacion Señor Serra Hamilton, y del de Propaganda, Señor Díez," *Boletín de Galerías Preciados*, no. 166, Year XVII (November 1966), 1.

20. "Acta de la Reunion," 23 February 1965, AGUN-JMM/144/431/002; "Análisis de la Situación actual de la Costa Brava y Estudio de una posible Acción de Relaciones Públicas en pro de la misma," n.d., AGUN-JMM/144/009/002.

21. Kuisel, *Seducing the French*. See also Poiger, *Jazz, Rock and Rebels*.

22. See introduction, note 50.

23. Moreno, *Yankee Don't Go Home*, 174–81; de Grazia, *Irresistible Empire*, chap. 8; "La Libre Empresa y Vd.," *Noti-Sears*, no. 39, Year VI (July–August 1977).

24. This is likewise true of Portugal's and Greece's contemporaneous transitions. For a recent analysis of precisely how the 2008 global economic crisis has sparked such reevaluation, see Cavallaro and Kornetis, *Rethinking Democratisation in Spain, Greece, and Portugal*.

25. Palomares, *The Quest for Survival after Franco*.

26. Pavlović, *The Mobile Nation*, 3.

27. For Spanish "disremembering" of Francoism, see Casanova, "Disremembering Francoism." For a recent analysis of women's rights struggles and Francoist legacies in the transition, see Mahaney, "Feminism under and after Franco."

28. Kowalsky, "Rated S"; Kornetis, "Documenting Post-Authoritarian Subcultures in the European South: The Cases of Pedro Almodóvar's *Pepi, Luci, Bom* and Nikos Zervos' *Dracula of Exarchia*."

29. For labor activism under Franco, see Ruíz, *Historia de Comisiones Obreras (1958–1988)*. For two examples of such lawsuits, see "Case before Labor

Magistrate due to Termination of Don José Luis Muñoz Martínez," 6 December 1972–3 January 1973, AHT-AS, Folder 0063–0014; and "Case before Labor Magistrate due to Termination of Don Anselmo Lanzas Alamín," 13 May 1971–24 May 1971, AHT-AS, Folder 0019–0020.

30. For "yellow" syndicates, see Carvajal Soria and Martín Criado, "Venderás en domingo. Las luchas por el tiempo en el sector de grandes superficies comerciales (1976–2011)." For complaints, see Comisiones Obreras de El Corte Inglés, *I Conferencia de CC.OO. de El Corte Inglés*, 16, 18, 51.

31. Author's observation; Javier Romera, "Llegan más cambios a El Corte Inglés: Las mujeres se ponen pantalones," *El Economista.es*, 7 May 2007, https://www.eleconomista.es/empresas-finanzas/noticias/207996/05 /07/Llegan-mas-cambios-a-El-Corte-Ingles-las-mujeres-se-ponen-los -pantalones.html.

32. Carvajal Soria and Martín Criado, "Venderás en domingo," 65–67, 71–74.

33. For El Corte Inglés's rise to dominance in modern-day Spanish retailing, see Cuartas, *Biografía de El Corte Inglés*, chap. 27; and Toboso, *Pepín Fernández*, 360–63, 386–94.

34. Toboso, *Pepín Fernández*, 421–34.

35. His choice to invest in El Corte Inglés was unsurprising, for while he had been a founding investor in both Sederías Carretas and El Corte Inglés, he had broken with Pepín Fernández in the mid-1940s, but remained nominal president of El Corte Inglés's board of directors through to 1960. See Cuartas, *Biografía de El Corte Inglés*, 221–26; Zafra Aragón, *Méritos, errores, ilusiones y personajes de Galerías Preciados*, 33; Toboso, *Pepín Fernández*, 168–71, 302–3.

36. Toboso, *Pepín Fernández*, 302–10, 315, 320–22.

37. Toboso, *Pepín Fernández*, 288–97; Cuartas, *Biografía de El Corte Inglés*, 372.

38. For the sale to RUMASA, see Toboso, *Pepín Fernández*, 372–78; Zafra Aragón, *Méritos, errores, ilusiones y personajes de Galerías Preciados*, 205–13.

39. For a detailed description of Galerías Preciados's subsequent sale to various investors through 1995, most notable among them the Venezuela-based Cisneros Group (1984–1987) and the English Mountleigh Group (1987–1992), see Toboso, *Pepín Fernández*, 376–86, chap. 12; and for an insider perspective on this process, particularly in its financial dimensions, see Zafra Aragón, *Méritos, errores, ilusiones y personajes de Galerías Preciados*, chaps. 7–14.

BIBLIOGRAPHY

Locating archival collections and often short-lived historical periodicals represents a special challenge for the historian of modern Spain, particularly when researching the Franco era. These resources are not always well-publicized and, notwithstanding the Franco regime's well-known centralist impulses, are sometimes scattered across multiple repositories. In consequence, the published and unpublished sources consulted for this book are listed here in four sections, respectively detailing the archives, the magazines and bulletins, the newspapers, and the other published primary as well as secondary sources on which this analysis draws. The intent is to save the reader the trouble of combing through the book's citations simply to determine what archives, magazines, and newspapers proved useful when pursuing this research—and which might likewise be useful to other scholars with thematically similar interests—by listing them separately.

Archives

Archivo de la Historia del Trabajo, Fundación 10 de Mayo–CC.OO. (Madrid, Spain)
    Almeida-Salorio Law Offices Collection
    Galerías Preciados Collection
Archivo General de la Administración (Alcalá de Henares, Spain)
    Comisaría de Abastecimientos y Transportes Documentation
    Ministry of Information and Tourism Records
Archivo General de la Universidad de Navarra (Pamplona, Spain)
    Personal Papers, Gregorio Marañón Moya
    Personal Papers, Joaquín Maestre Morata
Archivo Regional de la Comunidad de Madrid (Madrid, Spain)
    Auxiliary Library
    Galerías Preciados Internal Records Collection
Fundació Cipriano García–Arxiu Històric de CC.OO. de Catalunya (Barcelona, Spain)
    Clandestine Press Collection
    Comisiones Obreras Department Store Organization Records

Worker's Biographies Oral History Collection
National Library of Catalonia (Barcelona, Spain)
    María Freixas i Bru Family Budget Books Collection
Rockefeller Family Archives (Sleepy Hollow, New York)
    International Basic Economy Corporation (IBEC) Records Collection

Magazines and Bulletins Consulted

Actualidad Económica
Alta Costura: Revista de la Moda
AMA: La Revista de las Amas de Casa Españolas
Ana María: Revista para la Mujer
Arte Comercial: Revista Técnica de Publicidad y Organización
Arte y Hogar
Astra: Revista moderna para la mujer
Blanco y Negro: Revista Ilustrada
Boletín Autoservicio COVIC
Boletín de Botas
Boletín de Sederías Carretas y Galerías Preciados
Boletín Oficial de Estado
Butlletí Portaveu Mensual del "Centro de Dependientes del Comercio y de la Industria"
CONAUTA: Revista Técnica del Autoservicio
Cortty: Boletín de El Corte Inglés
Cuadernos para el diálogo
Distinción: Revista Gráfica Española
Don: La Moda Masculina Española
El Hogar y la Moda
El Siglo–Periodico Quincenal, Organo de los Grandes Almacenes de este Titulo
Escaparate: Revista del arte decorativo comercial
Funcionarias: Revista para la mujer
Galerías
"Gay": Revista Mensual de Almacenes Siro Gay
Hogares Modernos
¡Hola!: Semanario de amenidades
Hombres Dunia
I.P.: Información de la Publicidad
ICA: Industria y Comercio de Alimentación

Idea: Al servicio de las relaciones públicas
Interviú
La Familia SPAR: *Revista para el ama de casa y la familia*
La Moda Elegante: Periódico de las Familias
Medina
Men's Modes: The Custom Tailor's Journal (Edición en Español)
Meridiano Femenino
Mujer: Revista Mensual del Hogar y de la Moda
Noti-Sears: Revista para los empleados de Sears Roebuck España, S.A. y sus familiares
PK *Press*
Quid: Revista Musical
Relaciones Públicas
Revista Jorba
Revista VéGé
Señor: La Revista del Hombre
SEPESA: *Revista de la Industria y del Comercio de la Alimentación*
SPARCO: *Boletín de Enlace de los Sparistas Españoles*
Tele-radio: Revista semanal de TVE-RNE
Telva
Teresa: Revista para todas las mujeres
Triunfo
Ventanal
Vivir a Dos
Warehousemen and Draper's Trade Journal

Newspapers Consulted

A.B.C.
El Economista.es
El País
La Nación (Buenos Aires)
La Vanguardia Española
New York Times
The Southern Cross (Buenos Aires)
The Times (London)
Wall Street Journal

Published Works

A Guide to Window-Dressing. London: W. H. & L. Collingridge, 1883.

Abella, Rafael. *La vida cotidiana bajo el régimen de Franco.* Madrid: Ediciones Temas de Hoy, 1984.

———. *La vida cotidiana durante la guerra civil: La España nacional.* Barcelona: Editorial Planeta, 1973.

Alcalde, Ángel. "El descanso del guerrero: La transformación de la masculinidad excombatiente franquista (1939–1965)." *Historia y Política* 37 (2017): 177–208.

Alferez, Antonio. *Cuarto poder en España: La prensa desde la Ley Fraga 1966.* Barcelona: Plaza y Janés, 1986.

Almacenes Jorba. *1911–1961—Bodas de Oro—Almacenes Jorba.* Barcelona: Agustín Núñez, 1961.

"Almacenes Siro Gay y Filiales." In *Cincuenta Años de Almacenes Siro Gay, 1906–1956.* N.p., 1958.

Alonso Tejada, Luis. *La represión sexual en la España de Franco.* Barcelona: Luis de Caralt, 1978.

Alonso, Luis Enrique, and Fernando Conde. *Historia del consumo en España: Una aproximación a sus orígenes y primer desarrollo.* Madrid: Debate, 1994.

Altabella, José. "Historia del Periodismo Español: Programa y fuentes." *Documentación de las Ciencias de la Información* (November 1987): 11–52.

Althusser, Louis. "Ideology and Ideological State Apparatuses (Notes towards an Investigation)." In *Essays on Ideology.* London: Verso, 1984.

Amador Carretero, Pilar. "La mujer es el mensaje: Los coros y danzas de sección femenina en hispanoamérica." *Feminismo/s* 2 (December 2003): 101–20.

Anderson, Benedict. *Imagined Communities: Reflections on the Origin and Spread of Nationalism.* London: Verso, 2006.

Anuario de la Prensa Española. Year I. Madrid: Delegación Nacional de Prensa, 1943–1944.

Anuario de la Prensa Española. Year II. Madrid: Delegación Nacional de Prensa, 1945–1946.

Anuario de la Prensa Española. Year III, Vol. 2. Madrid: Ministerio de Información y Turismo, 1954.

Aragüez Rubio, Carlos. "La Nova Cançó catalana: Génesis, desarrollo y trascendencia de un fenómeno cultural en el segundo franquismo." *Pasado y Memoria: Revista de Historia Contemporánea* 5 (2006): 81–97.

Auslander, Leora. *Taste and Power: Furnishing Modern France*. Berkeley: University of California Press, 1996.

Babiano, José. "Mujeres, trabajo y militancia laboral bajo el franquismo (materiales para un análisis histórico)." In *Del hogar a la huelga: Trabajo, género y movimiento obrero durante el franquismo*, edited by José Babiano, 25–76. Madrid: Los Libros de la Catarata, 2007.

Baudrillard, Jean. *Selected Writings*. Edited by Mark Poster. Stanford CA: Stanford University Press, 1988.

Bauer, Olga. *Cortesia y Etiqueta Modernas*. 5th ed. Madrid: Aguilar, 1967.

Benería, Lourdes. *Mujer, economía y patriarcado en la España de Franco*. Barcelona: Cuadernos Anagrama, 1977.

Benet, Josep. *L'intent franquista de genocidi cultural contra Catalunya*. Barcelona: Publicacions de l'Abadia de Montserrat, 1995.

Benson, Susan Porter. *Counter Cultures: Saleswomen, Managers, and Customers in American Department Stores, 1890–1940*. Urbana: University of Illinois Press, 1986.

Bernecker, Walter. "The Change in Mentalities during the Late Franco Regime." In *Spain Transformed: The Late Franco Dictatorship, 1959–75*, edited by Nigel Townson, 67–84. London: Palgrave Macmillan, 2007.

Bhabha, Homi K. *The Location of Culture*. London: Routledge, 1994.

Bowlby, Rachel. *Carried Away: The Invention of Modern Shopping*. New York: Columbia University Press, 2001.

Brenan, Gerald. *The Face of Spain*. London: Serif, 2006.

Breward, Christopher. *The Hidden Consumer: Masculinities, Fashion, and City Life (1860–1914)*. Manchester, UK: Manchester University Press, 1999.

Buisán Pérez, Alfonso. *Memorias*. Vol. 2. Mexico: Servicios Editoriales de Aguascalientes, 2008.

Bunk, Brian D. *Ghosts of Passion: Martyrdom, Gender, and the Origins of the Spanish Civil War*. Durham NC: Duke University Press, 2007.

Cabana, Francesc. *Cien Empresarios Catalanes*. Madrid: LID Editorial Empresarial, 2006.

Cabrera, Miguel A. "Developments in Contemporary Spanish Historiography: From Social History to the New Cultural History." *Journal of Modern History* 77 (December 2005): 988–1023.

Callahan, William. *The Catholic Church in Spain, 1875–1998*. Washington DC: The Catholic University of America Press, 2012.

Campmany [*sic*], Maria Aurelia. *Carta Abierta al Macho Ibérico*. 2nd ed. Madrid: Ediciones 99, 1974.

Capmany, María Aurèlia. "Cartas Impertinentes." In *La Liberación de la Mujer: Año Cero*, 31–44. Barcelona: Granica, 1977.

Carr, Raymond, and Juan Pablo Fusi Aizpurúa. *Spain: Dictatorship to Democracy*. London: George Allen & Unwin, 1979.

Carrillo-Linares, Alberto. "Movimiento estudiantil antifranquista, cultura política y transición política a la democracia." *Pasado y Memoria. Revista de Historia Contemporánea* 5 (2006): 149–70.

———. *Subversivos y malditos en la Universidad de Sevilla (1965–1977)*. Seville: Fundación Centro de Estudios Anaduces, 2008.

Carrión Jiménez, Carmen, and Javier Hernando Carrasco. "'Medina,' prototipo de la prensa femenina de postguerra." *Estudios Humanísticos: Geografía, Historia, Arte* 7 (1985): 163–80.

Carvajal Soria, Pilar, and Enrique Martín Criado. "Venderás en domingo. Las luchas por el tiempo en el sector de grandes superficies comerciales (1976–2011)." In *Conflictos por el tiempo. Poder, relación salarial y relaciones de género*, edited by Enrique Martín Criado and Carlos Prieto, 49–82. Madrid: Centro de Investigaciones Sociológicas, 2015.

Casanova, Julián. "Disremembering Francoism: What Is at Stake in Spain's Memory Wars?" In *Interrogating Francoism: History and Dictatorship in Twentieth-Century Spain*, edited by Helen Graham, 203–22. London: Bloomsbury, 2016.

Casares, Francisco. *Conferencia que el secretario de la Asociacion de la Prensa D. Francisco Casares ha dado al personal de Sederias Carretas, S.L el 15 de Noviembre de 1941*. N.p.

Castillo Castillo, José. "¿Es España sociedad de consumo de masas?" *Anales de Sociología* 1 (1966): 7–18.

———. *Sociedad de Consumo a la Española*. Madrid: EUDEMA, 1987.

Castillo, Greg. "The American 'Fat Kitchen' in Europe: Postwar Domestic Modernity and Marshall Plan Strategies of Enchantment." In *Cold War Kitchen: Americanization, Technology, and European Users*, edited by Ruth Oldenziel and Karin Zachmann, 33–58. Cambridge MA: MIT Press, 2009.

Cavallaro, María Elena, and Kostis Kornetis, eds. *Rethinking Democratisation in Spain, Greece, and Portugal*. New York: Palgrave Macmillan, 2019.

Cazorla Sánchez, Antonio. *Fear and Progress: Ordinary Lives in Franco's Spain, 1939–1975*. Malden MA: Wiley-Blackwell, 2010.

Centre d'Estudis sobre les Èpoques Franquista i Democràtica (CEFID). *Catalunya durant el franquisme—Diccionari*. Vic: Eumo Editorial, 2006.

Chase, Michelle. *Revolution within the Revolution: Women and Gender Politics in Cuba, 1952–1962*. Chapel Hill: University of North Carolina Press, 2015.

Ciarlo, David. *Advertising Empire: Race and Visual Culture in Imperial Germany*. Cambridge MA: Harvard University Press, 2011.

Cieraad, Irene. "The Radiant American Kitchen: Domesticating Dutch Nuclear Energy." In *Cold War Kitchen: Americanization, Technology, and European Users*, edited by Ruth Oldenziel and Karin Zachmann, 113–36. Cambridge MA: MIT Press, 2009.

Claret Miranda, Jaume. *El Atroz Desmoche: La destrucción de la Universidad española por el franquismo, 1937–1945*. Barcelona: Crítica, 2006.

Cobble, Dorothy Sue. "Recapturing Working-Class Feminism: Union Women in the Postwar Era." In *Not June Cleaver: Women and Gender in Postwar America, 1945–1960*, edited by Joanne Jay Meyerowitz, 57–83. Philadelphia: Temple University Press, 1994.

Cohen, Lizabeth. *A Consumers' Republic: The Politics of Mass Consumption in Postwar America*. New York: Vintage Books, 2004.

Comisiones Obreras de El Corte Inglés. *I Conferencia de CC.OO. de El Corte Inglés*. Barcelona: CC.OO. de El Corte Inglés, 1980.

Connickie, Yvonne. *Fashions of a Decade: The 1960s*. New York: Infobase, 2007.

Crespo MacLennan, Julio. *España en Europa, 1945–2000: Del ostracismo a la modernidad*. Madrid: Marcial Pons, 2004.

———. *Spain and the Process of European Integration, 1957–1985*. Hampshire, UK: Palgrave, 2000.

Crossick, Geoffrey, and Serve Jaumain. *Cathedrals of Consumption: The European Department Store, 1850–1939*. Aldershot, UK: Ashgate, 1999.

Crumbaugh, Justin. *Destination Dictatorship: The Spectacle of Spain's Tourist Boom and the Reinvention of Difference*. Albany: State University of New York Press, 2009.

Cruz, Jesus. *The Rise of Middle-Class Culture in Nineteenth-Century Spain*. Baton Rouge: Louisiana State University Press, 2011.

Cuartas, Javier. *Biografía de El Corte Inglés: La Historia de un Gigante*. Barcelona: Libros Límite, 1992.

Daudet, Elvira. *Los Empresarios*. Barcelona: DOPESA, 1974.

Davis, Fred. *Fashion, Culture, and Identity*. Chicago: University of Chicago Press, 1992.

de Certeau, Michel. *The Practice of Everyday Life*. Berkeley: University of California Press, 1984

de Grazia, Victoria. "Changing Consumption Regimes in Europe, 1930–1970: Comparative Perspectives on the Distribution Problem." In *Getting and Spending: European and American Consumer Societies in the Twentieth Century*, edited by Susan Strasser, Charles McGovern, and Mattias Judt, 59–83. Cambridge: Cambridge University Press, 1998.

———. *How Fascism Ruled Women: Italy, 1922–1945*. Berkeley: University of California Press, 1993.

———. *Irresistible Empire: America's Advance through 20th-Century Europe*. Cambridge MA: Belknap, 2006.

de Grazia, Victoria, and Ellen Furlough. *The Sex of Things: Gender and Consumption in Historical Perspective*. Berkeley: University of California Press, 1996.

de Sena, Enrique. "Un Hombre de la Plaza Mayor." In *Cincuenta Años de Almacenes Siro Gay, 1906–1956*. N.p., 1958.

de Urzaiz, Jaime. *Teoria y Técnica de las Relaciones Públicas*. Madrid: Libreria Editorial San Martín, 1971.

Debord, Guy. *Society of the Spectacle*. Detroit: Black & Red, 1983.

del Arco Blanco, Miguel Ángel. "Hunger and the Consolidation of the Francoist Regime (1939–1951)." *European History Quarterly* 40, no. 3 (July 2010): 458–83.

del Campo, Salustiano, and Manuel Navarro. *Crítica de la planificación social española, 1964–1975*. Madrid: Miguel Castellote, 1976.

Delgado Gómez-Escalonilla, Lorenzo. *Diplomacia Franquista y Política Cultural Hacia Iberoamérica, 1939–1953*. Madrid: CSIC, 1988.

Deutsch, Tracey. *Building a Housewife's Paradise: Gender, Politics, and American Grocery Stores in the Twentieth Century*. Chapel Hill: University of North Carolina Press, 2010.

Díaz Silva, Elena. "El Año Internacional de la Mujer en España: 1975." *Cuadernos de Historia Contemporánea* 31 (8 October 2009): 319–39.

Domènech Sampere, Xavier. "La otra cara del milagro español: Clase obrera y movimiento obrero en los años del desarrollismo." *Historia Contemporánea* 26 (2003): 91–112.

Edles, Laura Desfor. *Symbol and Ritual in the New Spain: The Transition to Democracy after Franco*. Cambridge: Cambridge University Press, 2011.

Eiroa San Francisco, Matilde. "Relaciones internacionales y estrategias de comunicación de la España de Franco ante la coyuntura de 1956." *Historia y Comunicación Social* 12 (30 May 2007): 5–22.

El Corte Inglés. *Reglamento de Régimen Interior*. Madrid: El Corte Inglés, 1977.

Erwin, Kathleen. "Heart-to-Heart, Phone-to-Phone: Family Values, Sexuality, and the Politics of Shanghai's Advice Hotlines." In *The Consumer Revolution in Urban China*, edited by Deborah S. Davis, 145–70. Berkeley: University of California Press, 2000.

Eslava Galán, Juan. *Los Años del Miedo*. Barcelona: Editorial Planeta, 2010.

Espuny i Espuny, Francina. *El moviment estudiantil a Barcelona (1965–1975)*. La Garriga: Malhivern, 2010.

Falcón, Lidia. *Los dereches civiles de la mujer*. Barcelona: Nereo, 1963.

———. *Los dereches laborales de la mujer*. Madrid: Montecorvo, 1964.

———. *Mujer y Sociedad: Análisis de un Fenómeno Reaccionario*. Barcelona: Fontanella, 1969.

———. "La Opresión de la Mujer: Una Incógnita." In *La Liberación de la Mujer: Año Cero*, edited by Ana Balletbo, et al., 45–58. Barcelona: Granica, 1977.

Fernández Areal, Manuel. *La Libertad de Prensa en España, 1938–71*. Madrid: Cuadernos para el Diálogo, 1968.

Fernández García, Ana María. "Galerías Preciados (1943–1975): A Spanish Cathedral of Consumption and Its Display Strategies during the Franco Years." In *Architectures of Display: Department Stores and Modern Retail*, edited by Anca I. Lasc, Patricia Lara-Betancourt, and Margaret Maile Petty, 265–79. London: Routledge, 2018.

Ferrer Andreu, Vicente. "Distribución regional de la renta en España, (1947–1970)." *Revista Española de Economía* 5, no. 3 (September–December 1975): 89–102.

Ferry, John William. *A History of the Department Store*. New York: Macmillan, 1960.

Fink, Carole, Philipp Gassert, and Detlef Junker, eds. *1968: The World Transformed*. Cambridge: Cambridge University Press, 1999.

Finlayson, Iain. *Tangier: City of the Dream*. London: HarperCollins, 1992.

FOESSA-Fomento de Estudios Sociales y de Sociologia Aplicada. Madrid: Editorial Mediterráneo, 1967.

Folguera Crespo, Pilar. "El Franquismo. El Retorno a la Esfera Privada (1939–1975)." In *Historia de las Mujeres en España*, edited by Elisa Garrido González, 527–48. Madrid: Editorial Síntesis, 1997.

Fomento de Estudios Sociales y de Sociologia Aplicada—Fundación FOESSA. "Breve estudio estadístico del INFORME SOCIOLOGICO SOBRE LA SITU-

ACION SOCIAL DE ESPAÑA, Madrid, 1966." *Información Documental* 9 (1 June 1967): 1–14.

———. "Situación Social Española: 1966." *Información Documental* 6 (3 December 1966): 1–9.

Forcano, Eugeni. Email correspondence with author, 16 September, 2008.

Forcano, Eugeni, Daniel Giralt-Miracle, and Roser Martínez Rochina. *Eugeni Forcano: La meva Barcelona*. Barcelona: Lunwerg, 2010.

Fouce, Héctor. "De la agitación a la Movida: Políticas culturales y música popular en la Transición española." *Arizona Journal of Hispanic Cultural Studies* 13 (2009): 143–53.

Fox, Stephen. *The Mirror Makers: A History of American Advertising and its Creators*. Urbana: University of Illinois Press, 1997.

Freeman, Roger, and Paquita Freeman. *A Visitor's Guide to Madrid*. León: Editorial Everest, 1971.

Fundación FOESSA. *Efectos sociales queridos y no queridos en el desarrollo español*. Madrid: Fundación FOESSA, 1967.

———. *Estudios sociológicos sobre la situación social de España, 1975*. Madrid: Euramérica, 1975.

———. *Informe sociológico sobre la situación social de Madrid*. Madrid: Euramérica, 1967.

———. *Informe Sociológico Sobre la Situación Social en España, 1966*. Madrid: FOESSA, 1966.

Gallego Ayala, Juana. *Mujeres de papel: De ¡Hola! a Vogue: La prensa femenina en la actualidad*. Barcelona: ICARIA Editorial, 1990.

Ganzabal Learreta, María. "Nacimiento, evolución y crisis de la prensa femenina contemporánea en España." *Ámbitos* 15 (2006): 405–20.

García Ruescas, Francisco. *Historia de la Publicidad*. Madrid: Editora Nacional, 1971.

———. *Problemática de las Inversiones Extranjeras en España*. Madrid: Gráf. Brasil, 1967.

Gilmour, David. *The Transformation of Spain: From Franco to the Constitutional Monarchy*. London: Quartet Books, 1985.

Ginard i Ferón, David. "Las Condiciones de Vida durante el Primer Franquismo. El Caso de las Islas Baleares." *Hispania* 62/3, no. 212 (2002): 1099–1128.

Gómez Alén, José. "Las Comisiones Obreras de Galicia y la oposición al franquismo (1962–1978)." In *Historia de Comisiones Obreras (1958–1988)*, edited by David Ruíz, 259–88. Madrid: Siglo Veintiuno de España, 1993.

Gómez Pérez, Rafael. *El Franquismo y la iglesia*. Madrid: Ediciones Rialp, 1986.

González Iglesias, Julio. *Historia General de la Higiene Bucodentaria*. Madrid: Yeltes, 2003.

González, Manuel-Jesús. *La Economía Política de Franquismo (1940–1970): Dirigismo, mercado y planificación*. Madrid: Tecnos, 1979.

Gorsuch, Anne E. *All This Is Your World: Soviet Tourism at Home and Abroad after Stalin*. Oxford: Oxford University Press, 2011.

Gould Levine, Linda, and Gloria Feiman Waldman, eds. *Feminismo ante el Franquismo: Entrevistas con feministas de España*. Miami FL: Ediciones Universal, 1980.

Grandío, Antonio Javier, and J. Carles Maixé-Altés, eds. *Vegalsa-Eroski: Homenaje a un emprendedor, Ventura González Prieto y la distribución alimentaria en Galicia, 1945–2007*. Vigo: Vegalsa-Eroski, 2008.

Guerin, Joseph R. "Limitations of Supermarkets in Spain." *Journal of Marketing* 28 (October 1964): 22–26.

Guibernau, Montserrat. *Catalan Nationalism: Francoism, Transition, and Democracy*. London: Routledge, 2004.

Hall, Richard H. "Professionalization and Bureaucratization." *American Sociological Review* 33, no. 1 (February 1968): 92–104.

Hamilton, Shane. "Supermarket USA Confronts State Socialism: Airlifting the Technopolitics of Industrial Food Distribution into Cold War Yugoslavia." In *Cold War Kitchen: Americanization, Technology, and European Users*, edited by Ruth Oldenziel and Karin Zachmann, 137–60. Cambridge MA: MIT Press, 2009.

Harrison, Joseph. *An Economic History of Modern Spain*. New York: Holmes & Meier, 1978.

———. "Spanish Economic History: From the Restoration to the Franco Regime." *Economic History Review* 33, no. 2 (May 1980): 259–75.

Hartmann, Susan M. "Women's Employment and the Domestic Ideal in the Early Cold War Years." In *Not June Cleaver: Women and Gender in Postwar America, 1945–1960*, edited by Joanne Jay Meyerowitz, 84–100. Philadelphia: Temple University Press, 1994.

Holguín, Sandie. "National Spain Invites You: Battlefield Tourism during the Spanish Civil War." *American Historical Review* 110, no. 5 (December 2005): 1399–1426.

Hollander, Anne. *Sex and Suits*. New York: Alfred A. Knopf, 1994.

Hooper, John. *The New Spaniards*. 2nd ed. London: Penguin Books, 2006.

Horowitz, Daniel. "Consumption and Its Discontents: Simon N. Patten, Thorstein Veblen, and George Gunton." *Journal of American History* 67, no. 2 (September 1980): 301–17.

Hosgood, Chris. "The Shopkeeper's 'Friend': The Retail Trade Press in Late-Victorian and Edwardian Britain." *Victorian Periodicals Review* 25, no. 4 (May 1992): 164–72.

Ibarra Güell, Pedro, and Chelo García Marroquín. "De la primavera de 1956 a Lejona 1978. Comisiones Obreras de Euskadi." In *Historia de Comisiones Obreras (1958–1988)*, edited by David Ruíz, 111–40. Madrid: Siglo Veintiuno de España, 1993.

Intercontinental Group of Department Stores, *Intercontinental Group of Department Stores, 1946–1996*. Essen: Karstadt, 1996. Accessed 30 January 2013. http://www.igds.org/publicarea/aboutigds/IGDS%201946%20%201996.pdf.

Jackson, Kenneth T. *Crabgrass Frontier: The Suburbanization of the United States*. Oxford: Oxford University Press, 1984.

Jiménez Artigas, Sonia, José Luis Pineiro Alonso, and Antonio José Ranedo Fernández. *Galerías: Ayer, Hoy y Mañana*. 2 vols. Madrid: Universidad Autónoma de Madrid, 1992.

Kaplan, Temma. "Luchar por la democracia: Formas de organizacion de la mujeres entre los años cincuenta y los anos setenta." In *Mujeres, regulación de conflictos sociales y cultura de la paz*, edited by Anna Aguado, 89–107. Valencia: Institut Universitari d'Estudis de la Dona–Univeristat de València, 1999.

Klimke, Martin, and Joachim Scharloth, eds. *1968 in Europe: A History of Protest and Activism, 1956–1977*. London: Palgrave Macmillan, 2008.

Kornetis, Kostis. "Documenting Post-Authoritarian Subcultures in the European South: The Cases of Pedro Almodóvar's *Pepi, Luci, Bom* and Nikos Zervos' *Dracula of Exarchia*." In *Gender and Consumption in Southern Europe since the Long 1960s*, edited by Kostis Kornetis, Eirini Kotsovili, and Nikolaos Papadogiannis, 153–72. London: Bloomsbury, 2016.

Kornetis, Kostis, Eirini Kotsovili, and Nikolaos Papadogiannis, eds. *Gender and Consumption in Southern Europe since the Long 1960s*. London: Bloomsbury, 2016.

Kowalsky, Daniel. "Rated S: Softcore Pornography and the Spanish Transition to Democracy, 1977–82." In *Spanish Popular Cinema*, edited by Antonio Lázaro-Reboll and Andrew Willis, 188–208. Manchester, UK: Manchester University Press, 2004.

Kroes, Rob. "Americanisation: What Are We Talking About?" In *Cultural Transmissions and Receptions: American Mass Culture in Europe*, edited by Rob Kroes, Robert W. Rydell, and Doeko F. J. Bosscher, 302–18. Amsterdam: VU University Press, 1993.

Kuchta, David. "The Making of the Self-Made Man: Class, Clothing, and English Masculinity, 1688–1832." In *The Sex of Things: Gender and Consumption in Historical Perspective*, edited by Victoria de Grazia and Ellen Furlough, 54–78. Berkeley: University of California Press, 1996.

Kuisel, Richard. "Coca-Cola and the Cold War: The French Face Americanization, 1948–1953." *French Historical Studies* 17, no. 1 (Spring 1991): 96–116.

———. *Seducing the French: The Dilemma of Americanization*. Berkeley: University of California Press, 1993.

Laver, James. *Taste and Fashion from the French Revolution until To-day*. New York: Dodd, Mead, 1938.

Lazaga, Pedro, dir. *Las Muchachas de Azul*. Ágata Films, 1957; DVD, Divisa Home Video, 2004.

Leach, William. *Land of Desire: Merchants, Power, and the Rise of a New American Culture*. New York: Pantheon Books, 1993.

Lears, Jackson. *Fables of Abundance: A Cultural History of Advertising in America*. New York: Basic Books, 1994.

Lechado, José Manuel. *La Movida: Una crónica de los 80*. Madrid: ALGABA Ediciones, 2006.

Lieberman, Sima. *Growth and Crisis in the Spanish Economy: 1940–93*. London: Routledge, 1995.

Linz, Juan J. "An Authoritarian Regime: The Case of Spain." In *Cleavages, Ideologies, and Party Systems*, edited by Erik Allardt and Yrjö Littunen, 291–342. Helsinki: Academic Bookstore, 1964.

———. *Totalitarian and Authoritarian Regimes*. Boulder CO: Lynne Rienner, 2000.

López Sainz, Celia. *La Cortesía en la Vida Moderna*. 3rd ed. Madrid: Editex, 1965.

Lundin, Per. "Introduction." In *The Making of European Consumption: Facing the American Challenge*, edited by Per Lundin and Thomas Kaiserfeld, 1–16. New York: Palgrave Macmillan, 2015.

Lurie, Alison. *The Language of Clothes*. 2nd ed. London: Bloomsbury, 1992.

Madorrán Ayerra, Carmen. "The Open Window: Women in Spain's Second Republic and Civil War." *Perspectives on Global Development and Technology* 15 (2016): 246–53.

"Madrid, Trasunto de España." *Guía Annual de la Industria y Comercio de Madrid* 67 (1956/1957): lxix–lxxi.

Mahaney, Kathryn L. "Feminism under and after Franco: Success and Failure in the Democratic Transition." PhD diss., The Graduate Center, CUNY, 2018.

Maixé-Altes, J. Carles. "Americanización y consumo de masas, la distribución alimentaria en España, 1947–2007." Munich Personal RePEc Archive. Accessed 1 August 2012. http://mpra.ub.uni-muenchen.de/14786/.

———. "Interpreting the Early Stages of the Self-Service Revolution in Europe: The Modernization of Food Retailing in Spain, 1947–1972." Munich Personal RePEc Archive. Accessed 1 August 2012. http://mpra.ub.uni-muenchen.de /18164/.

———. "La modernización de la distribución alimentaria en España, 1947–1995." *Revista de Historia Industrial* 41 no. 3 (2009): 109–44.

Maravall, José María. *The Transition to Democracy in Spain*. London: Croom Helm, 1982.

———. *Dictatorship and Political Dissent: Workers and Students in Franco's Spain*. New York: St. Martin's Press, 1978.

Marsá Vancells, Plutarco. *La mujer en el periodismo*. Madrid: Torremozas, 1986–1987.

Martín Aceña, Pablo, and Elena Martínez Ruiz. "The Golden Age of Spanish Capitalism: Economic Growth without Political Freedom." In *Spain Transformed: The Late Franco Dictatorship, 1959–1975*, edited by Nigel Townson, 30–46. New York: Palgrave Macmillan, 2007.

Martín Gaite, Carmen. *Courtship Customs in Postwar Spain (Usos amorosos de la postguerra española)*. Translated by Margaret E. W. Jones. Lewisburg PA: Bucknell University Press, 2004.

Martin, Morag. *Selling Beauty: Cosmetics, Commerce, and French Society, 1750–1830*. Baltimore MD: Johns Hopkins University Press, 2009.

Marwick, Arthur. *The Sixties: Cultural Revolution in Britain, France, Italy, and the United States, c. 1958–1974*. Oxford: Oxford University Press, 1998.

———. "Youth Culture and the Cultural Revolution of the Long Sixties." In *Between Marx and Coca-Cola: Youth Cultures in Changing European Societies, 1960–1980*, edited by Axel Schildt and Detlef Siegfried, 39–58. New York: Berghahn, 2006.

Matés Barco, Juan Manuel. "La economía durante el franquismo: La etapa del desarrollo (1960–1974)." In *Historia Económica de España*, edited by

Agustín González Enciso and Juan Manuel Matés Barco, 764–771. Barcelona: Ariel, 2006.

May, Elaine Tyler. *Homeward Bound: American Families in the Cold War Era*. New York: Basic Books, 2008.

McGovern, Charles. "Consumption and Citizenship in the United States, 1900–1940." In *Getting and Spending: European and American Consumer Societies in the Twentieth Century*, edited by Susan Strasser, Charles McGovern, and Matthias Judt, 37–58. Cambridge: Cambridge University Press, 1998.

Méndez de la Muela, Gregorio. "Evolución del turismo náutico en España en los últimos treinta años: Recreación o status social, una aproximación a la sociología del turismo náutico." PhD diss., Universidad Complutense de Madrid, 2004.

Merino, Ignacio. *Biografía de la Gran Vía*. Barcelona: Ediciones B, 2010.

Miley, Thomas Jeffrey. "Franquism as Authoritarianism: Juan Linz and His Critics." *Politics, Religion & Ideology* 12, no. 1 (March 2011): 27–50.

Miller, Michael B. *The Bon Marché: Bourgeois Culture and the Department Store, 1869–1920*. Princeton NJ: Princeton University Press, 1981.

Miller, Montserrat. *Feeding Barcleona, 1714–1975: Public Market Halls, Social Networks, and Consumer Culture*. Baton Rouge: Louisiana State University Press, 2015.

Molina Luque, J. Fidel. "Quintas y servicio militar: Aspectos sociológicos y antropológicos de la conscripción (Lleida, 1878–1960)." PhD diss., University of Lleida, 1996.

Molinero, Carme, Javier Tébar, and Pere Ysàs. "Comisiones obreras de Cataluña: De movimiento sociopolítico a confederación sindical." In *Historia de Comisiones Obreras (1958–1988)*, edited by David Ruíz, 69–110. Madrid: Siglo Veintiuno de España, 1993.

Monés, Nèlida, Marta Carrasco, Estrella Casero-García, and Delfín Colomé. "Between Tradition and Innovation: Two Ways of Understanding the History of Dance in Spain." In *Europe Dancing: Perspectives on Theatre, Dance, and Cultural Identity*, edited by Andrée Grau and Stephanie Jorban, 144–67. London: Routledge, 2000.

Montero García, Feliciano. "Las Publicaciones Periódicas de Acción Católica durante el Franquismo." In *Catolicismo y comunicación en la historia contemporánea*, edited by José Leonardo Ruiz Sánchez, 31–54. Seville: Universidad de Sevilla, 2005.

Moradiellos, Enrique. "Franco's Spain and the European Integration Process (1945–1975)." *Bulletin for Spanish and Portuguese Historical Studies* 41, no. 1 (2016): 67–78.

Morcillo, Aurora G. *The Seduction of Modern Spain: The Female Body and the Francoist Body Politic*. Lewisburg PA: Bucknell University Press, 2010.

———. *True Catholic Womanhood: Gender Ideology in Franco's Spain*. Dekalb: Northern Illinois University Press, 2000.

Moreno, Julio. *Yankee Don't Go Home: Mexican Nationalism, American Business Culture, and the Shaping of Modern Mexico, 1920–1950*. Chapel Hill: University of North Carolina Press, 2003.

Muñoz Ruiz, María del Carmen. "La construcción de las relaciones de género en el franquismo y sus conflictos: Los consultorios sentimentales." *Arenal: Revista de Historia de las Mujeres* 10, no. 2 (July–December 2003): 219–39.

———. "Las revistas para mujeres durante el Franquismo: Difusión de modelos de comportamiento femenino." In *Mujeres y Hombres en la España Franquista: Sociedad, Economía, Política, Cultura*, edited by Gloria Nielfa Cristóbal. Madrid: Editorial Complutense, 2003.

———. "Mujer Mítica, Mujeres Reales: Las Revistas Femeninas en España, 1955–1970." PhD diss., Universidad Complutense de Madrid, 2002.

Nash, Mary. *Dones en transició: De la resistència política a la legitimat feminista, les dones en la Barcelona de la transició*. Barcelona: Regidora de Dona, 2007.

———. "Towards a New Moral Order: National Catholicism, Culture and Gender." In *Spanish History since 1808*, edited by José Álvarez Junco and Adrian Shubert, 289–301. London: Hodder Education, 2005.

Nevett, T. R. *Advertising in Britain: A History*. London: Heinemann, 1982.

Nicolás Lazo, Gemma. "La reglamentación de la prostitución en el Estado español. Genealogía jurídico-feminista de los discursos sobre prostitución y sexualidad." PhD diss., Universitat de Barcelona, 2007.

Nielfa Cristóbal, Gloria. "El debate feminista durante el franquismo." In *Mujeres y Hombres en la España Franquista: Sociedad, Economía, Política, Cultura*, edited by Gloria Nielfa Cristóbal, 269–98. Madrid: Editorial Complutense, 2003.

———, ed. *Mujeres y Hombres en la España Franquista: Sociedad, Economía, Política, Cultura*. Madrid: Editorial Complutense, 2003.

Nolan, Mary. "Negotiating American Modernity in Twentieth-Century Europe." In *The Making of European Consumption: Facing the American Challenge*, edited by Per Lundin and Thomas Kaiserfeld, 17–44. New York: Palgrave Macmillan, 2015.

Ofer, Inbal. "La Guerra de Agua: Notions of Morality, Respectability, and Community in a Madrid Neighborhood." *Journal of Urban History* 35, no. 2 (January 2009): 220–35.

———. *Señoritas in Blue: The Making of a Female Political Elite in Franco's Spain*. Eastbourne, UK: Sussex Academic Press, 2010.

Oldenziel, Ruth, and Karin Zachmann, eds. *Cold War Kitchen: Americanization, Technology, and European Users*. Cambridge MA: MIT Press, 2009.

———. "Kitchens as Technology and Politics: An Introduction." In *Cold War Kitchen: Americanization, Technology, and European Users*, edited by Ruth Oldenziel and Karin Zachmann, 1–29. Cambridge MA: MIT Press, 2009.

Otaola González, Paloma. "La música pop en la España franquista: Rock, ye-ye y *beat* en la primera mitad de los años 60." *ILCEA: Revue de l'Institut des langues et cultures d'Europe et d'Amérique* 16 (2012). Accessed 17 May 2014. http://ilcea.revues.org/1421.

Pack, Sasha D. *Tourism and Dictatorship: Europe's Peaceful Invasion of Franco's Spain*. London: Palgrave Macmillan, 2006.

———. "Tourism and Political Change in Franco's Spain." In *Spain Transformed: The Late Franco Dictatorship, 1959–1975*, edited by Nigel Townson, 47–66. New York: Palgrave Macmillan, 2007.

Paff Ogle, Jennifer, and Mary Lynn Damhorst. "Dress for Success in the Popular Press." In *Appearance and Power*, edited by Kim K. P. Johnson and Sharron J. Lennon, 79–102. Oxford: Berg, 1999.

Palomares, Cristina. *The Quest for Survival after Franco: Moderate Francoism and the Slow Journey to the Polls, 1964–1977*. Brighton, UK: Sussex University Press, 2006.

Park, Jennifer. "Unisex Clothing." In *Encyclopedia of Clothing and Fashion*. Vol. 3, edited by Valerie Steele, 382–84. Detroit: Charles Scribner's Sons, 2005. Accessed 22 October 2008. Gale Virtual Reference Library.

Pasdermadjian, H. *The Department Store: Its Origins, Evolutions, and Economics*. London: Newman Books, 1954.

Pavlović, Tatjana. *The Mobile Nation: España Cambia de Piel (1954–1964)*. Bristol, UK: Intellect, 2011.

Payne, Stanley G. *Fascism in Spain, 1923–1977*. Madison: University of Wisconsin Press, 2000.

———. *The Franco Regime, 1936–1975*. Madison: University of Wisconsin Press, 1987.

———. *Spain's First Democracy: The Second Republic, 1931–36*. Madison: University of Wisconsin Press, 1993.

Pérez Díaz, Victor. *The Return of Civil Society: The Emergence of Democratic Spain*. Cambridge MA: Harvard University Press, 1993.

Pinilla García, Alfonso. "La mujer en la posguerra franquista a través de la revista *Medina* (1940–1945)." *Arenal: Revista de historia de las mujeres* 13, no. 1 (January–June 2006): 153–79.

Poiger, Uta G. "A New, 'Western' Hero? Reconstructing German Masculinity in the 1950s." *Signs* 24, no. 1 (Autumn 1998): 147–62.

———. *Jazz, Rock and Rebels: Cold War Politics and American Culture in a Divided Germany*. Berkeley: University of California Press, 2000.

———. "Rock 'n' Roll, Female Sexuality, and the Cold War Battle over German Identities." *Journal of Modern History* 68, no. 3 (September 1996): 577–616.

Pollack, Benny, and Graham Hunter. *The Paradox of Spanish Foreign Policy: Spain's International Relations from Franco to Democracy*. New York: St. Martin's Press, 1987.

Preston, Paul. *Juan Carlos: Steering Spain from Dictatorship to Democracy*. New York: W. W. Norton, 2004.

———. *The Spanish Civil War: Reaction, Revolution, and Revenge*. New York: W. W. Norton, 2007.

———. *The Triumph of Democracy in Spain*. London: Methuen, 1986.

Puertolas, Clotidle. "Masculinity versus Femininity: The Sanfermines: 1939–1978." In *Constructing Spanish Womanhood: Female Identity in Modern Spain*, edited by Victoria L. Enders and Pamela B. Radcliff, 95–122. Albany: State University of New York Press, 1999.

Puig, Núria. "La ayuda económica norteamericana y los empresarios españoles." *Cuadernos de Historia Contemporánea* 25 (2003): 109–29.

Radcliff, Pamela Beth. "Citizens and Housewives: The Problem of Female Citizenship in Spain's Transition to Democracy." *Journal of Social History* 36, no. 1 (Autumn 2002): 77–100.

———. *Making Democratic Citizens in Spain: Civil Society and the Popular Origins of the Transition, 1960–1978*. New York: Palgrave Macmillan, 2011.

———. "La Transición española: ¿un modelo global?" In *¿Es España diferente?: Una mirada comparativa (siglos XIX y XX)*, edited by Nigel Townson, 243–81. Madrid: Taurus, 2010.

Rappaport, Erika D. "'A Husband and His Wife's Dresses': Consumer Credit and the Debtor Family in England, 1864–1914." In *The Sex of Things: Gen-*

der and Consumption in Historical Perspective, edited by Victoria de Grazia and Ellen Furlough, 163–87. Berkeley: University of California Press, 1996.

———. Shopping for Pleasure: Women in the Making of London's West End. Princeton NJ: Princeton University Press, 2000.

Reid, Susan E. "This Is Tomorrow! Becoming a Consumer in the Soviet Sixties." In The Socialist Sixties: Crossing Borders in the Second World, edited by Anne E. Gorsuch and Diane P. Koenker, 25–65. Bloomington: Indiana University Press, 2013.

Richards, Thomas. The Commodity Culture of Victorian England: Advertising and Spectacle, 1851–1914. Stanford CA: Stanford University Press, 1990.

Rimby Leighow, Susan. "An 'Obligation to Participate': Married Nurses' Labor Force Participation in the 1950s." In Not June Cleaver: Women and Gender in Postwar America, 1945–1960, edited by Joanne Jay Meyerowitz, 37–56. Philadelphia: Temple University Press, 1994.

Roberts, Mary Louise. "Gender, Consumption, and Commodity Culture." American Historical Review 103, no. 3 (June 1998): 817–44.

Rodríguez Jiménez, Francisco Javier, Lorenzo Delgado Gómez-Escalonilla, and Nicolás Cull, eds. U.S. Public Diplomacy and Democratization in Spain: Selling Democracy? London: Palgrave Macmillan, 2015.

Rodríguez López, Sofía. "La Falange Femenina y Construcción de la Identidad de Género durante el Franquismo." In Actas de IV Simposio de Historia Actual, Logroño, 17–19 de octubre de 2002, edited by Carlos Navajas Zubeldia, 488–92. Logroño: Instituto de Estudios Riojanos, 2004.

Rodríguez Salcedo, Natalia. "Public Relations before 'Public Relations' in Spain: An Early History (1881–1960)." Journal of Communication Management 12, no. 4 (2008): 279–93.

Rodríguez, Sergio. Busque, compare y, si encuentra un libro mejor, ¡cómprelo!: Los anuncios que se quedaron en nuestra memoria. Barcelona: Random House Mondadori, 2009.

Rodríguez-Vigil Reguera, José María. "Grandes almacenes, centros comerciales y otros espacios de consumo contemporáneos: Panorama internacional y estudio del caso asturiano." 2 vols. PhD diss., University of Oviedo, 2017.

Roig Castellanos, Mercedes. La mujer y la prensa: Desde el siglo XVII a nuestros días. Madrid: M. Roig, 1977.

Rosendorf, Neal Moses. "Be El Caudillo's Guest: The Franco Regime's Quest for Rehabilitation and Dollars after World War II via the Promotion of U.S. Tourism to Spain." Diplomatic History 30, no. 3 (June 2006): 367–407.

———. *Franco Sells Spain to America: Hollywood, Tourism and Public Relations as Postwar Spanish Soft Power.* London: Palgrave Macmillan, 2014.

Rubin, Eli. *Synthetic Socialism: Plastics and Dictatorship in the German Democratic Republic.* Chapel Hill: University of North Carolina Press, 2008.

Rubio Mayoral, Juan Luis. *Disciplina y Rebeldía: Los estudiantes en la Universidad de Sevilla (1939–1970).* Seville: Universidad de Sevilla, 2005.

Ruiz Franco, Rosario. *¿Eternas menores?: Las mujeres en el franquismo.* Madrid: Biblioteca Nueva, 2007.

———. "María Telo y la participación de mujeres juristas en la Comisión General de Codificación (1973–1975)." *Asparkía: Investigación Feminista* 17 (2006): 165–80.

———. "Pequeña historia de ayer: La memoria histórica a través del testimonio de Mercedes Formica." *Trocadero: Revista del departamento de historia moderna, contemporánea, de América y del arte* 16 (2004): 19–34.

Saarikangas, Kirsi. "What's New? Women Pioneers and the Finnish State Meet the American Kitchen." In *Cold War Kitchen: Americanization, Technology, and European Users*, edited by Ruth Oldenziel and Karin Zachmann, 285–311. Cambridge MA: MIT Press, 2009.

Sáenz de Heredia, José Luis, dir. *Relaciones Casi Públicas.* Arturo González, 1968; DVD, Divisa Home Video, 2003.

Sánchez Hernández, María F. "Evolución de las publicaciones femeninas en España. Localización y análisis." *Documentación de las Ciencias de Información* 32 (2009): 217–44.

Sanchez Moreno, José. *Distinción y Etiqueta Moderna.* 2nd ed. Barcelona: Sociedad General Española de Librería, 1944.

Scanlon, Geraldine M. *La polémica feminista en la España contemporánea (1868–1974).* Madrid: Siglo XXI de España, 1976.

Schutts, Jeff. "Die Erfrischende Pause: Marketing Coca-Cola in Hitler's Germany." In *Selling Modernity: Advertising in Twentieth-Century Germany*, edited by Pamela E. Swett et al., 151–81. Durham NC: Duke University Press, 2007.

Sederías Carretas y Galerías Preciados—Normas. Madrid: Sederías Carretas y Galerías Preciados, 1953.

Seregni, Alessandro. *El Anti-Americanismo Español.* Madrid: Editorial Síntesis, 2007.

Serrano Sanz, José María, and Eva Pardos. "Los años de crecimiento del franquismo (1959–1975)." In *Historia económica de España, siglos XIX y XX*, edited by F. Comín, M. Hernández, and E. Llopis, 369–95. Barcelona: Crítica, 2002.

Shannon, Brent. *The Cut of His Coat: Men, Dress, and Consumer Culture in Britain, 1860–1914*. Athens: Ohio University Press, 2006.

Siegelbaum, Lewis. "Modernity Unbound: The New Soviet City of the Sixties." In *The Socialist Sixties: Crossing Borders in the Second World*, edited by Anne E. Gorsuch and Diane P. Koenker, 66–83. Bloomington: Indiana University Press, 2013.

Siegfried, Detlef. "Understanding 1968: Youth Rebellion, Generational Change, and Postindustrial Society." In *Between Marx and Coca-Cola: Youth Cultures in Changing European Societies, 1960–1980*, edited by Axel Schildt and Detlef Siegfried, 59–81. New York: Berghahn, 2006.

Solé i Sabaté, Josep M. *La repressió franquista a Catalunya, 1938–1953*. Barcelona: Edicions 62, 1985.

"Spain." In *Censorship: A World Encyclopedia*, edited by Derek Jones. London: Fitzroy Dearborn, 2001.

Stappell, Hamilton. *Remaking Madrid: Culture, Politics, and Identity after Franco*. London: Palgrave Macmillan, 2010.

Stehrenberger, Céline Stephanie. "Folklore, Nation, and Gender in a Colonial Encounter: *Coros y Danzas* of the *Sección Femenina* of the Falange in Equatorial Guinea." *Afro-Hispanic Review* 28, no. 2, Equatorial Guinea Issue (Fall 2009): 231–44.

Steinbach, Edward H. "A Comparative Study: Domestic Versus International Personnel Policies and Procedures, Sears of the San Francisco Bay Area versus Sears of Barcelona, Spain." Master's thesis, San Francisco State University, 1977.

Strasser, Susan. *Satisfaction Guaranteed: The Making of the American Mass Market*. New York: Routledge, 1989.

Strasser, Susan, Charles McGovern, and Mattias Judt, eds. *Getting and Spending: European and American Consumer Societies in the Twentieth Century*. Cambridge: Cambridge University Press, 1998.

Tamames, Ramón. *Estructura Económica de España*. Vol. 2. 12th ed. Madrid: Alianza Editorial, 1978.

Tango, Cristina. *La transición y su doble: El rock y Radio Futura*. Madrid: Biblioteca Nueva, 2006.

Taylor, Chloë. "Biopower." In *Michel Foucault: Key Concepts*, edited by Dianne Taylor, 41–54. London: Routledge, 2011.

Thomas, Hugh. *Eduardo Barreiros and the Recovery of Spain*. New Haven CT: Yale University Press, 2009.

Tiersten, Lisa. *Marianne in the Market: Envisioning Consumer Society in Fin-de-Siècle France*. Berkeley: University of California Press, 2001.

Toboso Sánchez, Pilar. "Grandes Almacenes y Almacenes Populares en España. Una Visión Histórica." Working Paper. Fundación SEPI Programa de Historia Económica, 2002. Accessed 10 September 2018. ftp://ftp.fundacionsepi.es /phe/hdt2002_2.pdf.

———. "Las mujeres en la transición. Una perspectiva histórica: Antecedentes y retos." In *El movimiento feminista en España en los años 70*, edited by Carmen Martínez Ten, Purificación Gutiérrez López, and Pilar González Ruiz, 83–88. Madrid: Ediciones Cátedra, 2007.

———. *Pepín Fernández (Galerías Preciados), César Rodríguez y Ramón Areces (El Corte Inglés): Tres grandes empresarios del comercio en España*. Mexico City: Centro de Estudios Históricos Internacionales–Universidad Autónoma Metropolitana-Iztapalapa, 2006.

———. *Pepín Fernández, 1891–1982, Galerías Preciados, El pionero de los grandes almacenes*. Madrid: LID Historia Empresarial, 2000.

Townson, Nigel. "Introduction." In *Spain Transformed: The Late Franco Dictatorship, 1959–1975*, edited by Nigel Townson, 1–29. New York: Palgrave Macmillan, 2007.

———, ed. *Spain Transformed: The Late Franco Dictatorship, 1959–1975*. New York: Palgrave Macmillan, 2007.

Tusell, Javier. *La Transición Española: La Recuperación de la Libertades*. Madrid: Historia 16, 1997.

Tye, Larry. *The Father of Spin: Edward L. Bernays and the Birth of Public Relations*. New York: Crown Publishing Group, 1998.

Un futuro para España: La democracia económica y política. Paris: Éditions de la Librarie du Globe, 1967.

Valiente, Celia. "An Overview of Research on Gender in Spanish Society." *Gender and Society* 16, no. 6 (December 2002): 767–792.

van Ruler, Betteke, and Dejan Verčič. *Public Relations and Communication Management in Europe: A Nation-By-Nation Introduction to Public Relations Theory and Practice*. Berlin: Walter de Gruyter, 2004.

Vázquez Montalbán, Manuel. *Crónica sentimental de España*. Madrid: Grijalbo, 1998.

———. *Crónica sentimental de la transición*. Madrid: Editorial Planeta, 1985.

———. *La penetración americana en España*. Madrid: Cuadernos para el diálogo, 1974.

Vincent, Mary. "Camisas Nuevas: Style and Uniformity in the Falange Española 1933–1943." In *Dress, Gender, Citizenship: Fashioning the Body Politic*, edited by Wendy Parkins, 167–88. Oxford: Berg, 2002.

Vollmer, Harold M., and Donald L. Mills, eds. *Professionalization*. Englewood Cliffs NJ: Prentice-Hall, 1966.

Walker, Nancy A. *Shaping Our Mothers' World: American Women's Magazines*. Jackson: University Press of Mississippi, 2000.

Whitaker, Jan. *Service and Style: How the American Department Store Fashioned the Middle Class*. New York: St. Martin's, 2006.

Wiesen, S. Jonathan. *Creating the Nazi Marketplace: Commerce and Consumption in the Third Reich*. Cambridge: Cambridge University Press, 2011.

Wilensky, Harold L. "The Professionalization of Everyone?" *American Journal of Sociology* 70 no. 2 (September 1964): 137–58.

Williams, Rosalind H. *Dream Worlds: Mass Consumption in Late Nineteenth-Century France*. Berkeley: University of California Press, 1991.

Winchester, Ian K. "Hombres Normativos: The Creation and Inculcation of Martial Masculinity during the Franco Regime in Spain (1939–1975)." PhD diss., University of New Mexico, 2016.

Woodworth, Paddy. *Dirty War, Clean Hands: ETA, the GAL, and Spanish Democracy*. Cork, Ireland: Cork University Press, 2001.

Yan, Yunxiang. "Of Hamburger and Social Space: Consuming McDonald's in Beijing." In *The Consumer Revolution in Urban China*, edited by Deborah S. Davis, 201–25. Berkeley: University of California Press, 2000.

Zafra Aragón, Manuel. *Méritos, errores, ilusiones y personajes de Galerías Preciados*. Madrid: Ediciones Académicas, 2006.

Zimmerman, M. M. *Los Supermercados*. Madrid: Ediciones Rialp, 1959.

Zimmerman, Patrick. "Faer Asturies: Linguistic Politics and the Frustrated Construction of Asturian Nationalism, 1974–1999." PhD diss., Carnegie Mellon University, 2011.

Zola, Émile. *The Ladies' Paradise*. Translated by Brian Nelson. Oxford: Oxford University Press, 1995.

appliance culture, 19, 85–89, 96–97, 103, 108–9, 208, 241n8, 262n73, 263n78

Arce, Roberto, 147

Areces, Ramón: American business trips, 15; on consumer credit systems, 35; early career at El Encanto, 14, 42, 217; managerial style, 42, 46, 55; relationship with Cesar Rodríguez, 14, 228; role in modernizing retailing, 13. *See also* El Corte Inglés (department store)

Arias Navarro, Carlos, 20

Arte Comercial (journal), 87

El Arte de Vender (employee handbook), 37

Arte en el Hogar (magazine), 78

Association of Public Relations Technicians (ATRP), 146

Association of Spanish Advertisers (AEA), 146, 151

Astorga Alda, Rogelia, 118, 271n21

Astra: Revista moderna para la mujer (journal), 107; haute-bourgeois pricing and content, 78; launch of, 89; role in aspirational mass consumer society development, 89–90, 108

Asturian culture, 192–93, 301n47

ATRP (Association of Public Relations Technicians), 146

attitudinal professionalization, 147

Auserón, Luis, 215–16

Auserón, Santiago, 215–16

autarkic policies, 15, 18, 81, 133, 261n63

automobiles, 8, 190–92, 208, 211, 299n35, 299n37, 300n38

autoservicios (supermarkets). *See* supermarkets *(autoservicios)*

Auxilio Social (Social Aid) program, 73, 75

Aycuens (window dresser), 32, 33

Azpiazu, Joaquín, 50

Balearic Islands, 254n5

Ball, Lucille, 80, 109–10

Barceló, José Luis, 91

bargain-priced retailers, 31, 33, 35, 184

Barreiros (automobile maker), 192, 300n38

Basque terrorist attacks, 20

Bastida, Asunción, 72

Batista, Fulgencio, 297n20

Baudrillard, Jean, 4

Begoña, María, 62

Belier, Alice, 80

Bella Aurora beauty products, 81–82, 84, 95, 261n64

Benito Sánchez, Jesús, 197–98

Bernays, Edward R., 143

Bernecker, Walter, 214

Bhabha, Homi K., 95, 138

Big Bear (supermarket chain), 113, 118, 119

black market, 15, 28, 68

Blasco Zaldívar, Manuel, 134

Bliss, Robert, 152, 176

Boletín de Botas (internal employee bulletin): apolitical nature of, 53; concern with company's reputation, 46–47; cultural representations in, 192–93, 301n47;

Club de Publicidad de Barcelona (professional advertisers' association), 144

code of conduct handbooks: of American retailers, 40; company reputation concerns, 43, 46–47, 246n58; development of, 37; as models of Francoist fundamental ideology, 51–52; paternalistic control of, 8, 26, 40–46; political alignment of, 26–27, 48–53; reinforcing gendered differences, 62–64, 252n111, 252n113; treason clauses, 43–48, *44*, 246n58. *See also* bulletins (internal employee bulletins); *Normas de Sederías Carretas y Galerías* (code of conduct handbook); workplace culture

Cohen, Lizabeth, 267n128

Colman, Prentis & Varley (ad agency), 154

Comisaría de Abastecimientos y Transportes (CAT). *See* CAT (Comisaría de Abastecimientos y Transportes)

Comisiones Obreras (CC.OO., workers commissions), 19–20, 227

Commissary-General for Supply and Transport, 87

CONAUTA (journal), 136–37

Conde, Cesar, 188

Conde, Eduardo, 14

Conde, Fernando, 182, 235n40, 241n8

Confecciones Fargas (clothing manufacturer), 290n74

Consejo de la Hispanidad (Hispanic Cultural Council), 53

consumer diplomacy, 6, 177, 186–87, 225

consumer press: audiences of, 7, 68, 76–79, 217; censorship of, 17, 19, 173, 238n74, 239n84; concern with global status, 159, 162–64, 177–78; constructing an imagined/aspirational mass consumer society, 7–8, 68–69, 217; cost of, 68, 78–79, 104–5, 259n50; defined, 255n11; distribution rates, 260n52–53; expansion and growth (boom era), 140–42, 159; expansion and growth (early Franco era), 67–69, 89–90, 107–10; focus on foreign fashion, 164–75, 177, 181–82; focus on foreign products and innovations, 7, 69–71, 142, 159–64, 217; impact on mass consumer society development, 2–3, 67–71, 142–43; integration into international community through, 70–71, 142–43; on menswear, 164–67; pricing for ad space, 261n60; reinforcing Francoist gender norms, 166–67, 175; reinforcing Francoist ideology, 8, 69; religious publications, 254n3; sociopolitical impacts of, 2–3, 69–71; subverting Francoist gender norms, 142, 167–75, 177, 181–82; on unisex fashion, 169–75; variety of, 68–69, 89–90, 107; on youth culture and fashion, 167–75. *See also individual publications*

El Corte Inglés (*cont.*)

28; impacts on sociopolitical changes, 2; incorporation of, 29, 242n15; labor disputes at, 227; manufacturing division, 29, 216; menswear collections, 162, 187–88; policies and programs, 37, 246n49; political alignment of, 50, 53; social structures and activities, 196–98; transforming urban spaces, 188–90; window displays of, 32; workplace culture at, 49–50, 54–55, 62–63, 216–17, 246n49; youth clothing sections, 10, 172

Cortty: Boletín de El Corte Inglés (internal employee bulletin): elements of, 35; on importance of parking to store planning, 192; launch of, 184; paternalistic nature, 184; on women workers, 200; on youth culture and fashion, 167, 169, 173, 177

counterculture, 167–68, 215–16, 218, 219

Creaciones (magazine), 259n49

credit systems (consumer): at Almacenes Jorba, 35–36, 98, 100; in Britain, 98–100; criticism and distrust of, 35, 98–100; as foreign innovation, 35–36; impact on gender norms, 70, 98–100, 103, 109; impact on mass consumption, 4, 35, 98, 103, 109, 110, 238n75; at Sears, 208, 220; in the United States, 36

Crisán, Vasilie, 207

Crossick, Geoffrey, 229

Crumbaugh, Justin, 156–57, 195

Cruz, Jesús, 253n2

Cuartas, Javier, 253n117

Cuba, 14, 186, 297n20. *See also* El Encanto (Cuban department store)

Cuban Revolution, 186, 228

Curso Fémina CCC courses, 96, 98

Damhorst, Mary Lynn, 62–63, 251–52n110

Danamask (makeup company), 96

Danegoods (Danish frozen foods company), 116

DANIS (ad agency), 144, 145, 148

Davidoff, Leonore, 255n9

Davis, Fred, 173

de Alzate, Vera, 80–81

Debord, Guy, 4

Le Défi Américain (Servan-Schreiber), 157

de Grazia, Victoria, 9, 19, 80, 268n133

Delgado, Jaime, 166

democratization: flaws in Spanish transition, 225–28; impact of fashion on, 165, 175; impact of supermarkets on, 139; limits of mass consumption to, 5–6, 12; multicausal transitional model, 4, 222–23; role of mass consumption in, 4, 12, 221–24; scholarly debates on, 3–4; Spanish process of, 2, 20–21, 202, 210

department stores: advancing consumer diplomacy, 186–87, 225; challenges of cosmopolitanism for, 192–201; characteristics of, 13–14; continuing impacts of Francoism on, 227–28; cultural regionalism highlighted by, 192–93; development of, 27–28; employee exchanges, 9, 182, 187, 205, 213, 219; expansion and growth (boom era), 9, 183–85, 193–94, 210–13; expansion and growth (early Franco years), 25–26, 27–32, 65–66, 107, 216; focus on professional development and technical mastery, 37–39, 185, 188, 206; foreign product exhibitions, 5, 183, 187, 213; foreign products and innovations adopted by, 7, 9–10, 14, 28, 32–36, 64–65, 179–83, 187–88, 202, 207–9, 211–13, 217; history of, 12–15; impact of automobile culture on, 190–92; impact of Francoism on, 48–53; international affiliations, 10, 26, 65, 187–88; international integration, 66, 181–83, 221–22; international integration illustrated by Sears, 201–10, 213; meanings of, 230; modern cosmopolitan aspirations of, 183, 184–88, 219, 221–22, 224; modern cosmopolitan identities claimed by, 9, 183, 186, 188; policies and programs, 36–54; political alignment of, 53–54; professionalization of, 26, 69; reinforcing Francoist ideology, 8, 26–27, 217, 221, 248n78, 251n108; role in development of mass consumption, 2–3, 7–8, 26, 181; selling consumption as aspirational, 7–8; sociopolitical impacts of, 1, 2–3, 25–27, 66; threatened by sub-versive consumerism, 182; tourists served by, 4, 224; transforming urban landscapes, 181, 188–92, 211, 299n32; undermining Francoist gender norms, 219–21; undermining Francoist ideology, 27, 209–10, 216; undermining notions of exceptionalism, 5, 66, 187, 204–5, 213–14; wages at, 39, 228, 245n44, 249n85. *See also* bulletins (internal employee bulletins); code of conduct handbooks; *individual stores*; workplace culture

department stores (American): employee handbooks of, 37, 38; influencing Spanish retailers, 7, 14, 33, 64–65, 179–82; role of freedom of choice in, 47; welfare work initiatives, 40, 41. *See also* Sears, Roebuck and Co. (department store)

Dermiluz (makeup producer), 82

Destape (cinematic nudity), 11, 210, 220, 227

Dichter, Ernest, 156

diet and nutrition, 6, 110, 122–23, 136–37, 138

Dill Scott, Walter, 143–44

diplomacy: during boom era, 2; consumer diplomacy, 6, 177, 186–87, 225; economic impacts of, 7, 17–18; Franco regime-United States relations, 6, 7, 79, 103; initial Spanish isolation, 107, 216; during postwar years, 15; rehabilitation efforts, 25, 89, 96, 108, 182

Domenech (window dresser), 32

domestic abuse exposé, 74

Don: La Moda Masculina Española
(journal): audience of, 288n65;
biannual frequency of, 291n83;
censorship of, 173, 220, 291n83;
concern with international
prestige, 159, 163; cost of, 288n65,
291n83; founding of, 10, 159;
haute bourgeois content of, 159,
288n65; on importance of fashion
to identity, 165; international
focus of, 159, 162, 164; reinforcing Francoist gender norms,
166–67; subverting Francoist
gender norms, 142, 177; on unisex
fashion, 169–72; unisex fashion
photo editorial, *171*

Dupont, Lidia, 266n113

Dusek, Edmund, 304n74

economatos (low-price company
stores), 133, 138

economy: autarkic policies, 15, 18, 81,
133; during the boom era (1959–
1973), 2, 9, 18–19, 22, 141–42, 181,
217–18; foreign investment, 2, 9,
18, 129, 157, 181, 225; global expansion, 223; impact of diplomacy
on, 7, 17–18; impact of public
relations on, 153; impact of youth
culture on, 220; during postwar
isolation period, 27–28, 76–78;
in postwar Western Europe,
183; recession (1970s), 20, 229,
240n90; during recovery period
(1950s), 25–26, 35, 85

EEC (European Economic Community), 18, 19, 126, 135, 148, 158,
177, 192

Eisenhower, Dwight, 19, 239n80

El Encanto (Cuban department
store): arson attack, 186; credit
services of, 35; employee handbook of, 38; founding of, 13; influence on Spanish retailing, 1, 14–15,
42, 64–65; *interesado* employee
rank, 14, 64–65; international
affiliations, 26, 186; paternalistic
policies of, 14, 42, 217; Pepín
Fernández's career at, 1, 14, 217,
297n18; Ramón Areces's career at,
14, 217; social club, 41, 64

Eléxpuru, Manuel de, 144–45

Elizalde, Graciela, 97

escalators, 28, 33, 65, 243n27

Escaparate (journal), 32–33, 47, 87,
243n24

Escobar, Manolo, 178

Estatuto de la Publicidad (regulatory charter), 141, 145, 146, 147,
149–50, 218

Europe: advertising industry in,
143–44, 156; counterculture in,
167–68; diplomatic ties with
Spain, 108; fashion industry in,
72, 80–82, 96, 105, 106–7, 108,
163–64; food retailing industry
in, 113–15, 136–37; model American home exhibits in, 97; shaping
Spanish mass consumer society, 3,
6; Spanish integration into, 2–3,
136–37, 159, 178, 181, 201, 223–24;
supermarkets in, 114–16, 127–30

European Common Market (EEC),
18, 19, 126, 135, 148, 158, 177, 192
European Community for Advertising Organizations (CEOP), 146
European Economic Community
(EEC), 18, 19, 126, 135, 148, 158,
177, 192
exceptionalism: advertising industry
undermining, 141, 145–46, 156–
59; consumer press undermining,
70, 88–89; cosmopolitanism of
boom era undermining, 182; and
cultural stereotypes, 156–59, *161*;
department stores undermining,
5, 27, 66, 187, 202, 204–5, 213–14;
fashion industry undermining,
80–84, 159; under Francoism,
3, 215; hybrid cultural identities
undermining, 219, 310n5; mass
consumption undermining, 3, 12,
218–19, 222; supermarkets undermining, 113, 139

Fabra Carbó, José María, 291n83
Falange: anti-American sentiment of,
101; consumer press reinforcing,
75; feminine ideals, 73; and the
Franco regime, 16, 247–48n72;
masculine "man-warrior" ideal,
17, 106, 166–67; sociopolitical
project of, 257n33; totalitarianism
of, 50. *See also* Franco regime;
Sección Femenina (Falange)
Fama (ad agency), 144
La Familia SPAR (magazine), 125,
126, 132, 280n89

fashion industry: Bond Street fashion, 142, 162; boom era changes,
141–42; Carnaby Street fashion,
10, 106, 142, 162, 169; concerns
over place within international
community, 70, 159–64, 176, 177–
78, 289n71; fashion as form of
personal expression, 168; fashion
imposing discipline on bodies,
251–52n110; focus on American
fashion, 69–71, 79–81, 96, 108;
focus on British fashion, 10–11,
96, 105, 106, 142, 162, 169, 187–88;
focus on European fashion, 72,
80, 96, 105, 108; foreign focus
of, 70–71, 149, 164–65, 176–77,
261n63; National Fashion Show,
67, 163–64, 255n13; reinforcing
Francoism gender norms, 106,
164, 166–67, 175; subverting
Francoist gender norms, 167–75,
181, 220; subverting Francoist
ideology, 11, 165, 220; undermining exceptionalism, 80–84, 159;
unisex fashion, 10–11, 165, 169–75,
171, 177, 181, 209, 219–20. *See also*
menswear; youth fashion
femininity: Francoist ideals, 11, 16,
58, 73, 221; increasingly liberal
notions of, 18; linking of fashion to acceptable roles, 256n17;
National-Catholic ideals, 16,
71–73, 256n21–22; National
Movement's model of, 256n21;
Sección Femenina's model of, 16,
70, 84, 94, 125, 256n21, 257n27;
self-abnegating/self-sacrificing

femininity (*cont.*)
  ideal, 16, 70, 84–86, 92–95, 103,
  125; submissive domestic ideal, 16,
  58, 72–73, 85–86, 109–10, 256n21,
  257n27. *See also* gender norms
  (Francoist); women
feminism, 92, 199–201
Fernández, Gustavo, 203
Fernández, José Manuel, 32, 38, 64, 185
Fernández, Ramiro, 203
Fernández Rodríguez, José "Pepín":
  on commerce as a social function, 25, 48; on consumer credit
  systems, 35; and the decline of
  Galerías, 228–29; early career at
  El Encanto, 1, 14, 42, 217, 297n18;
  expectations of employees, 14, 37,
  41, 42, 43, 51, 246n58; on female
  workers, 59–60, 200; following
  the Cuban Revolution, 186;
  foreign-influenced methods of,
  14–15, 38, 41; impact of rationing
  on, 28; importance of world-
  class reputation to, 1, 33, 46, 65,
  246n58; managerial style, 14–15,
  42, 47, 55, 217; relationship with
  Cesar Rodríguez, 312n35; retirement of, 229; role in modernizing
  retailing, 13; Silver Medal for
  Merit in Work award, 53; supporting Franco regime, 8, 53, 215,
  221, 235n35; ties to Almacenes
  Botas, 253n117; ties to Fulgencio
  Batista, 297n20
Fernán Gómez, Fernando, 61
Ferrer, Fernando, 202, 306n86
firing practices, 46, 61, 251n108

FOESSA (sociological institute), 225
Font, Lina, 102–3
Fontcuberta, Joan, 145
food distribution and retailing:
  focus on diet and nutrition, 6,
  122–23, 136–37, 138; foreign influences on, 112–16; Franco regime's
  streamlining of, 87, 121–22;
  impact of supermarkets on, 137–
  38; professionalization of, 111, 112,
  133–34; professional trade journal
  (*ICA*), 87, 126, 136, 263n81;
  transformations in, 111–13, 138–
  39; viewed by Franco regime in
  nationalistic terms, 6. *See also* grocers (traditional grocery stores);
  supermarkets *(autoservicios)*
Forcano, Eugeni, 299n35
Formica, Mercedes, 74
Fraga Iribarne, Manuel, 9, 19, 20,
  145, 146, 149, 156, 157, 176, 205
France: appliance culture in, 86;
  fashion industry in, 72, 80, 105;
  public relations industry in, 154;
  supermarkets in, 115, 137
Franco, Francisco: cabinet changes
  made by, 17–18, 26; in the Civil
  War, 1–2; death of, 2, 20; impact
  on economic boom, 18; as paterfamilias of the Spanish people,
  215; *Señor*'s profile of, 105; years of
  dictatorship, 2
Franco regime: autarkic policies of,
  15, 18; cabinet changes, 17–18, 26;
  collapse of, 20; decline of, 210;
  diplomatic isolation of, 107, 216;
  diplomatic rehabilitation efforts,

25, 89, 96, 108, 182; diplomatic relations with the United States, 6, 7, 79, 103; efforts to join European Common Market, 19, 158; goal of establishing global prominence, 3, 9, 148–49, 176, 221; militarized discourse of, 48–49; modern struggles with legacy of, 226–28; repression under, 2, 12, 15–16; scholarly treatment of, 4, 233n12; sociopolitical project of, 50–52, 75, 257n33; tensions with minority regional cultures, 20. *See also* CAT (Comisaría de Abastecimientos y Transportes); exceptionalism; gender norms (Francoist); National-Catholicism

Freixas i Bru, María, 77, 86, 241n8, 259n44

Friedan, Betty, 201

Funcionarias: Revista para la Mujer (magazine), 107; audience of, 68, 90, 103; circulation statistics, 92; contributors to, 91; focus of, 87–88; launch of, 68, 87, 90; legitimizing married women's careers, 90–92, 103; reinforcing traditional female domesticity, 87–88, 94–95; role in aspirational mass consumer society development, 108; tensions in reconciling gender norms, 95–96; on women's right to work, 108

Gable, Clark, 79
Gadé, Analía, 61

Galeras, África, 206

Galerías Preciados (department store): adapting to changing gender norms, 182; advertising during postwar shortages, 27, 241n4; bypassing Francoist import restrictions, 81–82; celebrating Dwight Eisenhower's visit, 239n80; consumer magazines published by, 34–35; decline of, 2, 228–29; declining sense of community at, 198; employee exchanges of, 182, 187; escalators, 33, 243n27; expansion and growth (boom era), 183–84, 228; expansion and growth (early Franco years), 26, 28–32, *30*, 36, 41, 216; film portrayals of, 61–62; focus on company reputation, 46–47; focus on professional development and technical mastery, 37–39, 185, 246n47; foreign products and innovations adopted by, 32, 33, 38, 64–65, 183, 187; hiring practices, 32, 36, 38, 54, 198; images of, *191*; impact on mass consumption, 181; international affiliations, 65, 151, 187, 298n26–27; interpreters corps, 186, 203; labor disputes, 227; launch of, 2; mail-order department, 29; manufacturing division of, 29, 216; modern cosmopolitan aspirations of, 185–87; modern cosmopolitan identity claimed by, 188; political alignment of, 26–27, 50–54; reinforcing Francoist ideals, 26–27, 221; reinforcing gendered differences, 59–63, 200; sold to El

112, 130–31; competing with self-service stores, 130–31, 138; complementing self-service stores, 131, 138, 278–79n72; criticisms of supermarkets, 119, 270n7; in Europe, 114–15; impact of food retailing changes on, 112, 119, 120; traditional methods, 112, 130; in the United States, 113. *See also* food distribution and retailing; supermarkets *(autoservicios)*

Haasenstein & Volger (Swiss ad agency), 144
Hall, Richard, 146, 147, 151
Hamol Company, 81
handbooks. *See* code of conduct handbooks
Heatherton, Joey, 289n66
Helios (ad agency), 144
Hernández, Ramón, 187
hipermercado (hypermarkets), 137
hiring practices: at Almacenes Botas, 31–32; at Galerías, 32, 36, 38, 54, 198; at Sears, 202–3
El Hogar y la Moda (magazine): circulation figures, 79, 260n53; consumer orientation of, 71; pricing for ad space, 261n60; relaunch of, 68–69
¡Hola! (magazine), 78, 259n50
Hollywood star system, 69–70, 79–81, 108, 261n63, 289n66
Hotel Florida, *189*, 190
Hourez, Fernand, 149
Huguet, Jaime, 164

Hujar, Ted, 203
humor columns: addressing policies, 55, 250n89–90, 251n98; in employee bulletins, 55–58, 250n89–90, 251n98, 304n71; women portrayed by, 59. *See also* cartoons and comic strips
hypermarkets, 137

IBEC (International Basic Economy Corporation), 115
ICA: Industria y Comercio de Alimentación (journal): Alberto Ullastres' speech in, 126; focus on technical mastery, 87; on global status, 136; importance of, 263n81; launching of, 87
IGDS (International Group of Department Stores), 26, 65, 187, 213, 298n26–27
La Ilustración Femenina (magazine), 74
import restrictions, 81–82, 89, 298n26
incomes: at department stores, 39, 228, 245n44, 249n85; gender differences, 61, 228; gender equality reforms, 200; during postwar years, 15, 28, 39, 68; rises in, 8, 9, 18, 19, 235n40, 238n75; seamstressing work, 77
interesado, 14, 64–65
International Basic Economy Corporation (IBEC), 115
International Group of Department Stores (IGDS), 26, 65, 187, 213, 298n26–27

International Public Relations
   Association (IPRA). *See* IPRA
   (International Public Relations
   Association)
International Women's Year (1975),
   200–201
I.P.: Información de la Publicidad
   (journal), 147, 148, 149, 154, 155
IPRA (International Public Relations Association): annual conference (1966), 140, 152–53, 156,
   158–59, *160, 161,* 176; international
   networks of, 152–54, 219; Joaquín
   Maestre Morata joining, 10, 141,
   151; role in professionalization, 10,
   140–41, 145, 151–52
Italy, 80, 81, 115, 261n63

Jaumain, Serve, 229
Jorba (department store). *See* Almacenes Jorba (department store)
Jorba-Preciados (department store):
   cultural regionalism highlighted
   by, 192–93; financing of, 228;
   founding of, 183; naming of,
   295n7; sports club of, 196, 302n51,
   302n58. *See also* Almacenes Jorba
   (department store)
Juan Carlos (king of Spain), 20, 223
Jurado, Rocío, 292n88
J. Walter Thompson (ad agency),
   154, 177, 287n49

Kentie, Jetty, 186
Kenyon & Eckhardt (ad agency), 154
Kevend, Roderick, 206
Keyser, John, 152

Khrushchev, Nikita, 97
King Kullen (supermarket chain),
   113, 118, 119
Komol hair dye, 93, *93,* 95, 265n101
Kowalsky, Daniel, 220
Kuisel, Richard, 224

The Ladies' Paradise (Zola), 13
Laver, James, 251–52n110
Leblanc, Tony, 61
Lecturas (magazine), 78, 259n50
Ledbetter Lee, Ivy, 143
Legrain perfumes, 81, 105
León, Luís de, 73
Linz, Juan, 8, 50
Llerandi González, Marisol, 200
Llorens, Eduardo "Edy," 204–5
Loewe (Spanish designer), 166
López, Jorge, 210
López Rodó, Laureano, 18
Louis XVI (king of France), 72
Louis XVIII (king of France), 72
Lurie, Alison, 165, 251–52n110,
   268n138
Luz Morales, María, 167

Macrina (Jorba advice columnist), 34
Macy's (department store), 32, 35, 38,
   64, 187
Maestre Morata, Joaquín: at the
   1966 IPRA conference, 140,
   156, 158–59; collaborations of,
   152, 286n38; at DANIS, 145; on
   foreign tourism, 224; founding
   SAE de RP, 148; impact on public
   relations field, 145, 148, 156, 176;
   IPRA membership benefits for,

151–52; joining IPRA, 10, 141, 145; joining PRSA, 141, 145

Maestro-Amado, Ezequiel Puig, 209

magazines. *See* consumer press

mail-order services (department stores), 26, 29

Maixé-Altés, Joan Carles, 129, 134

Makro Cash and Carry (hypermarket), 137

Mantua, C. A., 101–2, 268n133

Marañón Moya, Gregorio, 7

Marbá, Jaime, 210

Marie Thérèse (Duchess of Angoulême), 72

Marinalba (hair tonic), 82, *83*

Market Basket (supermarket chain), 276n59

Marqueríe, Alfredo, 65

Marshall Plan, 15, 97

Martín Aceña, Pablo, 223

Martínez, Diego, 135

Martínez, Roldán, 156, 157, 205

Martínez Ruiz, Elena, 223

Martín Gaite, Carmen, 85

Marxism, 248n78–79

masculinity: consumer press reinforcing Francoist norms of, 164, 166–67; consumer press subverting Francoist norms of, 142, 167–75, 177; Falange's "Man-Warrior" ideal, 17, 106, 166–67; fashion reinforcing Francoist norms of, 106, 164, 166–67, 251–52n110; fashion subverting Francoist norms of, 106, 142, 164–75, 177; Francoist ideals, 11, 16–17, 166; impact of foreign consumption on, 11; importance of fashion to, 106, 165–66; National-Catholic ideals, 11, 17, 142. *See also* gender norms (Francoist)

mass consumer society: advertising industry shaping, 2–3, 25; as aspirational, 7–8, 28, 68–69, 71, 97–100, 103–4, 108–10, 217; consumer press shaping, 2–3, 34–35, 67–71, 84–89, 106–8, 142–43; defined, 4; department stores shaping, 2–3, 7–8, 26, 36–37, 66, 181; developed through modernization, 2–3; emergence of, 140, 210–13, 217–18; fashion shaping, 69–71; full realization of, 8; impact on national identity, 12; international orientation of, 69–71, 84–89, 96–98, 214, 217–18; multiple factors in development of, 223; role in sociopolitical changes, 4, 10–12, 214, 216, 221–22; role of discourse and meaning in, 230; supermarkets shaping, 2–3, 112–13, 218

mass consumption: as agent of sociopolitical change, 4, 11–12, 25–27, 182–83, 214, 221–23; centrality of class performance to, 254–55n8; defined, 4; development in the United States, 47, 254–55n8; expectations of access to, 103–4; impact of credit systems on, 4, 35, 98, 103, 109, 110, 238n75; internationalization through, 64–66, 71, 223–24; limits of democratizing effects of,

mass consumption (*cont.*)
5–6, 12; local backlash to, 224–25;
as an other-centered act, 70, 84–
86, 92–95, 103, 214; for personal
pleasure, 82–84, 90, 95, 103, 126;
pervasiveness of in modern life,
4; politicization of, 5, 8, 26–27, 37,
47, 51–52, 75–76, 221, 233n11; role
in democratization process, 4, 12,
214, 221–24; scholarly debate on,
233n11; shifting understandings of
availability, 97–100; transformations in accessibility, 19, 86–89,
103–4, 109, 110, 235n40; undermining exceptionalist conceptions, 3, 12, 218–19, 222
Matrat, Lucien, 151
Maxwell, Marilyn, 82, *83*
McCann-Erickson (ad agency), 141,
145, 154–55, *155*, 177, 218, 222
Medina (journal), 107; audience of,
68; consumer orientation of, 71;
publication dates, 71; traditional
gendered content of, 72, 74–75
Menaje (magazine), 261n60
Mencía Sanz, Agustín, 55–56, 63
Méndez González, Jesús, 38
Men's Modes (journal), 163, 168,
292n92
menswear: concern with international status in, 106–7; impact
of unisex fashion on, 169–75;
impact of youth fashion on, 168–
69, 173; imposing discipline on
bodies, 251–52n110; international
focus of, 105–7, 162–64; shifting
social views on, 104; as subverting

normative Francoist masculinity, 106, 164–65; as symbol of
normative Francoist masculinity,
106, 251–52n110; ties to countercultural movements, 106. *See also*
consumer press (men's)
Meridiano Femenino (women's
digest), 78, 259n50
Merino, Ignacio, 299n32
Mestre y Ballbé (textile manufacturer), 106
military service, 48–49
Miller, Montserrat, 131
Ministry of Information and Tourism (MIT): advertising charter,
145, 146, 176, 218; advertising
regulatory body, 146; censorship
of the press by, 11, 239n84, 291n83;
economic impact of, 18; impact
on democratization process, 223;
role in Spain's international integration, 222; tourist campaigns, 19
La Moda Elegante (magazine), 72
modernity: aspirations of, 149,
184–88, 219, 221–22, 224; foreign
standards of, 9, 159, 205; mass
consumer society developed
through, 2–3; myth of modernization, 9; relation to democratization process, 222; through
transformation of food retailing
industry, 112–13, 229; tourism as
symbol of, 157, 195
Molina, María Pilar de, 105
Molina Romero, Luis, 201
Morcillo, Aurora, 16, 35, 73, 82–84,
95, 256n22

Mortes, Vincente, 152–53

La Movida countercultural movement, 215

Las Muchachas de Azul (film), 61–62

Mujer: Revista Mensual del Hogar y de la Moda (magazine): as aspirational literature, 79, 109, 217; audience of, 68, 76–78; careers for women at, 74; cartoons, 264n87; censorship of, 173; circulation figures, 79; cost of, 77–78, 259n50; covering American appliance culture, 85–86, 96–97; focusing on thrift-mindedness, 76–78; focus on foreign fashions and lifestyles, 69, 79–81; launch of, 71; political alignment of, 75, 76; pricing for ad space, 261n60; promoting domestic tourism, 76, 258n37; reinforcing Francoist gender norms, 72–73, 75, 84–86, 93, 221, 256n22, 264n87, 266n110, 266n113; reinforcing Francoist ideology, 75; value placed on technical mastery, 87

Municipal Markets Institute (Barcelona), 278–79n72

Muñoz, Agustín, 134

Muñoz Ruiz, María del Carmen, 34, 95

NAFC (U.S. National Association of Food Chains), 128

National Advertisers' Syndicate, 150

National Advertising Institute (INP), 146

National-Catholicism: abolishing coeducation, 17, 172; advertising challenging, 82–84; consumer press challenging, 142, 175; consumer press reinforcing, 71–73, 75–76; defined, 50; department stores emulating, 50–52; fashion challenging, 142, 172, 175, 181, 209–10; feminine ideals, 16, 71–73, 256n21–22; impact of foreign consumption on, 11; masculine ideals, 11, 17, 142; patriarchal hierarchies under, 16–17, 172, 220; unisex fashion challenging, 172. *See also* Franco regime

National Fashion Show, 67, 163–64, 255n13

National Movement political party, 16, 72–73, 256n21. *See also* Franco regime

Nestlé Company-sponsored sweepstakes, 93–94

Neville, Edgar, 289n67

Nixon, Richard, 97

Nonell, Carmen, 74

Normas de Botas (code of conduct handbook): concern for store reputation, 43; development of, 37; influence of Galerías's *Normas* on, 37, 53–54; international origin of, 64; treason clause, 46, 246n58. *See also* Almacenes Botas (department store)

Normas de Sederías Carretas y Galerías (code of conduct handbook): customer service importance, 40, 46, 246n58; development of, 37,

norms, 177; on unisex fashion, 169, 172; on youth fashion, 168

Plá y Deniel, Enrique, 17, 82

Polo, Carmen, 53

Pond's Cold Cream, 70, 82

Portugal, 4–5

poverty, 7, 19, 64, 68

Prat Gaballi, Pedro, 144, 145, 146, 176

press (consumer). *See* consumer press

Press Law (1938), 17, 238n74

Primo de Rivera, José Antonio, 52

Primo de Rivera, Pilar, 16, 73

prostitution, 17

PRSA (Public Relations Society of America), 141, 145, 151

Pryca (French hypermarket), 137

publications. *See* consumer press

Publicidad Tiempo (ad agency), 154

Publicitas (ad agency), 144

public relations: boom era changes, 140–41, 148, 175–76; concern over global status, 177–78; criticism of international affiliations, 157–58; culturally reductionist discourses of, 158–59; development of, 140–41, 143–44, 145, 151, 176; international affiliations, 150–56, 176, 218; professionalization of, 151, 176–77, 218; SAE de RP, 148, 150–52, 158–59, 224; and tourism, 224; in the United States, 141, 143. *See also* advertising industry

Public Relations News, 152

Public Relations Review, 148

Public Relations Society of America (PRSA), 141, 145, 151

Publidis (ad agency), 219

Puerto, Pablo del, 14

Puig, Jaime, 156

Puig, Núria, 154

Quid (magazine), 167, 292n88

Radio Futura (band), 215–16, 220

reforms: in the advertising industry, 146, 147; as diplomatic efforts, 182; economic recovery following, 18; following Francisco Franco's death, 20; of food retailing laws, 279n79; limits to, 17–18, 225–28; to women's legal status, 18, 74, 126, 199–201

refrigerators, 19, 85–86, 97, 262n73, 263n78

Relaciones Casi Públicas (film), 178

Relaciones Públicas (journal), 147

Revista Jorba (magazine), 107; advertising Jorba's credit service, *99*, 100; as aspirational literature, 98, 109; audience of, 90, 265n103; circulation of, 34; content features of, 33–34, 94; covering American appliance culture, 97; impacts of, 34–35; launch of, 33, 90; othering of American culture in, 100–103; reinforcing Francoist gender norms, 34, 93–94; women portrayed in, 59. *See also* Almacenes Jorba (department store)

Riba, Ana, 309n119

Ribalta, Enrique, 118

Riney, John, 203–4, 205

Rodríguez, Cesar, 14, 228, 312n35

ideal of submissive domesticity, 16, 256n21, 257n27; influence of, 85; *Medina* (journal), 68, 71–72, 74–75, 107; *Teresa* (journal), 74, 90; *Ventanal* (magazine), 71, 78; *Y: Revista de la Mujer Nacional-Sindicalista* (magazine), 71

Sederías Carretas (department store): advertising cutbacks, 27; employee discounts, 64; employee social club, 66; escalators at, 28, 65; expansion and growth, 26, 28–31, 65–66; female managers at, 59–60; Francisco Casares' 1941 speech at, 25, 51–53; growing into Galerías Preciados, 2; launch of, 1, 46; political alignment, 26–27, 235n35; reinforcing Francoist ideology, 26–27, 51, 248n78; sociopolitical impacts of, 2, 66; wages at, 39, 245n44. *See also* Galerías Preciados (department store); *Normas de Sederías Carretas y Galerias* (code of conduct handbook)

Segura, Pedro, 17, 82

Selfridges & Co. (department store), 13, 187, 230

self-service grocery stores. *See* supermarkets *(autoservicios)*

Senda (magazine), 79

Señor: La Revista del Hombre (magazine): concern with international prestige, 106, 109, 163; constructing an aspirational mass consumer society, 106–7, 217; cost of, 104–5; elite focus of, 104–5, 268n138, 291n83; focus on inter-national fashion, 105, 162; Hollywood interviews of, 289n66; on importance of fashion to identity, 105–6, 165; launch of, 67, 104, 107, 253n2; political alignment of, 104–5; on progress through fashion, 214; reinforcing Fran-coist gender norms, 106, 166–67, 175; subverting Francoist gender norms, 106; on youth fashion, 168

SEPU (Spanish Fixed-Price Company), 33

Seregni, Alessandro, 101

Serrano Súñer, Ramón, 53, 247–48n72

Serrell, Georges, 152

Servan-Schreiber, Jean-Jacques, 157

Sevilla, Carmen, 109, 219, 310n5

Shirley's Institute of Barcelona, 96

shortages and rationing, 15, 27–28, 64, 68, 77, 87, 216, 254n5, 259n46

Shuster, Francis, 152

Siegfried, Detlef, 167–68

Siro Gay (department store). *See* Almacenes Siro Gay (department store)

Soberano (Spanish cognac), 167, 291–92n87

soccer teams (company sports clubs), 195–97

social clubs: colonizing workers' lei-sure time, 39, 42–43, 54, 296n11; declining interest in, 198; foreign influences on, 41, 64–65; inter-store tourism, 194–95; as social structure fostering community, 39, 42–43, 194–98; sports teams of, 195–97, 301n48, 302n51, 302n58

unions, 19–20, 227
unisex fashion, 10–11, 165, 169–75, *171*, 177, 181, 209, 219–20
United States: advertising industry in, 143–44, 154–55; American celebrity culture, 69–70, 79–81, 101, 103, 108, 261n63, 289n66; anti-American sentiment in Spain, 12, 19, 101–4; appliance culture, 19, 85–89, 96–97, 103, 108–9, 208, 241n8, 262n73, 263n78; automobile culture in, 190; consumer diplomacy of, 6, 177, 225; counterculture in, 167–68; department stores in, 33, 37, 38, 40–41, 47, 64, 187; diplomatic relations with Franco regime, 6, 7, 17, 79, 103, 109; export of consumerism to Europe, 9; fashion industry in, 69–71, 79–81, 96, 108; fears of economic colonialism by, 224–25; gender norms during postwar years, 267n128; household management methods in, 88; pursuit of soft power through consumer culture, 6; shifting public sentiment toward, 101–4, 110; supermarkets in, 113–15, 118, 128–29; Supermarket USA exhibition, 6, 86–87, 88, 128, 275n55; treaty with Spain (1953), 7, 101, 186
Urquijo Bank, 229
Urzaiz, Jaime de, 197

La Vanguardia Española (newspaper), 202, 207

van Well, Adriaan, 114
Vázquez Montalbán, Manuel, 225
VéGé (Dutch supermarket chain), 115, 129
Velasco, Conchita, 178
Venero, Samuel, 47
Ventanal (magazine), 71, 78
Verdú, Vicente, 165–66, 168–69, 172, 173, 175, 294n107
Verkoops Gemeenschaap (Dutch supermarket chain), 115, 129
Vigil, Manuel, 164, 290n74
Viñas Bona, Juan, 148
Vivir a Dos (magazine), 172

welfare work initiatives, 40, 41, 216–17
West Berlin Industrial Fair (1950), 86
Wilde, Cornel, 289n66
Wilensky, Harold, 146, 151
window displays, 14–15, 28, 32–33
women: consumption as an other-centered act for, 70, 84, 92–95; consumption for personal pleasure, 70, 82–84, 95, 103, 126; continuing problems with gender equality, 227–28; double burden faced by, 94–95, 108; expectation of marriage, 60–62, 72; expectations of domestic technical mastery, 69, 87–88, 120–26; extradomestic employment, 70, 90–95, 108; in Francoist patriarchal hierarchies, 92–95, 167; impact of supermarkets on status of, 122–26; labor rights of, 18, 103, 108, 126, 200–201; legal reforms impacting, 18, 74, 126,